1977

Thi.. .... .pt

Richard Barber was born in Essex in 1941 and was educated at Marlborough College and Corpus Christi College, Cambridge. His first book, *Arthur of Albion*, originated as a Trevelyan scholarship project. *The Knight and Chivalry* won him the Somerset Maugham award in 1970. His other work includes *Henry Plantagenet, Samuel Pepys Esq., Dictionary of Fabulous Beasts, The Figure of Arthur, King Arthur in Legend and History* and *Cooking and Recipes from Rome to the Renaissance*. He lives in East Anglia and divides his time between writing and publishing books of local interest through a small publishing house (Boydell Press), which he helped to found in 1969.

THE KNIGHT
AND CHIVALRY

Richard Barber

Rowman and Littlefield
Totowa, New Jersey

First published in the United States 1975
by Rowman and Littlefield, Totowa, N.J.

First published in Great Britain
by Longman Group Ltd. 1970
Copyright © Richard Barber 1970, 1974

Library of Congress Cataloging in Publication Data

Barber, Richard W
    The knight and chivalry.
    Bibliography: p
    Includes index.
    1. Knights and knighthood. 2. Chivalry. 1. Title
CR4509.B37   1975   940.1'7   74-34075
ISBN 0-87471-653-5

Printed in Great Britain

CONTENTS

PART V: CHIVALRY AND THE STATE

LIST OF ILLUSTRATIONS

The author and publishers would like to thank the above for supplying photographs for use in this volume

MAPS (drawn by John Messenger)

ACKNOWLEDGMENTS

This book has benefited from much advice and help, without which it would contain much less of interest and far more errors. I should like to acknowledge the encouragement and assistance of many friends.

In editorial matters, Professor Edward Miller and Miss Madeline Blaess of the University of Sheffield and Professor R. J. Taylor of the University of Sussex have made expert and most helpful criticisms of both substance and treatment. Dr Roy Strong has been an admirable guide to sixteenth-century chivalry, Mr Kevin Crossley-Holland has offered valuable suggestions on the problems of poetry translation, and Miss Elizabeth Dunn has given expert guidance on the question of orders of knighthood. Mr Eric Elstob has discussed many of the literary themes; Mr S. R. M. Wilson and Mrs G. C. Hargrove have read and criticised parts of the work in manuscript; and Mlle Marina Dimitropulos-Kantakuzenos and Miss Anne Riches have kindly obtained photographs for me.

I also gratefully recognise the unfailing assistance of the staff of the London Library, the British Museum and Cambridge University Library. Mrs Evelyn Rowe patiently succeeded in turning an illegible manuscript into a respectable typescript.

Finally, a special debt is owed to Mr John MacCallum Scott for his enthusiasm for the idea of this book, to Miss Juliet O'Hea for moral support during the writing of much of it, and most of all, to my parents for their encouragement and forbearance during the past six years.

Note to the Second Edition

For this new edition, which has been entirely reset, a number of changes to the text have been made, particularly in chs. 1, 7, 13 and 18, and the bibliography has been brought up to date. An appendix on the Order of the *Banda*, based on a paper read to the British branch of the International Arthurian Society in September 1971, has also been included.

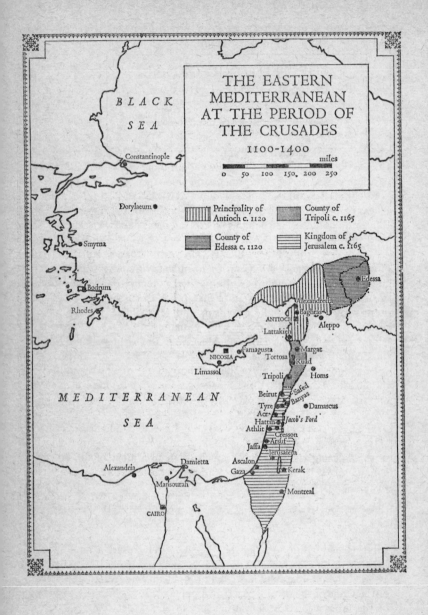

THE EASTERN
MEDITERRANEAN
AT THE PERIOD OF
THE CRUSADES
1100-1400

miles

0   50   100 150   200 250

| | Principality of Antioch c. 1120 | | County of Tripoli c. 1165 |
| | County of Edessa c. 1120 | | Kingdom of Jerusalem c. 1165 |

BLACK

SEA

Constantinople

Dorylaeum

Smyrna

Bodrum

Rhodes

Edessa

Alexandretta

Baghras

ANTIOCH

Aleppo

Lattakieh

Famagusta

Margat

NICOSIA

Tortosa

Ruad

Limassol

Homs

Tripoli

MEDITERRANEAN

Beirut

Safed

Banyas

SEA

Tyre

Acre

Damascus

Hattin

Jacob's Ford

Athlit

Cresson

Jaffa

Arsuf

Ascalon

Jerusalem

Alexandria

Damietta

Gaza

Kerak

Mansourah

Montreal

CAIRO

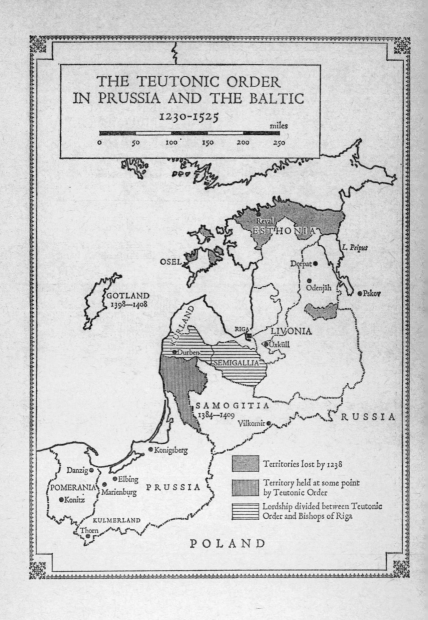

THE TEUTONIC ORDER
IN PRUSSIA AND THE BALTIC
1230–1525

miles

0   50   100   150   200   250

ESTHONIA

Reval

OSEL

L. Peipus

Dorpat

Odenjäh

Pskov

GOTLAND
1398–1408

KURLAND

RIGA

LIVONIA

Durben

Uxküll

SEMIGALLIA

SAMOGITIA
1384–1409

Vilkomir

RUSSIA

Konigsberg

Danzig

Elbing

POMERANIA

Marienburg

PRUSSIA

Konitz

KULMERLAND

Thorn

Territories lost by 1238

Territory held at some point
by Teutonic Order

Lordship divided between Teutonic
Order and Bishops of Riga

POLAND

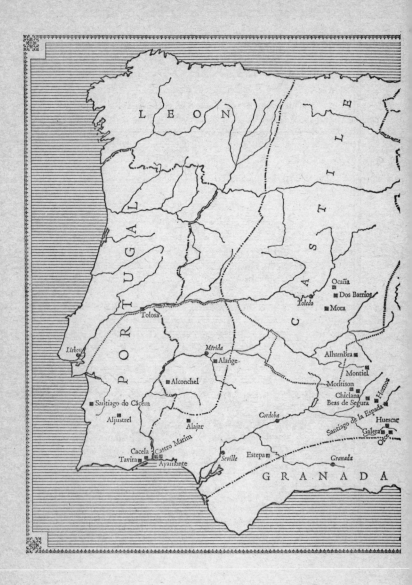

L E O N

C A S T I L E

P O R T U G A L

Tolosa

Lisbon

Mérida
Alange

Alconchel

Santiago do Cácem
Aljustrel

Alajar

Cacela Castro Marim
Tavira
Ayamonte

Ocaña
Dos Barrios
Toledo
Mota

Alhambra
Montiel
Montison
Chiclana
Beas de Segura

Cordoba

Seville   Estepa

Santiago de la Espada   Huescar
Galera
Orce
Granada

Hornos

G R A N A D A

NAVARRA

A R A G O N

Paracuellos

MEDITERRANEAN

SEA

Montesa

Socovos
Moratalla
Caravaca
Aledo

THE MILITARY ORDERS
IN SPAIN
1165-1492

miles

0   50   100   150   200

■ Castles of the Order of Santiago
········· Moslem frontier in 1170

PART I
The Feudal Warrior

I

The Knight

The figure of the knight at once dominates the mediaeval world and distinguishes it from the classical era. The knight inherited both the lands and status of the magnate of the Roman world in his luxurious villa and the political power of the infantry soldier of the Praetorian Guard. His roots were barbarian; his ideals were in sharp contrast to the Roman order, ideals born of the three turbulent centuries between the end of the western Empire and the accession of Charlemagne. Above all, two characteristics stand out: in war, he fought on horseback where the Roman legions had fought on foot; in peace, he held his land because he was a skilled fighter.

In the Roman wars of conquest and defence, the legions had occasionally encountered light horsemen. They were not unusual among the Germanic tribes, but rarely caused any great reverses of fortune; they were little esteemed as auxiliary troops when the Romans did think fit to hire them. Mounted bareback, with a loose cloth as saddle and a very primitive bit, and lacking stirrups, their light javelins were difficult to use accurately, and they were too easily unseated to make a really effective charge. It was only with the advent of the Goths that cavalry began to count. The new enemies, nomads whose life was lived on horseback, were at first raiders and plunderers; for this they needed the horseman's speed and mobility. By the late fourth century, they considered it more honourable to fight on horseback, and no longer used horses as a means of transport, dismounting on the field of battle. It was their overwhelming triumph at Adrianople in 378 that sealed the fate of the infantry. Using javelins and swords, their cavalry surprised the Roman army on the flank, and drove it into confusion. The Romans, unable to deploy properly and thus to resist the impetus of the Goths with a wall of shields, were massacred.

However, even with the advent of the Huns (who were so inseparable from their horses that a Roman writer called them shaggy centaurs) the new style of cavalry warfare found favour only in the

17

eastern Empire. The mounted archers of the Parthians which became the model for Byzantium were almost unknown in the west. Of the Germanic tribes, only the Visigoths, and to a lesser extent the Lombards, were successful horsemen; and the Franks and Anglo-Saxons remained very skilled in infantry tactics as late as the eleventh century. It was the Frankish infantry that broke the onslaught of the Arab cavalry at Poitiers in 733: 'The men of the north remained as motionless as a wall, and frozen together like a block of ice, they put the Arabs to the sword.'[1] But the Franks had already experimented with horses in the field, and perhaps learned from their Arab adversaries.

Another advantage of the change to cavalry was that it meant fewer men to find provisions for; and in an age when supplies had to be found *en route* by pillage and foraging, this was a major consideration. The feeding of horses did mean some problems. Already in 755 the annual review of the levies had been postponed from March until May, when the spring grass was abundant. And though a far smaller force was required, it was not simply a matter of re-training as many picked infantry as were needed. The future knight had to spend a considerable amount on his equipment: even in the ninth century a horse cost six times as much as a cow – a modern equivalent might be £500 – and armour possibly as much again. The only detailed summons to one of Charlemagne's vassals to survive, from *c*. 806, specifies shield, lance, sword, dagger, a bow and a quiver, besides all 'warlike equipment of clothing and victuals'.[2]

A slight superiority in mobility and striking power would not have been enough to ensure that the horseman would supersede the foot-soldier. At this point, however, technical developments vastly increased his usefulness. The most important was the use of stirrups. The stirrup first appears in China at the end of the fifth century, and may have come originally from nomadic tribes on the eastern borders. In the simple form of two iron rings suspended on thongs, they were adopted by the Chinese, but the idea did not spread further until late in the seventh century; contacts between east and west were slow, and the fashion was by no means universal in China itself until considerably later. At the end of the seventh century it appeared in Iran just before the Arab conquest, and in Hungary, where Arab tribes from central Asia had settled. Its progress continued to western Europe, though exactly how it came to Carolingian France (perhaps by way of the Arabs in their invasions of the early eighth century) remains a mystery. The Vikings and Byzantines only learnt of it by the ninth century, but the German tribes had acquired the secret at about the same time as the Franks.

Once the idea of using stirrups had reached France, it was quickly adopted and developed. Parallel innovations such as the use of the lance in rest and the long pointed shield followed: and it was from the Franks, now leaders in military technology, that the Byzantines acquired these (as well as the crossbow, another originally eastern invention, in the succeeding century). All these innovations amounted to a revolution in warfare. Shod horses could negotiate rough, difficult terrain which earlier riders had had to avoid, and could move more swiftly in bad conditions elsewhere. Stirrups transformed the part that cavalry could play. They gave the rider much better balance and a surer seat, opening the way for the development of the heavy lance, used 'in rest' as a battering ram, to replace the thrown javelin. The old style and the new appear side by side in the Bayeux Tapestry; the lance held in rest came into use very shortly after the introduction of the stirrup, as the use of lances with a crosspiece shows; these were designed to be pulled out and used again instead of being thrown. Warfare rapidly became a duel between cavalry with infantry support, and the spectacle of two armies meeting in a full-scale charge was soon to become the climax of most battles.

Even in the heyday of the knight, however, cavalry were not always used as mounted troops. There are numerous examples of battles won by cavalry dismounted for the actual battle, and just as many where rash action by mounted troops against infantry over unfavourable ground proved fatal. For the knight was not simply a good horseman; his efficiency in the field depended also on his skill in all kinds of fighting. To explain the superiority of cavalry forces, whether mounted or dismounted, we must return to a simpler explanation: mounted troops usually arrived in better condition on the battlefield. This was at least as important an element as the brute force of the cavalry charge.

The knight's military power explained only half his pre-eminence. He was a powerful figure in peacetime as well as in wartime, and had begun to emerge as such in the great transition from classical to mediaeval society during the centuries once known as the Dark Ages. This period was marked by violence and anarchy such as even pre-Roman Europe had scarcely known. The internecine wars of the Merovingians in France, the heathen domination of Germany, the wars of Visigoth and Saracen in Spain, Goth and Lombard in Italy, in their various and separate times and theatres, made the birth of the new society a harsh one. The marks of this ordeal by fire and the sword can be traced in many mediaeval attitudes of mind, from the great concept of the sanctity of the established order down to small superstitions stemming from the terror the invaders had once inspired.

The period of transition falls into two great phases, the watershed being the reign of Charlemagne and the breathing-space of civilisation which the military victories of his house made possible. Up to this point, men had looked back to the Roman Empire as the great example of peace and prosperity, even if it was an inheritance largely misunderstood. Charlemagne's reign was the new starting-point for laws and social institutions. In the earlier period, the veneer of Roman customs was clearer, if weak in practice when tested against the realities of a barbarian world. The Romans had relied on the imperial administration to provide those elements of order which were now so conspicuously lacking: the great legions of the Empire encamped on the German frontier guaranteed the peace of the pro-consul in retirement at his Gaulish villa, the safety of the merchant trafficking in Spain. The men who held power or wealth in the Roman empire had no need for more immediate protection, and little contact with, or respect for, the realities of military life. The glorious ancient days of the Republic, the conquering forays of the early Empire had faded in men's memories: military service was a burden fit only for hired menials. Let barbarian fight barbarian, one under the Roman eagles, the other in his rustic skins; if peace could be bought by hiring soldiers, it was worth the price. How the price became more than the Empire could raise, and the other causes of Rome's decline, are not part of our present theme; but when the barbarians overran Gaul and Spain, the heart of the Roman Empire in the west, there was no tradition of military service which might have inspired a stouter, individual resistance. The Roman *equester ordo* (order of 'knights'), descended from the cavalry troops of the Republic, had become a class of wealthy financiers and administrators whose military connections were entirely dissolved. It was not in the Roman world that the mediaeval knight had his origins.

The barbarian invaders, on the other hand, were a nomadic society for whom war was commonplace, necessary and almost a welcome alternative to their pastoral life. Their incessant movement in search of new pastures meant that they grouped naturally into close-knit tribes, never more than a few thousand strong, and the personal bond was much more important than in a more settled society. They relied only on each other for security in face of danger, and the hierarchy was of the simplest: a chief and a few chosen companions-in-arms were their leaders. This structure of the tribe remained unchanged until the era of settlements began; and Tacitus' picture of it as it was in the late first century AD remained true until as late as the Carolingian wars with the Saxons in south Germany:

No business, public or private, is transacted except in arms. But it is the rule that no one shall take up his arms until the state has attested that he is likely to make good. When that time comes, one of the chiefs or the father or a kinsman equips the young warrior with shield and spear in the public council. This with the Germans is the equivalent of our *toga* – the first public distinction of youth. They cease to rank merely as members of the household and are now members of the state. Conspicuous ancestry or great services rendered by their fathers can win the rank of chief for boys still in their teens. They are attached to the other chiefs, who are more mature and approved, and no one blushes to be seen thus in the ranks of the companions. This order of companions has even its different grades, as determined by the leader, and there is intense rivalry among the companions for the first place beside the chief, among the chiefs for the most numerous and enthusiastic companions. Dignity and power alike consist in being continually attended by a corps of chosen youths. This gives you consideration in peacetime and security in war. Nor is it only in a man's own nation that he can win name and fame by the superior number and quality of his companions, but in neighbouring states as well. Chiefs are counted by embassies and complimented by gifts, and they often virtually decide wars by the mere weight of their reputation.

On the field of battle it is a disgrace to the chief to be surpassed in valour by his companions, to the companions not to come up to the valour of their chiefs. As for leaving a battle alive after your chief has fallen, *that* means lifelong infamy and shame. To defend and protect him, to put down one's own acts of heroism to his credit – that is what they really mean by 'allegiance'. The chiefs fight for victory, the companions for their chief. Many noble youths, if the land of their birth is stagnating in a protracted peace, deliberately seek out other tribes, where some war is afoot. The Germans have no taste for peace; renown is easier won among perils, and you cannot maintain a large body of companions except by violence and war.[3]

The emphasis on companionship and the investing of arms in public ceremony are commonplaces of primitive societies in many parts of the world. Yet they were in sharp contrast with Roman practice and thought, not only by reason of the uncouthness of one and the civilisation of the other. The toga which marked the Roman's coming of age was a legal, almost administrative distinction; the German's shield and spear were practical. The companions of the chief were chosen for strength and skill in fighting, not for their subtlety or political acumen: and yet they were the chief councillors of the tribe by virtue of their position.

This war-based organisation remained appropriate long after the nomadic existence, which in itself entailed so much fighting, had been exchanged for a settled life as farmers. Wars which had been fought for booty were now fought for political reasons, to gain control of land. War remained 'the normal thread of every leader's career and the *raison d'être* of every position of authority'.[4] In the troubles of the dying Empire, when the *pax romana* failed, the magnates acquired hired soldiers, providing their own security in face of the collapse of public order. The *bucellarii*, as they were called, were in a position of power only because of ever-present danger; they were a nuisance to be tolerated, not companions of equal rank. Although apparently similar to the *bucellarii*, the small group around the Merovingian chieftains in France known as *gasindi*, and a similar band around the kings called *antrustiones*, derived from Germanic predecessors; the name *gasindi* implies fellowship, the comradeship of Tacitus' *'comites'*. The royal warriors were also bound by an oath to their leader. To the *antrustiones* were given the great positions of state, as *comes* – meaning comrade in classical Latin, count in mediaeval Latin – or as duke (*dux*, leader) or margrave with more specifically military duties.

Until the seventh century, the bond between leader and follower consisted of nothing more than an oath of personal loyalty. However, another form of personal dependence had been developing in this turbulent society, a tie arising out of the need for protection. Under the late Roman empire, magnates had provided themselves with a bodyguard by accepting the service of clients, a practice with political rather than military obligations which had now become a form of mutual defence and a source of security for both parties; the client was under the magnate's protection, and in turn furthered the latter's interests. Roman poets often wrote satires about clients and their patrons, showing the client as downtrodden and reduced to flattery; but this form of service was not servile, that is, free men did not regard it as tainted with slavery, but as a basically honourable contract.

In the chaos of the sixth and seventh centuries, this institution, under the name of 'commendation', became much more widespread. The most usual case was that in which a very poor man, simply in order to survive, bound himself completely to a lord in return for sustenance. The benefits and services changed all the way up the scale. It was a very flexible institution, whose strength derived from one chief characteristic of those troubled times: that loyalty was at a premium, whether from slave or boon-companion. The Merovingian kingship has been tersely described as 'despotism tempered by assassination'. A follower of King Guntram in the sixth century could remind him: 'We know where the axe is which cut off your brothers' heads, and its edge is still sharp; soon it will cut off your head, too.'[5] So it became just as important to have some kind of formal tie be-

22

tween king and lord, and lord and knight, as between starving peasant and provider.

Commendation, as a solemn contract in an age when the legal niceties were rarely observed, was soon symbolised in the ceremony of homage, an outward and visible sign of the relationship of the two parties. The suppliant placed his hands between those of his lord, in token of his obedience and the lord's protection. Later, the formula grew more complex; the would-be vassal knelt bareheaded and weaponless before his lord, and declared his intention aloud: 'Sire, I become your man.' This was followed by an affirmation of loyalty, and finally by an oath of loyalty, usually sworn on a relic. But the basic relationship of lord and vassal remained almost unchanged from the seventh century to the fourteenth; it coloured men's unconscious thought, and was reflected in other liaisons: lovers swore fealty to their beloved, their more serious companions did spiritual homage to Our Lady.

If loyalty was to flourish, more tangible bonds than those of oaths were needed. Just as the poor man who virtually enslaved himself expected his sustenance in return, so the great lords had their price. In theory, the grants made after homage had been paid were for maintenance, but a lord did not have to support his vassal as well as protect him unless this was a specific condition of the agreement. Hence the benefice, a simple means of maintaining the vassal by giving him sufficient land to feed himself, became the fief, a political as well as economic unit. Vassalage and benefices had originally been all-embracing institutions, capable of providing for the household servants of a lesser vassal (for example the cook, who would be granted a small corner of the benefice his employer had received from a higher lord) as well as for the *vassi dominici*, the great barons who were the king's direct vassals and who received estates which were almost principalities.

By the end of the eighth century, the system of vassalage was operating from the highest to the lowest levels of society. The earliest instances of full and formal contracts of vassalage that have come down to us involve the German princes who formed alliances with the rising Carolingian dynasty, such as Tassilo III of Bavaria in 757. The principal political use of the idea at this time was to ensure the loyalty of the great officers of state, the counts and margraves. At the other end of the scale, the Carolingian kings rewarded their servants and stewards by granting them estates, and men who were little more than serfs could hope to rise in the world by hard work in the royal service. Between these two groups came the freemen, a

23

yeoman class owning small holdings without any tie, and the new knights of the feudal army. The combination of military service and landholding was a new one, and to see how it arose, we must retrace our steps, to the early days of the Frankish kingdom.

The Franks, unlike the majority of the Germanic tribes, were accustomed to fighting on horseback. In the latter days of the Roman empire, they provided a number of mounted units, and under the Merovingian king Clovis, we find an edict about taking food and water for horses on a campaign in 507. Other units in Clovis' army were drawn from tribes which had traditionally provided horsemen for the Romans, such as the Alans of Brittany and the Alamans. Clovis' principal enemies, the Visigoths, were also horsemen, and the combats between them were dominated by cavalry action.

But the support of large and well-organised troops of cavalry required an efficient government and a central authority capable of raising large sums of money. With the degeneration of the Frankish kingdom into a web of small principalities continually at war with each other at the end of the sixth century, it was increasingly difficult to organise cavalry on a large scale. Instead, the military scene was dominated by small marauding war bands and by more or less defensive local levies based on the towns. The men who served in them were expected to provide their own equipment and provisions which meant that the poorer citizens were excluded. With the return of central authority under Pepin and Charles Martel, the war bands and the levies began to merge into one. The war band, supported by the magnate, was unreliable, since one man's gold was as good as another's; and an oath was at best uncertain assurance of loyalty in an age of anarchy. Pepin seems to have formalised the arrangement whereby warriors were paid not in gold, but in lands or benefices, which had originally had no military significance, and which had grown up under the Merovingian kings. In order to do this, both they and Pepin and his successors were reputed to have seized church lands, which confirms the idea that this was a novel approach, since they needed a new supply of land to carry it out. At the same time, the towns, which had been the basis of the earlier local levies and the focal points of warfare under the first Merovingian kings, were now declining in importance, and the economic basis of government was transferred to the countryside. With the return of a strong ruler, the independent magnates and their personal war bands were integrated into a formal structure of government, and used as the new source of local levies. From these varied and often obscure developments grew the military fief which was to become the cornerstone of mediaeval society.

At first, warrior service applied to a relatively small number of estates, and it seems to have grown only gradually throughout the period of Charlemagne's rule. But the troubles that followed the disintegration of the over-ambitious structure of the empire built by Charlemagne bore heaviest on the remaining freemen, who owed no such service. Until now, only the poorest among them had been forced to take refuge in the protection of vassalage, and agreements with private lords were only at this humble level. But now that the royal vassals had begun to show that the condition was neither dishonourable nor onerous, small landowners found that there were many advantages to be gained by doing homage and holding land from a lord who offered some hope of protection from Saracen, Dane or Hun. Hence in the early eleventh century, there emerged a radically different pattern of society. The royal vassals predominated, and the former freemen who had belatedly joined their ranks or become vassals of other lords were generally at a disadvantage, possibly because their protectors had driven a hard bargain in hard times. The various kinds of service by which the benefice was held became a single type: warrior-service. The vassal was the owner of the knights equipment, and he held his fief in return for his readiness to fight. As a German law-code put it in the fourteenth century, 'the fief is the pay of the knight'.[6]

In the process of disintegration, the threads of common political institutions which had bound France and Germany into one loosely connected state had snapped. The status of the knightly vassal evolved differently in each country. In France the relative weakness of royal authority until the twelfth century meant that the royal vassals were conveniently able to forget the royal claims to their land, and to set themselves up as free knights, or knights whose land was largely free with a few small fief-holdings, as in central France in the eleventh century. In Germany, on the other hand, the Ottonian emperors were able to enforce their title, and the new type of vassalage did not spread so quickly or widely on the east bank of the Rhine. As a result, the typical German knight was not a freeman, but the descendant of the old royal vassal, bound in person as well as land, even if he usually had a small freehold besides his fief.

The pattern varied from region to region, especially along the borders of the Empire. Namur has been closely studied in recent years: here in the eleventh century a group of about twenty noble families predominated, and freemen scarcely appeared outside these families. Towards 1150 a small group of knights appeared among the unfree vassals, and by 1200 had grown numerous, while about half the noble families had disappeared. On the other hand, in twelfth-century Burgundy all except two of a group of forty-three knights in the lands around Cluny were related to old noble families, and the number of knightly families remained remarkably constant.[7]

In countries beyond the sphere of Carolingian influence, a similar evolution took place from a very different starting point. In Normandy the descendants of Rollo's freebooting companions of the early tenth century were William the Conqueror's knights of the mid-eleventh century; in Spain, the freemen of the early eleventh century in Castile and León had become lesser knights a hundred years later, if they were rich enough to equip themselves. In these western kingdoms of Spain the feudal system failed to take real root. The 'knights' were armed freemen whose status had no connection with land, and the knighting ceremony was rare, if not completely unknown, before the thirteenth century. A social hierarchy based on the monarchy appeared, but it was founded on the extent of free-holdings and not on personal allegiances. Warfare was constant in Spain until the beginning of the thirteenth century, and a militia was needed, formed of the broader class of armed warrior produced by enforcing the old general duty of freemen to bear arms.

Thus the knight was not merely the warrior of an earlier age in a new guise. If he had been nothing more than that, he would have formed a much larger class. Equipment for mounted warfare was expensive, and only those who were prosperous could afford it. Hence the new class was a compound of men whose families were well-established without being noble, and of newcomers whose wealth had been won by adventure or ambition. The rise of the knight was apparent throughout Europe by 1050; and the distinction between them and the older nobility, whose roots go back to Merovingian and even Germanic princely families, was quickly blurred. The nobility had claimed special status by virtue of their descent; but at the moment in time at which pressure from the knights was strongest, the rules by which descent was traced were changing. The emphasis on the standing of the mother's and the father's family had been equal until the problem of inheriting fiefs appeared. Since these were passed on through the eldest son, descent in the father's line became paramount. Hence the knights were less sharply isolated by their lack of high birth than might have been the case if noble descent had been determined by a rigid set of rules. By the end of the twelfth century, nobles are knights, and knights are the highest social class, though the last traces of the dividing line only disappear in the late fourteenth century. By this time the knights' descendants had fully adopted the nobles' insistence on birth as the great criterion, while abandoning the knighting ceremony which had once been their proudest title.

Hence control of the land passed into the hands of one class. The predominance of the knights was complete in the eleventh and twelfth centuries. Political power was based almost entirely on force of arms; and the economic monopoly of agriculture had not yet been challenged by the towns. The knights were soldiers and rulers at once. Their power was increased by the weakening of the central authority during this period, caused partly by external circumstances, but also by the weakening of the king's hold over his vassals. The feudal hierarchy was no longer a perfect pyramid, as, in its purest form, it should once have been, with each vassal owing service to one lord only, his lord in turn doing homage to a higher lord or to the king. During the ninth century, this rule of exclusive service had been more and more frequently broken. The vassal felt that he could easily provide the necessary service for two or more benefices, either by creating his own vassals, or by keeping men trained in the arts of war as household knights, vassals who were supported as part of his household instead of receiving land. The ambitious lesser lords were not going to allow legal niceties to restrict them when their allegiance was at a premium; and a chronic shortage of skilled fighters had helped them to break down the old custom. By the tenth century, vassalage had become less a tie between man and man than a strictly commercial arrangement: if a man held several fiefs, the lord who gave most land had the greatest claim.

The old link had had a passionate loyalty derived from the old Germanic warrior tradition, reflected in the Anglo-Saxon *Battle of Maldon* as well as the *Chanson de Roland*. The lady Dhuoda might instruct her son in these high precepts in the ninth century as follows: 'Since God, as I believe, and your father Bernard have chosen you, in the flower of your youth, to serve Charles as your lord, I urge you ever to remember the record of your family, illustrious on both sides, and to serve your master simply to satisfy him outwardly, but to maintain towards him and his service in all things a devoted and certain fealty both of body and soul.'[8] Thereafter, as property became the predominant element in the relationship of lord and vassal, the personal side receded. The fief could be inherited, divided, and joined to other fiefs, despite the lawyers' insistence that the contract was from man to man: homage had to be renewed on the

27

death of the lord or vassal, when the fief was technically returned to the lord; the ceremony itself was a personal one; and only personal wrongs allowed the contract to be repudiated. As a result of the conflicting claims which the holding of several fiefs involved, a man with two lords would all too often have to choose between them in times when local feuds were common, and the vassal's oath came to be taken more and more lightly.

To counteract this problem, the solution of liege homage was devised. A vassal holding several fiefs would choose one (again, usually the lord from whom he held most land) as his especial lord, and swear a specific oath to serve him in preference to the others. The liege lord and his liegemen were bound in the same exclusive way as the earliest lords and vassals. The personal tie was revived, the vassal again being bound to defend his lord against all others. Though the idea of the special nature of liege homage persisted throughout the Middle Ages, it was soon debased in much the same way as simple vassalage before it. A man could become the liege vassal of a second lord with the consent of the original liege lord, and by the beginning of the thirteenth century this was generally accepted. England and the Kingdom of Jerusalem were exceptions, since liege homage there was the fealty sworn to the king irrespective of other feudal ties; elsewhere almost every lord was liege to his vassal, and ordinary vassalage was merely a less usual and less exacting form of the feudal contract.

The direct personal tie became less important as a more ordered society developed. In this society, the knight added to his roles as fighter and landowner a third, that of administrator. Justice, in early mediaeval society, was no theoretical abstraction, a high ideal that had to be translated into reality, but an eminently practical affair, concerned with personal and community relationships. The knight, as lord of his small and often self-contained world, became dispenser of justice and keeper of the peace, as the structure of society became more hierarchical and the freemen less numerous. The rise of a legal system based on the grass-roots manor court is difficult to chart; but it seems that if the possession of a castle was one possible criterion by which the future knight could be distinguished, the owners of manor houses within the villages with rights of jurisdiction were the other forerunners of the knightly class proper.[9] To some extent, these rights had been usurped from the king during the anarchy of the ninth and tenth centuries; but as central authority was reasserted, so the knights became the acknowledged administrators of justice at this local level, save in those matters reserved to the crown, controlling rather than replacing the old village assembly. This 'low justice' covered all manner of civil disputes, which would usually be questions of landholding, and some minor crimes; major offences were 'high justice' and hence within the scope of the royal courts only. However, all such rights of justice stemmed from property-owning, and it was only the knight's position as lord that gave him these powers: there was no connection as of right between knight-hood and jurisdiction, except in certain exceptional cases where a *de facto* situation had become the basis of law.

Yet within this new order, there were broad variations in personal circumstances. The castellans and their superiors were important figures, while many of the ordinary knights were no more than farmers, living directly off the land, even if closely related – and the knightly class was very closely intermarried – to greater lords. The real difference between them and the richer peasants was the inter-mittent summons to warfare, whether their lord's private feud or a greater royal quarrel, which took them into a wider and different world, and gave them a broader outlook. The need to avoid division of the fief if they were to maintain their status led them to send sons into the Church, and some inkling of the new intellectual ferment reached them through these contacts. Until the rural economy gave way to a money system, the lesser knight retained his close and practical contact with the land, which restricted his part in tour-naments, court life and the developing ideas of knighthood. Even in the later period the nobility remained obstinately rural in back-ground, never moving into the towns.

In their heyday in the eleventh and twelfth centuries, the knights had been in an almost unchallenged position. Only the clergy held comparable power as a class, and had some hand in government, but they lacked the knights' individual power as landowners. The thir-teenth century brought other changes besides the growth of the royal power: the new economic order was less favourable to agriculture as coinage was increasingly used, and the towns and new merchant classes stood outside the old hierarchy. The rise in prices throughout the next two centuries was not matched by an appreciable increase in the knight's income from his lands: no agricultural revolution came to the aid of the old kind of estate, with its small strip fields where the lord's land was hopelessly jumbled with the serfs' holdings, com-parable to that in the wool industry in England, where the East An-glian churches stand as evidence of the farmers' and wool-dealers' wealth. Not only were the lucrative rewards of trade forbidden to the knight by social convention, but the merchants themselves were hostile interlopers. And just when the one hope seemed to be alliance with this new moneyed class, the instinctive reaction of a threatened order prevailed: knighthood became more sharply self-conscious and exclusive in this period.

Hitherto, knights had been distinguished from the rest of society merely by their qualification in arms, which in turn had brought them relative wealth. Entry into knighthood and the attendant ceremony had been a simple formality that could be carried out by any knight for anyone's benefit. Nonetheless, it was acknowledged at a very early date that it was not advisable to knight men of low birth, and legal restrictions appear in Germany and Sicily in the twelfth century. In 1152 and 1179 German peasants had been forbidden to bear knightly arms on pain of a fine, and this purely practical measure was followed in 1186 by an order that sons of priests, as being illegitimate, and sons of peasants, as being unfree, were not to be knighted. Equally, Otto of Freising pours scorn on the Italians for knighting tradesmen and apprentices; but he refers to the towns of the north, because the Sicilian kingdom had preceded the Empire in imposing restrictions. Roger II in 1140 had forbidden the knighting of men who might disturb the peace, a move designed to prevent the raising of a rebellious force by wholesale dubbing and equipping of merchants or rich peasants. Though these measures were police regulations, both in Sicily and Germany, the implication that the king could control the practice of knighting remained; and the old right of any knight to make a knight of whomsoever he pleased, by which knighthood was a kind of apostolic succession, was replaced by the idea of hierarchy in which the king, as fount of all honour, had sole jurisdiction as to the making of knights.

The process by which knighthood became a hereditary right is an obscure one. It was partly based on the old Frankish law that only freemen might bear arms and serve in the national levies; as knight and freeman became more and more closely identified in the tenth and eleventh centuries, so the right to bear full arms was restricted to the knight only. Since personal freedom was hereditary, so knighthood too passed from father to son. In 1186 Frederick I implied in the edict already quoted that knighthood was to be restricted to the sons of knights. In 1231 Frederick II laid this down as law, both in his Sicilian and German domains: 'No one shall acquire the standing of a knight who is not of knightly family unless by grace of our special licence and mandate.' In 1235 the Cortes of Catalonia, in session at Tarragona, echoed his words: 'We decree that no one shall be knighted unless he is a knight's son.' By the mid-thirteenth century, both the law of Anjou and St Louis' legal collections insisted that both parents must be noble, though under certain conditions a peasant whose forebears had inherited a knight's fief four generations earlier could be knighted.[10]

Behind all this the hand of the Church can also be dimly discerned as it tried to restrain the knights by turning them into a lay order, with vows and ceremonies to match. So the restrictions which applied to holy orders – Alexander III had told the Bishop of Tours in the mid-twelfth century that neither bastards nor serfs should be ordained – were likewise to be preconditions for admission to knighthood; and even if the Church could not impose such restrictions effectively, it supported any effort to close the ranks of the knights and increase their standing.

From this period onwards the exclusive nature of the knightly caste was unquestioned, save in England. Those who contrived to join its ranks from below did so only by exercise of the royal prerogative; those who tried to do so under false pretences were duly punished. In France, under the regency of Blanche of Castile, Robert de Beaumont, a bourgeois, was fined £100 for having himself knighted.

Exceptionally, knighthood was the reward for great deeds of arms, in particular on the battlefield: more usually, it became another of the privileges put up for sale by a hard-pressed royal exchequer. After the defeat at Courtrai in 1302, Philip the Fair advertised his readiness to grant it for a fee. In France this could make sound financial sense to a rich merchant, as the knights had begun to acquire those exemptions from taxation which were to become one of the great abuses of the *ancien régime* in the eighteenth century, and the purchase of knighthood soon became a kind of quittance for future taxes by payment of a single lump sum. For an imprudent king, it was an easy way of raising money at the expense of future income, and similar schemes were used by Charles IV and his successors in Germany.

Likewise, in the early fourteenth century those fiefs which by their extent conferred nobility on their holder, could only be purchased by a non-noble on payment of a heavy tax, which made the fief 'free'; and this remained a possible means of entry into the French nobility until 1579, when titles attached to the tenure of a specific piece of land were abolished.

Despite these privileges, and the evident anxiety of wealthy non-nobles to make their way up the social ladder, the majority of the nobles, and particularly simple knights, grew steadily poorer during the thirteenth and fourteenth centuries. The freedom from ordinary taxes in France was more than offset by the expenses of feudal service and the heavy 'relief' payable on inheritance of a fief; Philippe de Beaumanoir in the 1380s reckoned a knight's lands to be worth one-sixth less than those of a non-noble. In England the exemptions were non-existent, and the feudal dues added to an already heavy burden. Conditions in Germany were unfavourable for other reasons, the chief being the incessant private wars and lack of political stability. The poor knight was a common figure throughout the Middle Ages, ranging from the younger son making his fortune in tournament and the old knight fallen on harsh days who could not find a dowry for his daughter (like the touching portrait of Enide's father in Chrétien de Troyes' *Erec et Enide*[11]), to the mercenaries and men of the 'great companies' fighting and plundering for a living or the robber knights turned to evil ways. Knighthood and wealth were by no means synonymous.

The special status of knighthood survived the mercenary instincts of the kings who were supposed to be its protectors. For reasons which we shall outline later, initiation into knighthood became a costly ceremonial process, which the poorer nobles were unwilling to undertake; and knighthood and nobility once again became separate concepts, having been for three centuries but facets of the same social idea. Nobility took on once more its hereditary form, requiring no formal admission or acknowledgment; knighthood became entirely a matter of membership of an order with a specific ceremony as its distinguishing mark. At the period in the mid-thirteenth century when the rulers of western Europe began to try to restrict the numbers of those who were exempted from taxes by reason of nobility, the old rule that a noble was a knight was no longer true. Hence nobility, once rarer than knighthood, now became dependent on it: to prove nobility, a man had to have a knight in his family. In Provence, grandsons of knights were regarded as having knightly privileges, but had to be knighted by the time they were thirty if they were to continue to claim these rights; in 1275 at Oppenheim in Germany a similar custom without the need for knighting at a specified age prevailed. By the early fourteenth century it was quite common for nobles to die as unknighted 'donzeaux' in France; of a group of fifty-six potential knights in the rebellion at Forez in 1314–15, only thirty-five were knighted before they were forty, and eleven died without being knighted at all.[12]

It was not only the cost of the actual knighting ceremony which acted as a deterrent. A new knight would have to acquire the basic equipment of war as well; and it was no longer a matter of a mere shirt of mail, helmet, sword and lance. Mail consisted merely of inter-linked metal rings forming a tough but pliable garment proof against cuts and stabs, and made up as a hauberk; it only covered the upper part of the body, with a coif over the head and neck. The conical helmet of four flat plates riveted together and shaped with a pro-jecting nasal was also a very simple piece of armour, within the average blacksmith's skill. The shield and sword were plain and prac-tical.

The knight of the late thirteenth century cut a very different figure. The helm had replaced the helmet, covering the head completely, and later to be equipped with a vizor to protect the eyes: the wearer was unrecognisable, and elaborate crests were worn to distinguish him from other knights in similar attire. The whole body was now en-cased in armour of varying degrees of flexibility. A series of plates attached to the basic mail armour protected the arms, legs, chest and back, and a quilted garment was worn beneath to lessen the dis-comfort. Besides this, the warhorse would bear a mail or cloth trap-per, often both, and a chamfron on its head, as protection. All this was extremely expensive, and not easy to obtain. In a strongly governed and peaceful country like England, only a knight who in-tended to make fighting his career, and to go in person to do his service rather than paying scutage (shield-tax) and other dues, was likely to regard the outlay as worthwhile. It was these men who continued to take up knighthood and to foster the traditions of their class as a whole. Their personal prestige stemmed from their achieve-ments as warriors, not from their financial or social standing, and they acquired something of the aura that sportsmen have today, while retaining their role as the focal point of the army. Men like these could not be raised by mere royal command, as Edward 1's experience in the feudal levy of 1282 showed; he had to excuse those who did not possess a horse, and allow them to pay a fine, even though they were possessors of land worth £20 a year. It was much easier to rely on paid troops, who might well be the same men as the feudal levy, but were at least likely to be properly turned out. In 1297 he specifically stated that he was only summoning a small number of knights in order that they should be better mounted and equipped.

This leads us to a problem which was never satisfactorily resolved, that of the relationship between the fief and the standing of the knight. It was all very well for Philip Augustus to try to enforce knighthood on fief-holders; but the fiefs were often split up, and a rich man might hold several parts of fiefs and still not fall under the terms of the enforcement. It is not uncommon to find fractions as small as one-tenth of a knight's fief in charters. Henry II had attempted a solution to the problem as early as 1180, when all who held land yielding more than £100 Angevin in his French domains were obliged to equip themselves as knights, although nothing was said about actual knighthood. It was only in 1254, under Henry III, that the full logic of this idea was applied in England, and tenants-in-chief holding land worth £60 or more per annum were not only to equip themselves, but were also to be knighted. The measure was undoubtedly aimed at increasing the numbers of titular knights, since as a class they had important administrative duties; though it was also a revenue measure, as fines payable for not taking up knighthood had been levied since the beginning of the century. There had been a vast decline from Henry II's day, when there were 5,000 landholders who could have been knights. By the end of the thirteenth century, even when the greatest possible pressure was exerted by the king, the total of English knights was unlikely to exceed 1,500, and only about 500 were capable of fighting. There were, however, still a number of landless knights: the Dictum of Kenilworth in 1266 includes provisions for dealing with those of Simon de Montfort's supporters who came from this class. The same proportion of knights to the whole population, estimated at one in 500 of all able-bodied men of full age, probably applies to France and Germany as well.

As knighthood became a matter of legal status, so the warlike character of the English knights was eclipsed by their duties in peacetime. The 'knights of the shire' became key figures in both local and central government. At the local level they were responsible for providing juries for the grand assize, and thus dealt with royal justice as well as their own manorial courts. By 1258 evasions and exemptions, and the persistent decline in numbers, meant that the grand assize could not be held in some counties because there were not enough knights available. And yet despite this the Provisions of Oxford, instigated by the barons in the same year, and probably supported by most of the knights themselves, gave the knights of the shire even greater responsibility in the sphere of local justice, a responsibility soon extended into what was in effect a complete review of all local administration. Quite apart from this, ordinary jury duty itself was not simply a matter of listening to skilled pleaders and assessing their prepared case; it often involved actual inspection of lands in dispute, administrative work connected with the court's decision, and police duties in criminal cases.

In central affairs, it was the knights of the shire who were the original members of the House of Commons. The four knights of the shire who brought their reports to Westminster in October 1258 were the forerunners of the most active part of the mediaeval parliament, though they quickly became public figures first and foremost, and knights only incidentally. In the country their standing as knights was a clear distinguishing mark; as members of parliament, they would have regarded 'knight of the shire' as a title having little to do with nobility or knighthood, and much to do with administrative duties. For this reason, parliament never became a class pressure group in the way that the estates of France did, and the knights as a body conscious of their identity did not appear in England. Indeed, within parliament they combined with their social rivals from city and borough, and became representatives of one part of the whole community. In France the same development took place in rather different circumstances. The English kings, being relatively poorer, relied largely on partly paid men to do the work of local administration and the purely professional civil service remained small, the rewards slight except for the great officers. In France the king's service became a means of livelihood for many French knights who found themselves in financial straits, and knighthood was the key to a political rather than military career.

Hence by the early fourteenth century the old feudal basis of knighthood had virtually disappeared. The summons to the feudal levy for forty days' service was a technical obligation, and the last two attempts at raising an English army by this method were in 1327 and 1385,[13] though it persisted elsewhere: in Liège an unsuccessful effort was made as late as 1435. Instead, a system of taxation based on landed wealth had become the means of raising revenue to pay a mercenary army. The distinction between the knight and the paid soldier after the late thirteenth century was merely one of name; both served of their own free will, though the knight had other financial means and was therefore not entirely dependent on warfare for his bread and butter. Furthermore the knight was also in many cases paid on a different basis, that of the *fief-rente*, whereby his military service was part of a feudal contract. Instead of land, however, he received a specified income in money. In an era which still thought in feudal terms this was a more natural arrangement than a straightforward salary and had the additional advantage of ensuring that men were easily available, since otherwise mercenaries had to be found for each separate expedition. Such arrangements could be made with either land-owning knights or household knights: as witness the agreement between the Count of Flanders and John Traiment de Noyelles in 1338. In return for £60 Paris per annum, John was to serve the count in all wars and tournaments, and was to receive in addition wages and maintenance in kind.

A century and a half later, nobility had become a much less rigidly defined matter. A clever lawyer could argue his way into it, which is much what maître Jean Boutaud in 1475 seems to have done, producing witnesses to swear that his family had always lived in a noble fashion, and had served in the king's armies. Another advocate, Jean Barbin, argued that his father was 'descended of a noble line, and as such held and reputed publicly and to the knowledge of all'.[14] Both cases succeeded; and it was the style of living and general esteem in which the family was held that decided the matter, rather than any question of formal knighthood. The two ideas had completely separated, even though the nobleman's duty to fight remained as a vestige of his former glories as a warrior.

This change had largely come about with the development of an economy in which money was more powerful than landed wealth. The lesser nobles depended not so much on landed fiefs as on the pensions, or 'fief-rentes', the reward of military allegiance or service at court, whether the King's court or some greater noble's. The outward and visible signs of their social standing were no longer the family castle, perhaps already a ruin, but their town house and country manor, neither necessarily fortified in any way. The old relationship between lord and peasant inherent in the older system had dissolved as well, partly because the state had taken over the knight's role as protector.

In times of peace knighting was neglected, and became purely honorific. In war it became a matter of military standing, and was more easily acquired by knighting on the battlefield. In times of anarchy the knights reappeared; but instead of being defenders, they became aggressors. If they had not always been a sure defence in times of trouble before, they proved a far worse menace now that they acknowledged no responsibilities. In Germany the 'robber knights' were partly excused by the needs of poverty. The Westphalian lords of the mid-fifteenth century had 'fields so unfruitful that they lie as desert, uncultivated . . . you could not watch without tears the way in which these fine knights had to fight, day in, day out, for their food and clothing, and risked the gallows or the wheel in order to avoid hunger and want'.[15] On the other hand, there was a strong and stubborn tradition of independence of authority, aggravated by the persistence of the idea of private war as a legal right. Even the Golden Bull of Charles IV in 1356, attempting to impose order on the riven Empire, confirmed that, provided due notice of

36

three days were given, private war remained the subject's inalienable right. In the early sixteenth century this right degenerated into little more than a system of legalised highway robbery in the hands of men such as Götz von Berlichingen, Franz von Sickingen and their associates, who declared war on Mainz, Nuremberg and other towns in turn, and were thus licensed to plunder their merchants at will. 'Knight' in such cases had come to mean merely an armed horseman; the wheel had come full circle.

Likewise, with the decline of ordered government in France in the Hundred Years' War, and particularly at the end of the fourteenth and beginning of the fifteenth century, the old instincts for plunder and rapine reappeared among the knights. It had been long enough since Bertran de Born sang the glories of war, war for no matter what cause; and he at least had wrested a castle of his own from his brother. A knight of the 'free companies' which ravaged France under the guise of greater political ends would have echoed his words cheerfully, but pleaded the same need as his German counterpart. Often unpaid and unprovisioned, whether living as garrison of a fortress or as a raider in enemy territory, he was forced to forage, and when foraging failed, to extort a living from the neighbouring peasants. This he did by the system known as *appatis*; at best this was a kind of local taxation, properly administered and accounted for, but when the same people had to pay it to as many as ten garrisons or companies, small wonder that they fled to the towns or eked out a living in the forests. The security which the knight's presence had once implied was now sold in the form of safe-conducts through the territory he controlled, and such documents were not cheap: 12s 6d for a month's safe conduct for a good ploughman who earned £3 in a year was no small sum. The sword had become a means of making one's future, and those who did not perish by it in the process might amass great wealth. Ransoms among the knights themselves were one matter, but to extort money from the common folk was another. Unfortunately, the latter was often easier; and it is not surprising that the knights as a class fell into disrepute during the fifteenth century.

By this time, however, the majority of so-called knights had no claim to the title: the few remaining knights who had adhered to the old practice and who had been ceremonially knighted, were a very small part of the class of armed warriors now termed knights. And the world of the lawless brigands who went under the once proud title was nearer to reality than that of the genuine knights, with their nostalgia for imagined glories of the past.

37

2

Knighthood

From the early days of knights who were simple fighting men to the extravaganzas of the most elaborate kind of chivalry, the ceremony of knighting was the central moment in a knight's life. Its roots lay in the initiation ritual, by which primitive societies marked the coming of age of adolescents. In Roman and Germanic society, the tokens of maturity were common to all free men; there was no idea of entry into an exclusive class restricted to the privileged few. The Roman's white toga and the German's spear and shield set the free man apart from the slave, but nothing more. Tacitus remarks of the German ceremony that 'no one shall take up his arms until the state has attested that he is likely to make good',[1] but he does not imply that the privilege is ever withheld, only that it can be delayed if the candidate is not yet ready for the field.

'When that time comes, one of the chiefs or the father or a kinsman equips the young warrior with shield and spear in the public council.'[2] In the eighth century, a very similar ceremony reappeared, as we learn from the meagre chronicles of the period. There seems little doubt that it was the direct descendant of the earlier German custom, as its form was specifically that of equipping with arms. Because of the change in ways of fighting, it was now the sword that was the symbolic weapon. Thus Louis the Pious, Charlemagne's son, was girded with the sword at Regensburg in 791, before going with his father on a campaign against the Avars; and in turn Charles the Bald underwent the rite at Chiersy in 838, when he was crowned and invested with part of the Empire. Louis II in 844 at Rome was girded with the sword during his coronation by the Pope, and among the insignia when Otto I was crowned at Aachen in 936 a sword figured prominently.

In the eleventh century, as records multiplied, lesser princes were described as being 'girded with the sword', a phrase which is used almost invariably until the early thirteenth century. The Norman kings introduced knighting to England, where the Anglo-Saxons had abandoned the custom of marking a freeman's coming of age; and from William I's knighting by the French king, we have a record of the knighting of each heir to the thone in turn. At Whitsun 1086 William I 'dubbed his son Henry to knight' (*dubbade his sunu Henric to ridere thaere*),[3] William Rufus having already been knighted. The custom continued in Germany and France likewise. Easter and Whitsun were the most favoured occasions for such ceremonies, when the monarch usually held solemn court; in England the crown-wearings on these days continued until the mid-twelfth century.

Until now the actual investiture had been performed by the father, except at the coronation of Louis II and Otto I. At Otto I's crowning, Archbishop Hildebert handed the new emperor his sword, admonishing him to eradicate with God's help all enemies of Christ, whether barbarians or bad Christians. In 1065 at Henry IV of Germany's knighting, and in 1098 at that of Louis of France, bishops were present; and in 1146 Gersa II of Hungary is said to have been given his weapons by bishops before a battle with the Austrians. The Church was thus taking a part in the making of a knight: and its role is confirmed by the appearance in the Pontifical of St Alban of Mainz of a prayer for the newly made knight. This order of service for the blessing of the sword was drawn up in the mid-tenth century, and it implies that the sword is laid for a moment on the altar just before the gospel is read at Mass. The usual form of prayer said over it ran:

> Hearken, we beseech Thee, O Lord, to our prayers, and deign to bless with the right hand of thy majesty this sword with which this Thy servant desires to be girded, that it may be a defence of churches, widows, orphans and all Thy servants against the scourge of the pagans, that it may be the terror and dread of other evildoers, and that it may be just both in attack and defence.[4]

The sword was then girded on by attendants (Plate II).

The Church's concern with the ethics of knighthood increased during the following century, and there was an attempt to adopt knighthood as an order of a quasireligious nature, of similar status to that of clerks in minor orders. The institution of the religious orders of knighthood proper in the early twelfth century, and the rise of the crusading ideal, both lent colour to the argument that knighthood was intended as the secular arm of the Church, for its protection and for the defence of the weak. A later prayer for the new knight underlined this: 'O Lord, who after the fall didst ordain three ranks of men to be in the whole world that Thy faithful people might dwell in safety and quietness secure from evil, hearken to our prayer. . . .'[5]

Geoffroi de Charny in the fourteenth century compared knighthood and priesthood as two great orders. And as this idea grew, so the original brief blessing, a formal ecclesiastical seal on a civil ceremony, became a self-contained church ritual. Frederick II of Austria was knighted by the Bishop of Passau at Vienna in 1232 after Candlemas in what seems to have been such a ceremony; and at the turn of the century counts Otto and Stefan of Bavaria were knighted by the Archbishop of Salzburg with 200 others. About the same time, chivalry acquired a patron saint in St George, and one of the manuscripts of the prayer for the blessing of the sword adds 'on St George's Day' after the title of the prayer.[6] A new order of service appears at about the same time, in the Pontifical of Guillaume Durand, Bishop of Mende, written about 1295. Here the sword is first blessed, followed by any other pieces of armour, a prayer is said, and the naked sword is given to the knight. It is sheathed and girded on; the knight then takes it out and brandishes it three times. The kiss of peace is exchanged, and the bishop gives him a light blow, saying 'Awake from evil dreams and keep watch, faithful in Christ and praiseworthy in fame'. The nobles standing by then put on his spurs, and if he is entitled to a banner, this is presented with a final blessing. The phrases of the service repeat the idea of protection: 'O Lord ... who didst wish to institute the order of knighthood for the safeguard of Thy people ...'; and there is a warning against the misuse of power: 'that he may not unjustly harm anyone with this sword or any other'.[7]

This ritual contains the essence of all later forms of granting knighthood, though the variations ranged from the elaborate knighting of a prince, to the simple words 'Be thou a knight' accompanied by a light blow either with the hand or the sword. The appearance of this *colée* or *paumée*, later to become the one essential act in the ceremony, is shrouded in mystery. It is only found in France and England before 1350, and even there is not universal. Llull's book on knighthood, written in Spain in 1265, knows nothing of it, and the many later translations of his book do not add the detail. The reference in the Pontifical is one of the earliest historical mentions of this procedure, though it appears in the French romances before this, at the beginning of the thirteenth century. Its exact meaning and origin seem uncertain; in the Pontifical, it is used to symbolise an awakening from sleep into the new life of knighthood. In *L'ordene de chevalerie*, a poem of the late twelfth century on the making of a knight, it is called 'a reminder of Him who has dubbed him knight, and ordained him'.[8] It is possible that it is related to the blow which freed slaves in the act of manumission, and to an obscure Germanic

40

custom of striking the witnesses to a legal act to make them remember the occasion (and also perhaps to wake them up!).

Until a squire was knighted he was technically not able to lead troops in battle. Hence there were occasions when knighthood was associated with the opening of a campaign or an imminent battle. Louis' girding on of a sword in 791 before the Avar campaign is the earliest example of this, and the giving of arms to Gersa II in 1146 before a battle is the first of numerous occasions on which knighthood was conferred on the field. In such circumstances it may not always have been possible to carry out the full ritual, and the very brief formula of a blow and the words 'Be thou a knight' may well have originated on such an occasion. When battle was expected at Vironfosse in 1338 between the armies of France and England, a hasty knighting took place by accident:

> The day passed until near twelve o'clock in disputes and debates. About noon a hare was started in the plain, and ran among the French army, who began to make a great shouting and noise, which caused those in the rear to imagine the combat was begun in the front, and many put on their helmets and made ready their swords. Several new knights were made, especially by the earl of Hainault, who knighted fourteen and they were ever after called *Knights of the hare*.[9]

Against this, most of the examples of knighting before a battle date from the fourteenth and fifteenth century, and seem to be inspired by slightly less theoretical ideas than fitness to bear arms. It was, first, one of the few occasions when the ceremony did not entail vast costs, and hence a poor squire would seek such an excuse wherever possible. Secondly, the knight was paid more for a day's fighting than the squire. And finally, a knight was less likely to have difficulty in raising a ransom, and was certainly in little danger of being killed out of hand instead of being taken prisoner.

The period of the Hundred Years' War provides numerous examples of the ceremony on the field of battle. In a foray into Scotland in 1335, Edward had made knights when expecting action at Annandale on 20 July; and in 1337, in anticipation of the war with France, the Black Prince made twenty knights on 11 March. A particular act of valour might be honoured by knighthood. On the crossing of the Scheldt in September 1339, Henry Eam was thus honoured, and being a poor squire was given lands worth £200 a year to support his new estate; and similarly Nele Loring was knighted and given lands for his part in the sea fight off Sluys. Before a great battle, the numbers might be considerable: at Aljubarrota, in 1385, Froissart

41

claims a total of 140 newly made Spanish knights, naming nine, and says that there were sixty created on the Portuguese side, who were placed in the front of the battalion to do honour to their new status. Knighting as a method of improving morale and making men eager for the fray is also mentioned at an attack on a stronghold near Ardres in 1380, when ten knights were dubbed and 'eager to do honour to their new knighthood, surrounded the tower of Folant, and immediately began the attack'.[10] The most scrupulous would-be knights, however, waited until they had in some way distinguished themselves, 'won their spurs', before their knighting. The phrase originated with those men such as Henry Eam and Nele Loring who owed their knighthood to a specific feat of arms; we find du Guesclin knighted after he had foiled an ambush by Hugh Calverley at Montmuron in 1354; and Pero Nino, 'the unconquered knight', was only knighted when he had seen thirteen years in the service of arms, aged twenty-eight. Most notable of all was the Black Prince at Crécy, where Edward iii refused to send him help – 'Let the boy win his spurs' – and knighted him after the battle.

There were other special occasions when knighting might be part of the proceedings. The journeys to Rome of the German emperors for their coronation by the Pope were frequently occasions for mass knightings: seven examples occur, though the ceremony was exploited for other ends, such as propaganda for imperial rights in Italy and the sale of titles to help the imperial treasury. From such a journey, the first contemporary record of dubbing by accolade occurs, when, on 31 December 1354, Charles iv knighted Francesco Carrara; the Emperor sat on horseback, and striking Francesco on the neck with the flat of his hand said, 'Be a good knight and true to the Empire.' Spurs were then put on by two of Charles's attendant nobles. A pilgrimage could be an occasion for knighthood: the Grand Master of the Teutonic Order knighted pilgrims to Prussia in 1377, and the tradition of knighting pilgrims to the Holy Sepulchre continued until the eighteenth century. The young Goethe witnessed the knighting ceremony at the coronation of a German emperor in 1765.

All this is a far cry from the reality of mediaeval knighthood, a reality which was nonetheless beginning to change by the time this new ritual appears. The words 'Be thou a knight', simple as they are, first appear at this period and are a sign of such a change. (The evidence for earlier French use of this custom derives entirely from romances: details of the ceremony are never given by historians. It is worth noting that Charles iv had been brought up in France.)

Earlier writers had almost always used words close to Tacitus, 'gird on the sword', or more rarely 'take up arms'. In 1106, a chronicler at Tournai speaks of 'making a knight'.[11] In 1198 Guy of Ponthieu, reporting on the knighting of the future Louis VIII which he had carried out, says that he had 'promoted and ordained him to knighthood'. By 1250 the idea of making a knight had become the usual one, and the Latin word *'miles'*, which had until now had a fairly general use as 'soldier', acquired the more specialised meaning of knight. The idea of knighthood as a special estate had been further strengthened by the royal and imperial ordinances which decreed that only sons of knights should be made knights. Originally little more than a restriction on the entry to the profession of arms, this now served to strengthen the feeling that knighthood was a corporation or fraternity. Indeed, to represent it as a kind of guild of soldiers aptly described one of its aspects. Yet this and the Church's efforts to make it an order are not quite enough to explain all its characteristics. The missing element, which begins to appear towards the end of the twelfth century, is a particular pride in descent, a kind of inherited glory, which finds its expression in heraldry.

The methods by which the fief was inherited had had considerable influence on the attitude of the nobles to ancestry. There is some evidence that the old way of tracing the family through the mother's line had survived into the tenth century. Now not only was this superseded, but the patriarchal side was heavily emphasised. The eldest son would normally inherit the fief; while the younger sons would have to go out and seek their fortune, as part of that society of *iuvenes*, men between knighthood and marriage, who are most distinct in northern France in the twelfth and thirteenth centuries. The best recommendation in such circles, until a knight had earned his own reputation, was his father's name as a warrior. It was probably for this reason that heraldic devices, originally personal, became hereditary, and the herald's interest in genealogy developed, an interest furthered by the exclusion from tournaments of men who were not qualified to become knights, again towards the end of the twelfth century. The original function of heralds had been to conduct tournaments, first proclaiming their place and date, and on the occasion announcing the combatants to the spectators, adding their own commentary on the deeds and renown of each. As the question of arms became more involved and more important, they kept records of armorial bearings, and from their knowledge of the conduct of business became officials with a recognised standing by the mid-thirteenth century. A hundred years later they appeared as diplomatic messengers, under the authority of the two chief officers of war, the marshal and the constable, doubtless becaue of their experience in proclaiming tournaments abroad.

The heralds had originally been involved with arms simply as a means of identifying combatants, a task which would have become increasingly difficult as armour covered the entire head and body. The first tournament shields were very simple, of a single colour with a simple device: the three leopards of Anjou, the three lions of England, the fleurs-de-lis of France, are examples. As the claims to use these individual devices were inherited by several sons, the practice grew of quartering the arms, taking those of both parents, especially since French law insisted that both parents had to be noble if a man was to be knighted. By the fourteenth century, only those who could lay claim to four noble grandparents were qualified to take part in tournaments, and the German 'tournament societies' could be even stricter. *Turnierfähigkeit*, the ability to take part in tournaments, was a jealously guarded privilege.

The rules of these societies were carefully framed to exclude 'robber knights', and as these might easily be nobles fallen on evil day, a moral censorship was also exercised. In 1434 Albrecht III of Bavaria was refused entry to a tournament because of his scandalous relationship with Agnes Bernauer; and in René d'Anjou's *Le Livre des Tournois* written in the 1450s, three main cases for exclusion are listed: perjurers and those who have broken their word of honour, usurers, and those who have married beneath their station. Thus secular knighthood adopted some of the characteristics which the Church had proposed for it some two centuries earlier.

The particular mystique of the word of honour, however, cannot be explained by religious influence. It was this, perhaps more than any other single feature, that distinguished the way of thought of the knight. If, as Francis I's motto after his Italian defeat ran, '*Tout est perdu fors l'honneur*' (All is lost save honour), little was lost. Honour was the shrine at which the knight worshipped: it implied renown, good conduct, and the world's approval. The 'word of honour' was the most solemn oath the knight knew, and this alone became the reason for the most extravagant exploits, fruit of a rash word spoken in the heat of the moment. Walter Manny's expedition into France in 1338 with a small band of forty horsemen was the result of his vow to be the first to strike a blow in the newly declared war. The whole world of romance depends on the convention that a knight's word once given can never be retracted for its incidents, and only the knight's lord could absolve such oaths. Usually they took a relatively harmless form: the holding of tournaments which outdid even those of romance – Moriz von Craûn's exploit of arriving in a ship on wheels at the tournament he had arranged outside his lady's castle pales beside the real splendours of the '*pas de l'arbre d'or*' at the wedding of Charles the Rash to Margaret of York in 1468. On the other hand a vow could be overridden by ducal or royal command; the Duke of Burgundy in 1454 annulled a vow by one of his knights to wear a piece of armour until he had found an opponent prepared to fight, and never to turn his horse's head back until he had killed an infidel.

René d'Anjou's second prohibition, that against knights who were usurers taking part in tournaments, marked another way in which knights were set apart. This was partly due to the rigid order of mediaeval society; if a merchant could not be a knight, then neither should a knight be a merchant. But there were deeper roots than this, in civil law. For the lawyer, working from late classical texts, *miles* meant soldier in general, as it had done in Roman days; but the same text could equally well seem to mean knight in particular. Thus when Giovanni da Legnano gathered the opinions of ancient authorities in his *Tractatus de Bello*, he used Justinian and the Roman lawbooks when he said that soldiers (*milites*) 'ought to abstain from the cultivation of the land, from the care of animals, from trade in commodities. They should not manage the business of other people; nor engage in civil duties.'[12] Towards the end of the fourteenth century Honoré Bonet writing *The Tree of Battles*, a work on the conduct of war, used this passage as the basis of his passage on the duties of a good knight and translated *miles* as knight, making the obligations of a Roman legionary part of a knight's way of life. Likewise, the romances about Alexander and Troy, which appeared in the twelfth century, and which describe classical heroes as though they were contemporary knights, gave knighthood a false classical pedigree, much on the lines of the eponymous Trojan founders of France and Britain. Knighthood was seen as an ancient institution, and proper pride was taken in its venerable age.

The realities of war, the ideals of the Church, the pride of noble families, the records of the heralds, and the researches of the lawyers all contributed to give the cult of knighthood an ardent following. Without the splendour of secular ceremonies and the flights of fancy of the romances, however, its flame would never have been so bright. The moment when a young prince came to take up knighthood was one of the occasions when the mediaeval love of pageant could be exploited to the full. Indeed, it was almost a duty so to do; in two

cases where chronicles only made brief mention of a knighting ceremony, a suitably full account was added at a later date to improve
appearance. In John of Marmoutier's biography of Geoffrey of
Anjou, we learn how he was knighted in 1129. After a ceremonial
bath and robing, gifts and horses were distributed to his companions;
while he received a Spanish horse which was said to be swifter than
the birds in flight, and a superb set of armour with a sword said to
have been made by Wayland the Smith himself. Likewise, when Lambert of Ardres described Arnold of Ardres' knighting in 1181, he
claimed that so much was given away that the new knight 'could
hardly call himself his own'.[13]

Apart from these romantic accounts, the real occasion was often
just as splendid. To make the occasion more impressive the prince
might be accompanied by a group of knights, as when Roger and
Tancred of Sicily were knighted in 1135 with forty others. In England
from 1223 onwards important heirs were frequently knighted with
others: Henry III's brother in that year had ten companions, Gilbert
of Clare in 1245 forty. The most splendid group was that at Edward
II's knighting in 1306, when 276 squires accompanied the twenty-
two-year-old prince. Because the palace was too small, the grounds
of the Temple were commandeered, and tents pitched there. All
expenses, save those of horses and armour, were paid, and the richest
garments provided. The night before Whitsun the prince and a few
chosen companions kept vigil at Westminster, the remainder at the
Temple; the prince was then knighted at the palace by his father,
and returned to Westminster to knight the other candidates. In the
press of the crowd, two knights were killed, several fainted, and
fighting broke out; only when the disturbance had been settled could
the prince proceed with the ceremony.

Such an occasion was by no means exceptional, save that Edward
had political reasons (the renewed war with Scotland) for requiring
so many knights at once. For splendour, the knighting of Louis
d'Anjou and his brother Charles by Charles VI at Saint Denis at
Easter 1389 easily matched it. Once again a religious establishment
(the monastery of Saint Denis) was commandeered to provide
enough room, and even so a temporary great hall, decorated within
like a temple, had to be erected in the main courtyard. The proceedings began on the Sunday, when at Mass the king administered
'the usual oath, [and] then bound on their swords and ordered M. de
Chauvigny to put on their spurs'. Three tournaments, one for knights,
one for squires, and a general one, followed, with dances and other
festivities each night; festivities which seemed to have disturbed the

46

monks somewhat, as the chronicler of Saint Denis records that 'the lords, in making day of night and giving themselves up to all the excesses of the table, were driven by drunkenness to all such disorders, that, without respect for the king's presence, several of them sullied the sanctity of the religious house, and abandoned themselves to libertinage and adultery'.[14]

At the other end of the scale were the occasions when ordinary squires of the royal household came to take up knighthood. There are frequent entries in the royal records of such events: in September 1248 William de Plessetis is told to send 'one silk robe, two linen robes, a cape and a bed and other things necessary to the making of a knight' to Marlborough in time for Christmas.[15] The ritual must have been very similar to that in *L'ordene de chevalerie*. The candidate's hair and beard were trimmed, and he took a ceremonial bath, after which he was laid on a bed for a short time; his robes were then put on: a white linen garment, with a scarlet coat, black surcoat and white belt. The actual knighting followed immediately, and as there was in any case the Christmas feast to follow, no special celebration was called for.

The Church had defined its ideas of the knight's duties in the prayers of the knighting ceremony, as a defender of the weak and of the Church itself. For those with little Latin, these ideals were set out in secular poetry, and enlarged upon. In a poem of the early twelfth century written by a clerk from the Rhineland, a series of simple commandments are given. He is to use wealth carefully, choose his company well, go frequently to church. Courage and readiness for battle are praised; he should not care too much for hunting, and 'should be interested in noble horses and also his sister's honour', avenging insults to himself as well. Above all, he should practise knightly deeds and 'seek whole victories'. The most interesting passage is that on love: 'A young knight should woo a noble woman, whom one can recognise as such by her noble bearing. He knocks at her door until she opens. He talks with her before the chimneypiece; she wants to talk away the sorrow from her heart. Whoever becomes too deeply in love and cannot tear himself away, loses his soul.' This homely vignette of a knightly courtship is a world away from the love of the troubadours, a practical view of life unaffected by romantic ideas.[16]

Even if romantic ideas gained wide enough currency for a preacher to say that 'no knight can be brave unless he is in love; love gives the knight his courage',[17] the older, simpler view of knighthood persists in the following century. In the prose romance of *Lancelot*, the Lady

of the Lake can lecture Lancelot on knightly duties and virtues without once mentioning love, and *L'ordene de chevalerie*, having depicted the actual knighting in great detail, has only a brief negative
list of things a knight should never do: never give false judgment;
never give evil counsel to ladies, but help them; fast on Fridays; hear
Mass every day and make an offering. In contrast to this simple
advice, great attention is paid in both works to the symbolic meaning
of each part of the knight's armour. As the hauberk safeguards the
body so the knight safeguards the Church; as the helm defends the
head so the knight defends the Church; as the fear of the lance drives
back the unarmed so the knight drives back the Church's enemies.
The two edges of the sword show that the knight serves both God
and the people, and its point shows that all people must obey him.
The horse that carries him represents the people, whom the knight
must lead, but who must support him and give him the wherewithal
for an honourable life.

This idea of knighthood as the bulwark of society against disorder
runs right through the manuals on the subject, and is partly a
justification of the knight's right to lead, partly a sanctification of the
feudal warrior. It is not enough to bear arms; the power given to the
knight must be used rightly if he is to be worthy of his knighthood. In
the late fourteenth century, Geoffroi de Charny, one of the foremost
knights of France, wrote of brigands as 'those armed men who are far
from being men-at-arms'.[18] He also saw the dangers of those who,
in an age when knighthood was becoming a rare title, sought
knighthood for the wrong reasons. The enthusiastic young knight was
welcome, as long as he realised that knighthood was hard work;
the middle-aged man had to be sure that he wanted the duties
as well as the honour; and as for the old men who would have
liked to have ended their days as knights, let them be sensible
about it.

Knighthood becomes inextricably bound up with the ideals of chivalry after the mid-thirteenth century, and the later manuals on it
belong to the ethics of chivalrous behaviour. In its original form
knighthood is a personal status which does not depend on the holding of land on the one hand, nor on belief in a certain code of behaviour on the other. Its distinctive character is supported chiefly by
the Church's ideas of it as an order with moral obligations towards
the society which supports it, combined with the adoption of
knightly descent as a test of nobility. It is a warrior caste such as can
be found in many societies, both feudal and non-feudal; and it is no
more than the basis for chivalry. Here the knight is soldier and lord;

later we will find him as knight-errant, lover and crusader: but we must still remember that chivalry and all its glories are only an extension of the original, simple institution of the recognised bearer of knightly arms.

3

The Heroic Age of Chivalry: the *Chansons de Geste*

The knights of the tenth century, preoccupied with survival in a hostile world, had little time or thought for literature; their songs and stories, like those in the camps of Troy during the historical Trojan wars, have not come down to us. The picture of those heroic days, both of chivalry and of the Greek epic, depends on later witnesses, both for its details and for the ideals which men held dear. Homer in his day preserved some of the real feelings of the men who fought these already legendary battles, and in the same way the old French poems known as the *chansons de geste* (*geste* being a deed or exploit) brought to life the battles of Charlemagne and preserved them in a literary form.

The *chansons de geste*, as far as they have survived, comprise a fragment and a complete poem from the late eleventh century, a group of fairly primitive poems of the twelfth century, and poems which gradually merge into the common stock of romance in the following years. Besides these we may place as both a yardstick and as another branch of the same literary form the Spanish *Cantar del mio Cid* (Song of the Cid), and the German heroic tale, the *Nibelungenlied* (Song of the Nibelungs). The latter, written in the early thirteenth century, reflects a much older society, some of its episodes belonging to sixth-century history. The fourteenth-century *Cantar del mio Cid* is set in the eleventh century, and the *chansons de geste* likewise deal with the Carolingian period, from the eighth century onwards.

The three great themes of the *chansons de geste* remained static from an early period. The defeat of Roland at Roncevaux, the deeds of William, Count of Toulouse, and the rebelliousness of the northern French barons under Charlemagne's successors, became established as the accepted subjects for such poems. Both authentic independent episodes and invented scenes were attached to them until they formed three great cycles, tenuously connected by a series of common figures. The chief characters largely belong to Charlemagne's family and two great clans: that descended from Garin de Montglane, the fearless, righteous heroes, and that of Doon de Mayence, the corrupted traitors. There is scarcely a single character who does not find a place in this scheme, though the general traits of the clan may not appear in each of its members: for example, Charlemagne is a grandiose, heroic figure, but his son Louis is presented as a simple, weak and indecisive character who has to be rescued from his own folly, and is far from a worthy descendant of the great Emperor.

In the form in which these poems have come down to us they date from the early twelfth century or later, with the exception of the great *Chanson de Roland* and the fragment *Gormont-et Isembart*. Hence they largely belong to an age when knighthood was already a well-established institution, and when the crusading movement had already achieved its first triumphs. The attitudes they reflect are only a decade or two earlier than those of the romances, as are their expressions and turns of phrase; and there is a literary element, however crude they may seem beside the romances, which nonetheless brings them close to the calculated inventions of the latter. Even in the *Chanson de Roland*, the earliest complete poem, the story is treated as a triptych in which the death of Roland, Charlemagne's victory, and the avenging of Ganelon's treachery balance and complement each other. The very fact that almost all the tales have been cast in the form of cycles is another mark of a conscious idea of literary method.

Yet the material of the *chansons de geste* belongs to a much less sophisticated world than the enchantments of romance. For this reason it is easy to be deceived by the stories into taking the actual poems to be the original raw material of epic. In that case one would have to account for a remarkable burst of literary activity in France about the year 1100, centring on events which had happened two or three centuries earlier, for all the historical events which these poems celebrate belong to the years 716–943. Furthermore, the records of this period are never detailed enough in style to enable a poet, however scholarly and assiduous in his research, and with access to a multitude of lost sources, to provide such lifelike accounts. Above all, there are certain details in many of the poems which are too much at variance with the story to have been invented, and yet ring true as history.

There is only one convincing explanation for this mixture of literature and history in the *chansons de geste*: that the versions we possess are descendants of a tradition which goes back to contemporary poems on the events of Charlemagne's time. This is supported by studies of modern societies where the epic still flourished in recent times, notably in Serbia. Long poems composed on recent political events were recited by local bards; their methods, notably of variation at each telling and repetition of stanzas for emphasis, are echoed in the old French epics. And beside these recent works, this traditional poetry dealt with the events of five centuries ago with some degree of historical accuracy. Indeed, it has been argued that variation (which the surviving scripts of the *chansons de geste* provide to a remarkable degree) was essential to keep the oral poetic tradition alive; no audience wanted to hear exactly the same version told again, and the older version would be forgotten as the poet learnt or invented some new phrase, metaphor or even episode. Finally, there is the parallel of the twelfth-century German *Nibelungenlied* already mentioned, where events of the sixth and seventh century (again a period in which the style of historical works was terse and not given to great detail) are described in terms which imply the use of material handed down by tradition and including details unknown to orthodox historians.

Thus the *chansons de geste* reflect in varying degrees the whole formative period of knighthood. The historical background of the eighth century and the knightly attitudes of the late eleventh century predominate respectively in the matter and the point of view. Two of the cycles, those based on the *Chanson de Roland* and the *Chanson de Guillaume*, share a common theme: the struggle between Frank and Saracen in southern France and Spain in the eighth century. Despite Charles Martel's great victory at Poitiers in 733, the Saracens continued to threaten the safety of the south, through their presence in Spain and their raids from the sea and from their bases on the Mediterranean coast. Charlemagne's aggressive imperial policy, which consisted of reducing hostile enemies on his frontier to client-states, was bound to bring him into conflict with the Moorish kingdoms beyond the Pyrenees. Only the Saxons on his German borders caused him more anxiety; from 777 onwards the Saracens ranked as a problem of the same order, and expeditions of varying sizes set out almost every year until 814.

The *Chanson de Roland* celebrates the first and probably greatest of these forays. In 778, in response to an appeal from Spain – though it was not because Charlemagne was 'moved by the cries and complaints of the Christians under the heavy yoke of the Saracens', as a contemporary chronicler has it, for the appeal came from Muslim emirs engaged in a feud with others of their religion – Charlemagne moved into Spain, hoping to establish his influence over his allies and thus secure the frontier. Pampeluna and Gerona fell, but Saragossa was resisting him successfully when news came from Germany of fresh Saxon attacks. As the Spanish expedition had engaged most of his military resources, this meant retreat, and as he recrossed the Pyrenees his rearguard was ambushed in the narrow pass of Roncevaux, on the Spanish side of the mountains, by the Basques (probably with Saracen assistance, though the early chroniclers know nothing of this). Among those who fell were the king's seneschal and count of the palace, as well as 'Roland, duke of the Breton march, and many others'. There were at most 1,000 horsemen involved in the encounter; trapped in the steepsided defile, they must have been an easy prey, unable to manœuvre. Charlemagne was unable to avenge the disaster, not so much because the enemy had disappeared into their native mountains, but because of the more urgent threat from Germany.

William of Orange belongs to the same era; his prototype was probably William, count of Toulouse, the first of a series of powerful magnates to bear that title, who defeated a renewed Saracen onslaught on the banks of the Orbieu, between Carcassonne and Narbonne, in 793. Both he and Roland remain shadowy figures in history, and the only early chronicle to relate their deeds at length is that ascribed to Turpin, Archbishop of Rheims and Roland's supposed companion at Roncevaux, which is really a twelfth-century confabulation.

The third cycle, of the rebellious barons, is a more diffuse group. *Gormont et Isembart* is not strictly part of it, dealing with a victory of Charles III over the Northmen in 881: the tradition that all great battles were fought against the southern infidels is so strong that the traitor Isembart's allies have become Saracens. The real cycle is centred on Raoul de Cambrai, to whom the *Geste des Lorrains* was connected by thirteenth-century writers using a tenuous genealogy. Here again historical notices are very sparse. In 943, the chronicler records, after the death of count Hubert II of Vermandois, there was war between his sons and Raoul, son of Raoul de Gouy; and the only other detailed record again draws on a literary source akin to the *chanson de geste*. Likewise, Garin de Lorrain and Girart de Roussillon or de Vienne are shadowy figures, and it is only with difficulty that their historical counterparts can be identified.

If the historical background to the *chansons de geste* is obscure, so are their literary antecedents. If we accept the idea of oral tradition as the missing link between the actual events and their written versions, there still remains the problem of who wrote the poems we now have. It is not a question of not having authors' names: the enigmatic Turoldus appears at the end of the *Chanson de Roland*, and in *Raoul de Cambrai*, Bertolai is presented as the original author. It is a question of what kind of men we are dealing with. If the writers, or even the recorders — who would have refashioned the poems somewhat were clerics, we must make due allowance for clerical attitudes; while if they were jongleurs themselves, the poems are more valuable to us as witnesses of knightly society and its ethics.

We start with poems 'born on the spot relating notable contemporary dates or facts'.[1] This is the skeleton of all our poems: the main course of action and the main traits of the characters belong to this period. The elaboration and connection of this material was the work of jongleurs in the following centuries, who omit details, invent new ones, and weld earlier unconnected pieces into longer works. Such refashioning would be largely an unconscious effort to arrange the material in a more easily memorable form, and to adapt to their audience's tastes. Of these poems nothing survives. The *Chanson de Roland*, first and also finest of the surviving poems, comes from the last phase when the literate men who wrote the legends down probably gave them a more polished style and borrowed literary turns of phrase in order to gloss over the weaknesses which repetition had introduced; and made from crude recital, elegant reading. To this phase belong the subtleties of tragedy and patriotism which, without changing the stories, emphasise and alter details to heighten the effect. Occasional echoes of Latin learning appear, culled from the meagre repertory of eleventh-century education.

Hence the *chansons de geste* were the product of a society still not literate, but which had moved beyond the most primitive stage of oral records, and which knew of literature, even if only as a mystery for clerks. They were scarcely affected by theory or by earlier works; instead, it was their immediate surroundings, the great baronial halls where the jongleur recited them to a simple musical cadence (Plate III), that shaped them. The *rapport* between an audience of fighting men, capable of appreciating the subtleties of their descriptions of battles, and the minstrel was essential: to see them on the cold printed page invites misunderstanding.

The themes and heroes which held the rough fighters spellbound were close to their own enthusiasms and way of life. Warfare is central to all of them: the hero is a good fighter in battle. And as in warfare loyalty to the leader is paramount, so fidelity and treachery are the twin poles of virtue and vice for these early knights. The *Chanson de Roland* has become the epitome of the *chansons de geste* as well as the chief masterpiece among them. It is built on two great episodes: Charlemagne's retreat from Spain and Roland's death, and Charlemagne's revenge on Baligant and Ganelon. Roland's death is the key to the action. It is encompassed by Ganelon, who, sent on an embassy to Spain after Roland has insulted him, arranges that the Saracens shall fall on the emperor's rearguard. He will see that Roland is in command of it; for not only is Roland his enemy, but the implacable foe of peace; Charles will never weary of going to the wars 'while Roland still bears sword'. Ganelon favours peace, and has said so at the council with which the poem opens: thus there is a subtle equation between the pacifists and the traitors. Ganelon's scheme succeeds: Roland is named leader of the rearguard, and with him go Oliver, his friend and companion, and the warlike Archbishop Turpin. The trap is set, and when Oliver sees that not one but five armies confront them he begs Roland to summon Charlemagne by blowing his ivory horn (Plate IV). In a famous scene, Roland refuses and Oliver insists:

> 'Roland, my friend, blow your ivory horn
> For Charles to hear as he rides through the gates
> Of Spain. Be sure, the Franks will soon return.'
> 'Let it please God,' Roland quickly replied,
> 'No man on earth shall ever say of me
> I blew my horn for fear of pagan troops;
> My kin shall never be reproached for that.
> When in the battle's heat I take my stand,
> I'll deal seven hundred—no, a thousand strokes—
> And Durendal's bright blade shall run with blood.
> The French are brave, they'll do as vassals should;
> Our Spanish foes come only to their graves.'[2]

'Roland is fierce, and Oliver is wise'; but the hero is Roland, not Oliver, and it is his boast that he will destroy the entire heathen army, despite its evident folly, that wins the poet's admiration, rather than Oliver's practical caution. The least hint of fear must be shunned:

'And damn the man whose heart admits despair',[3] and bravery is what a baron's reputation and position depend on: 'If the King loves us it's for our valour's sake.'[4]

So Roland goes willingly to his almost certain death, because of an ideal courage and trust. To object that it is not in the emperor's best interest that he should do so, is to make the argument too subtle. Roland has been given a task to do: when he was given command of the rearguard, he declares that Charles shall not lose even a mule unless it is bought with the sword.[5] This is all that counts: the task he has been entrusted with by his lord. When, having destroyed four of the pagan armies, he is overwhelmed by the last attack, and Oliver rebukes him for his foolhardiness, he cannot see what he has done wrong, nor why he should not now summon help, since his resources are at an end. And as he dies, his last thoughts before he commends himself to heaven are that his emperor should see that he had carried out his charge well, now that the Saracens have fled:

> He turned his head to face the pagan host;
> For he desired that Charles, and all the men
> Of France, should see his dying glance and say
> That he died as he lived, a conqueror.[6]

If faithfulness is the subject's great virtue, justice is that of the lord. Charlemagne must do justice to his dead vassal by avenging him; first on the Saracens, second on the traitor. The battle against Baligant, Marsile's new ally, is a huge set piece, as emir rides against peer, Frank against Paynim, culminating in the duel between Charlemagne and Baligant. Once the heathen are defeated, their leaders slain, and the idols down, he can return to France, and deal with Ganelon. For one terrible moment it seems as though the traitor will be forgiven: there are many of Ganelon's kin to declare that it is better that he should live to serve the king. But a champion comes forward to support the king's angry reply, 'False traitors are ye all', and Ganelon's supporters are vanquished. With their death, 'the Emperor's debt of vengeance now is paid';[7] though the business of empire goes on, and a new summons to war ends the poem – leaving the way open for a continuation.

Of the central characters of the poem, Roland, Oliver and Ganelon are the most individual; Charlemagne and Turpin represent ideals rather than personalities. Roland, too, has a large measure of the ideal hero in him. His courage is unsurpassed – 'There's none so valiant beneath the heavens broad' – and his appearance handsome and gay:

> Now Roland rides through passes into Spain
> On Veillantif, his swift and sturdy horse,
> Bearing such arms as well become his ways.
> Fearless the baron goes, grasping his spear—
> Its head so proudly pointed at the sky,

And to its tip a snow-white pennon laced.
The golden fringes reach down to his hands.
His heart is bold, his face is clear and gay.[8]

This proud appearance betrays a proud heart within: when at the beginning of the poem he offers to go as messenger to the Saracens, Oliver retorts:

'You're fierce in mood and proud in your heart;
I fear you'll start some dangerous argument . .'[9]

It is this ferocity and tenacity that makes him a superb fighter; only at the turn of the battle at Roncevaux does his heart fail him, and then it is from grief at the sight of so many good knights slain, not from fear. War is all that he lives for: his speech against the proposed peace is not reasoned counsel, but an impassioned plea for the existence he loves. 'Roland is fierce . . .'

'. . . And Oliver is wise'. Oliver is the foil to the hero's impulsive bravery, and is one of the few characters on the French side for whom no historical roots have been found. His country, the 'Vale of Runers', is mythical; yet his name is found linked with Roland's from the beginning of the tenth century. If he is an entirely invented character, he belongs to the jongleur's inventions, not the later literary refashioning. But he was probably brought in less as a foil than as the type of the perfect companion. It is easy to see only the contrast between his wisdom and calculation and Roland's headstrong, berserker ways, and forget the close links that bind them. The poignant moment when Oliver, dazed and blinded by his wounds, strikes Roland in his confusion, and Roland answers him with uncharacteristic gentleness, reveals the depth of the bond:

The blow strikes home; then Roland stares at him
And asks, his voice as always soft and mild:
'My friend, can you have meant to strike that blow?
Look, I am Roland, look, your dearest friend;
And, Oliver, you did not challenge me.'[10]

Oliver is second only to Roland in battle once the fray begins; but he lacks the high zeal of his companion. If he is a more attractive character, his example does not fire the spirit as Roland's does.

Ganelon is likewise a more complex being than Roland. Roland cannot understand his stepfather's devious mind, which sees threats everywhere. He sees Roland's recommendation of him as ambassador as a plot to encompass his death (the last envoys were killed) and

Roland makes matters worse by laughing outright at his fears. Being cunning himself, he expects others to be equally cunning: hence his success with the Saracens, when he at first defies them and then waits for his treacherous conversation with their envoy to bear fruit. But cunning is not a virtue in this heroic world, and treachery is the foulest of crimes: so Ganelon meets his gruesome end, dragged apart by four stallions. If he had his good points – he has served Charlemagne well, and is as fine a figure of a man as any of the barons – they are all marred by his betrayal: 'A man right noble he'd seem, were he not false.' Yet there are still human touches to his conduct: his first thought, when he is faced with almost certain death, is of his wife and son: and his kinsmen's loyalty to him costs them their lives. Roland and Oliver have no such ties, and Roland's cause finds but one lone champion besides the Emperor.

Charlemagne himself dominates the poem. He is an ideal figure to the extent that he never gives orders himself but always asks his barons their advice, as though the embodiment of empire could not stoop to a personal decision. Even in the duel with Baligant, the two rulers of Christendom and Islam seem gigantic allegorical figures, isolated and apart from the throng of the general battle. He is a focus for men's reverence: the dying Oliver thinks of him and 'la douce France' which he rules, as much as of Roland, and Roland's last earthly thought is of 'Charles his Lord.'

Roland serves Charles as warrior first, as a Christian second; Turpin, the representative of religion, is a warrior as well. His warlike ways are more in evidence than Roland's Christianity. He breaks canonical laws about bloodshed, and he does not even trouble to observe the letter of the law by using a mace, that standard weapon of warrior-bishops. Indeed, he shines more as a fighter than as an archbishop: an ideal cleric from the fighting man's point of view, he belongs entirely to the world of the barons. His exhortation to the troops is brief and to the point: by the sword one can win a martyr's reward in heaven. Yet he has an aura of real Christianity, soothing the quarrel between the two champions, and dying as he goes to fetch Roland some water, though he himself is more in need of help than the count.

The other *chansons de geste* do not present us with such sharp characters, polished manners, and subtle motives. Even the cycle of Guillaume d'Orange, despite some fine scenes, tends to portray everything in black and white, and only Guillaume and his wife stand out vividly. Whereas Roland has his moments of weakness, and Ganelon his moments of humanity, Guillaume and the treacherous barons whom he opposes are contrasted in the crudest terms. We are merely told that Erneis d'Orléans is a traitor; ample justification for Guillaume to stride up to him at Louis' coronation, and to kill him in the church – not with a sword, for that would mean bloodshed on hallowed ground, but with a blow of his fist.

This very simplicity is at times more revealing than the *Chanson de Roland*'s subtleties. Guillaume goes to reproach the king for giving fiefs to his favourites, and finds no satisfaction in promises of other men's lands or indeed of a quarter of the Kingdom. Guillaume wants not simply a reward for his services, but the fair and proper reward. For his story is above all that of a great warrior, but of a warrior who is also just, faithful to his wife and family, and a wise counsellor: he is, in a word, the ideal baron rather than a heroic figure on the scale of Roland. In the competition for glory, he is always in the forefront: so much so that his nephew Bertrand complains: 'You get everything – all the battles and all the glory. Your prowess makes ours appear as nothing.' He has conquered Provence, Champagne and Burgundy and overthrown most of the king's enemies almost singlehanded; and when he finally claims his reward, he asks for lands held by the Saracens, which he will have to conquer.

The main part of the poems about Guillaume d'Orange is concerned with his war with the heathen. He takes Orange, and makes it his chief residence: and here he weds the lovely Saracen princess Orable, christening her as Guibourc. It is for her sake that the Saracens make war on Guillaume; there is little religious element in the count's wars, though the maxim put forward in the *Chanson de Roland* that 'pagans are wrong and Christians are right' still holds good. If there were monsters among Roland's foes, such as Chernubles of Munigre, whose hair sweeps the ground, and whose home is a desert land, sunless and black, there are apparitions as strange among Desramé's men: 'What is this strange army of beasts who come at us?' Guillaume demands as King Agrapax is killed, 'a squat creature two feet high, with hairy face, shining eyes and sharp claws like a griffin's'. Yet Rainouart, who kills this nightmarish creature, is a Saracen by birth, like his aunt Guibourc and cousin Vivien; and these converted heathen are the heroes of the Christian side.

In the *Chanson de Roland*, Marsile, the heathen king, and Charlemagne are both described in council, at the beginning of the poem, in very similar terms: both are imposing figures with a noble and valiant following and wise counsellors. Nor is the attraction of the heathen as people denied in either poem: there is Margaris of Seville on the one hand:

> *His handsome face wins all the ladies' love*
> *And every girl that looks at him grows gay;*
> *She cannot keep from smiling for pure joy.*
> *No pagan knight can match his chivalry.*[11]

And on the other there is Orable-Guibourc, a second Helen, whose beauty is at the root of Guillaume's war with the Saracens. It is only the errors of their faith, the laws of the three idols that they worship, that makes them treacherous and deceitful. No attempt is made to understand the Muslim religion; the three images which the Saracens are supposed to worship are absurdities, with no counterpart in the real Islam, a monotheistic religion which abhorred idolatry. There is sympathy on a human level, but no intellectual contact.

Guibourc, Guillaume's wife, is a very individual character. Her counterpart does not occur anywhere else in the *chansons de geste*, nor in the later romances. For she is an eminently practical figure, yet dearly loved by Guillaume. The exotic princess becomes a woman who can welcome her defeated husband home in his blackest hour, and find the means to comfort him. This scene, when Guillaume returns alone after the great defeat at Aliscans, having lost his nephew Vivien and 15,000 men, is more poignant than all Roland's heroics: Guillaume seated at the lowest place in the hall, because he cannot bear to sit at the high table as he used to do with his men around him; Guibourc's tender care mingled with courage, which makes her send him on his way again into the darkness in search of help. But its poignancy is because it is homely, familiar, and down-to-earth; it is a scene from the Scandinavian epics or from the *Nibelungenlied*, where woman is a helpmeet and equal. 'La belle Aude' in the *Chanson de Roland* is much more fitted to this world of heroic knighthood; she appears only to die of grief at the news of Roland's death, expressing the blind devotion that such a knight inspires.

As a warrior, Guillaume can be brutal as well as fierce: in a macabre scene at the battle of Aliscans, he fights with Aerofle and cuts off his leg and thigh, then proceeds to mock him, saying that he should get a crutch now, and everyone will see that he is one of the Count of Orange's victims. He seizes Aerofle's splendid horse, Folatise, and gallops round as Aerofle watches in despair and agony before Guillaume returns to give him his death blow; and for the sake of Folatise he abandons his faithful steed Baucent to be hewn apart by the Saracens.

If a mixture of idealism and vivid reality is typical of the legends of Guillaume d'Orange, there is almost no idealism at all in *Raoul de Cambrai*. Raoul is scarcely a hero at all. He is a fine warrior, it is true, but all is ruined by lack of self-restraint: 'a man who cannot hold himself in check is good for nothing,' his chronicler declares. His career is almost an exemplary tale, a warning. He slowly alienates all his best followers, until only a like throng of evildoers accompanies him: Bernier, his faithful companion, bastard son of the man Raoul has killed, puts up with his misdeeds for as long as he can. In the culminating horror, Raoul attacks a nunnery at Origny, and orders his tent to be pitched in the church, his bed to be made up against the altar, and his hawks to be mewed to the crucifix. This is too much even for his followers, and he gives way with a bad grace. Later, despite the pleas of the abbess, he takes offence at an imagined slight, and burns the nuns alive in their nunnery, including the abbess, who is Bernier's mother. Even now, Bernier comes to Raoul to reproach him, rather than rebelling at once, and only when Raoul actually strikes him does he turn and utter a *défi*, the formula by which a wronged vassal disowned his lord. Bernier becomes his deadliest enemy; and when Raoul's pride leads him into fresh battle, and into a blasphemous declaration that no power on heaven and earth, not even God and all the saints, can prevent him from killing a knight whom he has at his mercy, it is Bernier who appears as an avenging angel and who, when he refuses to stay his hand, strikes him down.

If the relationship between Guillaume and King Louis showed how a vassal should not be rewarded, that between Raoul and Bernier shows how a vassal should not be treated. Bernier asks for no more than that his lord should not wrong him, and serves him until there can be no question of making amends. In both cases, the central part played by the feudal bond in the plot reflects its importance in real life, and the familiarity of the listeners with the correct procedure in such relationships, and the occasions on which a vassal could lawfully 'defy' his lord. The true working of the relationship between vassal and lord is shown in Roland's loyalty to the trust which Charlemagne has placed in him, and in Charlemagne's deep grief for his dead warriors, whom he carefully bears away with him for burial in 'la douce France' as custom demanded.

Lastly, there is the relationship between warriors on equal terms and between the family, 'compagnonnage' and the ties of blood. The high regard for the kinship of uncle and nephew, particularly when the latter is a sister's son, which can be traced back to Germanic society, is remarkable throughout the *chansons de geste*. Roland is Charlemagne's nephew; Guillaume has two nephews, Bertrand and Vivien, both of whom prove worthy of him. Sons, on the other hand, are less highly regarded: indeed, Charlemagne's son Louis drives his father to despair in the *Couronnement Louis*, the opening of the story of Guillaume. 'Compagnonnage', blood-brotherhood from childhood, which was to find its epitome in the romance of *Amis et Amiloun*, the classical mediaeval example of friendship, is at its most poignant in the *Chanson de Roland*, but it is best summed up in the famous words from *Garin le Loherains*:

> There is no worth in mantles or furs
> Nor wealth in coins, in mules or asses
> But riches lie in friends and kindred;
> One man's heart's worth a country's gold.[12]

As are, the poet might have added, a swift horse and a well-tempered blade. Throughout the *chansons de geste*, these essential parts of a warrior's equipment play a special part, and almost acquire a life of their own. Roland tries to destroy his sword Durendal lest it falls into heathen hands: Charlemagne's sword Joyeuse is almost magical in its properties. Elsewhere, it is the horses that are highly prized: Guillaume's Baucent is almost capable of understanding speech, though he does not belong to the race of fairy horses of the romances.

If we compare the *chansons de geste* with the Scandinavian epics, we will find many points of similarity, and the Anglo-Saxon heroic poems reflect the same qualities. Only the context varies: the *chansons de geste* are firmly Christian, the northern poems heathen or converted in name only. What is perhaps missing in the northern poets is the sense of a 'grand design', a right order of society, in which the warrior, like everyone else, has his pre-ordained place: he is different only in that he is the chief glory of his nation. In the northern poems, we are in a narrower, more personal world, which does not look outwards beyond the confines of the warband, the chosen few comrades-in-arms: in *The Battle of Maldon*, Byrthwold sums up this attitude in the famous lines at the end of the poem:

> Mind must be the firmer, heart the more fierce,
> Courage the greater, as our strength diminishes.
> Here lies our leader, dead,
> An heroic man in the dust.
> He who now longs to escape will lament for ever.
> I am old. I will not go from here,
> But I mean to lie by the side of my lord,
> Lie in the dust with the man I loved so dearly.[13]

There is only one fierce virtue here, that of loyalty. Roland holds to the same ideal, but in a more complex world, where loyalty is concerned with not only a warrior's lord, but with the emperor and with Christ. The feudal warrior has to bear in mind more demands on his allegiance than the heroic simplicity of Byrthwold's creed.

The *chansons de geste* and their ideals arise directly out of the nature of feudal society. There is no alien magic here; there are no high concepts of love or abstract notions of duty. Roland and Guillaume obey the ordinary rules of feudal conduct; because they move on an heroic plane, with heroic tasks to accomplish, what in mere mortals would be simple obedience to duty becomes heroic. And in this lies the concept of chivalry of the *chansons de geste. Chevalier* by itself still means little more than horseman or knight; but the poet never speaks of a bad *chevalier* – it is always a matter of a good, courageous, valiant or bold *chevalier*, and the adjective *chevalerus* denotes a quality of strength and boldness combined. *Chevalerie* itself means the state of being a *chevalier*, of knighthood. It also means prowess, but it turns up in unexpected places and Ganelon can call the idea of killing Roland *gente chevalerie* – a fine deed of arms. There is a rudimentary idea of fair play, but it is scarcely more advanced than that of the *Nibelungenlied*: to kill a man from behind, or with a thrown javelin, is regarded as cowardly, but to fight two against one is by no means bad conduct. Before attacking, it is usual to issue a challenge, and in the *Chanson de Roland* the duels within the battles take on a formal and slightly unreal air. A defiant threat is followed by a course with lance in rest, and the fight is continued on horseback with swords until one or both are dismounted. If there is a pause, both sides call on each other to surrender but all the fights continue to the death, whereupon the victor insults his vanquished foe. Part of this is poetic stylisation, part an epic tradition with parallels in Homer; but there remains the beginning of a formal set of rules for warfare, the rudiments of chivalry proper.

Across the Pyrenees, the first fruits of Spanish secular literature took a form not unlike the *chansons de geste*. The *joglares*, like their French counterparts, were wandering minstrels, purveyors of news as well as entertainment, and the ballads they composed on the events of the day formed the basis for the Spanish *cantares de gesta*. The contemporary 'news poems' have not survived, and the earliest of the works that have come down to us is, like the *Chanson de Roland*, a distinctly polished work. Indeed, the *Cantar de mio Cid* owes something to the French *chansons de geste*, for in its earliest form it is at least forty years later than the *Chanson de Roland*; elsewhere the same phrases, the same metres recur in both French and Spanish works.

63

French and Spanish society were in very different stages of development, however, when the *chansons de geste* appeared. In France the Saracens had ceased to be a serious threat and warfare was internecine rather than national; and the classes were not so sharply defined as in Spain. Royal authority was at a low ebb, and there were strong memories of the Carolingian age. The Spaniards, and more particularly the men of Castile, to whom the Cid belonged, were faced with a continuous campaign against the Arabic kingdoms of the south, whom they had gradually forced back in the preceding centuries from a position of almost total control of the peninsula. The intensity of the struggle might wax and wane; alliance might even be made with the Arabic kings against Christian rivals; but it was an ever-present and therefore accepted part of life. This had produced a rather different society from that of France. In Castile, anyone could own horse and armour, and all those who could afford to buy such knightly equipment usually did so. There was no mystique to the profession of arms, and it was seen in an entirely practical light. The social hierarchy depended on wealth and political power instead. At the highest level were the *ricos hombres*, the immediate counsellors of the king; they and the *infanzones* or barons made up the royal court. Outside the royal circle stood the knights, and squires, small landowners who were not necessarily vassals but fought either for the king or in their own interest. Nationalist feeling in this less developed society was almost entirely absent.

The historical figure of the Cid is deeply rooted in these circumstances. Unlike the heroes of French epic, whose fame reached its height two or three centuries after their death, the Cid was celebrated almost at once. Rodrigo Diaz de Vivar was the son of a small landowner, born about 1043. Brought up at the court of the heir of Castile, he became a leading figure in Sancho's entourage when the latter became king, only to find himself out of favour when Sancho was murdered by his brother Alfonso in 1072, in the course of a civil war. In 1081 he was sent into exile, despite his great reputation as a warrior. By equal skill in the murky waters of frontier politics he succeeded in making himself master of Valencia in 1089 in alliance with a Muslim party, and later as sole lord from 1093 until his death in 1099. His relations with both Christians and Muslims were equally variable; at times he regained Alfonso's favour, at times he was allied to his bitter enemies. He fought the count of Barcelona and the king of Aragon as well as the Almoravide emperor and numerous petty Muslim kings, though his personal following was largely drawn from Castile.

This complex history of intrigue and counter-intrigue was reduced to a relatively simple tale in three main episodes: the exile of the Cid, his exploits and pardon, and the story of the marriage of his daughters. (The poem as it survives makes different divisions, possibly marking the end of a day's recital.) Because the writer was working relatively close to his subject, he treated it with considerable realism, a realism which can be traced back to the *Pharsalia* of Lucan, a Roman poet from Cordoba, which is a chronicle poem without parallel in classical literature. This difference of approach is vital to the development of the Spanish form of chivalry.

The Cid, or 'My Cid,' as he is usually called, owed his title to the Arabic word, *sidi*, lord, which he may have earned because of his position as an adventurer, without official standing either in Castile or elsewhere. He is a very different kind of hero from Roland. His humble birth is acknowledged: when an enemy asks:

> Since when might we receive honour   from my Cid of Vivar!
> Let him go now to the River Ubierna   and look after his mills
> And be paid in corn   as he used to do![14]

Much of the interest of the poem lies in the contrast between the great deeds of the Cid and the great pride of his noble enemies of Carrión, and when the brides they have rejected are claimed by the kings of Aragon and Navarre the Cid's triumph is complete. Yet he accepts the order of society as he finds it, objecting only to pride unmatched by deeds.

He is conscious of his obedience to the king, even though Alfonso has wronged him, and makes several efforts to regain favour by sending him part of the spoils he has won; but he does not sentimentalise over his duty or take anything except a very down-to-earth view of the situation. If it serves his purposes to treat the Moors well, he does so; if he needs their wealth he will take it, for that is why he fights them. When he gazes on the Moorish host that has come to besiege Valencia, and which so terrifies his wife and daughters, he calmly remarks that the more of the enemy there are, the greater will be the booty:

> This is great and marvellous wealth   to be added unto us:
> You have barely arrived here   and they send you gifts,
> They bring the marriage portion   for the wedding of your daughters.[15]

Pride in his family is a central theme in the poem, and with it that of vengeance. Doña Jimenez, his wife, and his daughters, Doña

Elvira and Doña Sol, are never far from his thoughts. One of the loveliest passages in the poem is the Cid's farewell to Doña Jimenez as he goes into exile, leaving her behind; a scene which even Guillaume and Guibourc could never have acted:

> My Cid went and embraced   Doña Jimena;
> Doña Jimena   kissed my Cid's hand,
> weeping   she could not hold back the tears.
> He turned and looked   upon his daughters
> 'To God I commend you   and to the heavenly Father:
> Now we part; God knows   when we shall come together.'[5]
> Weeping from his eyes   you have never seen such grief
> Thus parted the one from the others   as the nail from the flesh.[16]

Such emotion is only matched in the French epics by Charlemagne's grief for Roland or Guillaume's lament for Vivien. And the vengeance of the insult offered by the Cid's enemies, the lords of Carrión, to his daughters to whom they are betrothed occupies the last part of the poem. The lords of Carrión (who appear as cowardly and often comic figures) decide to make off with their dowries and abandon their brides once they have left the Cid's court at Valencia; they beat the girls and leave them for dead, but the crime is revealed. In a magnificent scene, the Cid obtains justice of the king. At first he demands the swords he has given them, the precious weapons Colada and Tison; they yield, glad to escape so lightly. But he then demands the dowry, which they have already spent, and they have to borrow to repay him. Lastly, he claims reparation for the insult, and a battle of words begins. Three of his followers challenge those of Carrión, and in the ensuing combat the two lords and another of their clan are overthrown. With the brilliant marriages of his daughters the poem closes:

> See how he grows in honour   who was born in a good hour
> His daughters are wives of the Kings   of Navarre and Aragon
> Now the Kings of Spain   are his kinsmen,
> And all advance in honour   through my Cid the Campeador.[17]

The Cid's other title, 'Campeador', appears in the Latin poems as 'Campidoctor', learned in battle. Battle, however, takes up less of the poem than in the French epics. There are no heroic duels, and the Cid kills the Moorish king Bucar not in the thick of the fray, but in ignominious pursuit; he does not hurl insults, but offers friendship. Only when this is spurned does the race between the two become earnest; the Cid's horse Babieca proves the swifter, and his master slays Bucar with a mightly blow. Realism prevails: we find Pedro Bermudez disobeying the Cid's instruction to wait for the signal before charging with the standard, and having to be rescued from the result of his rashness. If it were not for the Cid's remarkable record in real life, the poet could be indicted for never hinting that the Cid was not invincible, and he does win his battles with a superhuman ease which justifies his heroic status.

In this practical world there is no place for the monstrous enemies of French epic; no giants or witches bar the Cid's path. His wars are not even tinged with the idea of a battle for higher ideals, for *la douce France* against the Saracens, for God against the heathen. He treats the Moors as human beings, and we hear of the ransoming of captives, and even of their release if no ransom was forthcoming. He shares his booty with those Moors who are loyal to him, and his subjects regard him with affection.

If there is much that is historical and realistic in the *Cantar de Mio Cid*, and if it records historical details not mentioned elsewhere, it is nonetheless a work of fiction; the fiction of the *joglar* whose appeals for attention still remain in the poem, and the fiction of the two later poets who probably reworked it, one about 1140–50, the other about 1160. The fiction consists in the Cid's unwavering heroism, and loyalty to his family and followers, and in the struggle between him and the lords of Carrión. His place as sole leader is also imagined, since his second-in-command, Minaya Álvar Fáñez, was really an independent leader who sometimes made common cause with him. The Cid is thus a romanticised warrior in a setting which is realistic; his great virtues are a combination of courage and *mesure*, moderation. It is his deeds, not a set of abstract ideals, that earn him his place among the heroes of chivalry.

The *chansons de geste* continue as a living poetic form until the early thirteenth century, that is, throughout the formative period of chivalry. They are the material of the early knight's dreams, and reflect in turn the new developments in their world. The crusades become the subject of epic poems; rising Spanish nationalism invents a mythical Bernardo del Carpio to slay the intruder Roland at Roncevaux; and the last *chansons de geste* adopt the new romantic fashion. This was to prove fatal to their existence as a lively if unsophisticated poetry: *Huon of Bordeaux* and *L'Entrée d'Espagne* lead to the Italian fables of the fourteenth century, and eventually, as we shall see, to Ariosto's garden of wonders. But for the ordinary twelfth-century knight in Spain or France, the Cid and Roland each in his different way were the flowers of knighthood, models which their counterparts in romance could not yet rival. Fighting was all: 'Mio Cid Campeador' and 'Roland le preux,' stood out as leaders and heroes for one reason only, because they were great warriors.

PART II
Chivalry and Literature

4

Traditions of Love and Attitudes to Women

Knighthood is masculine, aggressive; a battle with rules and limits, in which courtesy is a matter of do as you would be done by. Its heroes and feats of arms are those of the *Iliad* as much as of the *Chanson de Roland*. The distinctive touch of chivalry is missing; the play awaits its heroine. The knight's lady is unlike anything before or since, unrivalled in her command over men's hearts. The love she inspires is half the worship accorded to a goddess, half the moonfaced longings of youth; her place is wholly with the divinities.

Chivalry and the worship of fair ladies are so intimately bound up as to become almost indistinguishable; the knight who aspires to military glory does not yearn to lead armies in Alexander's footsteps, does not dream of the gold of power, but longs to shine for his prowess as an individual, that he may earn the silver of his lady's love. It is the world of the early Renaissance portraits, where the close physical presence of the subject yields in one corner of the canvas to a sudden ethereal vista into an insubstantial heaven on earth. So the knights saw their ladies, real and physical presences in an idealised setting; the honest lady of some grey-stoned castle seemed to hold the keys to their paradise. Once her love was won they would be as sure against their opponent's spears as any hero of the romances, and from her all spiritual wealth would flow.

The idea of the lady as the source of inspiration behind knightly deeds is present throughout chivalric history from the early twelfth century onwards. The Provençal troubadour's idea that a man might grow in moral stature through love becomes simplified in the less subtle schools of northern France and Germany into the idea that the thought of his loved one will lend strength to a knight's arm, skill to his riding, and accuracy to his aim: to us, a commonplace, but unknown to the Roman or old French heroes, who thought of fatherland

71

or friend – *dulce et decorum est pro patria mori*, Roland's dying vision of *la douce France* and Charlemagne.

This change in attitude and its perpetuation are the vital difference between chivalry and a mere love of heroics, the softening, civilising element in a rough and ready world. The central philosophy of chivalry may have in it a certain contradiction, in that a lady's love and feats of arms are not achieved by the same means: the most polished lover is rarely the finest jouster. But this contradiction is essential to the nature of chivalry, for if we judge chivalry by, kill in arms and valour, the introduction of the worship of ladies may seem to mark a decline. To take this view, as some writers have done, and to see the *chansons de geste* and the Provençal poets as the twin peaks of chivalry's achievement is to misunderstand the entire nature of it, which lies in the humanising of the fighting man. On the other hand, the clerk has a great deal to do with chivalry, but when the intellect plays too large a part, from the fourteenth century onwards, it is no longer chivalry proper, a living ethos, but a decoration for palace masques.

The origins of chivalry have therefore much to do with a change in men's attitude to women. The lingering inheritance of imperial Rome offered a traditional attitude to women far removed from that of the knightly lover. The Roman lady was a minder of children, not to be seen in public; and only high birth or notoriety could bring her into prominence.

Here love was treated in a realistic fashion; Ovid's elegant cynicism in the *Ars Amatoria* and its effect on the twelfth century is one of the problems we shall return to; but in his original context, there is no difficulty of interpretation. He is writing verse for the amusement of the public, a take-off on more serious manuals in verse which is nonetheless both very amusing in its own right, and like all true humour, exceptionally acute in its observation. If he is outspoken, and talks boldly of the best positions for intercourse, and of 'successful' abortions, it is the climate of his circle in Rome rather than any self-engendered pornography; and this again is in the realist tradition.

Only in Catullus do we find an idealisation of passion: and it is an incomplete idealisation at that. No troubadour ever wandered into the tortured world of 'Odi et amo'; none dared curse his mistress in later years as bitingly as Catullus cursed Clodia – indeed, they hardly dared whisper that all was not perfect, lest the whole carefully contrived edifice should crumble on top of them. Raimon de Miraval alone makes so bold; and he does so in anger at the betrayal of a precious ideal rather than in the process of pouring out the bitter dregs of love. Lucretius points the moral for the Romans: 'a pretty face or a pleasing complexion gives the body nothing to enjoy but insubstantial images, which all too often fond hope scatters to the winds'.

Yet if the poets rejected the idea of woman as goddess, or at least made of her an idol with feet of clay, the religions of the later Roman empire went to the opposite extreme. The Empire was the great period of the importation of foreign cults to Rome. Eastern fertility cults are in strong contrast to the Grecian myths in that the male protagonists are subordinate to the mother-figure of the goddess, a psychological attitude foreign to the native Roman ideals of manliness and patriotism.

Christian tradition, on the other hand, was strongly biased against women. In its theology, the cult of Mary only began to grow in the sixth and seventh centuries, and scarcely appears in the imperial Christian period. In the circle around Charlemagne's court it had made some headway, as the *Carmen dogmaticum ad Beatam Virginem Mariam* of Hincmar shows; and the lovely *Ave Maris Stella* is a popular hymn of the ninth century. But the worship of the Virgin is little more than a variant of the cults of the individual saints, and holds no special significance until the early eleventh century. It is possible to make out a case for Mariolatry as preceding the growth of the chivalric idealisation of women; but to set up chivalry as a kind of secular answer to Mariolatry itself is excessive. What is much more in evidence is a new attitude within the Church towards women. The early fathers regarded woman as the serpent's ally in her relations with the opposite sex, sent to lure man from the paths of purity as Eve had once lured Adam; and chastity was at a premium, following the Pauline view. On the other hand, women as individuals were highly regarded by the Church; the pagan role of women as priestesses was transmuted into something more humane and practical. By the eighth and ninth centuries, the tradition of patronage and pious works which became the expected function of the mediaeval princess and noblewoman had become established; if it owed something to the classical idea of the mistress of the house as guardian of the domestic deities, there was a much more constructive force evident in the works of Radegunde of Tours, saint and queen, and of her successors in France.

Neither the classical nor the Christian tradition is adequate seed for the flower of the chivalric ideal; at best, they are the pollen, which, carried to alien blossoms, produced that seed. France is the garden where the flowering took place; and France in the tenth century

73

harboured the growth of another culture besides that of Christian Rome: the heroic tradition of the Northmen and Germans. From Ireland and England in Charlemagne's day had come the Celtic and Saxon teachers who led the Christian world in learning, and their ways of thought were akin to those of the German tribes. Women, whether endowed with Deirdre's magic in Irish myth or the warrior women of the *Nibelungenlied* in the German legend, enjoyed a very different standing in the north. They were treated with the respect due to equals, even if their influence in high affairs of state might be less. Very little actual love poetry has survived in any of these languages; the remaining fragments of Anglo-Saxon love poems are enigmatic, and there is nothing in Norse literature, so we know little of how the most cultured of these races set about their wooing. The legal status of women was certainly high; they could inherit and rule much in the same way as a man. The Northern attitude was honest and practical; it ascribed little special magic to women, though they do appear as mystical priestesses in Norse religion; but the lack of awe is balanced by a greater respect. Women can actively help men to greater deeds and valour by their solace and comfort. It is an unpassionate view; but it is a vast advance on the classical and early Christian ideas.

The Northmen who came to France in the tenth century were pagans when they settled there. Their religion was unusual in that it was dominated to an even greater extent than the Roman worship by its gods. Even the dominating female fertility goddess was absent, and the twin deities of Freyr and Freyja ruled instead. Of the pair, Freyr, who had absorbed the characteristics of a large number of minor fertility gods, was the dominant partner and was worshipped as the God of Plenty; Freyja was largely concerned with the hearth and home, though there was a darker, magical side to her worship in soothsaying and witchcraft. The myths do not centre on her, but on the heroic struggle between the gods and the powers of darkness, which will only end at the day of Ragnarok, when the gods are overthrown. This active but pessimistic religion has no Venus, no Diana, and none of the lesser goddesses who decorate Olympus: it reflects a society with little time for the contemplation of beauty and an obsessive concern with the struggle for existence.

It was this world that was inherited by the authors of the *chansons de geste*, thinly veneered with Christianity. Four or five generations separate the invading pagan Norseman from the Anglo-Norman clerk who wrote or copied the *Chanson de Roland*. This is an epic world, not concerned with women. High matters of state and the heroes who determine their outcome, politics and war, inspire their muse. We have seen how Roland's loyalties are to France and to Oliver, and how the fair Aude is a shadowy figure, whose only moment at the centre of the stage is when she dies of grief on hearing of the heroic end of her betrothed. Likewise, we have seen how Guibourc is a central character in the cycle of Guillaume d'Orange; her beauty, and the affection between Guillaume and herself are warmly depicted. But she has something of the Valkyrie in her, and their relationship is as much that of companions in arms as of husband and wife. It is for her heroism in the defence of Orange rather than her beauty that the poet admires her. Likewise in the other rare appearances of women in the *chansons de geste*, it is the ideal of the helpmeet, in the Norse tradition, that prevails; if the fight is no longer one for mere existence, but a war fought for God and the Emperor, the struggle is as paramount as ever.

In this harsh world of fire and bloodshed, the monasteries were islands of refuge where not only Christianity but also the scattered relics of pagan learning survived. The lyric poems of the Latin tradition are the only source of literature addressed to or involving the opposite sex during the period when the ideas of knighthood were germinating. The Latin poets had never ceased to sing their ladies' praise for long: in the sixth century, Fortunatus addresses Radegunde of Tours in lines scented with flowers but tempered with the deep respect due to a queen and a saint; in the ninth Sedulius Scottus works in the same vein. But it is nonetheless formal, the coin of homage paid to the great; and intimacies are out of place. The new mood that breaks in with the tenth century is a reversion to the classical Roman tradition, realist and cheerful, pleading and urging for sweet solace. From this it is a short step to the *Carmina Burana*, the most famous collection of the genre, set down in the thirteenth century; the poems are earlier, and among their anonymous, exquisite lines may be disguised one of the love songs Abelard wrote for Héloise. The freshness of these poems is their most astonishing virtue; they cannot be other than the first fruits of learning laid lightheartedly on pagan altars before more serious cares befell their authors. If the classical inspiration is there, it is in form and imagery, not in mood: by comparison, the most joyous of the poets is worldweary.

The earlier poems of the *Carmina Burana* are roughly contemporary with the first troubadour songs: many of them are later. And the attitude is totally different: 'goddess' is a compliment, to be sure, but little else. The poet calls her that only if he thinks she will yield the sooner for it, and addresses his song bluntly, directly. We are in a world where passion reigns, more powerful than ever, the world of the student-singers, impoverished and tipsy, but always with an eye for a girl. The girl may only be a serving-wench in a tavern, but her beauty earns her the title of goddess. And so we come closer to the roots of chivalric love; yet the search is not ended. The troubadours are much more oblique: they sing of their own feelings, into which their lady's beauty enters only as a cause, and though there may be longing in their verses, there is none of the urging, no 'Come live with me and be my love'. The Latin poets, too, are always conscious that their love is undoubtedly illicit, no more than a peccadillo perhaps, yet still a sin of sorts. They have half an eye on their clerical superiors even in their most abandoned moment, and the founts of love are all the tastier for it:

> Loving's no crime, for if to love were to go astray
> God would never have made of love so divine a joy.

This is not the troubadour's way of thinking; love was far too serious a subject to be treated as a diversion en route for the higher callings of scholarship and the religious life. There, even poets who turned cleric, such as Folquet de Marseille, who was to become a zealous bishop of Toulouse, never betray by the least flicker of their features that they are not in deadly earnest: here among the poets of the schools love is a pastime, not a high calling.

5

The Troubadours and the
Courts of Provence

With the coming of the troubadours, love is taken seriously for the
first time. Flirtation is no longer a mild amusement, passion a disease; Cupid's dart no longer leaves a flesh-wound, but strikes mortal
blows. There is a new intensity about poetry; it no longer moves at
an elegant and formal level, through which deeper feelings sometimes erupt, but aims consciously at a consuming, continuous fire.
From Guillaume IX, the first singer of the new style, to its last exponents in Germany two and a half centuries later, this is the hallmark of the songs, beneath the formulae and codes that grew like ivy
over the central stem, hiding it and sapping its strength, until only a
verdant growth on a hollow centre was left.

The southern half of France in the late eleventh century was a
fortunate land; despite the continual petty squabbles of its lords, it
had not suffered from the raids of Northmen, nor from the trial of
strength between Pope and Emperor. Independent of the French king
in all but name, its petty rulers could vie with each other in splendour, and each of their castles came to house its own court; not a
court in the grand manner, but still a place of leisure, where men
could think of things other than war and the state of their lands.
Above all, social intercourse came to be valued for its own sake. The
system of lordships and feudal tenure led to a monotonous existence,
each man guarding his own castle and meeting his neighbours only
on business occasions. Where security from the sword and from star-
vation was found and great affairs of state did not exclude pastimes,
as in the south, this isolation tended to break down, and the castles
became centres for purely pleasurable gatherings.

Peace and prosperity alone do not explain the appearance of such
a singular culture as that of Provence. The northern Italian towns
were equally flourishing; yet throughout the Middle Ages Italy resisted almost completely not only the courtly ideal in its original

form, but also the ideal of chivalry. Italy had mercantile prosperity and peace; her merchants were busier than ever; Provence had aristocratic peace, and her nobles were idle as they had rarely been before. Attitudes to money were also important. The Italian merchants traded with it, increasing their power. To the lords of the south, power was a matter of politics; their estates were defined, not by wealth, but by feudal bonds, and in less certain days the prosperity they afforded had been hoarded in coffers. Now that the need for such precautions was less pressing, the income from lands was used to buy luxuries and to hold great feasts.

We shall find generosity enthroned as one of the troubadour's principal virtues: for it was on the free-spending lords that not only their own existence depended, but the whole way of life that they championed. This transformation in habits begins at almost exactly the same moment that the troubadours first appear: in the north, Ordericus Vitalis dates what his clerical eye sees as a decline in morals from about 1085. He writes of the Angevin court under Fulk Nerra:

> But now men of the world sought in their pride fashions of dress which accorded with their perverse habits; and what formerly honourable persons thought a mark of disgrace, the men of this age find to be sweet as honey to their taste, and parade on their persons as a special distinction. . . .
> The customs of barbarians were adopted in dress and in the mode of life. They parted their hair from the crown of the head and on each side of the forehead, and let their locks grow long like women, and wore long shirts and tunics, closely tied with points. . . . Now almost everyone wears crisped hair and beards, carrying on their faces the tokens of their filthy lust like stinking goats.[1]

Geoffrey, prior of Vigeois, writing about 1175, describes even more extravagant fashions than those Ordericus decried. Contrasting the simplicity of olden days with the new flamboyance, he says:

> Nowadays the meanest would blush to wear such clothes. Rich and precious stuffs are woven, whose colours suit each man's mood; the borders of the clothes are cut into little balls and pointed tongues, until their wearers look like the devils in a painting.[2]

But it is his description of the festivities at Beaucaire in 1177 that shows the fashion for extravagance at its height:

> That summer, a multitude of local princes and celebrities held a foolish festival at the castle of Beaucaire. It was apparently to commemorate the reconciliation brought about by the King of England [Henry II] between Raymond of Narbonne and Alfonso of Aragon. But the King was for some

reason absent, and the princes held this inane feast in his name. The court of Toulouse gave a knight, one Raymond Dagout, a hundred thousand shillings, which he immediately divided into a hundred times a thousand and gave a hundred knights each a thousand shillings. Bertrand Raiembaus had twelve yoke of oxen plough the streets of the castle and sowed them with thirty thousand shillings. William Gros de Martel, who had three hundred knights with him (there were about ten thousand knights at that court), had all their food cooked in the kitchen with wax candles and torches. The Countess Sorgest sent a crown valued at 40,000 shillings; they appointed William Mita [or Ireta] as king of the jongleurs, unless he was absent for any reason. Raymond of Venoul had thirty horses burnt there in front of everyone for a boast.[3]

After descriptions such as these, it is hardly surprising that the southern lords lived in a more easygoing way than their northern counterparts as far as morals were concerned. The Church's organisation, like the king's (which to some extent used the same personnel), was weak in the Midi. Its puritanism, mild enough in all conscience, and its fiercer misogyny had no influence; and whereas in the north women taken in adultery were shut up in a convent, or if caught *in flagrante delicto* sometimes killed, in the twelfth century, the southern customs allowed a very great degree of licence without actually condoning the offence.

In such circumstances, as in the literary salons of the seventeenth and eighteenth centuries, the ladies of the castle came into their own as arbiters of taste. They could already inherit in their own right, under the law of the country, and we find them as great landowners: in the twelfth century, Ermengarde of Narbonne and Eleanor of Aquitaine wielded as much power as their male counterparts in times of peace. The sons of lesser lords and knights came crowding into these little courts to make their way in the social world; and the lady of the castle was at once the centre of that world and yet inaccessible. Her favour was important, but mere ordinary approaches were unrewarding or dangerous, so the man who could entertain and flatter her was at a distinct advantage. The poems of the *chansons de geste*, sung in long episodes to the monotonous sound of a crude string instrument, woke no echoes of glory in the hearts of princesses such as these; nor were the barons of the south as wholeheartedly warlike as their northern counterparts. Hence there was an audience for a new kind of song, a song to while away an idle hour. It could not be in Latin, for few women were educated in the classical tongue; and its spontaneous nature meant that it was not to be epic, but short and poignant, a verse that could equally be turned easily enough by nobles with more artistic talent than scholastic learning. The poetry that resulted could only be personal, immediate and concerned with the actual world rather than flights of fantasy or rhetoric: it was emotional rather than intellectual from the beginning and reflected the feelings of the poets themselves. Its roots are aristocratic, its metaphors feudal, but its problems within anyone's experience.

The remarkable thing about the lyric poems that resulted is their subtlety; it is part of a process of increasing civilisation that can be observed elsewhere in France, in the new scholastic arguments of the philosophers, in the artistic revival leading to the architectural triumphs of the twelfth and thirteenth centuries. Hence there is no need to search too hard for the forerunners of the troubadours; their great good fortune was that they were working free of the burden of tradition for an audience ready to appreciate novelty. The pattern of their work was shaped by the demands of this audience, rather than by a conscious harking-back to earlier poets and thinkers.

Guillaume IX of Aquitaine (1071–1127) is the earliest poet of the new tradition whose name and work has survived. He was not the first to work in the common tongue: fragments of popular language had been mixed into Latin verse since the eighth century, and the *kharjas*, Arabic songs with a refrain in Spanish, appeared in Andalusia in the tenth century. But there was no long tradition of written verse at the end of the tenth century, when Guillaume was writing, on which he could draw. If verse there was, it was sung and stored in the memories of jongleurs, minstrels who wandered from castle to castle, performing at dinner, reciting stories, singing verses and bringing gossip from the outside world. The network of their profession was wide enough to spread the Breton tales of Arthur as far as Italy by the early twelfth century. Those who could compose their own songs, instead of merely performing the compositions of others, must have attained some degree of social respectability for a man of Guillaume's standing to have joined their ranks. The troubadour poems undoubtedly belong to this tradition, for they were written to be sung in public, and to read them, divorced from their often haunting music, is to invite misunderstanding; the demands of the music, as with all song lyrics, affect the form of the verse, sometimes very strongly.

Guillaume's poems, and those of the other early troubadours, contain no small number of surprises if we expect them to consist of an unvarying longing for an unattainable, ice-hearted princess. The first group of Guillaume's poems are so obscene as to be untranslatable; they can only have been intended for drunken evenings among friends, written, like Peire d'Auvergne's satire on his fellowtroubabours, 'to the sound of pipes, amid gaming and laughter'. The view of women is coarser and bawdier, and more masculine, than anything that has survived in the *Carmina Burana*; they are erotic fantasies on the physical level. It is tempting to regard these as Guillaume's first work, and there are signs of a development, both in technique and attitude, which would make his 'courtly' poems later. If so, the astonishing lyric 'Farai un vers de dreyt nien' marks the transition. It is a nonsense-rhyme on the surface, first of a long line of such verses; to write such an enigmatic, sophisticated and yet world-weary poem at all is a radical departure. If it owes something to the mediaeval fondness for riddles, it is not a riddle that demands an answer. Guillaume is expressing his boredom with the conventional subjects for poetry, and with sensual love he has so far experienced; the shy humour is there to sugar the pill for his audience:

> I'll write a song about nothing at all,
> Not about myself, nor about anyone else.
> Not about love, nor about the joys of youth,
>   Nor anything else.
> I wrote it just now as I slept
>   In the saddle.

> I do not know at which hour I was born;
> I am not joyful and yet not sad;
> I am neither reserved nor intimate
>   And can do nothing about it:
> I was put under a spell one night
>   On a high hill.[4]

He goes on to describe his listlessness, and fears he will die of an unknown disease. He has a lady whom he has never seen, and to whom he is indifferent; indeed, he knows another much fairer and more gentle. Finally he declares his poem finished; he will send it to beyond Anjou, and the receiver will send the 'counter-key' back in return.

From this we come to the first 'courtly' poems. They do not contain the 'code of courtly love' fully fledged: indeed, to speak of such a code is to fall into a dangerous trap. The men of the Middle Ages loved to codify and classify, as witness the tradition of the encyclopedists from Isidore of Seville to Vincent of Beauvais. The writers who inherited the ideas propounded by the troubadours turned them into Latin treatises, to which we shall return; but this systematic approach is a difficult yoke to impose on the unruly subject of love, and was not the troubadours' invention. They recognised certain virtues, taught certain morals, and sought certain ends; but each

81

singer followed his own vision, and the ideals waxed and waned in each new poet's work. So Guillaume's poems merely contain the first phrasing of some of the ideas that later became common stock.

Guillaume's ideal of love is centred on the knightly class; he roundly declares that a lady 'commits a great and mortal sin if she does not love a loyal knight; but if it is a monk or cleric, she is wrong; by rights she should be burnt to death', implying that the smooth-tongued clerk was already a rival. His terms of praise for his lady, too, show that he was familiar with religious literature; but if some of the turns of phrase echo from this familiarity, he appeals for the physical consolations of love. The novelty here is the intensity of the feeling. He cannot live without his lady, whom he worships, 'for her I shiver and tremble, because I love her so deeply'. We are not quite at 'Vénus toute entière à sa proie attachée', but the hunt has begun. Guillaume sees 'joy d'amour' as the salvation of mortal man:

> No man can ever dream what that joy
> Is like, neither by wishing or desiring it
> Nor by thinking of it nor imagining it
> Such a joy can never find its match
> And he who would praise it worthily
> Would not succeed in the space of a year.[5]

Guillaume stands alone; if there were contemporary singers, time has used them harshly, for there is no record of them left. The troubadours who succeed him are numerous enough for two general trends to appear. One refines the abstract idealising mood of his later poems until the rarefied atmosphere leaves the reader breathless in the fantasies of *trobar clus*, deliberately obscure verbal feats; the other takes his realistic side, which had been a mere ploughshare of obscenity, and beats it into a sword of social criticism. The aesthetic school was centred on the court of Ventadour and Eblo II, the count, seems to have been its leader. Unfortunately his verses, written shortly after Guillaume's, have not survived; his poetic heir was Bernart de Ventadour, whose delicate verses probably reflect his master's ideas. Bernart, wrongly famous as the lover of Eleanor of Aquitaine, wife of Henry II of England, pays homage to his lady in a feudal relationship where the poet becomes the lady's vassal, an idea which re-echoes down to *The Faerie Queene* and persists as a poetic image beyond the demise of chivalry itself. (The vidas, or lives of the troubadours, which precede their works in most manuscripts, are thirteenth-century embroiderings on the content of the poems; so Bernart, addressing a panegyric to Eleanor, becomes her lover.) The relationship is not a rewarding one; all Bernart's poems reflect a personal world where suffering predominates over recompense. Yet he draws comfort from his pangs, and shows how *joy d'amour*, the lover's ecstasy, feeds on frustration and despair. The object of his desire remains explicitly the carnal possession of his beloved; yet the desire outstrips its end in importance, and we are face to face with the particular twist of troubadour love, its self-denying, contradictory longing.

Rilke's *mot*, that the troubadours feared nothing so much as the attainment of what they longed for, seems even closer to the mark with Jaufré Rudel, renowned for his apocryphal love of the Countess of Tripoli, to whom he sent sweet love songs, without having seen her, and finally went himself, only to die in her arms a moment after glimpsing her fabled beauty. (The vidas again! The story has gained such force that one is tempted to believe it against the evidence; but history says no.) Jaufré was not quite so impractical, if his own story of being caught in bed with his mistress is true. The shame of this exposure led him to seek a higher love, and this he found in the idea of *amor londhana*, love from afar. The first verse of his most famous lyric, 'Lanquan li jorn son lonc en mai', enshrines the essence of his mood:

> When the days grow long in May
> I love to hear the distant bird;
> When I have left off listening
> It reminds me of my distant love
> And I go dull and bent with longing
> So that song, flower and hawthorn
> Might as well be winter frosts for me.[6]

He and his lady are separated by space as well as the lady's resistance, hope is dead and only desire remains. 'He speaks truly who says that I am hungry for distant love, because no joy pleases me as much as the enjoyment of distant love.' This is the nearest to a mystical or philosophical approach that the troubadours were to come until the declining days of their art. Once again, it is a personal, introspective world, where the poet himself occupies the foreground. Of his lady we learn nothing; she is a shadowy divinity, to be worshipped unquestioningly.

At the opposite extreme to Jaufré, we find the pungent attacks of Marcabru. In deliberately obscure but razor-edged poems, he sets about the exponents of false love, calling down the wrath of Heaven on an impious generation like some stern prophet. But he is not a religious prophet; his idol is pure love, the undefined opposite to the garish world he paints. He brands the love current among his fellows as promiscuous, disturbing the peace of honest men. The only difficulty is that he names the exponents of this coarse and sensual love as the school of Ventadour; and such poems as survive from this source are far from licentious. His attack is perhaps two-pronged: against his rivals as a poet, and against the practices of the courts he had visited. So his poems became tirades against the nobility and their lax morals – he himself was probably of humble birth – and if his often coarse language reflects reality, it is a reality distorted by jealousy and the moral attitude he adopts. What he attacks is not adultery but licence, adultery being at worst a venial sin, and in these circles scarcely a sin at all. His rejection of the grossness of carnal love does not necessarily mean that a decline in morals was taking place, but is rather a measure of the increasing civilisation of his surroundings.

To see Marcabru as an early representative of some popular resentment against the nobility, a forerunner of Wat Tyler, is to ignore his use of the most refined poetic devices, current only within the very circles he is supposed to despise. His search for rich images, the technique of 'mixing' words – *entrebescar les mots* – regardless of immediate sense, foreshadow the later thickets of this *trobar clus*, poems so full of allusions that it seems doubtful whether their authors really understood them, their attraction being that of a crossword puzzle in rhyme. Such poems are not Marcabru's best, at least to our ears, and are a very marginal note in the development of chivalry.

If Marcabru is in some ways a split personality as a result of his refinement of the ultimate ideal on one hand and his description of reality on the other, troubadour poetry was not a movement with a single stream. While there are poets who live entirely in Venus' realm, others come to prefer the arts of Mars. Bertran de Born's political squibs, such as his *sirventes* to Henry II's sons, are in the realistic manner; while in the thirteenth century the Italian Sordello singing of the ecstasy of unfulfilled love, until his friend Bertran d'Alamanon feared that he was mad, is the heir of Jaufré Rudel. And between the two the joys of physical love, casual or passionate, are reflected throughout the troubadours' poetry. If we concentrate here on the more high-flown fancies, it is because these are the most original of their ideas, and the most influential for later chivalry, at the risk of portraying the poets as moving in a rarefied atmosphere where the chief tenet was that the least carnal desire was 'th'expense of spirit in a waste of shame' when they were well grounded in reality.

Equally it is a mistake to make of this exaltation of restraint a paean to purity and hence to connect them with the contemporary Cathar heresy, whose *perfecti* abstained from all carnal pleasures. They sought rather the prolongation of sexual pleasure beyond the act of love itself by means of restraint.

The later troubadours move further into the realms of what was later to be known as 'platonic' love, and the movement that had a sensual beginning draws to a spiritual end. The search for technical improvements that had led to *trobar clus* continued with Peire d'Auvergne, who says of himself 'he would be master to all troubadours if only he would make his words a little clearer; people can scarcely understand them,' and meaning has almost as little place in the rich language and complex verse forms of *trobar ric* as it had in the parallel obscurities of *trobar clus*. The artificiality of the verses was matched by a slavish following of the 'formula' of courtly love: Elias Cairel admits to his lady: 'If I have sung of your worth and wisdom, it was not because I loved you; I did it to gain honour and profit, as jongleurs addressing a noble lady do.'[7] Raimbaut d'Orange, even more original in technique, mixes prose into his poems; while Arnaut Daniel, his brilliant and wide-ranging successor, who produced one of the most unprintable as well as some of the most dazzling troubadour poems, sums up the artificiality of *trobar ric* in a wry self-portrait:

> *I am Arnaut, who gathers the air into sacks*
> *Who uses oxen from the yoke to hunt the hare*
> *Who swims in swift rivers against the current.*[8]

The turn of the twelfth century was possibly the richest and most productive period for the troubadour poets. Yet no great figures emerge; competent poets there are by the dozen, some with considerable claims to our attention, such as Peire Vidal, Raimon de Miraval and Uc de St Circ. The reaction against *trobar ric* after the *ne plus ultra* of Raimbaut d'Orange's efforts failed to produce the real new impetus which was needed; the formulae begin to grow a little stereotyped. Raimon de Mirval, whom a later poet[9] was to call the greatest singer of all, is nonetheless systematic, almost didactic in his approach to love. His anger is reserved for those who have betrayed his ideal rather than wronged him personally; it is in this mood that he reproaches his lady for her infidelity. And he esteems *pretz*, worthiness won through love's service, above *joy d'amour*. His lesser contemporaries, more concerned with form and expression, tended to work over the familiar themes in increasingly eccentric imagery,

85

replacing obscure language by tortuous ideas. The figures of lover and lady in the *chansons* of the thirteenth century have been neatly described as 'puppets refashioned by the dozen'.[10]

The troubadours were very dependent on the whim of their masters: one count might heap them with honours, and his successor chase them out of the gate. Yet certain courts were particular havens for them; and the decline of their art is directly connected with the rise and fall of these. Poitiers, capital of the county of Poitou, had been one of the greatest centres in the south throughout the twelfth century; at its most brilliant under Guillaume IX, Guillaume X and Eleanor, it became less important after the latter's marriage to Henry II of England, though Richard I was acclaimed count in 1172 and always preferred the southern parts of his domain. Richard wrote a few verses himself, elegant enough of their kind; but the Plantagenets were not the best of patrons.

Ventadour and Narbonne, Orange and Limoges all had their moments of popularity; and Barcelona and Castile across the Pyrenees were for long periods places where the troubadours were welcome. Yet the real strength of the movement was with the minor lords, castellans who could barely have maintained a court in harsher times, who were amateurs themselves: men such as Blacatz d'Aups in Provence, a fierce partisan of the old modes and styles. The ladies of the court, too, remained ardent supporters of the poets to the end; in the declining days of the troubadours in Provence the court of Aix had several patronesses of their art, the most notable being Guida de Rodez, whose praises were sung by Blacatz, Sordello and others. Once their patronage disappeared, and the troubadours had to seek favour in the more preoccupied courts of greater princes, their livelihood became much harder to find.

With the horrors of the crusade against the Cathars, the civilisation of Provence which had flourished in the same easy atmosphere and rich soil was to wither and die. In the fifty years after 1200 the fair land the poets had known and loved was to pay dearly for its independence. If the Cathars were a thorn in the flesh of the Church, the unruly nobles of the south, who had owed neither political nor cultural allegiance to the north, had aroused the enmity of the kings of France. Church and State in formidable alliance were too much for the lords of the south, with no central figure or organisation on which to base their resistance. The violence and atrocity of the attack at Beziers and elsewhere, and the terrors of the Inquisition, aroused passionate resistance, but it was unco-ordinated and spontaneous, and the prolonged sieges of the Cathars in their mountain fortresses at Montségur and elsewhere increased the damage to Provence as a whole; Languedoc was heavily ravaged after the abortive revolt of 1242. The poetic tradition needed patrons and peace for the writing of verses; the clash of arms had been an inspiration only for Bertran de Born and his ilk.

The troubadours of this last era come mainly from Provence and northern Italy. Their efforts are more carefully orthodox, and platonic love in Guillem de Montanhagnol becomes pure adoration of the Virgin with Guiraut Riquier, though the transition from profane to sacred had come as early as the last decade of the twelfth century, with Folquet de Marseille's lovely dawn hymn and its refrain:

> The shadows flee, the light draws near;
> The sky is calm and clear.
> The dawn no longer hesitates,
> The day in fair perfection waits.[11]

But the later poets address our Lady a their *domna*: thus Guiraut Riquier:

> God, in whose power it lies, had made me standard bearer
> For my Lady, Lady of the Pure, in Love's high kingdom.[12]

And on this note, the last of the major poets of the south ends his swan-song. The tradition lingers for another half-century; but its autumn leaves are drab and soon fallen.

The last troubadours moved to Italy, where their inheritance was handed on to the poets of the Sicilian court and of the *dolce stil novo*, Guinizelli and Cavalcanti; so through Petrarch it finally returns to Renaissance France by way of the Lyons poets, Scève and Louise Labé, finding renewed life as a theme for royal pageants.

The fame of the troubadours did not need such cataclysms to spread it abroad; they had long ago found imitators in Italy and, more important for our present purpose, in northern France, The trouvères, working while the original ideas were still developing, remained on a more down-to-earth level, and their art never developed into a really distinctive style. But it was through them that the ideas of the troubadours entered the active world of chivalry, and were subtly metamorphosed from the abstract to the concrete. The knight wearing his lady's favour in a sixteenth-century tournament was still subscribing to the troubadour idea that love is an improving force: instead of moral prowess, however, he wore the favour so that the thought of his lady would lend physical strength to his arm, a notion which came about in the more literal schools of northern France.

That man could become more noble through love is the essential discovery of the troubadours: personality and love are connected for the first time. From enthroning the lady as a superhuman creature, it was a short step to endowing her with the power of granting gifts, albeit in an indirect way, through the effect of the love she inspired. Troubadour poetry is not about women, their beauty or charms; it is about the lover and his longings. The highest praise is measured in terms of her influence on the admirer, and so the qualities of the lover loom large in their philosophy.

We start with the lover and the lady. It was assumed that they were both noble; nothing is said of their attachment, whether they were married to others or were both unmarried. The lover may have adored his lady from childhood up, a common theme; or equally, passion may have struck suddenly, at the meeting of two pairs of eyes. The love which resulted was not designed to lead to marriage, so whether they have partners was incidental; but they had to be free from other liaisons within the convention. Marcabru is particularly scornful of these who entertain more than one lover at a time, and only in very lax circles was it permitted. It was not an equal relationship: the beloved was always regarded as a superior being, the lover attempted to win her favour by noble acts. In the Provençal tradition these do not seem to have included deeds of arms, and more civilised ways of paying court, such as the composing of songs, and the cultivation of wit and good manners were preferred. If a lover was adept at pleasing his lady, she might in due course recognise his suit, and grant him some token of his favour, perhaps after several years. After a similar period of waiting, she might admit him to more physical joys, and it was not unknown for her to surrender herself completely. It was made plain, however, that this was incidental to the real nature of this type of love; the extended attentions of the earlier stages were the really important element, and many suitors sighed in vain for their ladies' kisses and caresses.

On a higher plane, it was the harmony between lover and beloved that was all-important: 'Any lover who rebukes his beloved for not giving him what he desires, or who asks things which she should not grant, is indeed a fool.' Jaufré Rudel renounces all hope of consummation: 'Since there is never a chance of my seeing her, no wonder I long for her so.'[18] Partly because the Church frowned on such affairs, but largely because it added spice to the intrigue, and intensified the excitement, secrecy was regarded as *de rigueur*. It also offered dramatic possibilities for concealment, suspicion and watchfulness for the *losangiers*, the jealous rivals who would betray everything to the world.

Despite the implied though remote possibility of union with the beloved, and despite the solace of harmony of minds, the usual state of the troubadour was represented as one of ceaseless yearning. It was from this yearning that the lover should acquire the qualities which brought him nearer to the heights on which the beloved moved. Any lover worth his salt was at once *cortes*, a word that meant both courteous and courtly, and implied a knowledge of the conventions. Certain things were not *cortes* – falsehood in love, miserliness, infidelity and lack of restraint or secrecy. These were the vices which the courtly code was designed to suppress: and their strange mixture only makes sense when we take love, and the effect of each *on* love, as the criterion. *Cortesia* was a vital aspect of troubadour love, but it was a negative virtue. The lover's *cortesia* consisted in not being miserly, but not necessarily in indulging in lavish exhibitions; in not being boastful, but not necessarily in keeping total secrecy; in not being too forward, but not in waiting on his mistress' every word – the term used is *mezura*, the golden mean.

However, more positive virtues were admired in a lover: *pretz* and *jovens*. A lover was *pretz* when he had earned esteem through his love; the word is akin to prowess, and implies accomplishment, a stage beyond mere keeping of rules. The lover had learned to please his lady, and had earned admiration for his skill in correct behaviour. *Jovens*, literally youth, was a more complex word, embracing generosity and lightness of heart, and it was linked with the *joy d'amour* which is the lover's prize. A lover who is *jovens* was not only accomplished, but had attained the state of mind which rewards that accomplishment. Generosity came into the catalogue of virtues for altogether more practical reasons. The troubadours depended on their audience for a living, and gifts to them counted in the service of love much as alms did in the church. It is the last and subtlest twist to a long tradition of skilled writers reminding their patrons of their needs.

Finally, there is the question of *joy d'amour*. This embraced so wide a range of emotions, from physical satisfaction to an almost mystical ecstasy that it can only be defined in reverse as 'the one true end of love'. In its purest sense it was associated with the restraint and yearning of *fin' amors* and unconnected with an ultimate reward. The striving towards and the achievement of harmony between lover and beloved were both part of it; and very often it was the wounds of love that produced it. The masochistic attitude is made explicit in one of the last troubadours, Hugo Brunec, lamenting its passing:

> *And now I see with its own fulfilment*
> *That love dying which once wounded sweetly.*[14]

This is the key to the apparent chastity of some of the troubadours' desires: they do not fear the attainment of their goal, they prefer the sweet torment of hope to an uncertain joy which leaves no further conquests, no new horizons, once it has been tasted.

But such exalted pinnacles of pleasure were not for all and sundry: and out of this arises the debate over *fin' amors* and *amars*, as Marcabru would have it. For pure love was too high an ideal for the ordinary courtier of the castle where the troubadours sang; seeing this new fashion in love all the rage, he might imitate, and the result would probably be what the later writers called mixed love and what the Church called adultery. Marcabru might call down heaven's wrath in fierce invective, but a necessary by-product of his high visions was their corrupted reflection in lesser men. The troubadours' concept of love is not implicitly adulterous; the practical result more often than not was. For troubadour love was not a means of wooing a bride, and never could be in a feudal world where marriages were political or financial alliances; rather, it provided an outlet for feelings that society thus ignored. Equally, it fell into adultery as though into the gap between vision and reality. *Amars* may have been what happened: *fin' amors* was not affected as an ideal, and we shall find the paradox repeated in other branches of chivalry.

We have looked at the possible reasons for the appearance of a new attitude towards women; the more difficult question of why it took this direction remains. There are almost as many theories about 'the origins of courtly love' as there are scholars who have studied it, and the answers can only be very tentative. A great many elements in the troubadour songs can be found elsewhere, and explained as borrowings; but no consistent pattern appears, and to admit them all would be to make Provence the centre of a far-ranging network of intellectual activity, which is hardly justified by any other evidence. Again, even if all the other ideas are ascribed to outside sources, one central theme, that of the lover's yearning and suffering, of what we know as passion, remains obstinately original.

Broadly, the possible influences on the shaping of the ideals of courtly love are three: mysticism and philosophy, Latin poetry and Arabic literature. The mystical and philosophical systems such as that propounded by St Bernard are on another plane altogether. St Bernard, writing just after the first generation of troubadour poets, treats carnal love more sympathetically than the early fathers had done: though it is purely selfish, 'that love by which man loves himself, for his own sake and before all else.'[15], it is a step on the road to that divine love in which God is loved for his own sake. St Bernard's divine love is echoed by phrases in the troubadours, but they never move beyond an erudite simile: usually their invocations of heaven are forerunners of the modern pop song:

> *A smile from your eyes*
> *Is my paradise*

to translate the trouvère Thibaut de Champagne somewhat freely. And if we look closely at the ecstasy of the troubadours, it is not a mystical ecstasy: Etienne Gilson neatly describes it as 'a paralysis induced by passion'.[16] It is temporary escape from the pangs of love into a numbered awe before the splendours of the beloved's spiritual and physical beauty, which has little relation to the beloved's attitude, to any spiritual union, or indeed to any spiritual achievement at all. The troubadours' attempts to introduce a mood of ascetic renunciation, to achieve more intensity of feeling, were in direct opposition to the ends of their desire; worship in spiritual terms only, from motives which were never purely spiritual, was doomed to confusion. Hence mysticism and religious poetry lend formulae and phrases, but not the essence of their thought, to the troubadours.

None of the early Provençal poets, and few of the later ones, are likely to have read any non-Christian philosophy. However, the Christian philosophers had inherited a great deal from the ancient world, and much of their work is almost a-religious in attitude. They discuss the relations of body and soul in similar terms to those of Plotinus, the Alexandrian writer of the fifth century AD, and the tradition known as neoplatonism was still predominant. In the system proposed by Plotinus and his successors, all things ascend towards the One, a progress helped or hindered by the proportion of finite being and of essential good in each individual. The attraction to sensible beauty is one step on the ascent towards the contemplation of innate, ideal beauty, which is for Plotinus the highest state to be attained in this existence. The idea of yearning as the driving force behind spiritual growth is essential to this view of life, and this does offer a close parallel with the lover's attitude to his lady, which may begin with a carnal desire, but ends in spiritual improvement. As with mysticism, however, the parallel is more a result of the general nature of human love, another facet of a universal truth, than of direct borrowing. The same applies to any parallels with the Augustinian tradition as expressed in works such as Alcher of Clairvaux's *De spiritu et anima*, where a systematic analysis of love in similar terms to that of the troubadours appears. The Church's doctrines on love, though admittedly part of the general cultural background of the time, were unlikely to come to the troubadours in such a way as to influence them over details. Again, the troubadours were consciously exploring love in non-philosophical but intelligent and serious terms; though love is seen from a different angle, its essence remains the same, and some of the results must therefore be related.

The only civilisation which had tried a similar approach to the subject before was the Arabic culture, particularly in Spain. Arab theology did not regard love as a link between the human and divine: man was not created to love God, but only to praise him. Hence the Arab view of love was not complicated by religious dogmas, and human love was the only type of love for writers such as Ibn Dawoud of Bagdad. Ibn Sina, or Avicenna (987–1030), was working within the terms of his own philosophical system, Neoplatonic in its basis, when he came to write his *Risala fi'l-'Isq* (Treatise on Love), and it was attacked in the east for unorthodoxy. In eleventh-century Spain a more liberal atmosphere meant that his writings were studied with interest, and from here they passed on to Latin Christendom. The Treatise on Love sees restraint in love-making as essential if the animal side of man's nature is not to have the upper hand; but, although the first Latin translations of Avicenna were made about 1130, this work does not seem to have been among them, either then or in later years.

Arab writings on love are refinements of sensual love, and if they arrive at a type of spiritual love, it is not connected with a higher religious love. In the ninth century, Ibn Dawoud sees chaste love as the highest type, not because the flesh is evil, and such a love will be purely spiritual, but because renunciation perpetuates desire. His successors could not elaborate further on these ideals without treading the paths of heresy, and the Andalusian poets are much readier to sing of the pleasures of the flesh. Lip-service is still paid to the supremacy of spiritual love; but the lover does not grow more noble in his lady's service (she is as often as not a young slave-girl anyway), and the yearnings are quickly satisfied or drowned in wine. It is a more realistic, easygoing world; *pretz*, fame in the world's eye, would have found no seekers, and *cortesia* would have seemed an exaggerated fantasy.

The troubadour songs owe something in their form to the Arabic songs; but there are only broad parallels between them, and how the latter could have reached Provence when intellectual contacts with northern Spain, let alone the kingdoms of the south, were few and far between, must remain a mystery. At home in Provence there was another rich source of song forms in music, the School of St Martial at Limoges whose Latin hymns or tropes, embellishments inserted into the ordinary sung Mass, were renowned: these were related to Latin secular poetry, and occasionally the tunes were interchangeable. The more daring choristers might sing the secular, ribald version of their part, in strict harmony with their fellow-worshippers. The barrier between secular and religious music was much slighter, and it is not surprising to find the troubadours borrowing from this source, to lend again and enrich it in turn.

Given the circumstances of increased leisure and greater education, and the new status of women which we have outlined above, the lyric poetry of the troubadours was a spontaneous growth. (All three are reflected in the richer, more flattering fashions for women which appear about 1140.) The seed may have come from any one of the established traditions we have examined: what finally grew out of it was something entirely original, compounded from any ideas to hand, but to see courtly love as something adopted from elsewhere is to misunderstand it entirely. It reflects closely the life of the courts of southern France: the eternal fidelity of the lover, the superiority of the loved one, mirror the relationship of lord and vassal; the love for another man's wife is the result of a society where courting and love matches were almost unknown, and marriage was a political and procreative institution only. As to the means of attaining one's goal, the quest for *cortesia* and *pretz* is an echo in peacetime of the feudal virtues sought in war: courage and loyalty are the equivalent of *cortesia*, fame is the spur for both warrior and lover. Some of its other points are discoveries about the psychology of love which remain true for most civilisations: the danger that a love affair will wane after its consummation, the pleasure that can be found in the pangs of love, the lover's hesitation before his mistress. Even the complex idea of *pretz*, and the lover's gain in moral worth is only an elaboration of Housman's:

> *O when I was in love with you*
> *Then I was clean and brave*
> *And miles around the wonder grew*
> *How well did I behave.*

6

The Minnesingers

The striking and attractive songs of the troubadours found an appreciative audience wherever the southern language was readily understood; and it was not long before the more difficult transplantation of their art to northern France and to Germany began. Even without the barrier of language, conditions were less favourable: the social world of the north was more practical, less inclined to the easy southern ways. Eleanor of Aquitaine was to exclaim in impatience at her first husband: 'I have married a monk, not a king!', and her habits more than once shocked the French court. Both in northern France and across the Rhine, the lesser lords could not keep court in the style of their Provençal counterparts. King and Emperor were the centres of society, and only when they or a powerful magnate deigned to take an interest did the arts flourish.

Fortunately such men did exist: courts such as Champagne, Thuringia and Austria all provided such patronage at various times, and we find the bishops too, the protectors of the wandering scholars, offering their hospitality. Yet even where interest was shown in the new and foreign songs, the singers were moving in a different world, with its own traditions that merged with theirs to form a native style.

The first imitators of the troubadours were a group of northern French poets known by the northern version of the word, trouvères. These poets worked in an area of France already notable for its devotion to the knightly arts, Champagne and the Flemish borders. We shall return to the court of Champagne as a home of knightly romance, and to Flanders as an especial haunt of the tourneyers: here was the audience, here the rich reward. Yet the purely troubadour element appears only in the first generation of trouvères, among poets such as Chrétien de Troyes, Gace Brulé, Conon de Béthune. By the early thirteenth century, the older traditional forms native to the region, the *pastourelle* and *chansons de toile*, in a simpler lyric form, appear as well; and we are on the road to the Arcadian shepherdesses of the seventeenth and eighteenth centuries by way of such incongruous episodes as René d'Anjou's tournament known as the *Pas d'Armes de la Bergière*, where the setting of the tournament included the king's beloved dressed in pastoral costume, and with a real flock of sheep to guard in the midst of the heat and fury of the lists. But such diversions were not the real rivals of troubadour songs and love: it was the preference of the northern knights for epics to while away the long evenings, rather than lyrics brief as the Provençal dawn, that determined the issue. Into these longer poems the fruits of troubadours poetry were assimilated; and the echoes of the songs die away.

Folksong proved more attractive than troubadour themes in France; in Germany the verdict was reserved. A native lyric poetry untouched by the idea of *fin' amors* appeared briefly in the decades after 1150. The surviving poems derived from an older tradition, and their themes were those common to much of early European poetry: a conversation between lovers, a woman's complaint on her lover's absence, a dawn song. Some poems are preserved in the largely Latin anthology of the *Carmina Burana* and themes and patterns of the vernacular songs may well be echoes of earlier Latin lyrics rather than folksongs. One is to be found in the Tegernsee letters, a collection of model epistles to be copied as required: here, in a Latin love letter supposed to be written by a girl, the writer inserted a verse in German:

> You are mine, I am yours;
> Of this you should rest assured.
> You lie hidden
> In my heart's prison
> And, now the small key is lost,
> There, for ever, you are locked.[1]

Love and its pleasures are simple, uncomplicated by ideas. The verses, too, are simple, too simple for increasingly sophisticated tastes. The first three German lyric poets whose names are known to us, 'der von Kürenberc', Dietmar on Aist, and Meinloh von Sevlingen, show what native talent might have made of the love song in the absence of the Provençal influence. Kürenberc's metaphors are drawn from knightly surroundings and pastimes; but his ladies are human, pleading and hoping that love will endure in the hearts of their fickle knights. If they are proud and unyielding, the knight says 'Then she shall remain without my love' and goes in search of a warmer welcome, instead of throwing himself at her feet. In his most famous song, a lady sees her lover as a falcon, unsure whether she really has his love:

I trained myself a falcon through a year's long days.
When he was safely tamed to follow my ways
And his plumage shone golden, painted by my hand,
With powerful wingbeats rising, he sought another land.

Since then I've often seen him, soaring in fair flight,
For on his feet my silken jesses still shine bright
And his plumage gleams with scarlet and with gold.
May God grace lovers and reunite them as of old.[2]

When Kürenberc speaks as a man, women are fit subjects for conquest rather than adoration: 'women and falcons are easily tamed'. The pathos and high feeling are always on the woman's side; it is unmanly to be sentimental or subservient.

With Dietmar von Aist an occasional echo of new ideas creeps in: he can discreetly hint that his long service of his lady had made him a better man, and therefore more deserving of a reward. And he tosses and turns at night, thinking of 'the lady whom I'd like to love me'. The old forms of conversation and of the lady speaking alone continue in both his verse and that of the yet more courtly Meinloh; but they lack the sharp clarity of Kürenberc, while the poems addressed to the lady are more fiery and sharply drawn. Meinloh brings in the idea of *dienst*, service, which was to become an inseparable compound of *minne*, high love or *fin' amors: minnedienst*. With him, we are at the true beginning of *minnesang*, 'the songs of high love'.

There is one particular event within Meinloh's lifetime which marks the new epoch, the knighting of Heinrich VI at Mainz at Whitsun 1184. An international gathering on this scale was unknown since Charlemagne's day. Thanks to Frederick Barbarossa's able rule Germany was at peace, a rare enough state of affairs throughout the Middle Ages, and preparations had gone on without interruption for several months. All the lands under Frederick's rule were represented: and these included Burgundy, the kingdom of Arles and Italy. These fiefs of the Holy Roman Empire led a political existence with little direct connection with Germany, and their magnates rarely appeared at the Imperial Court except on business. Now for once they gathered for more social purposes, and there were knights from France as well. For an occasion of this kind, with its tournaments and festivals, Mainz was full of noble ladies, and to complete the court, all kinds of squires, minstrels and other members of the lords' retinues. It was they above all who benefited from the generosity proper to such occasions; this time the casual expenditure of fortunes

1 (*left*) Warrior, from the tenth-century Silos Apocalypse: a stark and practical figure

2 (*below*) Making a knight: Matthew Paris' drawing comes from his history of the eighth-century king Offa, but depicts a ceremony of the mid-thirteenth century

3 Accolade on the field of battle, from a fourteenth-century Arthurian romance

4 Charlemagne sets out against the Saracens. Twelfth-century miniature

Minnesingers: 5 (*left*) Walther von der Vogelweide; 6 (*right*) Hartmann von Aue

7 Lovers in conversation. Subjects like these were a favourite theme for secular ivories; this mirror case would have adorned the room of a noble and wealthy lady

8 The magic fountain at dawn. This miniature, more than any other, captures the haunted atmosphere of the late romances, an unreal world evoking half-forgotten dreams. The scene comes from *The Book of the Lovelorn Heart,* by René d'Anjou

9 Marshal Boucicaut as St George, from the Boucicaut Book of Hours.
Boucicaut was equally at home in the pageantry of secular chivalry, for
which such a costume might have been appropriate, and in the world of the
crusade to which the allegory refers

10 (*above*) A
tournament, from a
treatise on the various
kinds of sin, among
which tournaments
were included: note
the devils ready to
seize the knights'
souls if they were
killed

11 (*left*) Departure for
and return from a
tournament,
fourteenth century

12 The Duke of Brittany armed for the tournament. By the mid-fifteenth
century, crests and trappings had become extremely ornate

13 The famous feat of
arms at St Inglevert
in 1389

was almost on a scale with that at Beaucaire in 1177, as the lords vied with each other to make the greatest impression.

We know for certain of three singers present: Guiot de Provins, and Doetes de Troyes from Champagne, and Heinrich von Veldeke from Limburg in Belgium. Guiot was a trouvère of some repute, who later described the feast in his poems; of Doetes de Troyes' work nothing survives. Veldeke, who was likewise to include in his version of the *Aeneid* a brilliant portrait of these days, of whose marvels 'men could talk until Doomsday without lying', is on the other hand a key figure in the development of *minnesang*, and with him the young Emperor in whose honour the gathering took place. Heinrich VI, conscious of his imperial status, sings of an equal passion where man and woman are partners, not adoring and adored. But he is a minor figure compared with the more radical Veldeke. His *Aeneid* is based on an old French poem, not directly on Virgil, and turns the Trojans into models of chivalry; Eneas and Lavinia might be lovers from the court of Champagne. His poems, too, derive from the trouvéres. Whether the great festival at Mainz affected his writing greatly we cannot tell; all the poets of this generation who show knowledge of troubadour or trouvére poetry come from the west of Germany, in areas where contact with France and the south was common. On the other hand, the nobles who flocked to Mainz heard the new songs for the first time, and certainly acquired their taste for such poetry about this period.

By the end of the century, there was no doubt as to the success of the new style. Veldeke's assertion that 'from love all good things come' is taken up and affirmed by Friedrich von Hausen and most of the others. Von Hausen is the first to acknowledge the complete superiority of his lady, a shadowy angel mirrored dimly in the poet's thoughts of despair and devotion. At its height, *Frauendienst*, the service of women, becomes a more intense experience in the hands of the German poets, an intensity which makes it liable to become entirely fantastic, as with Ulrich von Lichtenstein the following century, to whose adventures in tournaments we will return: but he is a law unto himself, a baroque figure from the ends of the empire. The greater poets saw *Minne* as an overwhelming, all-consuming force, but did not follow their arguments to their absurd end in real life.

The golden age of *Minnesang* was the first quarter of the thirteenth century. German writers had absorbed the Provençal ideas, and proceeded to go beyond them in their own ways. At the Thuringian court, Heinrich von Morungen stood 'bewitched by great love'; and his insubstantial beloved appears to him in dreams rather than in cold daylight. At times he followed a Provençal model very closely as in the poem where he sees himself first as a child grasping at a mirror that delights him and breaking it, and again as Narcissus, bound by what he sees in the mirror of the spring to love for ever. (The practice of *contrafacta*, writing a poem to an existing melody, accounts for the similarity of some German and Provençal poems, though the evidence is not always clear. There may have been imitation of metrical forms as well, which made it possible to sing a poem to an existing French tune. For instance, Jaufré Rudel's poem on p. 83 and Walther von der Vogelweide's 'Nu alrest lebe ich mir werde' can be sung to the same melody.) Here even the rhyme scheme and the number of lines is the same as in the original; the difference in content is barely more than that of a free translation. Yet Morungen's version is undoubtedly the greater poem; his images are sharper, his handling of the theme surer.

The great rival to Thuringia as a poetic centre was Vienna, ruled at this period by the Babenberg dukes. Here both 'the nightingale of Hagenau' and 'the nightingale of Vogelweide' sang. Reinmar of Hagenau, whom Gottfried von Strassburg mourns as the possessor of 'the master-secret of all music' represents classical *Minnesang* at its purest. His range of subjects is narrow: the unconditional and hopeless service of love through the lady is his dominant theme, which he dissects out until each nerve lies exposed in a fine pattern:

> These long days when I've sweetly sighed
> For my true love's love are still renewed and endless.
> And I still marvel how my pride
> Regrets so little years of service spent and fruitless;
> Her messengers never come
> With comforting words; sadness and sorrow is all they bring.
> How shall I endure this pain a moment more?
> Her heart is cold; that is my grief.
> Could I but fire her, I would swear her lifelong love.[3]

Love's fulfilment is as distant as for the most austere troubadours; but he still persists in his task. But there is a subtle shift in his reasoning: he argues that the lady loves him secretly and is fearful only of her reputation. He does not find the consolation in *joy d'amour*, the ecstasy of unfulfilled love with which the troubadours sustained themselves, though he still consoles himself, and answers his many critics, with the honour to be won through a lady's love. Even if his opponents disagreed with his idealised picture of love, they acknowledge his artistic skill, and particularly his poems in praise of his lady. Walther von der Vogelweide, his greater rival, in a generous elegy on a man whom he admired but did not like, quotes with approval Reinmar's famous line – 'O woman, greeting: how pure a name!'

Reinmar was keeper of the 'master-secret' not only for Gottfried, but also for a whole school of later poets. Here the terms of love-service became rigid and codified. The same theme of almost hopeless love within the private universe of poet and lady takes on an exclusive and esoteric air, as his successors seek for the *Minne* which he so finely analysed. *Minne* becomes a religion in itself; yet it does not contradict Christianity for lady's beauty is also God's creation, and *Minne* is the feeling inspired by contemplation of this handiwork. *Gotes bulde,* divine favour, and *êre,* honour, are the chief goals of the lover beside his lady's love; the striving for both worldly and spiritual reward leads to one end, the old troubadour ideal of worth through love. The German poets, despite their more vivid imagery, make of this a more abstruse ideal. The troubadours never exclude love's fulfilment so vigorously: the world is still peopled by the jealous watchers who may prevent it, but it remains a possible goal. The idea of love as suffering had already arisen in Provence, but it was the Minnesingers, and Reinmar first and foremost, who made the two inseparable: 'Love without suffering cannot be.' The hopeless, introspective nature of their emotion demands an impossible goal; and in later days, their goddesses are specifically married women. Ulrich von Lichtenstein, as he describes his extravagant pursuit of his beloved, can speak of his 'dearest wife' in the same breath. *Minnedienst* has become a courtly ritual, to be performed as a diversion from reality, however earnest it may at moments seem.

Reinmar and his successors were poets of an artificial convention, as the troubadours were, and no one had questioned the carefully contrived mythology of Provence. In Vienna the fantasy had not struck such deep roots. Walther von der Vogelweide extends the range of *Minnesang* and turns his verses to other ends besides. To us the result is more appealing, but he breaks the charmed circle in the process. There *is* a natural world outside the castle, which is more than the setting for a maying expedition. In returning to the roots from which the native German poetry of the mid-twelfth century had sprung, he saved the courtly lyric from the eclipse which it suffered in the knightly world of France. Yet his poems are not so different from those of, say, Thibaut de Champagne, or Charles d'Orléans in a later age; the background of courtly society no longer permeates them in the same way; instead a new and timeless charm distinguishes them:

Under the lime tree, amongst the heather,
Down in the hollow where we lay
Ah, passer-by, ah tell me whether
The grasses lie in disarray.
At the wood's edge, in the vale,
Tandaradei,
Sweetly sang the nightingale.

The meadow path was soft and easy
For there my love awaited me.
Ah, Blessed Mary, he received me
And my heart still sings its ecstasy
All his kisses seemed one kiss,
Tandaradei,
See how red my mouth is.

He made. as rich as I could wish for,
A bed from meadow flowers and grass;
And as you walk the path which I walked,
You'll smile, perhaps, there, as you pass.
From the roses you still may,
Tandaradei,
See the place where my head lay.

If anyone knew we'd lain together—
Which God forbid! – I'd die of shame.
And what he did, ah, no one ever,
Except for us, shall know that game;
Except for us and one small bird,
Tandaradei,
And he, surely he will keep his word.[4]

As the barrier separating the knightly world from that of burgher or peasant gradually disappear, there arise new divisions. The troubadour Peire Vidal had depicted the Germans as rough and unmannerly, and praised the ways of his native land in contrast; so Walther can defend German men as the most courtly of all, the women as angelic. Walther is the first German poet to extend the range of his subject matter to politics. His greatest poems are those on the state of the Empire, torn between two claimants to the Imperial Crown, as far about the Provençal *sirventes* as Ciceronian eloquence above a demagogue's taunts. It is this broader, wider view that characterises his work; and he himself had tasted life outside the charmed circle of court and castle. He 'learnt his singing and rhyming in Austria', but left Vienna in 1198 on the death of Duke Frederick, his patron, from an accident in a tournament. He then led a wandering existence, begging his way as necessary, like the Irish scholars before him. In 1203 he was in the company of Wolfger of Passau, who gave him a fur coat at the first great Church festival after he entered his service, just as another pauper singer, who went by the name of the Archpoet, had put in a Latin plea for one from Frederick Barbarossa's Chancellor half a century before. In the end he seems to have pleaded successfully for a fief, where he settled at some time after 1220.

Broadly speaking, Walther's poems are at their most courtly during his wanderings, though his later patrons may have demanded an occasional verse in a lighter vein. He starts by singing of one lady only, his own personal lodestar; but she soon disappears, and the heresy that *Minne* is a matter not confined to the elegance of court life creeps in. Then, briefly, he takes up Reinmar's universal theme of the divinity present in all women, finds it too artificial, and turns aside to an increasing concern with politics, a phase which corresponds with his years of wandering.

After Walther, *Minnesang* divides into two schools of thought, both claiming him as their genius. The traditionalist theoretical poets predominate, becoming more and more involved with the nuances of the central situation of *Minne* until rhetoric turns to cold hair-splitting as they search for the last shadow of refinement that can be wrung from the old themes. A little great poetry does emerge in the process, but only three poets had any hand in it: Neidhart von Reuenthal, Ulrich von Lichtenstein and Gottfried von Neifen. Neidhart makes rather pedantic play on his surname, 'of the Vale of Sorrows', in his more formal poems, quite in the old vein, but his really original work arises from the introduction of new subject matter, in that many of his poems are in peasant settings, descriptions of village dances and conversations, moving outside the framework of courtly convention.

All that could be done with *Minnesang* proper was to make of it a baroque fancy, in the manner of Ultrich von Lichtenstein's exploits. The poems embedded in the phantasmagoria of his book, entitled simply *Frauendienst*, are in the classic style and almost normal compared with the strange adventures he undertakes in his lady's service; his successors, however, transfer the eccentricities to their poetry. The complexities of metre are occasionally put to enchanting use, as with the dancing lilt in Burkhard von Hohenfels's poem:

> *Welcome, soft breezes!   Come now who pleases!*
> *Maidens entrancing,   join youths in dancing,*
> *Follow my paces:*
> *In gayest attire, you beckon Love's fire   with smiles and sweet faces.*[5]

More often, they are part of an overwhelming rush of images, which make the established themes seem a cornucopia of poetic visions. But description without conviction soon palls, as the competition for richer echoes, more intricate modes, increases. Satire, which Neidhart had directed against the rough ways of the peasants, was turned against the gates of love itself: and the last shreds of reality fell away. Towards the end of the great interregnum in the Empire which began in 1254, the burghers adopted the chivalric fashions and made of them the closely regulated art of *Meistergesang* which emerged about 1300. In the turbulent days that followed until Rudolf of Habsburg began to restore order, there was little time for the ways of knighthood, and much for those of war. Germany's contribution to the lyric poetry of chivalry was brief, eloquent, without lasting inheritance.

The most obvious and yet the most striking feature of the theory of *Minne* is its almost complete dependence on the Provençal *fin' amors*. The same premise lies at the roots of both: the lover's moral improvement through the spiritual love he bears his lady. Given this, the code cannot really vary in any great degree: if the love becomes passion in the modern sense it leads to physical union as well as spiritual, while it cannot diverge into pure friendship in the other direction. *Minne* tends to become a more generalised emotion, as in Reinmar's eulogy of the fair sex as a whole, of which his own lady is merely the fairest and most virtuous representative. The emphasis tends to be on love itself, its genesis and nature, rather than on the ancillary virtues which the troubadours delighted in. The moral rewards and ecstasies are less prominent; *hôher muot*, the equivalent of *joy d'amour*, rapidly becomes a state of mind inspired by circumstances rather than the lady herself; spring or, for Lichtenstein, a good horse or a noble banquet, inspiring the feeling. The relationship of lover and lady is in the foreground instead.

Service (*dienst*) and faithfulness (*triuwe*) are the cardinal points of this relationship. It is a service which for Frederick von Hausen (following Bernart de Ventadour), and later for Ulrich von Lichtenstein, begins in childhood: Ulrich declares that he has loved his lady since he was twelve. The terms of the relationship are set out more sharply in the German poets. The lady is guarded by jealous watchers who prevent the lover from gaining free access to her, but also exclude all rivals. The poet rarely accuses his beloved of unfaithfulness, or even admits that she might have other admirers. It is only the ice within her heart that keeps him at a distance, and he hopes that his lyrical ardour will be able to melt that. Occasionally, under the spell of the romances, he may resort to deeds as well. This, and the increasing physical descriptions of the lady, mark the decline of *Minnesang* with poets such as Tannhäuser: where the troubadours become more obscure and abstract as time goes on, the German poets come down to earth, and demand to 'pluck the roses' in return for their efforts in the tournament. For Veldeke or Reinmar, however, the lady offers no more than a token of favour, a smile, a word in private, as her part of the contract.

The setting of the *Minnesang* poems is exactly parallel to that of the troubadour lyrics: a courtly society where life is governed by conventions. These conventions were a matter of fashion, so much so that they almost seem a poetic fiction, yet the rules were so respected by the poets that they must have had some ground in reality. A poetry which had no such ground 'would indeed be an unheard-of phenomenon'. How seriously was the game played? We have too few independent witnesses to be able to tell, and most of them have a moral axe to grind. The attitudes struck by Reinmar and others may appear to be elegant poses; nonetheless, they are poses which arise from an exaggeration of real emotions, a dissection of the soul under the microscope true enough to its own premises, but out of scale with the rest of the world.

As *Minnesang* disappears at the end of the thirteenth century into contests of technique on the one hand and social satire on the other, it closes the great arc described by the lyric poetry of chivalry and the social convention of love attached to it. Rising from obscure origins, it starts as a mixture of high spirits and low morals in Guillaume IX's first poems and in some of Marcabru and Cercamon's work, rapidly climbs into the ethereal world of Jaufré Rudel's *amor londhana*, and remains in these high regions until the inspiration and impulse evaporated completely in the south. The trouvères make it a little more mundane, but the Minnesingers briefly restore it to its old pretensions, at about the same time that it rises to its most abstruse in Provence. From then on the mode and mood change; poetry is a decoration to the knight's existence, not the oracle from which all truth proceeds. The idea of love-service survives, as an old but active custom which good knights ought to observe, well into the fifteenth century, long after the original social and poetic impulses which gave it life have failed. The decline is slow, almost imperceptible: the accepted ideas of knightly society as to love in 1250 would have been perfectly understood in 1450, despite the fact that no lyric poetry actively advocating such ideas had been written in the interval. For this enduring preservation of the high ideals we must turn to the romances.

103

7

The Romances of Chivalry

From troubadour love the rest of chivalry takes its cue. Transmitted to northern France through Eleanor of Aquitaine and the court of Champagne, it inspired the trouvères, whose less subtle verse gains in clarity what it lacks in richness. Its direct effect here was brief because the north had fewer poets interested in working in the lyric tradition. For the northern courts were already producing literature of a very different kind, with a very different ancestry. The Celtic romances of Arthur and his court, with the *chansons de geste*, had produced a new epic poetry, on to which the courtly ideas were grafted.

The earliest of the major poems in this tradition, the *Tristan*, is a tale of what we now call passionate love. Later writers confused it with the ideas of courtly love, but the Tristan story is *not* courtly. Its idea of love as an overwhelming, dark, supernatural and tragic force is at loggerheads with the troubadours' concepts. Tristan actually loses *pretz* by falling in love with Iseult; and there is little *cortesia* in his actions. We are in a new world, a world of myth rather than manners. The figures of Tristan, Iseult and Mark are too close to their Celtic kin of the Irish legends for courtliness to do more than put a veneer of a different civilisation on them without destroying the force of the story. The tension arises from Tristan's dual allegiance: to Iseult through love, to Mark through duty. The conflict is engendered by the feudal bond, which had moulded the approach of the troubadour to his lady, but here the love bond is opposed to the feudal bond instead of imitating it.

The new ideas from the south and their rapid acceptance may explain why the *Tristan* poems, after several versions had appeared in the mid-twelfth century, later disappeared into a mere variation on the main Arthurian romances, a huge compilation on which Malory drew for his *Boke of Sir Tristram*. By the time the story reached him the tension between Mark and Tristram is caused not by Isode, but by the wife of one Sir Segwarides, whom they both love before Isode is wedded to Mark. Isode is no more than Tristram's lady; the passion that sings through earlier and later versions of the tale has disappeared. For chivalric love does not make passion its ideal; instead, devotion, fidelity, service are its lodestars, inherited from the troubadours' concern with those restraints which prevent love from becoming passionate.

Another poet of the mid-twelfth century who wrote on the Tristan legend was the first master of French romance, Chrétien de Troyes. Working at the sophisticated court of Champagne, whose countess, Marie, Eleanor of Aquitaine's daughter, was an enthusiastic follower of the southern poets, he nonetheless represents a new development in the ideas of chivalry. The writers of the *chansons de geste* were expert storytellers, heirs of local, almost tribal traditions who kept to a realistic, active world, whose only touches of fantasy were the giants and monsters fighting for the enemy, and whose heroes were moved by simple emotions of loyalty and hate. The troubadours were lyric poets, and hence preferred to move in an introspective world where feeling was paramount, and the setting of their love merely ornamental. Chrétien offered a very different atmosphere. He is international where the jongleurs are national, analytical where the troubadours are subjective. Drawing on the love of action of the knights and the longing for love stories of the ladies, and blending both with the newly current 'Breton tales' of Celtic marvels and enchantments, he created a new world and cast a spell over chivalry from which it never quite awoke.

Chrétien's earliest 'story of adventure', as he himself calls it, was written about 1160. The story of *Erec et Enide*[1] is known to English readers from Tennyson's *Enid*: the knight 'forgetful of the tilt and tournament' for love of the fair maiden he has married. At once there is a difference in ethics between Chrétien and the Provençal poets for the greater part of the action takes place after Erec's marriage, and the crux is how Enide can prove her faith to him in the series of adventures that befall them. Here for the first time we meet the unequal heroic combats, the magical adversaries, and enchanted castles that are the stock in trade of the romances; here too tournaments and knight-errantry come into their own. For it is essential to the style of the romances that the knight should wander forth in search of adventures; the duels and marvels that befall him are rarely hindrances to his journey, but are usually its very purpose. Erec sets out to retrieve his reputation and to test his wife's love for him, and in the course of his adventures does both; on these threads are strung the individual episodes which are the real matter in hand.

The adventures of Erec conform to certain rules which condition all later chivalric romances. For instances, the hero is never defeated unless suffering from a handicap, such as wounds from a recent combat. This is common to all heroic folk-tales: the central figure of such tales may commit all kinds of pillage and rape, as in the Irish epics, but his prowess remains unquestioned. Erec is harsh to his wife, though only while he suspects her fidelity, yet he is generous and courteous to the rest of the world. Chrétien overlays the basic simplicity of his marvels with other touches which become commonplace later. Even the most hardened brigands attack one by one so that the hero can dispatch them individually, without having to resort to impossible feats; unknown knights with no reason to be aggressive fight each other without a challenge. In the latter type of combat, the protagonists are often within an ace of death, but never actually expire. Thus Erec not only overcomes Guivret le Petit in such an encounter, and is greeted warmly by him when he learns Erec's identity, but meets him again on a dark night and is nearly killed by Guivret because he is already badly wounded. Such episodes do not represent any knightly custom of real life, being largely devices to heighten the tension of the story; but their spirit was inherent in the *pas d'armes* which copied the romances, and in the chivalric episodes of the Hundred Years' War.

In all this, love seems to have disappeared into the background. In a sense, it has become part of the adventures: Erec's meeting with Enide in her father's threadbare house and his winning of her by defeating Yder in the duel for the sparrow hawk tell us nothing about the subtleties of love, but spin more golden threads into the texture of the romance. It is in the picture Chrétien paints of Enide and Erec's adoration of each other, Erec's forgetfulness of knighthood in her arms, and her unswerving loyalty in face of his trials, that his skill is apparent. It is a new window on the ways of men's hearts. Chrétien is concerned with what actually happens, not with the artificial theories and stylised courtships of the troubadours. Yet the troubadour influence is remotely there. Erec, at a pause in the battle for the sparrow hawk, looks towards his lady 'as she softly prays for him. While he sat and looked at her, great strength was recruited within him. Her love and beauty inspired him with great boldness.'[2] The lover wins physical, not moral, prowess, from his lady's eyes; for his moral worth is taken for granted in this magic world, and the power of love is needed more urgently as a charm to give might to his sword.

Chrétien's second work, *Cligès*, takes us into a new realm again: he exchanges the wilds of Wales for the imperial courts of Constantinople, and instead of physical adventures gives us spiritual debates.³ *Cligès* is the history of two pairs of lovers: Alexander and Soredamors, Cligès' parents, and Cligès and Fenice. The setting is a mixture of classical and Arthurian, but the predominant influence is classical: the figure of Thessala, the witch, is out of Virgil, not from Celtic romance, and many details of the plot rely on classical legend. However, the main interest of the romance is in its study of love, and here Chrétien strikes another new note. He portrays the effect of love on Alexander, Soredamors, Cligès and Fenice in turn, but he does so as a detached observer and analyst of their feelings. The result is a series of introspective but acute monologues based on Ovid's ideas on love as the twelfth century understood them, but illumined by Chrétien's gift of bringing them vividly to life. Here is Soredamors wrestling with her pride when she discovers that she loves Alexander:

'Why do I think of him so much, if he pleases me no more than other men? I do not know; I am all confused: for I never thought so much about any man in the world, and if I had my will I should see him all the time, and never take my eyes from him. I feel such joy at the sight of him; is this love? Yes, I believe it is ...'⁴

But this love is still turned towards marriage; it is Alexander's wooing of Soredamors that is depicted in the smallest detail, dwelt on as the copyist might dwell on the jewelled colours of the illuminations to his manuscript. Love and marriage are one and indivisible; and Fenice, loving Cligès but betrothed to his uncle, bewails her fate as hopeless:

'I would rather be torn limb from limb than that men should speak of us as they speak of the loves of Iseult and Tristan, of whom so many unseemly stories are told that I should be ashamed to mention them. I could never bring myself to lead the life that Iseult led. Such love as hers was far too base; for her body belonged to two, whereas her heart was possessed by one ...'⁵

No clearer indictment of the morality behind the story of Tristan could be found; and Chrétien is fond of comparing his characters favourably with Tristan: for instance, Cligès knows far more about hunting than Tristan ever did.

So *Cligès* is in some respects a deliberate 'anti-Tristan', even though Chrétien boasts in the introduction of having written about King Mark and the fair Iseult. But he does now draw a high moral, and is more concerned to show that love admits of no division of affection. Fenice living with Cligès as his mistress he approves, so long as Fenice does not also give herself to Alis, his uncle. As she is the latter's wife, Chrétien has recourse to Thessalia's witchcraft to keep his heroine pure. Cligès marries Fenice in the end, and this is the only fitting end to the story.

However, Chrétien's moral attitude is to some extent conditioned by his story. The tension arises not from the subtleties of divided loyalties, but from the obstacles to the union of Cligès and Fenice. That he held no absolute brief for even the fairly broad morality of *Cligès* is shown by his next work the *Chevalier de la Charrette*, or *Knight of the Cart*,[6] admittedly written 'since my Lady of Champagne wishes me to undertake a romance'. There is a slightly defensive note about his insistence that 'the material and the treatment of it are given and furnished to him by the Countess, and he is simply trying to carry out her concern and intention'. For this is the story of Lancelot and Guinevere, morally a Tristan and an Iseult without even the love potion to excuse them. The love of the troubadours, existing only outside marriage, is sung by the poet of the married heroes, Erec and Yvain: but he is more interested, given his subject, in the relationship between the two than in the ethics of the affair. Lancelot's complete subservience to Guinevere as his lady is the most remarkable feature of the story. He rides in shame in the hangman's cart (from which he earns the nickname of the title) purely to reach Guinevere more quickly when his horse has been killed. Even after Guinevere has surrendered herself to him, she still commands his every movement; whether her whim is for her lover to play the coward or the hero in a tournament, Lancelot obeys with equal alacrity.

Chrétien's famed skill in characterisation and psychology fail him here: Lancelot and Guinevere have become little more than archetypes of the courtly lover and his lady. Though they are made of flesh and blood – Lancelot hesitates an instant before getting into the cart – they are not human beings in the same way as his previous characters. Chrétien loves to keep his protagonists anonymous (we only learn Enide's name after Erec has won her) and Lancelot spends half the story described only as 'the best knight living wherever the four winds blow'. But whereas Chrétien had previously depicted his heroes and heroines in glowing colours, here he is concerned to get on with the story, and scarcely pauses to dwell on their beauty. His skill in storytelling does not fail him, but there is a sense of unease about his handling of the subject, only to be confirmed when we reach the end and find that one Godefroi de Leigni finished the story under his direction.

With *Yvain*, Chrétien's masterpiece, we return to the old ground of the wooing and winning of a bride within the knightly conventions, and of the history of the marriage.[7] The parallel with *Erec et Enide* is close; the construction, and even the length of the sections, are very similar. A long introduction brings us to the hero's marriage; no particular question is posed, and the story is a simple adventure. Then the crisis is reached with the danger of Yvain falling into slothful ways, described in a short passage of some three hundred lines. His adventures and their resolution, the core of the story, form the longest concluding section. If the pattern is repeated, Chrétien profits from his familiarity with the scheme to weave a more subtle web of adventures and a more involved plot. The world of *Yvain* is that of Lancelot's journey to the land of Gorre in the *Chevalier de la Charrette*, enchanted, magical and spellbinding for the reader, who is carried breathless from one marvel to the next as soon as Calogrenant starts his tale of the spring in the forest of Broceliande at which, if water is poured from it on to a stone, a tempest arises and a knight appears to overthrow the challenger. Chrétien plunders every mythology to hand, pagan, Christian, Celtic, to embellish his story; the easily consoled widow may be Jocasta, the tame and devoted lion belongs to Androcles, and the fountain comes from Breton lore. And beyond this, he draws his characters in bold strokes: Yvain, generous, noble, impulsive; Laudine, haughty, clever, yet truly loving; and Lunete (her confidante) shrewd and devoted. Only once does he fail to convince us that he knows exactly how their minds work, and that is in Yvain's desertion of Laudine after a mere fortnight of marriage, and his forgetfulness. Chrétien merely says 'as the year passed by my lord Yvain had such success that my lord Gawain strove to honour him and caused him to delay so long that the whole year slipped by'. Though this is the hinge on which his plot turns, it demands no greater suspension of disbelief than the marvels which precede and follow it.

Yvain remains a highly moral work. Punishment is meted out for Yvain's forgetfulness, and Laudine's determination not to forgive him is only softened by Yvain's great deeds in his disguise as the Knight of the Lion; he has to earn forgiveness through the quality of his knighthood. Chrétien's message is that knighthood practised aright brings its own salvation with it. The cycle of sin and redemption is closed within an earthly limit.

Perceval or *Le conte del Graal* takes us beyond the secular boundaries of chivalry to which Chrétien has so far kept, where the supernatural is mysterious but amoral. The old scenery remains, and with it the magical adventures, still separate from divine retribution; but the

109

ultimate goal has changed. Chrétien did not complete the story, his longest and most ambitious undertaking; and the riddles he left unanswered, notably that of his concept of the Grail itself, have perplexed scholars for several generations. We can only assume that Perceval was to achieve the Grail quest and his spiritual journey in the finished version.

Beneath the perhaps deliberate obscurities of the adventures, Chrétien found a new direction. *Perceval* is the moral tale of a knight's education, both worldly and spiritual. The hero does not begin as an accomplished warrior but as a raw simpleton, who has to be taught everything about the world of chivalry. In the process Chrétien's view of the real functions of knighthood emerge, as Perceval comes first to maturity in physical skills, and then grows to his full moral and spiritual stature. Yvain and Erec never progressed beyond the moral experience, but here Chrétien treats both the physical and moral qualities of knighthood as though they could only find fulfilment in the spiritual end. Charity and faith supersede the thirst for glory, prowess and love as the ultimate goal.

Religious and secular chivalry are not exclusive in *Perceval*. Prowess and loyalty are cardinal virtues: maidens still insist on their lovers proving themselves, and oaths once pledged, however fantastic or impossible, are still kept at all costs. Indeed Chrétien's attention is divided between Perceval and his secular foil, Gawain, who plays the same part as in *Yvain*, the most peerless of knights in all things earthly, polished, courteous, fearless of danger. Perceval has these virtues too; and there is no insistence on his chastity, such as we shall meet in later poets. From the very first, however, he has a religious aura, which is totally foreign to Gawain: Gornemans knights him thus: 'The good man took the sword, girded him with it, and kissed him, telling him that with the sword he had given him the highest order that God had created and ordained, the order of knighthood, which ought to be blameless.'[8]

His mother's advice is largely religious in tone: succour the weak and helpless, and always turn aside to pray and hear mass. Such advice as she does give him on courtly ways he later misinterprets completely. Gornemans likewise tells him to avoid killing other knights, and to succour the helpless. Again, Perceval misinterprets Gornemans' worldly advice, which is simply not to talk too much. His uncle the hermit, much later in the story, repeats their religious advice, and adds the virtue of humility. This is a far cry from the hectic search for fame and hatred of idleness because it damages a knight's reputation which provides the crux of the matter in *Yvain*

110

and *Erec*, and further still from Lancelot's adoration of Guinevere.

Chrétien's world is the backbone of all the later mediaeval versions of the Arthurian romances, and for many stories in which Arthur is a mere figurehead or absent altogether. The court of these tales became the paradise of which all secular knights dreamed, and the themes the birthright of every storyteller. So his influence on the ideal of knighthood was immense, both directly and indirectly. The very concept of knight-errantry is almost Chrétien's own; the events that merely happened to the heroes of the Celtic romances are now something to be sought after. Knighthood implies activity, activity to win one's beloved, activity to make a reputation and maintain it. For Chrétien, the greatest sin is sloth. His heroes are all too ready to fight the first comer, without inquiring who it may be, but on a higher level, we have seen how sloth and the fear of loss of fame is the hinge on which both *Erec* and *Yvain* turn.

In the carefree world of these romances, this diligent search for glory seems the only obligation a knight has to recognise beyond his lady's commandments. The attempts in *Perceval* to make a moral code out of knightly ideals are prophetic, but at odds with the rest of the story; the knights and the adventures still predominate, not the hermits and the sermons as in some later versions. (Knowing what the story of Parzival became in other hands, it is almost impossible not to read into Chrétien's story religious details which were never intended: one feels that Chrétien only realised the religious possibilities as he worked on the story.) Otherwise, knights have little duty to the world around; damsels in distress may profit from their assistance, but none of the duller chores of real life intrude. Chrétien's knights have forgotten their feudal duties, and have no truck with the holding of land. Before we dismiss them as pure escapist fantasy, however, there is one point to be considered. His heroes are always young, by implication not yet required for responsible duties. Knighthood may become the burden of lordship in later years, but for Chrétien's heroes its essence is this very youth and freedom. It does not reject responsibility, but is rather something to be enjoyed before responsibility becomes unavoidable. And it was as such that knighthood was practised by the 'young king', Henry II's eldest son, Richard Cœur de Lion, William Marshal, Philip of Flanders, and others of Chrétien's contemporaries: an outlet for youthful exuberance.

Thus knighthood begins, by the end of the twelfth century, to become something apart from the social and feudal status we have already studied. It is this distinction that defines chivalry: the ideals of the knightly class pursued for their own sake. We shall hear little more of the feudal duties of a knight; henceforth chivalry is a prelude to or distraction from those burdens. So the escapism of the romances is paralleled in real life, and fantasy is increasingly chivalry's keynote. The romances themselves become more and more elaborate with Chrétien's successors, even though the flights of fancy which Chrétien took over from his Celtic predecessors die away into more prosaic sequences of jousts and tournaments.

The closest heirs of Chrétien were the German poets of the late twelfth and early thirteenth century. Chrétien's work was not the first to find its way across the Rhine from France: there were already versions of the Tristan story and of the Trojan legends taken from the French, and we have seen how troubadour and trouvère poetry won followers among German poets. Hartmann von Aue's adaptation of Chrétien's *Erec* is the first German romance of chivalry to survive. Hartmann came from the borders of southern Germany and Switzerland, and probably wrote his *Erec* in the last decade of the twelfth century, some thirty years after Chrétien. He prefers the splendours of knighthood's estate to Chrétien's poetic economy, and expands the text with long descriptions of the marvels of his hero's equipment or the luxuries of a great feast. The result is in a curious way simpler; the subtleties of Chrétien's psychology disappear under the elaborate trappings, and are replaced by an insistence on the high nature of knighthood itself. He followed this some years later with a version of *Yvain* (transcribed as *Iwein*) in which the same traits appear, though the details are less lavish and more acutely observed. The technical skill at his command was of a very high order; and this was to prove fatal to later imitators, who, dazzled by the outer brilliance, failed to perceive the central unity of his tales.

Between the two translations, Hartmann produced works of his own, based on Latin legends. *Der arme Heinrich*, the story of which comes from a Latin moral tale for use in sermons, is his masterpiece. It tells of a knight who has all the chivalric and Christian qualities save that of spiritual humility. His forgetfulness of God is punished by a terrible leprosy, which, he is told, can only be cured by the blood of a pure maiden willingly sacrificed for him. When he at last finds his paragon, the miracle is accomplished without her death; he marries her, although she is a poor man's daughter, and is restored to his former estate. He has learnt his lesson, and Hartmann allows his hero to return to his old ways and to a life of chivalry, although he remains conscious of the favour God has shown him. This is one of the rare examples where a moral tale is told, not against the knight's

112

scale of values as a whole, but as an example of one particular sin. The clergy were apt to condemn the whole panoply of secular knighthood as vainglorious, and to see it as an entirely unrewarding occupation, preaching a powerful contempt of the world instead. Hartmann counters this with the idea of *mâze*, moderation, and shows that it is only the abuse of knighthood, or its pursuit at the expense of one's devotions that really contravenes the Church law's, a point not often enough made by its champions, who preferred to regard their world as beyond the sphere of the Church.

The reconciliation of divine and knightly ideals was an exercise at which the German writers were adept. The greatest of the German romancers, Wolfram von Eschenbach, combines the highest philosophical themes and adventures in the manner of Chrétien with consummate skill in his *Parzival*, written in the first decade of the thirteenth century. Chivalry becomes an ideal within which all man's highest aspirations are fulfilled, crowned by its own religious order, the knights of the Grail, and yet remains a real and actual experience.

Wolfram was a Bavarian knight, from the village now known as Wolframseschenbach. His family were *ministeriales*, knights in imperial service who remained officially of unfree status. Of his life we know only what he himself tells us: that he was poor – 'at home the mice rarely have enough to eat' – that he had various misfortunes in love (though he implies that he was happily married), that he was widely travelled in Germany. He came at some point in his journeyings to the court of Hermann of Thuringia, where Veldeke and Walther von der Vogelweide had also been honoured guests. His view of courtly life is not entirely approving; he has some sharp words for the disorderliness of Hermann's halls, where every insolent fellow who pretended to sing or make verses gained easy entrance. Addressing the Landgrave, he says 'you would need someone like Keye [King Arthur's uncompromising seneschal] to deal with an unruly mob like that'.[9] And in another passage he attacks the morals that all too often lay behind the outward show of courtly love, saying that he would not care to take his wife to King Arthur's court, where everyone's thoughts were always occupied with love. 'Someone would soon be telling her that he was transfixed by love for her, and blind with the joy it caused him; if she could cure his pain, he would always serve her. I should take her away from there before anyone had a chance to do this.' Wolfram's wry humour marks him as a man with a down-to-earth view of life, at first blush an unlikely guide through Chrétien's exotic forests and spellbound adventures.

113

Chrétien's *Perceval* was left incomplete; what he did complete lacks that sureness of touch that is the hallmark of his earlier romances. The story has become too important, the adventures serve only to further it; and the hero has outgrown the achievements of a mere paragon of earthly virtue. It is perhaps unfair to compare it to Wolfram's work, which is almost too complete, telling of Parzival's father Gahmuret and of his son Loherangrin at its opening and close, but Wolfram does base his story on Chrétien's (despite his mystifying references to one Kyot), and the differences are revealing.

The theme which Wolfram makes central to the story, Parzival's courtly and spiritual progress, is only vaguely explored in Chrétien. The old folk-tale of the prince brought up in ignorance, the 'pure fool' of noble birth, was merely another inherited *motif* from the Celtic past with which to embellish another romance. Wolfram turns this into a deeply felt heroic example, yet does not preach or point a moral. Indeed, his portrait of Parzival's innocence is delightful and natural. The boy, kept from the ways of knighthood that have caused his father's death, is brought up by his mother in the depths of the forest, ignorant of the glittering world that is his birthright, ignorant even of the simplest ideas about life: he has learnt who God is, and that 'His love helps all who live on earth'. When he meets a knight who has fled into the deep forest to escape his pursuers, he can only imagine that this superior being is God: and although he is naturally disillusioned, his natural instinct for knighthood has been aroused.

Wolfram makes great play with the idea of an inherited nobility: Parzival's nature predisposes him to knighthood. From his father's family he inherits love as his destiny: from his mother's, the service of the Grail. This idea of a place in life at once fore-ordained and inherited is at the root of Wolfram's idea of society, which he conceives as a series of orders, of which knighthood is the chief. Man should not question his appointed lot, even if it be a less honourable one than knighthood.

So Parzival sets out: dressed in fool's clothing, and with the briefest of advice from his mother. She hopes that his attire will draw mockery and send him back to her; and he has misunderstood her advice. This provides the matter of his first adventures, and the wrongs he unwittingly inflicts will have to be atoned for later, including the killing of Ither, a knight who had done him little harm, but whose splendid armour he covets. It is not until he reaches the castle of Gurnemanz that he finds a mentor who is prepared to educate him in matters of chivalry. His fool's attire, which he still wears beneath the real armour, is taken from him, and with it his foolish ways. Gurnemanz instructs him in courtesy and, more important, in the ethics behind courtesy. 'Never lose your sense of shame', is his first precept, and the second to show compassion to those who suffer. Parzival remembers, but does not understand: he has learnt the outward forms but not the inner meaning.

His second series of exploits starts auspiciously. He wins the heart of Condwiramurs, and marries her. The contrast with Chrétien is sharp. Perceval and Blancheflor are deeply in love but their ties are only casual. Here Parzival and Condwiramurs are bound by the ideal love to which *Minne* aspires, the conjugal love of marriage and passionate physical love. When Condwiramurs comes to Parzival's room at dead of night to pour out her troubles to him, they do not even kiss; it is an astonishing scene, when such a visit means only one thing in every other romance. And when they marry, their love is so ethereal, 'they so shared togetherness', that Parzival does not think of making love to her for three nights after the wedding. The strength and joy of their earthly love shines clearly through the lovely scene when Parzival, now at the end of his adventures, comes to meet his wife at the edge of the lands of Munsalvaesche, the Grail castle in the grey light of dawn, and finds her asleep with their twin sons. The seneschal wakes the queen; clad in only her shift and a sheet hastily flung round her, with one impetuous movement she is in Parzival's arms. Parzival embraces her; the children wake, and he stoops to kiss them too. The old seneschal and the attendant ladies discreetly retire with the children, and leave the pair alone to prolong the night until the sun stands high in the heavens.[10]

In this ideal marriage Parzival fulfils one half of his nature, the steadfastness in love inherited from his father. Most heroines of the romances are only truly won at the end of the tale: even Erec and Enide, Yvain and Laudine do not find the fullness of joy until their adventures are over. To Parzival, Condwiramurs is both the lady of his love-service and his sustaining hope in his adventures. At one moment, like Chrétien's hero, we find him sunk in ecstasy over three drops of blood on the snow, which remind him of his beloved. If we remember that she is also his wife, the difference between Chrétien and Wolfram is evident. The idea for this relationship may well be evolved from Chrétien's married heroes; yet what distinguishes it is Wolfram's complete acceptance of the situation. Chrétien cannot quite believe that knighthood and marriage are compatible; for Wolfram they are the most natural companions in the world. Even Gawan, whose adventures occupy about half the romance, and whose deeds and character are much closer to his French counterpart, ends by marrying the proud Orgeluse. Orgeluse is in the French romance an irrational, scornful figure; and it would seem difficult even for Wolfram to make her a convincing character. Yet she becomes entirely human in his hands; her pride and scorn are partly the result of the loss of her lover, partly a test by which she will find the hero who can revenge her on her lover's killer.

Parzival's other inheritance takes us into the moral and religious spheres which are notably absent from Chrétien's unfinished poem. After a time, Parzival asks Condwiramurs to let him go in search of his mother; 'loving him truly, she could not disagree', and he sets out on a quest which, though he does not know it, is to lead not to his mother, but to his fulfilment of his part as guardian of the Grail. (Wolfram's idea of the Grail is a curious one: a stone of strange powers that fell from heaven during the struggle between Lucifer and the Angels. It has no particular associations as a relic, but its quality is such that it attracts all that is highest and best in men.) It is a task for which he is not yet ready: for though he comes to Munsalvaesche, the Grail castle, he heeds only Gurnemanz's warning that curiosity is rude, and does not ask the crucial question on seeing the Grail borne in procession, and the agony of the Grail-king, Anfortas. Anfortas has broken the laws of the Grail community in pursuing earthly love without permission, and lies wounded between the thighs in punishment, until an unknown knight shall come and ask him: 'Lord, what ails thee?' Parzival may observe the outward forms of courtesy and suppresses his curiosity; but he forgets its inward essence, humility and compassion. He leaves the desolate castle, which had shone with all the show of a splendid feast on the previous night, in a dark and lonely dawn, with only the curses of the gatekeeper to speed him on his way. As if to show that men cannot judge between inward and outward courtesy, Parzival rides on to his greatest triumph yet at Arthur's court, only to have it shattered by the arrival of Cundry, the hideous messenger from the Grail castle who roundly curses him for his 'falseness', 'falseness' both to his nature and to his destiny.

However, Parzival can only ask the question when he is ready to do so: and his reactions to Cundry's message show that he is far from such a state of mind or spirit. In the grip of black despair, he curses God for not rewarding his faithful service, and departs in search of the Grail again. He is now farther than ever from it, seeking it despite God; the lesson he has to learn is not only compassion and humility, but penitence and the real nature of man's relationship to God. He sees it only in feudal terms as a contract by which man's service

116

earns God's favour. It is not until he comes, after long wanderings, to his uncle, Anfortas' brother, the hermit Trevrizent, that the way begins to clear. In Chrétien's version, Perceval is quickly brought to penitence, and goes on his way with no more than a brief lesson and prescribed penance.

Wolfram makes this scene the crux of his hero's development. The pilgrims who reproach him for bearing arms on Good Friday bring him out of the heedless, timeless mood in which he declares that 'he once served a lord called God, until He chose to scorn and disgrace me'. Though he gives his horse its head that God may lead him to Trevrizent, he still defies and challenges: 'if this is His day for giving help, let Him help, if He is so inclined', and he only admits to his state of mind gradually under Trevrizent's patient questioning. As his story unfolds, so does the seriousness of his offences appear: the killing of Ither, which he had dismissed as something done when 'I was still a fool' proves to be the murder of a kinsman; and his equally thoughtless abandoning of his mother has caused her death from sorrow. Finally, his failure to ask the redeeming question when he was the chosen knight to do this had condemned his uncle – for Anfortas proves to be such – to continued years of pain. Parzival now sees that though he has indeed been a valiant and skilful knight, his own sins are so great that he has no claim on God; the way lies not through deeds alone, but also through belief. (In a curious passage just before Parzival's triumph, Trevrizent seems to retract his earlier statement that the Grail cannot be won by strength of purpose alone. The most probable explanation for this is that this idea was too unorthodox, as he also retracts some equally unusual remarks about the 'neutral angels' who sided neither with Lucifer nor God.) 'God Himself is loyalty', and cannot be disloyal, which had been the burden of Parzival's complaint against him. The spiritual world cannot be conquered by earthly virtues and services. He departs, chastened; the seeds of penitence and redemption are sown.

When 'the story comes to its rightful theme' again, Parzival and Gawan fight a duel as strangers, in which Parzival is victor, though he recognises Gawan before they have done each other serious injury. This is a commonplace of the romances and a similar combat ensues with Parzival's half-brother Feirefiz, in which the combatants are equally matched; again, they recognise each other in time. In the meanwhile, he has also fought a mutual enemy of his and Gawan's, Gramoflanz. Each of these battles, at this stage in Parzival's spiritual progress, must represent more than another episode in the romance; at first sight they seem to reduce Parzival to Gawan's level, a mere knight-errant again. But in the wider symbolism of the poem, Gawan represents earthly chivalry, and Gramoflanz pride. Earthly chivalry and pride have to be overcome. And Feirefiz, Parzival's pagan half-brother from his father's marriage to the heathen Belakane, is the archetype of natural goodness; despite his strange black-and-white striped skin, he is as courteous as any of the knights of the Round Table, and as virtuous as any Christian. It is Feirefiz who is the one knight chosen by Parzival to go with him on his journey to claim the kingship of the Grail.

For Parzival's trials are now at an end; and on the day of Feirefiz's admission to the Round Table, a day of 'sweet pure clarity', the messenger from the Grail castle returns, to announce that he has been named as King of the Grail, in letters which have appeared on the magical stone itself. He rides to Munsalvaesche; the compassionate question is asked, Anfortas healed. The story moves swiftly to its end, telling how Condwiramurs rejoins Parzival, how Feirefiz is converted and married to the bearer of the Grail, Repanse de Schoye, and how Loherangrin succeeds his father. The two ways are reconciled: earthly and spiritual chivalry move in harmony.

Parzival is at once the greatest and most human figure in the mediaeval romances; in him chivalry is shot through with a warmth and natural ease which owes little to convention. By contrast, Gawan, the secondary hero of the story, is a formal figure, moving within a limited world, but perfect within his own established limits. The idea of *orden*, levels of achievement according to each man's power, enables Wolfram to transcend the old ideals of knighthood, and set a higher goal without contradicting these cherished images. For this is his real insight: that chivalry is not merely a matter of rules of good behaviour, of *Minnedienst* or even of religious service. Its strength lies in its appeal to man's better nature while remaining in close contact with the realities of life. The marvellous is only an outward trapping, corresponding to the splendours of court festivals: what matters is the effect of these great ideals on the mind and soul. Chrétien had started to explore the effect of idealism in love on men's minds; in *Parzival*, Wolfram extends and completes the search, until the way of chivalry becomes the way of Everyman to Salvation.

Wolfram's disrespect for courtly conventions, his inventiveness, sly humour (which recurs even at the most solemn moments) and his obscure and uneven style, won him harsh words from his great contemporary, Gottfried von Strassburg. In the middle of his *Tristan*, he breaks off to discuss his fellow poets, and the only one whom he

118

cannot praise is 'the friend of the hare', as he calls Wolfram: the breadth of Wolfram's ideas, as well as his weakness for strange pieces of secondhand alchemists' lore, earned him that title. Gottfried is singleminded compared with him, and his purpose is quite different: so different as to be almost diametrically opposite.

The story of Tristan and Isolde has come briefly within our purview in its old French version, an unpolished tale of elemental power. From this rough stone, Gottfried carves and polishes one of the masterpieces of erotic literature. Wolfram raises chivalry's idealism to its highest peak. Gottfried takes courtly love and infuses it with pure passion. The result is a romance in the old tradition, but which breaks some of the conventional rules by the very nature of the subject matter.

Like *Parzival, Tristan* begins with an account of the hero's father and his exploits. But as soon as Tristan himself appears, there is a great gulf fixed between the two tales. Parzival is potentially perfect, and seeks to fulfil that perfection; Tristan can do no wrong from the moment he is born. Image beyond all words of the perfect courtier and knight, every skill is at his command, no virtue is too taxing. Strong, handsome, gay, he turns his hand to chess, harping, the arts of venery, or war, speaks several languages, is at ease from the moment he sets foot in a strange court.

With such a beginning, we might well expect to find ourselves back in the world of Chrétien, amidst more extravagant fantasies than ever. Instead, the fantasies are kept to a minimum; the descriptions are extraordinarily real, yet nonetheless beautiful for it. The courtly world needs no apology, no excusing ethos: for Gottfried it is normal and natural. Tristan's loyalty to Mark, his duty to his subjects as ruler of Parmenie are part of this world; his adventures until he meets Isolde are purely chivalrous, and of a very simple type. The slaying of Morold, the Irish champion who comes to claim the annual tribute from Cornwall, belongs to the old heroic manner, as does the theme of the poisoned sword whose wounds only the dead man's relatives can heal.

Gottfried uses this perfect, self-contained world only as a starting-point. As with Wolfram, there are higher ends in view. Wolfram looks to a perfection to be gained by striving and effort, and spiritual pilgrimage; Gottfried's higher world is very different. Tristan and Isolde are already perfect. It is this that qualifies them for the transcending experience. The mysticism of love is his theme, and he speaks only to those 'noble hearts' who can understand his message.

119

The crux of the story, the famous scene where Tristan and Isolde drink the love-potion, thinking it is common wine, has been given many different meanings. Gottfried uses the idea skilfully. He leaves us uncertain whether the drink merely confirms a love already begun, or is in itself the *coup de foudre*. For his own purposes he is well enough content to let it be regarded as a supernatural force; by this excuse he can tell his story of open adultery, treachery and broken oaths as a special case, and invoke magic as the cause of each transgression. On the other hand, the 'noble hearts' who understood his true meaning could see the potion merely as surrogate of love's power, a symbol of its workings.

Tristan and Isolde's love puts their relationship above the everyday ways of the world. They are no longer subject to the ordinary laws of men, and can only be judged in terms of their fidelity to each other and to love's ideals. The conflict and tension that arises between the two worlds, their unresolved discontent, shows that this is not an intensified version of courtly love, but a more disturbing force. Passion is the word we have now come to use for this force, and it is a commonplace of our view of love. But to Gottfried's contemporaries, despite Chrétien's tentative descriptions of the symptoms, this was novelty indeed.

Tristan and Isolde are equal in love. There is no question of knight serving lady; instead, they are both servants of *Frau Minne*, Lady Love. Caution becomes impossible, compromise unthinkable once her mystic joys have been tasted. Love becomes the fountain of all goodness, and even provides them with physical sustenance. The climax of the poem is the episode in which the lovers, banished by Mark, take refuge in the 'fossiure à la gent amant', the Cave of Lovers. In this symbolically perfect retreat, whose every feature corresponds to one of Love's qualities:

> Their high feast was Love, who gilded all their joys; she brought them King Arthur's Round Table as homage and all its company a thousand times a day! What better food could they have for body or soul? Man was there with Woman, Woman there with Man. What else should they be needing? They had what they were meant to have, they had reached the goal of their desire.[11]

But if love is a higher ideal than those of the courtly world in which the lovers move, it affords them no protection. Its joys are balanced by its sorrows; and its sorrows stem from the lovers' concern for their reputation. When Mark discovers them lying with a naked sword between them and is persuaded of their innocence, they return to court 'for the sake of God and their place in society'. Mark represents the opposite side of love: lust and appetite aroused by Isolde's beauty. As such he cannot find peace either; a pitiful figure, he wavers between the unpalatable truth and the comfort of illusion. Despite its outward gaiety, the court of Cornwall which he rules is similarly tainted; suspicion is everywhere, misunderstanding and distrust abound. Only Brangane and Kurvenal remain loyal; and even their steadfastness is tested. Isolde, fearing lest Brangane should reveal their secrets, tries to have her killed, but repents as soon as she fears that the deed is really done. For loyalty exists only between the lovers themselves; all external claims are brushed aside, and there is left

> A man, a woman; a woman, a man:
> Tristan, Isolde; Isolde, Tristan.[12]

Their true world is an enclosed, charmed garden, the garden of the Cave of Lovers; in the everyday world, however splendid and gay, they move guiltily, forced to deny their desires, and the air grows thick with sorrow and evil.

Gottfried did not complete his poem; whether by design or accident, we cannot tell for certain. It ends with Tristan's thoughts as he is torn between the idea of marrying Isolde of the White Hands, whose love he has won during his self-imposed exile from Cornwall; and it seems likely that Gottfried was similarly torn between faithfully following the story as given in his original and the loyalty in love which had become both his main theme and the excuse for his hero and heroine's misdeeds. That this ideal meant a great deal to him is plain enough, and there are veiled references to personal experiences of such a love throughout the poem. Yet, even as a guiding light for those 'noble hearts' to whom he addresses himself, it is an uncertain star. Gottfried makes sensual love sublime by his artistry; it is the one way in which the great tale he tells comes to life, but the philosophy is incomplete and less subtle than that of the troubadours and Minnesingers. Indeed, it is scarcely a philosophy at all, though Gottfried would like us to think it was; it is a mysticism without a goal, the exaltation of emotion to the level of the divine through the element of suffering that emotion arouses. What he does tell us a great deal about is the psychology of love, how lovers behave and how their minds work; and his audience of 'noble hearts' are lovers who seek to find distraction for their own sorrows and perhaps a reflection of their own dilemmas.

In this lies the sharp distinction between Gottfried and Wolfram.

Gottfried is a superb poet, a master of style whose cadences ring true, describing the deepest secrets of the emotions in a story well suited to his ends; Wolfram is less technically accomplished, but has a far broader view of life, which he expresses amidst the unlikely paraphernalia of a knightly romance. Both, however, have risen too far beyond the conventions of the world about which they were writing for their successors to do more than admire their lofty concepts and to produce imitations of the outward forms from which the inner spirit is lacking. Wolfram and Gottfried represent, together with the greatest of the Minnesingers, a *ne plus ultra*. All that is left for later writers in the romantic genre to do is to compile immense fantasies, drawing on the inherited stock-in-trade of endless combats, strange adventures, mysterious beautiful damsels, prolonged quests that never seem to reach an end. The romances revert to type, and as Caxton says 'for to passe the tyme, thys book shal be pleasaunte to rede in, but for to gyve fayth and byleve that al is trewe that is conteyned herin, ye be at your lyberté'. Yet even without the high intent to which these stories had once laid claim, their fascination was such that they survived into a fifteenth-century renaissance of the chivalric spirit in Germany, and were avidly sought after, despite two centuries in which very little of real interest had been written.

The main stream of chivalric romance in the thirteenth century is the vast assemblage of Arthurian stories in French called the Vulgate Cycle. Drawing on all the main themes of Arthurian literature, it presents a vast panorama of every element in the romantic literature of the period. The huge scheme of the work, from the bringing of the Grail to Britain to the death of Arthur, is an extended set of variations on the themes provided by Geoffrey of Monmouth and Chrétien, with borrowings from Celtic and Christian legend, and numerous inventions by the many lands who contributed to it. With the *Prose Tristan*, it contains almost all the most memorable of the Arthurian stories. The Vulgate Cycle itself was complete by about 1230, and the major variations on it do not continue much beyond the middle of the thirteenth century. So the main body of the romantic tradition of chivalry remained fixed for the next 250 years. Only the details changed in the numerous translations into practically every European language; the stories of Arthur and his court were common ground for Spanish, Italian, Portuguese, French, German and English knights, and there are even pieces in Hebrew, Greek, Latin and Norse.

The great Arthurian heroes are the literary archetypes of the mediaeval knight. Again and again, in songs and tournaments, their names recur; and their parts in the history of Logres, Arthur's realm, reflect the development of the ideals to which all knights looked. Arthur himself, originally a warrior hero, never becomes a real knight-errant, except in the fantastic fourteenth-century romance of the *Chevalier du Papegau*, where a talking parrot leads him on his adventures. He is the fount of all honour, his court the magnet to which all knights are drawn. He is in many ways the knight's ideal monarch: generous, eager for the renown of his knights, concerned that there shall be adventures for them to undertake. Only in the opening and closing sections, where deep emotions and high affairs of state predominate, does he become a clear cut figure: and Arthur himself belongs to the great tragic heroes rather than to the world of chivalry. When we reach *La mort le Roi Artu*, the last of the five sections of the Vulgate Cycle, chivalry is only the backdrop; the drama derives from the division of loyalties and the inexorable workings of fate, even if Lancelot and Guinevere are lovers in the courtly tradition.

Gawain, one of Arthur's earliest companions, likewise fails to shake off his pre-chivalric characteristics. In the first romances he figures not unflatteringly, and indeed is almost the co-hero of Chrétien's *Perceval*. But as the moral tone of the romances becomes more and more high-minded, Gawain's unremorseful wenching and killing comes in for increasing disapproval. In the Vulgate Cycle *Queste del Saint Graal* he is the exemplar of the folly of worldly glory without God; and in *La mort le Roi Artu* it is his stubborn pride that drives the tragedy on to its last agonies, through his refusal to forgive Lancelot for his accidental killing of Agravain and Gaheriet in rescuing Guinevere from the stake. The simple warrior seemed uncouth in the light of the newer more polished ideals: and his casual *amours* were equally censured. Under pressure from those who saw chivalry as a potential religious ideal, secular knighthood had to clear itself of its worst faults, or stand condemned like Gawain.

Lancelot, on the other hand, who had never been anything other than a courtly lover and knight-errant, survived the contest with the religious standards in a better light. He was no longer the unvanquished hero, the model of perfection; but his standing was such that the main body of the Vulgate Cycle is still known as the *Prose Lancelot*, and many versions of the whole story bear his name. His romance with Guinevere is transmuted into a more passionate than courtly love. Where once his love for her had merely been a duty appropriate to his standing – the best knight of the court could only have the queen as his lady – here he loves her 'from the first day he was made knight' and receives his sword from her at his knighting. Though the element of service remains, Guinevere is no cool, remote commander of his affections, but a warm and human partner, jealous to the point of despair when she seems to sense a rival in the maid of Escalot.

So long as the story moves on a secular plane, he remains as before the perfect knight, faithful to his lady and all-conquering in joust and tournament. Before he departs for Arthur's court, the Lady of the Lake outlines the qualities of the perfect knight to him, one of the few moments when theory replaces example. She begins by explaining why knighthood was instituted: how all men had been equal, but as envy and greed increased, knights were appointed to defend the weak against the strong, and how 'the tallest, strongest, fairest and most nimble, the most loyal and the bravest, those full of goodness of heart and body', were chosen for this office. A knight should be 'merciful without being uncouth, affable without being treacherous, kind towards the suffering, and generous. He must be ready to succour the needy and to confound robbers and murderers, a just judge without favour or hate.' He must prefer death to shame. Chivalry was also instituted to defend the Church, the Lady of the Lake goes on, and she explains the allegory, familiar from religious writers, of how the knight's armour symbolises his duties and position.[13]

Unfortunately the high moral tone and complete absence of any mention of the service of fair ladies make this passage sound remarkably like one of the numerous homilies to knights by hermits in the *Queste del Saint Graal*; the knightly virtues of secular romance remain undefined. Lancelot, though he possesses most of the virtues listed above, plays a very different part. Once the religious marvels of the Grail appear he becomes a sinner who loves his lady and his reputation too well, and God too little. Whereas on the other hand Gawain is almost past redemption, a great deal of time and numerous homilies are devoted to Lancelot's salvation. He is the only knight, apart from the three elect, to approach the Grail, though the consequences are dire; and he does achieve repentance at the end of the quest. It only lasts so long as he and Guinevere are separated. They fall into their old sin as soon as they meet again, with Bors, one of the three knights of the Grail, condoning them. He fails to see that he cannot reconcile the worldly ideal natural to him with the alien mystical ideal he has learnt in the Grail quest. However, he remains great-hearted, forgiving and generous to the end, and his fate in the closing scenes sums up the temptations and virtues of secular knighthood, his good qualities being balanced by his sensuality and pride.

124

The new ideal is represented by Bors, Perceval and Galahad, who achieve the quest of the Grail. Bors and Galahad are unknown in early versions of the Grail story: Perceval's character and traditional adventures were insufficiently idealised for the author of the *Queste del Saint Graal*, and he is replaced as the protagonist by Galahad, the pure knight who also has something of the Messiah about him. He is a superhuman figure moving in an aura of mystical certainty towards his appointed goal, almost an incarnation of our Lord as knight-errant. And it says much for the author of the romance that he is nonetheless a clearly defined character. Perceval, in his traditional role as a naive innocent, represents redemption by faith: his purity shines through his foolish incomprehension. Bors, likewise, represents a type of the Christian knight: he earns his redemption by good works in expiation of his one casual sin. But because none of them play an important part in the stories outside the *Queste del Saint Graal*, being solitaries rather than brothers-in-arms and preferring dialogues with hermits to the glittering companies that belong to knighthood's very essence, they remain in the last analysis lay figures, symbolic characters from another world.

The *Queste del Saint Graal* stands alone in the romances as a deliberate attempt to bend the power of chivalry to new ends, the Church's ends. It is probably the work of a Cistercian monk, but a monk well acquainted with the matter of romance. Robert de Borron, whose less coherent version of the story was probably used by the writer of the *Queste*, had made of Chrétien de Troyes' mysterious Grail a Christian symbol; but the adventures attached to it remained pure adventures in the other world of romance. The atmosphere of Arthur's court within this other world, a centre of light continually threatened by the surrounding darkness and its marvels, corresponds to the knight's own conception of his place in life; but it also corresponds to the Christian life in this world as mediaeval churchmen saw it. In the *Queste* the two ideals are brought together. Knowing the connection between the Cistercians and the military order of Calatrava (see p. 282f. below), it seems surprising that the result is not some new military order of the Grail, a spiritual counterweight to the order of the Round Table. But the romances themselves as already established could not be easily reshaped to such an end; besides, the Cistercians, despite Calatrava, were no great lovers of the military orders. So a new vision of chivalry, where secular knighthood became the highest inspiration of the lay world, emerged.

At much the same time as the *Queste del Saint Graal* was written, perhaps a decade or so earlier, another writer had realised the power and spiritual wealth of meaning in the story of Percival, and had written the romance called *Perlesvaus*. It is a strange work, at odds with much of the 'accepted' story of Arthur in its plot, and showing a markedly individual idea of the role of Christianity in a knight's life. The Old Law of the Old Testament is set against the New Law of the New Testament, as sharply as heathen and Christian are distinguished in the *Chanson de Roland*. The romance opens at Arthur's deserted court: Arthur, forgetful of the New Law, has lost all desire to honour knighthood and encourage great deeds. Only the renewal of his faith and the achievement of the Grail can remedy matters. Perlesvaus' (Percival's) failure to ask the vital question at the castl of the Fisher King has already taken place, and it is this that has caused the decline of Arthur's court and kingdom. The New Law, which Arthur is to reintroduce and spread, is far from being the gentle teaching of Christ as opposed to Jehovah's tribal anger; it is to be imposed by force of arms. Again the climax of the romance is Perlesvaus' reception at a castle with rich hangings worked with images of Christ, and occupied by two Masters and a company of thirty clad in white robes with a red cross on their breasts, might well be an idealised version of a castle of one of the military orders. Percival is destined to be king, not of that castle, but of one nearby, as though the Masters were sovereign rulers themselves. Both the militarism and earthly splendours of the leaders of the New Law echo the ideals of the crusaders and of the military orders; there is also a strong element of Mariolatry which coincides with knightly attitudes. *Perlesvaus* is an unjustly neglected work, and possibly a very important one in the history of chivalry, but needs more attention from scholars before it can be really understood.

Later works on the Grail shrink back from the positive religious attitude of both the *Queste* and the *Perlesvaus*. The *Queste del Saint Graal* would not have achieved its standing as the accepted history of the Grail if it had not formed a part, though at odds in spirit, of the Vulgate Cycle as a whole. In the first of the many variations and compilations that followed, the *Roman du Graal*, conflict of mood within the cycle as a whole is partially resolved by making Arthur a more central figure and linking the Grail with the fate of Arthur's kingdom by means of the story of the Dolorous Blow. The Grail and the Holy Lance, with which Balain strikes King Pellean and thus lays waste his kingdom, have returned to the world of marvels – or rather miracles, for they are still firmly Christian. The deeper allegory and argument is fading, however; the new knighthood has found no answering chord in reality. The process of attrition continues down to Malory; both the Grail knights and the Grail itself diminish in importance, until religious chivalry reappears in romantic terms with Godfrey of Boulogne in Tasso's *Gerusalemme Liberata*, a hero far removed from ecclesiastical visions of knighthood.

Another of the great Arthurian tales, that of Tristan and Iseult, suffered similar changes at the hands of thirteenth-century writers. The *courtois* ideal may never have been positively proclaimed in the romances as the one true mirror of life, but courtesy, as adapted in the later works, predominates over all other ideals. It was Lancelot and Guinevere's romance that was the stumbling-block for the Grail ideal, and it was their courtly prowess which later writers re-emphasised. The same originally *courtois* ideas became grafted on to the legends of Cornwall, which, as we have already shown, were alien to the idea of courtesy in their passionate intensity; they lacked the *mezura* of the troubadours, and burned all the brighter for it.

The *Prose Tristan* has as its central thread the original story, but the characters and relationships are almost unrecognisable. Tristan is now the central figure, Iseult becoming his lady rather than his soulmate and partner in hardship. The old tension between feudal and amorous loyalties disappears. Mark is an evil and treacherous king, with scarcely a spark of humanity to redeem him; it is he who kills Tristan as he sits harping at Iseult's feet with a cowardly blow from behind. Instead, in the absence of these tensions the romance is entirely in the manner of knight-errantry. Tristan's growing fame and eventual place among the greatest knights of the Round Table are as important to the plot as his love for Iseult. Once again, the active ideal predominates over the passive and passionate basis of the story.

One figure in the *Prose Tristan* stands out as something new. Dinadan is Tristan's companion-in-arms; and as such we might expect him to be a minor hero in his own right. Far from it; he is a cheerful but keen critic of the whole business of knight-errantry. On meeting an armed knight who greets him in the conventional way of the romances: 'Sir Knight, you must joust with me,' Dinadan replies, 'Sir Knight, as you hope that God will send you good adventures, don't you know any other way of greeting a knight-errant than "you must joust with me"? It is not very polite, and besides, how do you know I want to joust with you?' 'I don't know,' says the other, 'but I still say you must joust with me.' 'Out of friendship or out of hatred, then?' 'I don't hate you, of course; all I want is a friendly joust to pass the time.' 'Then I don't think much of your friendship or your pastimes; take you friendship elsewhere, for I'd rather be your enemy.'[14]

Eventually the baffled knight agrees to leave Dinadan in peace; and the latter congratulates himself on having talked his way out of trouble yet again. The contrast between the singleminded, lumbering anonymous knight and Dinadan's quick-witted practical view of the matter is nicely done. On another occasion, he remarks to Agravain, just defeated and deprived of his horse, by a mutual enemy whom Dinadan has avoided, 'My cowardice keeps me alive, and your boldness is the reason why you're on foot now', and to Agravain's angry exclamation he answers: 'I am a knight-errant who sets out each day in search of adventures and the sense of this world; but I can find neither.' 'Let cowards be cowards and leave prowess to the bold' is his motto; and in love he is careful to take his pleasure where he can and never lose his heart to a girl.

Despite all this, his sallies are greeted with enthusiasm by his knightly audiences; Guinevere laughs at his wry attacks on love, Tristan at his barbed remarks about knight-errants. He is still part of the chivalric world, not a new breath of critical realism from elsewhere. His part is that of a jester; when the unpalatable truth must be faced he disarms it by laughter. The attacks he makes are not meant as attacks on the ideals of knighthood; he accepts that prowess *is* for the bold, and never suggests that the expert knight-errants would be better employed in other fields. His humour is at his own expense; he is making fun of his own shortcomings as knight and lover.

If the great heroes of the romances are the best guide to knightly ideals, those ideals are often put in more explicit terms. The relationship between knight and lady is the most apparently important of the ideals. The adventures undertaken by the members of the Round Table arise entirely from their desire for renown; and this renown is only valued when it increases their standing in their ladies' eyes. Guinevere may reproach herself for having robbed Lancelot of his honour since his passionate love for her prevents him from achieving the adventure of the Grail, but his answer reassures her: 'I would never have risen to such heights without you, because my knighthood alone would never have led me to begin or undertake affairs which others had abandoned as beyond their power; but my devotion to you, and the thought of your great beauty has made my heart proud, and I cannot find any adventure I cannot accomplish.'

The lady remains at the centre of the chivalric world, but it is interesting that most of the lesser heroes have no specific lady to whom they are attached. They are very ready to succour damsels in distress, but just as prepared to sleep with their host's daughter if she is willing. Lancelot's fidelity to Guinevere is the exception, not the rule. It is a high ideal, and fully worthy of its place, at the summit of chivalric love stories. Lancelot's words towards the end of his career are an echo of his first admission of love to Guinevere: he tells her how he has loved her from the day he first saw her, and that all his deeds so far have been for her sake. 'When I took leave of my lord the King, fully armed save for my helmet, and commended you to God and said that I would be your knight and friend wherever I was; and you answered that you wished me to be your knight and your friend. And I bade you adieu, my lady; and you said "Adieu, fair sweet friend".'[15] These four words had been his comfort and safeguard in all his adventures. Other knights may serve their chosen ladies well, but without the qualms that beset Lancelot when the maid of Escalot offers her love; and although service is much spoken of, the examples are few and far between; indeed, only Galehaut's love for the lady of Malehaut offers a parallel.

Thus secular chivalry devolves into a code of conduct and a purely self-engendered search for 'adventure'. (One curiosity is the sanctity of a knight's oath, however fantastic or unreasonable. But this 'ideal' of a perfect faith is in fact only a device to further the plot, as the numerous episodes which arise from such undertakings show.) In the world of marvels which lies outside the gates of Arthur's court, the knights are the dispensers of justice in an evil and hostile world; and they themselves are a compact group, 150 in all, of whom the chief heroes come from two families, of Ban (Lancelot, Hector, Bors and Galahad) and Utherpendragon (Arthur, Gawain and his brothers, Mordred). It is a narrow circle, self-consciously aristocratic; and it reflects the vision of the knightly class of themselves as self-appointed leaders. Arthur, inactive himself but attracting a brilliant circle to his court by his generosity and care for his knights, when necessary a brilliant leader in war, is again the real knight's ideal king. 'Adventure' is another strand in the tissue of wish-fulfilment; but it must bear some resemblance to everyday life, which perhaps explains the increasing number of tournaments in later romances, and the tendency to play down the purely miraculous elements. Furthermore 'adventure' is a justification of the knight-errant's existence; for almost all the episodes end with some good deed being achieved – an evil custom abolished, a knight or damsel rescued, a giant slain.

But these ideals belong only to the *Lancelot* proper. *La mort le Roi Artu* and the *Queste del Saint Graal* have other themes. *La mort le Roi Artu* is furthest from the idea of 'adventure'; it is a return to the tale which originally engendered the whole cycle. It is concerned with blood feuds and the idea of Fate, both of which were part of the knight's world, however chivalrous he might be; chivalry only appears at intervals. Though the writer is more concerned with the action and characters of his drama, in Lancelot's fate we find the weaknesses and virtues of knighthood reflected. Adultery and pride are balanced by a simpler greatheartedness: forgiveness of enemies, generosity, justice. These are the real, observed, qualities that any knight should attain, not a complex code of prowess and honour. It was not for this that the audiences of the Middle Ages prized the tale, but for its play with the idea of Fate, and the eloquent laments for Gawain, Arthur and Lancelot as each in turn goes to his long home.

On a less exalted level, the knight's chief asset is his skill in arms. Lancelot, 'the best knight in the world', derives his position from his expert handling of lance and sword. His victories in jousts and tournaments earn him honour; honour earns him Guinevere's love; and that love spurs him on, for honour's sake, to seek fresh victories. His magical qualities as 'best knight in the world', enable him to achieve many adventures, such as the ending of the enchantments of the carol, which condemned its hearers to dance until the spell was broken, and of the self-moving chess set which no one could beat. Yet he has only to appear for the spell to be dissolved; his reputation alone is sufficient. Against this, the idea of victory as being in God's gift must be set: Lancelot's skill is a reflection of his other virtues. When his virtues are insufficient, as in the *Queste del Saint Graal*, he is overthrown by divine judgment: and there is a faint echo of the ideas behind the trial by battle in the outcome of each joust and tournament. Guinevere exerts a much more direct influence on his fortunes in the field: for example, at the last tournament at Winchester, she commands him to do badly, until the third day, when she relents, and allows him to display his usual prowess. Lancelot may attain to some spiritual standing in the Grail quest, but his real place is where we first met him, as ardent suitor to the queen of chivalry.

Outside the Arthurian cycle, *Perceforest* is the most interesting of the French romances from a chivalric point of view. Its author had distinct ideas on the nature of chivalry, and saw it as a noble institution which had fallen on evil days. In olden times, he tells us, 'all those who were endowed with sense and good morals and bold at heart and strong and personable were regarded as gentle, wherever they came from, and became knights if they wished to.' He places great emphasis on the ceremony of knighting, which he describes in detail in its various styles, from the simple *colée* on the battlefield to the elaborate church ceremony. A knight's prime function is the search for honour, in his view: and he gives four rules for the knight errant. Never refuse a challenge: if you unhorse your opponent, offer to fight him with swords. Support the better cause in a war, to the death. Always support the weaker side in a tournament. Always help and assist those in need of aid. And as in the Arthurian romances there is a great order of knighthood, that of the *Franc-Palais*, which, like the Round Table, attracts the best among knights. If all this varies only slightly from the Arthurian romances, the similarities show how consistent the romantic theory of chivalry was.

English literature is little concerned with chivalry. French was the *lingua franca* of the knights, and the humbler origins of English writers before Chaucer meant that the world of chivalry lay outside their ken. With Chaucer and his successors we are already into the first stirrings of the new humanist world which was to replace the knightly ways of thought, and beyond the point at which original romances were being written. The one major exception to this rule is the famous *Sir Gawain and the Green Knight*. The anonymous poet took two stock themes of romances, no more, and interlinked them into a plot of great subtlety yet simplicity, in which the outcome of the magical challenge which Gawain has accepted depends on his success in resisting the seductions offered by the challenger's wife. The richness of the poetry almost obscures the poem's other great merit: a clearcut and uncompromising view of knighthood as the highest attainment of mankind. Gawain fights, not under the auspices of an earthly lady, but bearing the pent-angle of virtue on his shield and vowing himself as 'Mary's knight'. But it is an attainment inescapably tainted by human weakness. Gawain acquits himself with great honour, except when he is offered a magic belt which will guarantee his safety, which he accepts and keeps, thus breaking faith with his host. Like Wolfram's *Parzival*, the theme of the poem is a search for earthly perfection. Wolfram, the optimist, believes that it can be attained in the end: the Gawain poet denies this, but paints just as moving and human a picture of the attempt, a far cry from the artificial world in which chivalry usually moved.

Both in France and Germany, little original work graces the two centuries that follow the completion of the Vulgate Cycle and its many variations. On the other hand, the romances remain much more popular in France and England than in Germany, and there are numerous copies from all periods, made for every kind of patron from the Duc de Bourbon downwards, which vary from straightforward reproductions of the old text, to elaborations that make the cycle yet more entangled and unwieldy. The lesser romances outside the Arthurian framework, including the enchanting *Aucassin et Nicolette* and its companions in spirit, *L'Escoufle* and *Flamenca*, tell of a much less complex world, where love is supreme and the lovers usually happily united at the story's end. These are the forerunners, with Boccaccio's *Decameron*, of the fifteenth-century *nouvelle* or short story, where the *dramatis personae* are no longer exclusively knights and ladies.

The knightly romances probably survived with a very strong class appeal attached to them. The ordinary educated citizen would find them uninteresting; only the rich merchant's wife hoping for a noble alliance for one of her daughters would devour them avidly and spin her dreams from their golden threads. The same golden threads helped to bind the knightly class more closely together in an age that seemed to have less and less respect for their standing: and in Jean Froissart the chronicler's immense romance *Meliador*, all the nostalgia for the good old days which begins to characterise the chivalry of the later Middle Ages can be felt. Though he did not know it, this was the swan-song of the old tradition: by 1400 chivalry had no new visions to offer, and the poets and writers in search of high and noble histories, who had served it so long, turned to new sources of inspiration.

8

The Knight and the Clerk

The Provençal ideas on love, from which the view of love in the romances of chivalry derived, appeared for the first time in northern France at the court of Champagne; and it was there that Chrétien de Troyes was influenced by them. The knight's view of his own place and style as a lover derived chiefly from the romances; but another tradition of love literature that starts from the same place and circumstances is also very important for our understanding of the chivalric lover. It might well be called the clerk's view of love; it is erudite, given to doctrine, theory and allegory, and more often than not smacks of the schools and the library rather than the lists and my lady's bower. Indeed, it first appears in a book entitled *On the art of loving honestly*, a treatise by one Andreas the chaplain, who wrote it about 1186, ostensibly for the instruction of his friend, Walter, but in fact for the entertainment of the ladies of Champagne.

Andreas' work purports to be a sober, serious account of how to behave in matters of the heart; his real intentions, however, are obscured by the third part of the book, 'The reproof of love', in which he calls down heaven's wrath on womankind and its followers. This contradiction seems only explicable if we remember that Andreas, as a royal chaplain, was presumably a cleric of some standing, who could not afford to put his name to so immoral a work without some kind of excuse. His preface implies that if his friend is to enter these sinful ways, he may as well do it with a degree of polish. To see him as an advocate of the Dualist heresy of the separate nature of matter and spirit does not accord with the tone of his remarks, though he was condemned alongside the Dualist philosophers by the bishop of Paris, Etienne Tempier, in 1277. Equally, to see the whole of the first two parts as a satire is to twist the text to give it a meaning it cannot bear, so we must take Andreas seriously as an *arbiter elegantiarum*, noting in passing the way in which the mediaeval mind could accept such a two-principled work. For Andreas was undoubtedly taken seriously by his contemporaries, to whom his fulminations were

133

equally understandable as part of a religious misogynist literature with numerous impressive predecessors, from the Fathers of the Church down.

From the beginning he speaks of teaching, implying that he has a system to impart. As his treatise unfolds, this teaching emerges as a theoretical reworking of many of the themes which the Provençal poets had dwelt on. Andreas takes the ideas that they had used intuitively as a basis for poetry and deduces a logical system from them. The cornerstone of love is the relationship between a man and his lady. Andreas is not so chivalrously minded that he regards only knights and nobles as capable of love; in the eight dialogues which form the major part of the book, he divides lovers by rank into four classes – bourgeois, knight, noble, and higher nobles, with the addition of clerks for the men. The dialogues between men and women of the various classes are intended as examples of how such affairs should be conducted. A lover and his lady should not be at opposite ends of the social scale, and hence, although he casts his net more widely, it is on the knights that the main attention falls, though the clerks are often depicted as superior in wit and skill in such matters.

The lady herself is free to accept or reject the service offered. In the dialogues, we hear the lady of courtly love speak for the first time: cold, haughty, discouraging, she is a long way from Chrétien's warm-hearted heroines. But these attitudes are demanded by the part she has to play. She is there to educate her lover, consciously and deliberately, until his moral worth makes him a fit partner. The length of the trials he endures are all to the lover's credit, and he must treat his lady humbly and respectfully. She has sole dominion over him and his affections, for in her he honours the whole sex, and any advances to another woman are to be vigorously shunned. In the rules of the king of love (who appears in an allegorical tale at the end of the work) the second is 'Thou shalt keep thyself chaste for the sake of her whom thou lovest'. The lady is regarded as spiritually superior to her lover. The three causes of true love are beauty, chastity and eloquence, and riches, higher social standing or easy compliance have nothing to do with the real emotion. Indeed, a lady gains more honour 'if she takes a man who is none too good, makes him praiseworthy through her good character, and by her instruction adds him to the court of love, than if she makes some good man better'.[1]

The final object of the relationship between lover and beloved is to further the cause of love itself, not the mutual possession of each other as individuals. Love is seen as the source of all good: 'O what a

134

wonderful thing is love, which makes a man shine with so many virtues and teaches everyone, no matter who he is, so many good traits of character.' These virtues we have already met among the troubadours: *mezura* or moderation, the middle path of generosity, hospitality, modesty, courage, obedience and chastity. Love becomes a kind of secular morality, adopting the Christian qualities as its own.

The nature of this love is, on the other hand, very unchristian. Even if only spiritual, it is spiritual adultery, for it is emphatically love *outside* marriage. 'Everybody knows that love can have no place between husband and wife. They may be bound to each other by a great and immoderate affection, because this affection cannot fit under the true name of love. For what is love but an inordinate desire to receive passionately a furtive embrace?'[2] Jealousy is absent if the pair are married, that jealousy which 'lovers should always welcome as the mother and nurse of love'. In marriage too, physical love becomes a duty, and cannot be used as a means to spiritual improvement. And it is far from purely spiritual. The goal of love is 'the surrender of the whole person' on the woman's part, and 'the solace of the lower part' the cause itself of love. Not only the merely lascivious, but also the young, the old and the blind are excluded from it; and its physical nature is made quite plain.

However, love is also *passio*, suffering – that 'certain inborn suffering derived from the sight of or excessive meditation upon the beauty of the opposite sex'; and the agony will be but brief, as the troubadours found, if the goal is too easily or too often attained. So the same concept of *fin'amors, amor purus,* reappears, sensual but restrained, if not actually unfulfilled love; though *amor mixtus* is still love, it is on a lower plane. 'Moreover, no one was ever weary of the solace of the upper part of the body or sated with such intercourse; but in truth the delights of the lower part soon pall and prolonged usage makes him who practises it repent.'[3]

Andreas' ultimate ideal may be unequivocally a spiritual love, reflected in the physical, but his basis is practical ground. His actual advice is less concerned with the exalted side of love, than with the everyday details. The laws of the king of love illustrate the amount of purely social advice that Andreas offers:

1. Thou shalt avoid avarice like the plague and shall embrace its opposite.
2. Thou shalt keep thyself chaste for the sake of her whom thou lovest.
3. Thou shalt not knowingly strive to break up another's love affair.
4. Thou shalt not choose for thy love anyone whom a natural sense of shame forbids thee to marry.

5. Be careful to avoid any kind of falsehood.
6. Do not let too many people know of your affair.
7. Being obedient in all things to the commands of ladies, you must always try to ally yourself to the service of love.
8. In giving and receiving love's solaces let modesty be ever present.
9. Thou shalt speak no evil.
10. Thou shalt not reveal love-affairs.
11. Thou shalt be in all things polite and courteous.
12. In practising the solaces of love, thou shalt not exceed the desires of thy lover.[4]

There is little that is ethereal about these ideals; at best they are a kind of 'live and let live' philosophy. Much of the dialogue, too, is intended on this level, showing in a down-to-earth way how a good lover should behave. The world of the troubadours, where such elementary matters are taken for granted, is some distance behind us. Indeed, Andreas at worst turns love into neither a physical need nor a divine force but merely an amusing social game, where the technique and the virtuosity of the players are an end in themselves.

Andreas does not, therefore, owe anything to the troubadours. The troubadours were often, like him, clerics, but not trained in the more learned schools of northern France. For instance, there is very little, if any, trace of acquaintance with Ovid among them, while Chrétien de Troyes had translated both 'the commands of Ovid and the art of Love' for the very circle for whom Andreas wrote. It is from Ovid that this more practical attitude towards love derives; and perhaps the *Ars amatoria* gave him the idea of a textbook of love as well.

Another element foreign to the troubadours is the appearance of the lady as an active partner in the love affair. For the troubadours, working in a personal lyric vein, to put words into the lady's mouth was unthinkable; they might reproach her attitudes, but she herself does not express her feelings. Andreas' reversal of this stems from two causes: his choice of the dialogue form, of which it is an incidental result, and the nature of the social milieu. The leading lights of the court were the countess Marie, and her cousin Elisabeth of Flanders; and Eleanor of Aquitaine was Marie's mother. Marie had already commanded Chrétien to write of courtly love in the *Chevalier de la Charrette*, so her activity in the cause of the new ideas was well known. Hence the famous 'judgments' of the so-called courts of love are all attributed to the ladies of the court.

These courts of love are another of Andreas' literary devices. He uses them to lay down certain laws of love which fall outside the scope of his dialogues, but which he nonetheless wishes to discuss. It is to countess Marie herself that the judgment on the incompatibility of love and marriage is attributed, and some of the other verdicts bear the names of Eleanor and Elisabeth. The idea of such courts recurs in later Provençal and Italian romances of about 1210 and 1250 respectively: but such references, and the notion of a 'law of love' owe more to Andreas and to the mediaeval love of metaphor than to reality. It is possible, on the other hand, that themes such as those Andreas put forward were discussed as an elegant pastime, though again he is just as likely to have originated the idea as to have copied it. The legend of formal tribunals of charming yet fearsome ladies arraigning and pronouncing upon offenders arises from a misreading by Nostradamus (brother of the astrologer) of a fifteenth-century work, and must take its place as no more than a delightful fiction.[5] The only real court of love for which there is historical evidence is the *Cour Amoureuse* created at the French court in 1400; both it and the pageants and festivals which appear in the fifteenth century on the same theme were entirely based on literary ideas.

Perhaps more important than either Ovid or the ladies of Champagne was the effect of Andreas' clerical background. This is immediately obvious in the last part, 'De Reprobatione amoris', which has nothing to do with courtly love; and it pervades the first two parts of the book more subtly. The twelfth century's humanism found its greatest expression in treatises, treatises on moral, ethical, and philosophical subjects, written in a style which derived from classical antiquity, using invented dialogue or an imaginary friend seeking advice. Andreas is writing a treatise, perhaps a study in the manner of the schools of Chartres or Paris, on a secular subject. In an age when the universe was seen as systematic, such an approach was bound to appeal to his audiences. The dialectic of love immanent in the Provençal songs becomes explicit in Andreas' work: his message is not a new one, but by turning it into a code, he made it more easily memorable, and ensured its continuing popularity in later generations.

In Provence, the troubadours had made little distinction between clerks and knights, and had regarded both as equally likely to attain the grace of love; the more self-conscious society of the north, with a stronger tradition of scholarly learning, made the distinction clearly, as Andreas himself does. With the Albigensian Crusades, not only did the Cathar religion disappear, but the northern pattern of life was imposed on the south; a more rigid feudalism and the idea of a separate clerical class, looking to the university (in this case at Toulouse) as their centre of culture.

The dual culture of knight and clerk which developed as a result was reflected in the romances of chivalry on the one hand and the lyrical and allegorical poems on the other. Clerks might write the romances of chivalry, but the supremacy of the knight, whether in secular or religious guise, is undisputed. In the clerical tradition it is the lover's personal qualities, not necessarily in terms of virtue but rather of culture and savoir-faire, as opposed to skill with lance and sword, that count in his lady's eyes. It is a way of thought that leads us to the Renaissance ideal of the gentleman, influencing the ideals of knighthood gradually towards a broader view of life; and it develops into concepts such as Platonic love.

Chrétien de Troyes had translated Ovid in this vein; the version of Ovid, by Master Elia and Jacques d'Amiens, and the imitation of Ovid called the *Clef d'Amors* continued the directly Ovidian tradition after Andreas' work had appeared. Later manuals show his influence, with variations according to the author's taste. The *Breviari d'Amor* of Matfré Ermengaut is idealistic, avoids sensuality and sees love as a source of mystical illumination. By the end of the fourteenth century, the idea of jealousy is rejected as being unnecessary to true love, openness is preferred to secrecy, and married men are told to love their wives in the *Court d'Amour*, which may derive from the entourage of Charles d'Orléans.

Works which only set out to instruct were of less importance than the allegorical poems of the thirteenth and fourteenth centuries. The greatest of these is the *Roman de la Rose*, more popular and influential than any of the romances of chivalry. Over three hundred manuscripts are recorded, and sixteen editions between 1480 and 1538. It had a curious history, in that the author of the first part, Guillaume de Lorris, left it as an incomplete poem of over four thousand lines, with perhaps five hundred lines unwritten; and its success in this form was such that it was taken up by Jean de Meun, who, instead of rounding it off, wrote another eighteen thousand lines, spinning out the action to introduce excursions on all kinds of philosophical and social topics.

Guillaume de Lorris' romance uses a formula new to the literature of the period. It is the story of a dream, in which the actors are allegorical personages, such as Jealousy, Shame, Gossip, Fair Welcome, and even Nature and Love itself. The dreamer sees a fair garden, within which stands a Rose of surpassing loveliness; as he looks on it, Love fells him with the arrow of Beauty: and the rest of the poem concerns his intrigues to gain the Rose. His opponents are not overcome by deeds or spiritual exercises, but by fair words, intrigues and arguments. The lover's strength, whatever passing advice may be offered on fashion or the advantage of skill in jousts and music, is in his courteous manner and eloquent tongue: the clerk's virtues, in fact.

Love itself is much more to the fore. In the romances it provided the motive, but not the action; here it is the be-all and end-all of the poet:

> Love bears both the gonfanon
> And banner of fair courtesy
> He is well mannered, sweet,
> Frank and gentle, so that
> Whoever may decide
> To serve and honour him,
> No villainy nor treason
> Nor any evil thought may dwell with him.[6]

The goal of life is the lover's bliss, reflected in the dreamer's version of the dancers in the garden:

> Lord, what a pleasant life they led:
> Only a fool would not have envied them.
> Who could wish for a better existence?
> There is nothing more joyous in Paradise
> Than to have a fair and willing lover.[7]

How to attain this goal? The god of love has nothing very new to say to the dreamer turned lover.

> Whoever wants to devote himself to love
> Must study noble ways and habits.[8]

Love's high precepts are seasoned with a few useful hints in matters of fashion and in dealing with milady's maids – a little flattery and the odd present will put him in good standing with them. There is more than an echo of Ovid's worldly wisdom; but it is a foreign note, and we are soon back among the more solemn melodies of courtly manners, which pervades the whole of Guillaume de Lorris' part of the poem.

Jean de Meun's continuation is a dazzling display of an eloquent tongue; his never-ending fund of anecdotes to illustrate the action, including whole stories from classical mythology inserted bodily into the tale, would have entertained a whole court for months, let alone amused one lady. He is no longer writing a romance, but a piece of instructive and witty literature with a very loose plot as a framework

139

on which to hang his ideas, ideas for which he plunders any writer to hand. Guillaume, by sticking to the point of the Romance, the lover's progress to the conquest of the Rose, was still just within the pale of chivalric love. Jean, without contradicting Guillaume, merely by his display of immense learning, is on the side of the clerks, when he is not being openly antifeminist, again part of the clerk's tradition. The knightly virtues are quite incidental to his ponderings on the way of the world.

Nor is Jean de Meun the first to exalt the clerk's position as a lover. We have already noted the appearance of the clerk in Andreas' work. A group of poems from an older non-courtly source also praise the clerk at the knight's expense, going back as far as the beginning of the twelfth century, and owing something to the tradition of Latin secular verse. The oldest is *The Council of Rémiremont*, in which a nunnery devoted to the service of the God of love holds a debate as to the relative merits of wielders of the sword and the pen. The forms of religious usage are neatly parodied; Ovid is read instead of the gospel, and a lady-cardinal, sent by the God of Love, conducts proceedings – which inevitably declare in favour of clerks. Those 'nuns' who prefer knights have to do penitence or be ejected from love's community, and a terrible curse is laid on those who persist in this error. This accomplished mockery is reflected by three other poems where the debate is purely secular, between two girls on a spring morning. In each case the maiden who dares in this learned and witty world to prefer a mere rough knight is duly punished: two die of grief at the decision of the assembly, and one had to be carried away in a dead faint.

These poems are lighthearted, certainly, and *The Council of Rémiremont* is a purely humorous piece; yet they do reveal something of a new mood among the clerks. The idea of a clerk being as well versed as a knight in the courtly arts is no longer in itself ludicrous – it is only the way the idea is put that is amusing. For the clerks have begun to develop secular ambitions which are not merely political. By the beginning of the thirteenth century a profane literature in which the knight has ceased to be the central and dominant figure has come into existence; nor is it attached to any religious outlook on life. It is a literature independent of the ideals of any particular class, intellectual to some degree, but with a much wider potential audience than the chivalric romances, from the increasingly influential universities and their students to the new educated bourgeois class of the towns, who might occasionally marry into the landed aristocracy, but who had little sympathy with the irrelevant ideals of knighthood. For them, new ideals and ways of thought were needed.

So we find the story of the shepherd girl rejecting the knight's dubious advances in favour of the simple life sung again and again; old though the theme already was, it seems to have acquired a new popularity. And we find Jacques d'Autun addressing his wife as he leaves her, in homely but enchanting terms:

> Sweet lady, artless and pleasing
> I have to take my leave of you,
> But do so with a heavier heart
> Than man could ever imagine.[9]

He goes on to say that love 'did much to my liking when he made me your husband; he would have done even better to make me your lover'. Andreas' dictum that love in marriage is impossible dies hard, though the rest of the poem is a moving contradiction of it.

Indeed, such new ideas could never be completely independent of what had gone before. So Jean de Meun's part of the *Roman de la Rose* has a courtly framework, provided by Guillaume de Lorris' poem. The *dolce stil novo*, 'sweet new mode', of the Italian poets of the thirteenth century is founded on a legacy from the troubadours. The *Meistergesang* in German flows on from *Minnesang*. The mood is changed, however; the new stream eventually rejoins the old traditions in the Renaissance ideal of a gentleman, but in so doing washes away the remains of a distinct chivalric ideal. In the interval it shows up by contrast that ideal, and hence briefly claims our attention.

Italy, home of the beginnings of this new culture, had not been involved with the world of chivalry to any extent. Her cities had resisted the alien organisation of the Holy Roman Empire, whose ancient claims on them and against the Papacy had led to the wars of Guelf and Ghibelline, but the Empire had never become more than a shadow over the land. Even the feudal substructure of chivalry was usurped by the towns, either by the voluntary adoption of citizenship by the nobles, or by the victories of the towns over their enemies in the countryside. The internecine wars between them, and on the other hand their prosperous trade with all Europe, meant that they remained in a kind of uneasy equilibrium which prevented any one commune from mastering the rest, or, from poverty and weakness, falling completely to its neighbour. Such conditions were not necessarily unfavourable to chivalry: there are many political parallels with the turbulent, divided state of Provence during the heyday of the

141

troubadours. There, however, the basis of the feudal pyramid had been secure; the knights and lesser lords had formed the numerous small groups centred on each local court and castle. Their Italian counterparts were assimilated into the life of the communes without giving it any distinctly chivalric flavour. All that appeared in Italy were a few isolated tournaments in the early twelfth century, before the knights had lost their identity as a class.

The troubadours had had some influence in Italy; and in some ways the *dolce stil novo* is the renewal of their art which they themselves had failed to bring about. The poets of the new school had a reserve of learning and classical culture which the troubadours had lacked, a broader view of the world. Instead of merging with the active life as in northern France, love is separated from chivalry and courteous manners, and is no longer a force that affects the lover's achievements. The Italian poets make love an end in itself; no longer does the lover pretend to greater moral worth or strength through love. His gaze is focused only on the beloved, and the world of active life is a hindrance rather than a help to union with her. The lover's innate nobility or spirit – a nobility which has nothing to do with birth or riches – is his greatest asset: 'Love and a gentle heart go together', as Dante says in his *Vita Nuova*.

The derivation from the troubadours' ideas is clear enough, but the Italian poets have taken the opposite direction to the writers of northern France. The reasons for this are not far to seek. Dante's audience was drawn from the citizens of Florence, proud of their independence from feudal ways. The *Vita Nuova* makes no pretensions to a courtly background: its setting is the high timbered streets of Florence and the 'church where the Queen of glory was spoken of'. The adjective he uses most often for his beloved Beatrice is 'most gentle', not noble or courteous. And, the death of Beatrice apart, the events in the *Vita Nuova* are on so purely an emotional a plane that the whole work seems a series of moods rather than happenings; indeed it is, for the narrative serves as no more than a linking commentary on the sequence of lyrics it encloses. Introspection, not action, predominates, ideal triumphs over achievement.

Italian poetry of the Middle Ages is predominantly lyrical: its chivalric romances are Renaissance hothouse blooms with no roots in tradition. (But the romances were not unknown for all this: even St Catherine of Siena can refer in her letters to Christ as 'a knight sweetly loved', the redemption as 'a tourney of Life against Death'.) This in itself is one reason why individual emotion rather than social graces of the courtly manner is the keynote of Dante and his successors. On the other hand, once the initial break with courtliness is made, the Italian writers vary the same material without any dramatic degree of novelty. In ways, their world is as closed as that of the troubadours; yet it remains open to new ideas from intellectual sources, which had very little effect on chivalry. If Cavalcanti and Cino da Pistoia develop Dante's themes and forms, and in particular begin to give the sonnet that emphatic last couplet which makes it so much more dramatic, they do not widen the range of poetic subjects. Cavalcanti never reaches that beatific vision which is for Dante the counterweight of love's despair. The lord of love has decreed that his love shall be unrequited, and all he can look for is the occasional grace of a kind word, the moment of unwarranted hope. The argument is conducted in terms of mood and emotion: tangible imagery is rare, though a knight rides once across the landscape of his poems, a glittering sight enough but inferior by far to the idea of his lady's beauty.

Petrarch is the prince of such poets. Learned in his approach to poetry, he affected to despise the songs of love's bitter-sweetness which he had written in the 'vulgar tongue', and preferred his fame as a latter-day Cicero and as an antiquary, pursuing rare classical manuscripts. This cosmopolitan background, embracing Avignon of the Papacy in French exile as well as Italy, gives him new ornaments and decorations to his verse, and yet the poems themselves remain fresh. Petrarch seeking 'to flee the travail of his flesh and bones' is a pre-Renaissance, not a medieval figure, even if he is the contemporary of the knights of the Hundred Years' War. The second part of the *Roman de la Rose* and the *Divine Comedy* still have something in common, among which are a few echoes of chivalry. With Petrarch we are well into the new world of humanism: he is not only the scholar *par excellence* but also the first of the universal men of the Renaissance ideal, transcending class and convention by power of intellect.

9

Chivalric Biographies
and Handbooks

Chivalry draws its inspiration not only from the heroes of the romances, from the practical Gawain to the ethereal Galahad, but also from the heroes of real wars and tournaments. The *chansons de geste*, with their ideals rooted firmly in the world around them, are the most primitive form of these heroic examples whose deeds are used to inspire succeeding generations of knights; and as the concept of chivalry grows more complex, so Charlemagne and his paladins are replaced on the one hand by the heroes of the imagination and on the other by men inspired by the new ideas. The heroic biography plays an important part in the cult of chivalry: if Lancelot and Parzival are its gods, William Marshal and Boucicaut might fairly be called its saints, offering a more human and practical example to the aspiring knight.

The biography of William Marshal, written with the help of his squire by a jongleur at the end of the Marshal's long and brilliant career, is the only survivor of a possibly extensive number of poems on current events, most of which were composed as news items to be recited by travelling minstrels on their rounds. We know that the heralds used to proclaim the praises of their patrons at tournaments, and thus became deadly rivals of the minstrels whose task this had once been, and who had reaped generous rewards for it. The currency of such work would be brief, and only a figure such as the Marshal could expect (or afford) a more permanent record.

It is the only portrait from the life of a knight-errant in the twelfth century that has come down to us. William Marshal certainly deserved his posthumous fame; the account of his life is no artificial eulogy, for it was written largely at his dictation and rings true in most of its details; yet he stands out as a shining example of what a knight could be and do. From being a penniless newly knighted younger son in 1167, he became regent of England during Henry III's minority in 1216. If he owed his latter advancement to his qualities as statesman, his early career was made by his skill with lance and sword. In 1173 his reputation was already such that he was chosen to knight Henry II's eldest son. But his other virtues, generosity, courtesy and good faith were also regarded highly. At a tournament at Joigny, William was admired because he could sing so that the other knights could dance with the ladies while they waited for the tournament to begin. When a proper minstrel arrived, he sang a ballade with the refrain 'Marshal, give me a horse', which caused much amusement. As soon as the lists opened, William mounted his steed, and spurred it on against the first knight he could find, whom he unseated. Leading the victim's horse away, he presented it to the minstrel amid general applause.[1]

Other occasional verses have survived from a later period: *Le tournoi de Chauvency* by Jacques Bretel describes an event of 1285, at which Bretel was present as a minstrel. And from Germany there is Heinrich von Freiberg's account of another chivalric event of the same period, Johann von Michelsberg's journey to Paris in 1297 to challenge two French knights to combat. All three poems reflect the real influence of chivalric ideas on the customs of the time. The Marshal is as adept at singing and dancing as at tilting, but has no great lady-love to spur him on; while Jacques Bretel and Heinrich von Freiberg speak of the influence of love in purely platonic terms, though Bretel is a little insistent on the purity of knights' emotions.

In France jousts are recorded in sober prose from the early fourteenth century onwards, and find their place in history rather than literature. In Italy, on the other hand, with the revival of chivalric practices in about 1400, a custom of commemorating such occasions in verse reappears. As they were usually part of a larger event, a wedding or a feast, so the poems are more concerned with the splendour of the central figures and how they enhanced the prestige of the Medicis or the Gonzagas as the case might be, rather than with the actual chivalric deeds performed.

Even in the Marshal's biography much of the work is concerned with political events; and the same is true of two other biographies which might at first blush be expected to contain shining deeds of knighthood, the poem on the Black Prince by Chandos Herald (who decries jongleurs and proclaims his historical intent) written *c.* 1385, and the biography of du Guesclin. Chivalry provides no more than the occasional flourish: of a skirmish which no other historian felt worthy of mention, Chandos Herald can say, 'there were done such feats of arms as might compare with Roland and Oliver and the Dane, or Guy, who was so courteous'[2], but it merely means that he has forgotten the details. It is left to Froissart to emphasise the Black Prince's courtesy to John the Good after Poitiers:

> The prince himself served the king's table, as well as the others, with every mark of humility, and would not sit down at it, in spite of all his entreaties for him so to do, saying, that 'he was not worthy of such an honour, nor did it appertain to him to seat himself at the table of so great a king, or of so valiant a man as he had shown himself by his actions that day'.[3]

The biographer of du Guesclin, though writing at the same period, is a realist through and through. If he has a moral to convey to the rest of the chivalric world, it is that even the most unpromising squire can make good. There is something of the childhood uncouthness of Parzival in the description of du Guesclin's youth: how his strange, swarthy appearance made his parents reject him, and although the eldest son, treat him as a menial. Only the prediction of a visitor that he would have a great future persuaded them to relent; and even then his escapades, including running away from home and leading a gang of the village youths, were anything but knightly. In later years, this rough upbringing was reflected in his impetuousness, generosity and lack of the subtler points of courtesy. It was his feats of arms alone that made him a chivalric figure, though at moments, as when he scales the walls of Melun alone, he seems to belong to the *chansons de geste*. On the other hand, it was his military genius that earned him the post of Constable; and it is a reminder of the close connection of chivalry and war that this seasoned soldier could ever become one of its heroes.

His successors were portrayed in a very different light, acquiring a veneer of romance even during their lifetime. To see how this was possible, we must return to the world of literature, and the attitude towards fact and fiction of the writers who depicted Boucicaut, Lalain and Don Pero Nino. A suitable starting point is the passage where, at the end of his account of the quest for the Holy Grail, Malory says: 'The kynge made grete clerkes to com before hym, for cause they sulde cronycle of the hyghe adventures of the good knyghtes. ... And all thys was made in grete bookes and put up in almeryes at Salysbury.'[4] This pretence that fiction was not fiction at all was beloved to mediaeval writers, and particularly of writers on chivalric subjects. From the very roots of Arthurian romance to the deeds of Maximilian I disguised in fictional form, the borderline between the romantic dreamworld and the military reality was always

146

indistinct: history was subject to the vagaries of imagination, and the chivalric figments of the mind posed as sober truth. The range of variations is enormous: and chivalry is so subject to literary influence that the whole concept seems at moments to have existed only between the black letter lines, illuminated initials and intricate borders of a manuscript.

Fictional history has a more than respectable pedigree in classical writers, from Virgil onwards. In mediaeval times, the story of Troy was retold from the Trojan side, as a kind of prologue to the *Aeneid*, but couched in an unmistakably mediaeval idiom, with the heroine sighing in the delicate phrases of courtly love, and feats of arms being performed in the best knightly style. The effect on its audience, who were not particularly concerned whether the poem was history or not was to reinforce the idea that chivalry was of great antiquity, and that its roots were deep in the Roman world. By the fifteenth century, Jean de Wavrin could say of Henry v, 'well he kept the discipline of chivalry, as did the Romans in former times'. Heralds were supposedly instituted by Julius Caesar, and the great Roman treatises on warfare became works on chivalry, partly through the anachronism of translating *miles* as knight. So *Knyghthode and Bataile* turns out to be a paraphrase of Vegetius' work *De re militari*, and the *Book of Fayttes of Armes and of Chivalrye* is a translation by Caxton of a work by Christine de Pisan on military strategy and law.

However, the classical influence on chivalric ideals always remained slight, a marginal gloss on its origin. A far more important piece of pseudo-history was Geoffrey of Monmouth's *History of the Kings of Britain* (*c*. 1135), on which the Arthurian romances were founded. Geoffrey's work itself was supposedly based on 'a certain very ancient book written in the British language' presented to him by Walter, archdeacon of Oxford. It portrays Arthur as a successful military commander, and has no particular chivalric bent; and the process of transformation only begins in earnest in the works based on it, such as Wace's *Roman de Brut*, and with the use of Celtic material by the writers of French romance. In retrospect, however, it provided Arthurian chivalry with a very respectable historical basis, which was not called into question until Polydore Vergil and his successors turned a critical Renaissance eye on the 'Breton fables'.

Because critical examination of history was very rarely part of mediaeval thinking, the heroes of chivalry were just as real as the prosaic rulers and statesmen of more recent centuries to the mind of the knight. Hence much of literature's influence on chivalry, and chivalry's contribution to literature moves in this shadow world.

147

There was always a temptation to imitate the style of the romances when describing real events, to give the commonplaces of a tournament high-sounding heroic epithets. At the knighting of Jean d'Ibelin's eldest son in 1223, 'many gifts were given, much money spent, many jousts run, and imitations of the adventures of Britain and the Round Table and many other kinds of games held',[5] and the Round Table provided the framework for tournaments until the more learned allegories of the Renaissance supplanted it, whether it were a simple joust or an elaborate *pas d'armes* lasting a year.

Not that other literary ideals could not be used: the first of the literary heroes of chivalry is Ulrich von Lichtenstein, and his 'device' on his first series of tournaments was Frau Venus, deriving from the poems of the Minnesingers (Plate I). Within the imaginative framework of his adventures in love, Ulrich describes with some degree of truth and at least as much fiction his jousting exploits, of which he seems to have kept some kind of record. It is a remarkable book; but whenever we look at the detail closely, he has quietly exaggerated the number of contenders or the number of spears broken until the total reaches fictional proportions. It is the work of a successful man of the world – when Ulrich wrote it he was a highly placed court official – who is writing for his friends' entertainment, with a sly dig at the more extravagant ideas of courtly love, but who completely accepts the basic convention. He is proud of his thirty-three years as a chivalrous knight, and writes for instruction as well as entertainment. Yet his parting advice is disarmingly simple and far from the artificial emotion of his adventures. As usual, he sees the days of his youth as ideal: men are now out to deceive women. His advice is to return to a simpler way of life than that which he attempted: a knight should not seek God's grace, honour, ease and wealth all at once, as he did, but take each in turn.

If there is a little of everything in Ulrich's book – romance, autobiography, poetry, moral instruction – it is bound together by a literary chivalry. This literary chivalry reappears in Germany towards the end of the fifteenth century as an antiquarian interest in the ideals of knighthood, beginning with Püterich von Reichertshaufen's *Ehrenbrief* of 1462, which is indeed almost purely literary. Püterich says he is an old man, only occasionally visited by love – and anyway his wife will not let him do chivalric deeds. 'You old fool,' she says, 'leave it be and let the young folk compete for love.' So instead he writes a poem listing the nobles of Bavaria who are *turnierfähig* (qualified to take part in tournaments), and rounds it off with a list of his favourite reading. Not much of a knight; but he is a herald of the revival of chivalry under Maximilian I which takes exactly this anti-quarian turn as opposed to the Italianate, allegorical symbolism.

Apart from occasional purely imaginative works which use the name of a real person as their central character, such as *The Chatelain of Coucy*, and *Little John of Saintré*, whose heroes lived about fifty years before the romances were written, the other important group of literary portraits of chivalric heroes are the French biographies of the fifteenth century, which are chronicles written in a romantic idiom. The deeds of Lalain, Boucicaut, du Guesclin, and Bayart all received this treatment. Real episodes are woven into the conventional progress of a hero so that we find Boucicaut excelling in chivalrous games in his youth, 'and his manner was from then on lordly and haughty; and his bearing was upright, hand on hip, which suited him well. Thus he watched the other children at play, and never spoke much nor laughed too long.'[6] And at a suitable point that love which was the making of all good knights appears:

> When the winter was ended and the renewal of sweet spring came round in the season when all things rejoice and woods and meadows clothe themselves in flowers again, and the earth grows green, when the little birds in the branches sing loud and the nightingales give tongue, at the time when love is strongest in gentle lovers' hearts, and sets them on fire with pleasant memories which give birth to desire, desire which gives them pleasant torment and sweet languishing in fragrant sickness.[7]

Boucicaut is duly initiated into the ways of love, but his valiant nature cannot dwell for long in such soft arbours, and love becomes the motive for his first series of adventures and single combats. His travels in the East and in Prussia, and his appointment as marshal at the age of twenty-five, point the way to a more serious career; but before that come the jousts of St Inglevert in 1390, in which Boucicaut played a major part, and the foundation in 1399 of his Order, 'The White Lady with the Green Shield', whose avowed object was to protect defenceless and disinherited ladies against oppressive lords. The thirty knights were to wear a badge with the device from which the order took its name. It was the last of Boucicaut's purely chivalrous exploits, and was defunct within five years, while its founder went on to a political career as governor of Genoa, and as representative of French interests in northern Italy, a career which did not prove entirely successful. (He did not abandon his courteous ways. Once, in the streets of Genoa, he bade good day to two prostitutes, and when his companion pointed out his mistake, he said that he preferred to greet two prostitutes by mistake, rather than fail in politeness to one noblewoman.) He returned to France and was captured at Agincourt, dying in prison in 1421. His biography ends, however, on a less dark note, as it was written in about 1408: and the last part is an encomium of the marshal's personality and qualities which had curiously little to do with the world of chivalry: his religious devotion and wisdom figure as largely as his boldness and generosity.

A slightly earlier example of a similar biographical treatment is to be found in Jean Le Bel and Froissart, whose eulogies of individual knights amount to heroic lives in miniature. Sir Walter Manny was a compatriot of Froissart's in Hainault and like him enjoyed Queen Philippa's patronage after her marriage to Edward III in 1328. He is one of the six knights mentioned by both writers in their prologues. Knighted for his exploits on the Scottish campaign of 1333, it was he who led the first English troops into France in 1338 as a result of a vow to be the first to strike a blow. During 1342 he was active in Brittany, helping the countess of Montfort to defend her husband's territories. At one point, he and his men were besieged with her at Guingamp; after dinner one evening, Manny looked out of the window at the great siege engine which the French had built, and turning to his companions suggested that they go out and destroy it as a fitting conclusion to the entertainment, which they proceeded to do. As they retired, the enemy set out in pursuit: 'Sir Walter Manny, seeing this, exclaimed, "May I never be embraced by my mistress and dear friend, if I enter castle or fortress before I have unhorsed one of these gallopers." '[8] At which a skirmish ensues in which 'many brilliant actions, captures and rescues might have been seen'. Later in the same expedition, when two of his compatriots were about to be beheaded to satisfy Louis d'Espagne's wrath, Manny rescued them by a daring sally from the castle of Hennebont into the besieging army. Froissart also has his examples of the power of love for a knight: Eustace d'Aubrecicourt, one of the English allies, was 'much in love with the lady Isabella de Juliers. . . . This lady was greatly attached to Sir Eustace, for his gallant deeds of arms, which had been related to her; and she sent him coursers, hackneys, and letters full of love which so much emboldened Sir Eustace, and spurred him to perform such feats of chivalry and arms, that all those under him made fortunes.'[9] But the dénouement − he married her − is not within the chivalric conventions.

A better known example was offered by Jacques de Lalaing, of whom two chroniclers wrote memorials. Born in 1421, he was brought up in the entourage of the duke of Cleves at the Burgundian court, and distinguished himself at an early age in tournaments. From the age of twenty-four onwards he held a series of single combats and challenges, culminating in the *pas d'armes de la Fontaine des Pleurs* which lasted from November 1449 for one year. His death at the siege of Poucques in 1453 meant that these feats were still fresh in men's minds when the time for eulogies came. If the results are less overlaid with romance than the life of Boucicaut, it is because Lalaing's record needed few embellishments. Indeed, Jean le Fèvre de St Remy, who was herald to the order of the Golden Fleece (of which Lalaing was a member) does not gloss over the occasions when an opponent breaks more lances than his hero.

Lalaing is the exception among these exemplary knights. If we turn to a Spanish history in similar vein, *The Victorious Knight*, a biography of Don Pero Nino of Castile finished in 1449, the romantic prelude to a prosaic career reappears. Pero Nino began his knightly deeds at the age of fifteen in 1394, jousting with cane lances and bullfighting, 'and there was there no one who did such good service, as well afoot as mounted'. He soon took up a military career, and at the siege of Pontevedra we find him jousting again: 'Battle was given on a ground well chosen for those who would distinguish themselves in arms for the love of their ladies; for all the ladies and damsels of Pontevedra were there to look on from the height of the ramparts.'[10] Shunning a political career for the moment, 'since among ministers there are of necessity found certain deceiving ways, and matters which spring not from the same root as chivalry', he entered the service of love, and sought feats of arms.

Yet he saw nothing incompatible with chivalry in becoming captain of a galley in the Spanish fleet which was little more than a licensed corsair, raiding in reprisal the Barbary coast and the Mediterranean, as well as an expedition to Cornwall. He cheerfully returned to chivalry after this interlude, jousting in France and defeating two champions, and finally being knighted in 1407, at the end of his chivalric career. He continued in the royal service as sea-captain and minister, and these events take up most of the latter part of his story. *The Victorious Knight* is less an example to others than an ordinary biography written in an idiom which no longer has much to do with the subject, a formal decoration suitable to a successful career.

A more worthy close to the roll of heroes is the Chevalier Bayart, '*sans peur et sans reproche*'. His life, as described by the 'loyal servitor' Jacques de Mailles, begins as an idyllic story of chivalry, from the moment when he challenges Claude de Vauldres at a pas d'armes, and is told by the herald: 'Your beard is not of three years growth, and do you undertake to fight with Messire Claude de Vauldrè, who is one of the fiercest knights that you may hear of?' Bayart answers that he wants to learn, 'and God, if He please, may give me grace to do something which shall please the ladies'.[11] Which indeed he does, at the cost of his reluctant uncle, the Abbot of Esnay who has to provide him with arms. More serious considerations prevail, with his service in the Italian wars, though even here he contrives intervals in the lists. His virtues are in the traditional mould: courtesy, generosity even when he 'knew not how to come by ten crowns', and above all courage: at Milan he was so intent on the pursuit of his enemies that he was captured right inside the town, though the skirmish had begun some miles outside.

Yet the new ways are upon us: Bayart's duel with Alonso de Sotomayor was fought in the Italian fashion with rapiers, a fencing match and not an old-fashioned exercise with axe or sword. Bayart had also to resist suggestions by the duke of Ferrara that the best means of overcoming the Pope was by poison; and little quarter was shown in the ferocious battle between Italians, French, Spaniards and Germans. The latter with their fearsome pikes now dominated the field. Only Francis I maintains the old estate of chivalry, and the scene in which Bayart, a penniless knight, confers knighthood on the king is the epitaph for all those who had made their name by their knightly prowess:

> On the evening of the Friday, when the battle terminated to the glory of France, rejoicings were made in the camp, and the affair was spoken of in divers fashions. And some were found to have behaved better than others; but above all it was determined that the good Knight had approved himself such as he had even done on all former occasions, when he had been in similar circumstances. The King, desirous of doing him signal honour, received the order of knighthood from his hands. Wherein he did wisely; for by one more worthy it could not have been conferred on him.[12]

Just as the courtly love of the troubadours and romances had been codified by Andreas and his followers, so knightly examples both in romance and real life were the basis for books which purported to set out the ideals of chivalry, and to offer practical advice on how to become a good knight. Much of this advice goes no further than the ideas put forward in the early manuals of knighthood based on the original concept of the knight as purveyor of justice in the service for the blessing of the sword. The advice given to Lancelot by the Lady of the Lake is an elaboration of the themes of defence of the weak and destruction of oppressors, and the symbolism of the knight's armour emphasises this message.

The same kind of argument is the core of the most famous and popular of the manuals, Raimon Llull's *Le libre del Orde de Cavelleria*. Llull, brought up as a knight and courtier, devoted himself to plans for a crusade in North Africa after a mystical experience at about the age of thirty, in 1265. His book is therefore written from a religious standpoint, while retaining a firsthand understanding of knightly ways. He is interested in chivalry, not as a spiritual weapon, like St Bernard in his letter on the Order of the Temple, *De laude novae militiae*, but as part of the established pattern of Christian society. His object is stated in the prologue: 'May the knight through this book return to the devotion, loyalty and obedience which he owes to his order.' This order is an essential part of the hierarchy, coming below the prince and above the people. In serving the prince, the knight also serves God, and he must defend both the prince's honour and the Catholic faith. His greatest mission, however, is his duty to the people, to uphold justice.

So far, Llull's ideas are strictly orthodox; but he insists on a nobility of spirit, which must at very least mean that knights 'are less inclined to do evil', and at its highest means that nobility is open to those whose way of life and deeds are noble. The knight must be an example to others, and should lead a virtuous and religious life. When he places these qualities at the service of the commonwealth, as he should, he is not expected to serve only in war, but also as a royal official. 'To a knyght apperteyneth that he be lover of the comyn wele. For by the comynalte of the people was the chyvalrye founden and establysshed. And the comyn wele is gretter and more necessary than propre good and specyall.'[13]

Llull sets out his work as a treatise presented by an old knight turned hermit, to a young squire about to be knighted. It opens with a description of the institution of knighthood, giving a popular (but wrong) derivation of the word knight, *miles*, from *mille*, a thousand: 'Of eche thousand was chosen a man most loyal, most stronge, and of most noble courage.'[14] After the mission of the knight, he describes the knighting ceremony and the symbolism of the arms, in a passage which seems to be borrowed from the Lady of the Lake's speech. The remainder of the book deals with the virtues appropriate to knighthood, with suitable examples, and the privileges which he should enjoy. The relative brevity and clarity of the book won it a wide following: there are translations in French, English and Scots, and a Latin version seems to have been made. Caxton printed it in 1484 as *The Book of the Ordre of Chyvalry or Knyghthode*, adding his own epilogue.[15]

Llull wrote as philosopher rather than as man of the world.

Geoffroi de Charny, a distinguished French knight whose career was at its zenith in the 1350s, adopts an eminently practical approach to knighthood in his *Livre de Chevalerie*. He has no great theory to expound, but is merely offering the fruits of his experience, the experience of a man who had been standard bearer of the oriflamme of France, and whose ransom had been set as high as 12,000 crowns. Much of it is advice which might be addressed to young men of any age: young men-at-arms, while they ought to be gay and handsome, and versed in the social graces, should avoid drunkenness and vanity, neither be miserly nor spendthrift, and keep away from brothels, but they should also shun solitude and melancholy, and honour their world, if they are to become good knights.[16]

Charny paints a realistic picture of warfare and tournaments: a knight should be a good horseman before he tries his hand in the lists, and he gives us a sad little vignette of a knight who goes up to his lady, and is asked to joust for her. He cannot make his horse obey him and is unseated in the mêlée; muddy and dishevelled, he tries to keep out of her sight: there is no question of a prize for him! Again, Geoffroi emphasises the hardships of life in the field: 'to fast often, drink little, be badly paid and often in debt, get up early, often have bad horses and a hard end to the campaign'.[17] Poverty leads to the need to borrow to buy arms and horses; there is the danger of imprisonment, from which release may be difficult to obtain; and if the campaign is overseas, the hardships may be ever greater, as Geoffroi illustrates by examples from his own campaigns in the Levant.[18]

Charny's realism is overshadowed by the idealistic tradition in most poems which deal incidentally with knighthood: Langland's *Piers Plowman* repeats the concept of knights as agents of justice, summing up:

> Trewely to take   and treweliche to fyghte,
> Ys the profession and the pure ordre   that apendeth to knyghtes;
> Who-so passeth that poynt   ys apostata of knyght-hod.
> For thei shoulde not faste   ne for-bere sherte;
> Bute feithfullich defende   and fyghte for truth,
> And never leve for love   in hope to lacche seluer.[19]

And the tradition persists well into the fifteenth century with very little change: Alain Chartier in *Le breviaire des nobles*[20] produces a list of twelve virtues of knighthood based on those of Llull: nobility, loyalty, honour, righteousness, prowess, love, courtesy, diligence, cleanliness, generosity, sobriety and perseverance. Chartier's additions are interesting: by love he means not only the love of one's lady, which hardly appears in Llull, but the love of king and country. In courtesy, sobriety and generosity, the old virtues preached by the troubadours reappear – *cortesia, mezura* and *largesse*. Here a more strictly chivalrous ideal has been merged with that of knighthood Chartier's poem, though pedestrian enough, is the nearest we come to an all-embracing definition of chivalry, including that 'knightly system of virtues' of which one modern critic speaks,[21] whose ideas are the common stock of many writers, deriving from philosophical ideas then current. In the German writers 'God's favour' and honour had predominated; in the French writers, *courtoisie* prevailed. As the German influence lessened towards the middle of the fourteenth century, and chivalric fashions were set almost entirely by the French, so *courtoisie*, the attainment of all worldly virtues, becomes the keynote of chivalry. Much of *courtoisie* was concerned with questions of manners: hospitality and a warm welcome, 'debonnaireté' or gaiety and openheartedness, seemed to be as essential as loyalty, and generosity is as vital as compassion.

The sum total of these qualities gives us Chaucer's 'very parfyt gentill knight', gives us Boucicaut and Bayart, and gives us indeed the modern meaning of the word chivalry. But chivalry was not something which lent itself to teaching by handbook or learning by rote; it was both engendered by and learnt from the romances. Sir Ector's lament for his brother Lancelot at the end of Malory's *Morte d'Arthur* overshadows all the host of other expressions of these virtues which are to be found in mediaeval writers:

'A, Launcelot!' he sayd, 'thou were hede of al Crysten knyghtes! And now I dare say,' sayd syr Ector, 'thou Sir Launcelot, there thou lyest, that thou were never matched of erthely knyghtes hande. And thou were the curtest knyght that ever bare shelde! And thou were the truest frende to thy lovar that ever bestrade hors, and thou were the trewest lover, of a synful man, that ever loved woman, and thou were the kyndest man that ever strake wyth swerde. And thou were the godelyest persone that ever came emonge prees of knyghtes, and thou was the mekest man and the jentyllest that ever ete in halle emonge ladyes, and thou were the sternest knyght to thy mortal foo that ever put spere in the reste.'[22]

PART III
Chivalry in Action

10

The Tournament as Sport

For all his involvement with higher ideals, the knight remained first and foremost a warrior; and he acquired his skill in arms in two ways: in real warfare, and in practice in arms off the battlefield. Training for war has existed since time immemorial; but when the conduct of war plays so important a part in society as in Europe in the tenth century, such training comes to occupy a quite exceptional place. In the absence of a central organisation with the means to supervise such training, it developed a formal outline of its own: the tournament. Although this brought together the most enjoyable elements of war, its pomp, its camaraderie, its delight in the display of physical skill, all tournaments retained a strong element of practice in arms until the status of the knight in war proper began to decline, and they lacked sufficient impetus of their own to survive as anything more than a pageant once their relevance to real war had disappeared. Yet tournaments must be firmly classified as sport, despite their military and political overtones, in that they very quickly became an end in themselves: although spectators of all classes were present at tournaments, they were primarily for the enjoyment of the participants. The ancient world had known nothing like them; for although tournaments resemble circuses in their exploitation of physical skill and courage for entertainment, and in their military overtones, the social stigma attached to appearance in the arena, whatever the circumstances, was very strong.

Perhaps the greatest difference between the tournament and the circus was that the former stemmed from a primitive element in social life, and not from the theatrical inventions of civilisation. Indeed, the very nature of the tournament's origins meant that its decline could not be avoided once it became the place for peacock vanities rather than strong arms and stout hearts. It harks back to the military games which Tacitus describes among the German tribes, but the exact development of these into mock warfare remains uncharted. We can catch a glimpse of Frankish games on horseback, a kind of competition in horsemanship which re-appears later as the *buhurt*, a sport associated with and sometimes confused with the tournament, in which similar manœuvres, and occasionally very light armour and weapons, were used. But even the historians of the later Middle Ages, though much closer in time to the beginnings of the tournament, knew very little about it indeed. They could only produce, for the edification of their noble readers, descriptions of fictitious tournaments in the style of their own times, and the most arduous sifting of their fictions leaves nothing tangible whatsoever, save a clear *terminus ante quem*: the tournament did not come into being before the middle of the tenth century. Even the ambitious Georg Ruexner only takes us back to the year 938 for his first tournament, though his *Tournament Book; which is to say a true real and brief description of the beginnings causes origins and deriva-tions of the Tournament in the Holy Roman Empire* . . . provides us with a circumstantial list of those who took part in nine elaborate festivals in German towns before the year 1100, giving their shields and their varying fortunes in the lists. Yet if Ruexner, writing in the sixteenth century to curry favour with the Emperor Maximilian, is an extreme example, the myths had nonetheless begun to be woven in the thirteenth century, when the vogue first began, with the insertion of bald and apparently factual entries into older chronicles, which appear to record jousts under the Frankish kings Clovis and Pepin. Even the junketings attributed to Charlemagne's sons are part of these fancies.

After which it may be rather hard to accept the entry of a sober monkish chronicler of St Martin at Tours, under the year 1062, to the effect that one Godfrey of Preuilly was killed in a tournament in that year, a sport of which he had framed the rules. But at this point that myth conceals a certain degree of probability. It cannot have been much later than this period that these military games were formal-ised into a specific framework. That this took place in France is supported by the early name for such events: *conflictus Gallicus*. There is no means of saying whether Godfrey of Preuilly was re-sponsible for this development. His name is merely the head of an ever-increasing roll of tourneyers who come to our notice after this date. By the beginning of the twelfth century there can have been few knights who did not know what a tournament implied. A charter of Henry I's reign provides that a vassal shall carry his lord's 'coloured lances' to London both for war 'and when I want to go overseas for tournaments'.[1] As the opportunities for, and plunder from, private baronial warfare diminished, so the tournament grew in popularity.

The first great tournament of which we have reliable record is that held at Würzburg in 1127, described briefly by Otto of Freising and even this seems to have been more a military review than what we would now call a tournament. Although prohibitions on the tournament were supposedly issued by William and Henry I, it was not until the troubled times of Stephen's reign that the tournament first reached England; the king himself was reputed to be an enthusiastic participant. By 1130, there was sufficient following for this unchristian sport for Innocent II to be moved to prohibit it at the Council of Clermont, preaching that crusades were a better means of employing knightly exuberance than these wantonly fatal affairs. The theme was to be repeated many times: at the second and third Lateran Councils in 1139 and 1179, and by Eugenius III in 1148 at the Synod of Rheims; but the 'repugnant markets and festivals at which knights are wont to assemble by agreement and to fight together to prove their rashness and strength, which often leads to death and corruption of the soul',[2] continued unabated. Knights who died in a tournament were permitted the last sacrament and extreme unction, but not church burial. In 1163, even the Archbishop of Rheims, with Thomas Becket's support, was unable to beg an exemption from this edict. Very often an automatic excommunication was in force for all the combatants as well. Despite these measures, the tournament was practised by the crusaders themselves, the first example being at Antioch in 1156, and at about the same time it appeared in Italy.

The new sport was thus well established by the third decade of the twelfth century; and with good reason. It provided an outlet for the exercise of knightly prowess which could no longer be expended in the old way in a society that was becoming more orderly and subject to restraints. The knight still occupied the position and maintained the attitudes that the previous centuries had given him; his very nature was conservative. But the last Viking raids were long past; the crusades were an alternative for the very dedicated, the very rich or the very pious; and large-scale warfare was rare. Since the whole outlook of the conservative knightly class was warlike, alternatives to full-scale war were vital as an outlet for their energies. Private war was certainly not uncommon, but with the increasing weight of central authority, both royal and papal, against it, only a very determined or very powerful baron could hope to wage it with success. Hence the arrival of the tournament was opportune, although neither pope nor king welcomed the armed gatherings; it seemed only to be the familiar devil of civil war in another guise, and their ideal remained a peace uninterrupted by either baronial revolts or baronial tournaments. But the knights' enthusiasm was already too great, and the powers-that-be had to extend a grudging toleration to the new sport. This is not to say that kings themselves disliked tournaments; the reverse was more often the case, because they were in many senses the first knights of their realms. When royal policy was concerned, the king as statesman was obliged to frown on tournaments as a possible source of disturbances; the king as knight more often than not took part, and enthusiasm easily overcame statesmanship.

The rise of the tournaments coincided with a number of other developments in the mediaeval world; most notably and closely with the emergence of a new literary culture. The first great works in everyday language are more or less contemporary with the establishment of the tournament as an international sport, and the trouvères or troubadours were essential to its greatness and to the fame which participants so eagerly sought. No monastic scholar writing in Latin was going to record such vain events, except as examples of devilish temptation to be shunned by God-fearing men who abhorred loose living (which filled an otherwise uneventful year in their records very nicely): or, more usually, as incidents in a political conflict, for when the knights of two hostile lords met in the lists, the tournament could – and often did – become a war in miniature.

Because the new literature only began to flourish about 1150, we glean little about the tournaments before that date, except for the vague indications of their growth in popularity already mentioned. Other traces come from later writers; unless mere monkish ignorance of worldly affairs explains Matthew Paris' description in the 1220s of a tournament as being fought in 'linen armour'[3] (meaning perhaps a kind of padded overgarment), he may be thinking either of an earlier form of the sport or some kind of practice jousts.

The tournament was essentially two teams of knights, fighting under certain conditions, including a prescribed time limit (of part of one day) and prescribed weapons (either of war or with blunted points). From the very first, rules to prevent foul or dangerous blows were enforced, for the object was at least in theory friendly, even in the miniature war of the tournaments à outrance. Such rules must at first have been relatively simple, covering only the points of aim and means of holding a lance. But judges do not appear in early accounts; and if someone struck a foul blow, it is hard to see how redress was to be obtained. Only the rudimentary formal elements in a tournament distinguished it from a mere brawl; and the tone in which the Church thundered against them in the early days implies that mere brawls were often the result. There were no individual jousts; the contest was a *mêlée,* in which all the combatants took part; as a result, it was not uncommon for four or five knights to attack one, and the fighting was much rougher and cruder. Finally, the term 'lists' in the early tournaments did not imply an enclosure; until well into the next century it meant the barriers erected round the refuges, where a knight could retreat to rest or to repair his armour. The fighting might range over a wide area as a result and no set boundaries seem to have been arranged. If there were limits to the area of the contest, they were either very wide indeed – several square miles – or frequently ignored.

To achieve personal distinction under such conditions was a considerable achievement; and only as the world of the tournament became more orderly did the first heroes of the lists emerge into international renown. For this development there is a fairly clear turning point. In the decade 1170–80, two of the younger princes of northern Europe became passionate devotees of the tournament: Henry 'the young king', son of Henry II (so called because his father had had him crowned in 1710), and Philip, count of Flanders. Henry II had banned the tournament in England, and so his sons, the young king, Richard, Geoffrey and John, of whom three were ardent tourneyers, were forced to cross the channel in pursuit of knightly renown. The young king had been placed by his father in the tutelage of one of the greatest knights of his day, William Marshal.

This encouragement of the tournament did not come a moment too soon; for the older generation who composed the royal courts of France and England had no particular taste for such diversions. In England Henry's entourage was largely made up of royal officials or older men of substance with no time for mock wars, who regarded the ban on such affairs as admirable and necessary. In France Louis VII pursued his pious ends and his son, Philip Augustus, was not yet of an age to gather an entourage around him. Only in the minor courts did the tournament flourish; though Henry II's ban did not extend to his French dominions, and William Marshal won his first renown in tournaments in Maine, a more impressive centre than the local baron's castle was needed if the sport was to attain its full stature. Indeed the biographer of William Marshal said of the young king Henry after his death:

> It was the young king who revived chivalry, for she was dead, or almost so. He was the door through which she entered, her standard-bearer. In those days, the magnates did nothing for young men; he set an example and kept men of worth about him. And when the men of high rank saw how he

assembled all men of worth, they were astonished at his wisdom and copied his example. The count of Flanders did likewise, and so horses and arms, lands and money were distributed to young men of valour.[4]

William Marshal was an experienced tourneyer by the time he became tutor to the young king. His career had started at a tournament near Le Mans in 1167, only a few months after he was knighted. It was a considerable affair for the time; his lord, William de Tancarville, led forty knights into the lists, and the young king of Scotland, William the Lion, brought a sizable following. William Marshal distinguished himself at once, capturing several knights. Since the loser forfeited his equipment and horse, William did well out of the proceedings, but as he had virtually had to beg a horse from William de Tancarville before the tournament, he could hardly afford to lose. At the end of the day his share was four and a half horses with a corresponding number of horses for his squires, baggage horses and equipment.[5] Such success whetted his appetite for more. Within a few weeks he entered the lists again, meeting with rather stiffer opposition; he was just about to complete the capture of a knight he had unhorsed, when five knights came on him. He managed to drive them off, but his helm came unfastened, and turned round on his shoulders so that he could hardly get it off again in the refuge in the lists, and was ready to retire from the fighting when two knights rode past praising his prowess. On hearing this, he made good the damage and re-entered the fray with better success.[6]

From then on, his career as tourneyer was only interrupted by the more serious cares of real war. In 1168 he was in Poitou with his uncle, Patrick of Salisbury, when the latter was surprised and killed unarmed by the rebel Lusignan family, and he himself was wounded and taken prisoner. Queen Eleanor, whom they had been escorting at the time, arranged for his ransom, and became his patron. When her eldest son, Henry, was crowned by his father, it was partly this patronage and partly his knightly reputation that moved the choice of William as his tutor. Almost immediately the pair entered the lists together, but it was only at the end of the civil war of 1174 that tournaments really flourished. From 1176, when the young king left England again, until 1182, he and his court pursued glory in the lists without interruption. A brilliant circle of knights of like mind gathered round them in northern France and Flanders; and of these William Marshal was the most skilled and renowned tourneyer. There was a tournament of varying size at least once a fortnight; William's biographer depicts nine of the multitude that he entered during these years, all of exceptional magnificence.

Although individual prowess was supposedly the main object, the knights had to think of team tactics as well, since they fought alongside their masters as a retinue, and the element of profit made a successful team operation very rewarding in terms of ransoms. In 1176, during a visit to Flanders, the young king's knights came up against a disconcerting habit adopted by count Philip, which consisted of waiting until all the other combatants were thoroughly exhausted and then throwing his knights into the fray, thus taking many easy captives. He would have continued this trick for as long as he pleased had not William advised Henry to outbluff him by pretending not to take part at all and only appearing on the scene when Philip's own men were tired out. The tables were neatly turned, and Philip had to pay the ransoms for a change.[7]

This businesslike attitude to tournaments shows clearly in a later episode from this period, when William went into partnership with another knight, Roger de Gaugi, with the object of attending all the tournaments they could together, fighting as a pair, in search of profit and renown – profit being upmost in their minds. The venture was certainly profitable; between 1177 and 1179 they travelled independently of the young king, and during ten months captured 103 knights; there is no mention of their having to pay any ransoms themselves, and the surplus at the end must have been considerable.

William, always in the thick of the fight, had some amusing adventures which give some idea of what went on in these confused free-for-alls. At a tournament in north-eastern France, in the Eure valley, the knights of the young king's retinue were so successful in the first charge that they drove their opponents from the field, and forced them to take to their heels. Indeed, they chased them into the neighbouring town of Anet; and William, in hot pursuit, galloped into the narrow streets, only to find his way blocked by a large number of footsoldiers from his opponents' retinues. Undeterred, he charged them, and captured the French knight commanding them, whom he led back to the scene of the tournament. As they returned, the French knight saw a low overhanging drainpipe, which he seized and swung himself out of the saddle. It was not until William tried to hand over the knight to his squire when he had returned to his base that he found that he had only a horse and saddle.[8] Such pursuits of vanquished opponents were apparently an accepted feature of tournaments in these early days, as was the employment of footsoldiers in organised bodies.

The greatest of all the tournaments of this period was that held on the occasion of the coronation of Philip Augustus of France in November 1179. This is the first well-authenticated example of a tournament as adjunct to a state occasion: seven hundred years later, the theatrical pageants which accompanied royal weddings and other such festivals in Italy, still rejoiced in the name of 'tournaments'. The gathering at Lagny-sur-Marne must have seemed the apotheosis of their beloved sport to the knights who took part; and almost every knight of any standing from northern France was there. William's biographer estimates the number of knights at three thousand, a clear exaggeration; but the young king's entourage consisted of two hundred knights, of whom eleven were bannerets with their own followers, five were counts, and seventy were distinguished knights bachelor. There may well have been over a thousand participants, since thirteen other counts and the duke of Burgundy took part. Among them was Philip of Flanders, whose following usually rivalled that of the young king in brilliance.

Among such a concourse, individual prowess could hardly shine, and the tournament itself seems to have been even more of a confusion than usual. The young king led a charge which successfully routed his opponents, and pursued them through a vineyard, which was almost destroyed by the horses. But he became separated from the rest of his knights, and rashly attacked a large group of knights from the other retinues. He was seized by the bridle and almost captured; but William, whose special task it was to preserve his master from such disgrace, had by now caught up, and he and another knight fought off the would-be captors. When they rejoined the main tournament, the young king was nearly taken prisoner again, and William had to repeat the rescue. But the day ended badly for them, since Philip of Flanders, reverting to his old tactics of waiting until the others were exhausted, entered the fray and forced the young king's men to retreat from the field, unable to resist after their earlier exertions.[9]

Shortly after this, William fell into disgrace with his master; and as soon as word came that he was free of ties, he was immediately sought after by every ruler with an interest in tournaments. Philip of Flanders, the duke of Burgundy and the lord of Bethune all offered him £500 a year to join their respective mesnies, a vast sum for those days: but he preferred to refuse all offers and go on pilgrimage instead. The death of the young king in the following year, just after a reconciliation had taken place, was followed by a two-year absence on crusade in compliance with the dying man's last wish. This meant that his career in tournaments was over; when he returned in 1185, the political situation had changed. The new power of France under Philip Augustus could not brook the overbearing influence of its vassal in Normandy and Anjou, and the two countries were locked in the first stages of the conflict that was to overshadow the rest of the age of chivalry. William's skill was not required in real wars, and tournaments took second place to royal business as diplomat and administrator.

William Marshal's career as a tourneyer spans exactly the period when the sport found its permanent shape. As a young knight, he had fought in the earliest succession of tournaments of which we know; when he left the lists for the last time, there was no question that they were more than a passing enthusiasm or nine-days' wonder, but something which, by its nature and the inclinations of the society which produced it, was to endure for many years to come. Nor were their implications to remain merely social; the political and religious reverberations had already made themselves felt. We will deal first with the technical history, and return to its larger connotations later.

Until well into the thirteenth century, the tournament remained in practice, if not in theory, a miniature war. With no boundaries and no referees or judges, all sorts of outrages might occur, since the only tribunal was the general consensus of the participants; only later did the heralds responsible for announcing the tournament and organising the time and place have any effective say in the control of the actual fighting. Prizes were awarded by consensus of either the knights or spectators; but otherwise only those arrangements which had an obvious mutual benefit were generally adhered to, such as the refuges and the rules about foul blows and weapons. The latter were limited to sword and lance; but other weapons were sometimes introduced, as the Monk of Montaudon tells us at the end of the twelfth century, when in the list of the things he hates to see in the world he includes 'darts and quarrels [crossbow bolts] in tournaments'. Specific matters about which prior rulings had been made could also be enforced, such as the amount payable for ransoms. However, the word of honour did count for something, and agreements over surrender, although made in the heat of battle, were generally honoured, even if the defeated knight was usually handed over to the keeping of a reliable and sturdy squire.

The first signs of control appear in 1194, when Richard I licensed tournaments in England. Most of his restrictions were political, but in the stipulation that the earls of Salisbury, Clare and Warenne – three names which recur throughout the roll-calls of English tournaments

– should act as general controllers and licencers of tournaments, the germ of a more formal attitude to the sport is present. Furthermore, each separate tournament was to be attended by two knights and two clerks, who were to administer an oath to keep the peace and not to pursue feuds in the lists, and also to collect the royal taxes imposed on those who took part.

About the same time there came about a decline in the system of patronage and retinues which figures so prominently in the tournaments of William Marshal's day. The retinues remained, but in much diminished form; even allowing for the usual exaggeration on the chronicler's part, the essence of William Marshal's tournaments was the large number of participants. By the middle of the thirteenth century the numbers indicated are in the region of 100 a side, and as the years pass so this number decreases. At the same time, jousts are first recorded. These may have started as a reaction against the chance and brute force which decided the fortunes of the *mêlée*. Fighting man to man, skill was all that counted, and the joust had the added advantage of being the only way of settling an argument as to which of two knights was the better.

As a result, by 1225 the lists had become much more civilised. Skill becomes much more important than mere endurance. Instead of William Marshal and his friends trampling over the vineyards and indulging in a cheerful but crude free-for-all, we have the faintly fantastical figure of Ulrich von Lichtenstein. The tournament for Ulrich was essentially part of the apparatus of courtly love, another reason for seeking individual glory. A great lord with a well-organised retinue was the real victor and hero of the old-style tournament, even if individuals had their share of the plaudits. But in fighting for one's lady's honour, the individual combat was essential.

Ulrich's great series of jousts in Italy, Austria and Bohemia in 1227 marks the first emergence of this form into prominence. At the same time it is the first transformation of the tournament by alien ideals, in that the show of gallantry is as important as the display of skill. Ulrich's narrative of his adventures is circumstantial, though he does stray into romance at intervals. It is often difficult to distinguish truth and fiction in his story; for instance, when he says that he went dressed as Frau Venus in honour of his lady, this might well be a figure of speech; but he goes on to describe the issue of a challenge to the knights of northern Italy and Austria, specifically mentioning this costume, and his stay incognito in Venice during the previous winter while he had the costume prepared. The terms of the challenge were that each comer who broke three spears with him was to receive a gold ring; if defeated, the challenger was to bow to the four corners of the earth in honour of Ulrich's lady, while if Ulrich was beaten, the victor was to take all his horses. The itinerary was carefully specified so that knights could find him easily, and ended in a great tournament at Klosterneuberg. If we are to believe Ulrich's own account, he broke, in one month's jousting, between 25 April and 23 May 1227, a total of 307 spears, a quite respectable number (though Gahmuret in Wolfram's *Parzival* is supposed to break 100 in a single day!). Indeed, the success of the enterprise was such that, thirteen years later, Ulrich undertook a journey dressed as King Arthur in honour of a new lady, when she in whose honour the 'Venus journey' had been made proved too cruel. But the idea did not bear repetition, and it ended suddenly after a local ban on tournaments.

The system of fighting depicted in Ulrich's poems introduces a number of entirely new elements. Skill, for the moment at least, becomes much more important, since instead of seeing who can withstand the opponents' blows the longest, the contest is limited in scope and form. Furthermore, scoring is introduced, which implies the presence of officials to record and supervise the actual events of the lists rather than the general conduct of the whole event. Most important of all, the tournament is becoming divorced from the practical side of war. For the object in these contests was to break one's own lance squarely on the opponent's shield, while deflecting his blow. Unhorsing might result (and meant complete victory, whether the spear was broken or not), but any form of unnecessary damage was to be avoided. In a real battle, lances were of less importance; they were useless after the first impact, and skill in swordplay – or other weapons, such as maces and pikes – was equally essential to the good warrior. Even in later years, when swordplay became increasingly important in jousts, the lance was never entirely abandoned. Hence a skilful jouster was not necessarily a skilful warrior.

However, the joust was not a rival to the tournament proper, but remained a supplementary exercise. Among the knights themselves, it was more highly esteemed because of the opportunities for personal glory; but the onlookers continued to prefer the spectacle of the *mêlée*. Indeed, it was not until the early fourteenth century that the joust was firmly established through Europe as part of the sport. The speed with which it spread is very hard to gauge, since the chroniclers fail to distinguish between the two: and our only mirror of the times is therefore in literary works. These would tend to confirm that the joust originated in Ulrich von Lichtenstein's homelands in Styria, and moved slowly north and west. The word itself is

Germanic – *tijoste* – and the German romances have more scenes involving jousts than their French counterparts, which at first prefer to describe the enchantments and marvels encountered by knights-errant rather than an honest tournament. From the poets of both countries comes our reconstruction of the formal theory of the lists of this period, the basis for all later tournaments.

Any tournament was fought under certain preconditions. There were clear rules as to who was qualified to take part. Knights who had disgraced the order of knighthood were excluded at an early date, although at first only those actually guilty of criminal offences suffered under this proviso. With the rise of the courtly philosophy, those who had been guilty of unchivalrous behaviour suffered likewise; even if their most heinous sin was only to have repeated gossip about a lady, the offended party could denounce them and have them debarred from the lists. A knight could also be thrown out of the tournament (and beaten by the squires into the bargain) for such diverse offences as buying goods to sell at a profit, deserting his lord in battle, destroying vineyards and cornfields, and, more essential, failing to prove his pedigree back to four great-grandfathers. He must not only be noble, but also be prepared to live up to his status. Such was the theory. In practice only a knight who was obviously ill-equipped or unskilled was likely to be turned away. Tournaments were usually open to anyone with the means and inclination to join in, but as the sport developed, certain practical distinctions arose. Competitors were matched against each other according to their skill, and events were graded accordingly. The most skilled were those reserved for the very expert knights. The weapons used could be either the *armes courtois*, a blunted sword and a lance without a point or with a coronal, a small knob with spokes shaped like a crown, on the end, or *armes à outrance* could be specified, in which case neither lance nor sword were blunted. The latter occasions were reversed for genuinely hostile combats, perhaps duels over points of honour, or for knights who were skilled enough to use such weapons with a minimum of injury to each other, though the weapons could be changed from *armes courtois* to *armes à outrance* half-way through a tournament.

The events within the tournament itself were similarly regulated, particularly the taking of prisoners and the interference of squires and servants. In the best tournaments of the thirteenth century jousting only was employed, not the sword fight, and the prime object was to unseat one's opponent, who then became a prisoner, but was at liberty to escape from the custody of the victor's squires if he did not give his word, although his horse and armour fell to the victor. More common were combats in which prisoners, once taken, agreed not to escape. The loser was therefore more reluctant to surrender, and the question was usually settled by a sword fight once a knight was unhorsed. Under both sets of rules squires and servants could only bring in new horses and weapons; but a third type allowed what was really a general free-for-all. This probably arose in small affairs where there were difficulties in finding enough heralds and other officers to run the tournament properly, and to prevent the attendants from joining in on behalf of their masters was difficult. They were therefore allowed to take prisoners for the latter, and the result was a mere brawl. Finally, there were the squires' tournaments, known as *buhurts,* descendants of the exercises on horseback of the twelfth century. These gave the most trouble of all. In 1234 they had to be banned in England because so much ill will was aroused. In 1288, at the 'Fair of Boston', two gangs of squires, pretending to hold a *buhurt,* dressed as friars and canons, burnt down half the town, and provided an excuse for renewed measures against tournaments proper.

The varying terms corresponded with a variety of motives. The free-for-alls were usually run for profit, the object being to make as much as possible out of ransoms and perquisites such as the armour and horse of the loser; but these were not suitable occasions for the wearing of ladies' favours and for fighting in their honour. Such contests, with ladies presiding, had as their goal the winning of individual renown; the knight exerted himself to gain approval in the eyes of the fair sex, and a mob of servants taking prisoners for him would win him no *doux baisers* and little honour. Tournaments for honour alone, where prizes were offered for the knight who acquitted himself best in the lists were the most highly regarded form, for those held in honour of ladies tended to degenerate into shows of elaborate gallantry; but where an individual prize was offered, skill was for once paramount.

Technique within the lists was fast becoming a complex independent art. By Wolfram von Eschenbach's time – early in the thirteenth century – five distinct 'runs' in tournament and joust were recognised. Two of these, *z'entmuoten* and *diu volge,* we cannot reconstruct with certainty. Two refer to multiple combats or *mêlées.* *Zem puneiz* was the usual form of charge, in which the massive warhorses were put into a canter, and thundered head-on towards each other, the target being the knight to the left. The lefthand aim was based on the simple reason that it was easiest to hold the spear steady by having it in the right hand and bracing it across the body at an angle of about fifteen degrees. The usual point of aim in this case would be the shield fastening of the opposing knight, which he would have in this left hand; four nailheads on the outside of the shield showed where it might be struck with the greatest chance of unseating him and least likelihood of danger or injury.

This manœuvre, simple in theory, must have called for good horsemanship and aim as well as a firm seat and not inconsiderable strength: the lances were about twelve feet in length and averaged three inches in diameter, being thicker towards the butt end, and tapering towards the point. As the years passed, more and more aids to keep the knight in the saddle were allowed until, with bootlike stirrups and a high pommelled saddle, man and horse were almost inseparable, and only the breaking of the lance was possible.

A more violent tactic was to try to ride down one's opponent by charging horse to horse as well as attempting to unseat him with the lance. This led to the heavy horse armour of the later Middle Ages, when the beast became a primitive form of tank: the gay trappings portrayed in the miniatures concealed more practical coverings beneath. Another possible manœuvre imposed a much more severe test on the knights' horsemanship. If it was agreed to use *zem treviers* beforehand, the knights would at a given signal, swing forty-five degrees to the right as they charged, and strike their opponents on the open side, thus avoiding their lances. The manœuvre must be to the right: if performed with a leftward swing the opponent can move his lance to meet the blow and still keep it across his body, while if he does this to counter a righthand swing he loses the leverage and must support it with his extended arm alone. To do this successfully good timing was essential or chaos would ensue, especially as the order had to be given at the last possible moment to prevent the enemy from doing a counter-manœuvre and defeating the purpose.

Ze rehter tjost was the simple joust, ridden between two knights only, with the same points of aim as in the *mêlée*, the four nails of the shield and the gorge or throat-armour. If the second aim was correctly taken, it might lift off his helm, even if it failed to sweep him clean out of the saddle. But if the armour was faulty or the lance point splintered, it could be very dangerous.[10]

In all this the lance is the chief weapon. Until the middle of the thirteenth century, the sword was regarded as incidental, and the swordfight on horseback was unknown. It was only when the knights wished to prolong the issue beyond the breaking of three lances that the sword came into play. When one of the two was unhorsed, the other would dismount; otherwise both would dismount when the lances had been broken. The weapons were rebated, that is, blunted on both edges and with a rounded end instead of a point. If one knight failed to use the correct type of sword – and this could happen not only by guile but also by picking up the wrong weapon, and there were always sharp weapons to hand – the result could be fatal. An incident of this type at an English tournament at Walden in 1252 aroused considerable anger and unfavourable comment.

As the joust developed, it came more and more to resemble a rather crude form of fencing match or duel. A knight had to be able to break the three spears correctly at the outset; but the real business was done on foot. Due to the nature of swordplay and the armour, it became increasingly a trial of strength. Only a series of heavy buffets could bring a knight down without injury; and although injury was frequent enough, the skilled knight would fight until the sheer weight of his armour or the effort of heaving himself to his feet when knocked down had completely exhausted him. Hence the only alternative was to make the contest dependent on technical rulings. Elaborate means of scoring were therefore developed to give due weight to the accomplished rather than the purely strong knight. In John Tiptoft's set of rules for English tournaments, a late example drawn up in 1466, the system is carefully graded according to the degree of competence involved in each achievement. Unhorsing remained the most impressive feat; a knight who had unhorsed another would take precedence for the prize over all others. After unhorsing came striking 'coronal to coronal', that is, spear's tip to spear's tip; any knight who did this twice was a candidate for the prize. This was followed by striking the crest (on the helm) three times, by breaking the most spears, and finally by any knight who was generally held to have stayed in the field longest and to have fought the best. This system was the standard one for the last century and a half of jousting, and Tudor 'jousting cheques' which record the scores on this basis still survive.

If these definitions seem artificial at first, they would certainly encourage a good eye and a firm seat in the saddle. A strong practical streak remains in the rules: anyone striking the barrier of his opponent's saddle is to have one spear deducted from his total; anyone who strikes a horse is to be immediately expelled from the lists with dishonour; and anyone using a gauntlet which locks on to the spear (to give a steady and rigid grip) is to be disqualified.

As the object of the tourneyer changed, so did the organisation of the jousts. The feats of Ulrich von Lichtenstein and other knights who fought for their ladies' sakes were of no avail if there were no spectators to witness their triumph. So the few attendants of the early tournaments became a throng. Even in William Marshal's day we hear of ladies dancing with the knights before a tournament; but this was only a diversion to fill a few idle moments. The first step towards the establishment of the tournament as a formal social event is probably the curious institution of the mid-thirteenth century known as the 'round table'. It first appears in Flanders in 1235, and is certainly derived from the institution of the same name in the legends of King Arthur, just as Ulrich had chosen a legendary guise for both his 'journeys'. Tournaments were dangerous, and only too liable to arouse ill-feeling; and the round table may have started as a group of knights who met together before proceedings opened to swear mutual friendship and to agree on certain preconditions aimed at greater safety. Naturally, feasting would be called for beforehand and afterwards, and the affair might take three days instead of one. Such arrangements soon became standard for all tournaments.

The most marked development in the history of the tournament is its gradual restriction to a smaller and smaller group of knights. The decline in retinues, abolition of the squires' right to intervene and capture knights, and political restrictions all contributed to this trend. The costs, too, grew to huge proportions, partly as the cost of armour increased and partly as the pageantry involved grew more elaborate. Each knight was expected to retain heralds and minstrels, and the distribution of largesse was claimed by an ever-increasing circle of attendants. Hence from being a sport in which almost any knight could participate, it became an expensive hobby for the select few by the fourteenth century. Even before that, the knight who had ruined himself in tournaments was a familiar figure in the diatribes of the moralists attacking tournaments.

At the same time, the ethos of the tournament became more sophisticated. The virtues of the early tourneyers were chiefly a strong arm and a hard head; if they were also congenial company and liberal spenders, their success was assured. Towards the end of the twelfth century, the ideas of courtly love were adapted to the circumstances of the tournament, and the romantic ideals of the poets began to be reflected in real life. Honour and the lady's love were now the spur, and on the outcome of the lists depended the knight's success with his mistress. The old tournaments were more likely to end in a drinking bout than in elaborate social festivities and dances. Eventually the tournament itself was overshadowed by these, and became a mere adjunct of occasions such as weddings, knightings or coronations, a means of giving them added pageantry and colour.

The apogee of the tournament must be placed in the late fourteenth and early fifteenth century. Even if earlier ages had been more enthusiastic and more attentive to what actually happened in the lists, it was at this time that it was most highly regarded and at its most splendid without being a mere pageant. Despite its international following, it was in Flanders and northern France, where it had first appeared, that it remained most popular. King René of Naples, later duke of Anjou, was an ardent champion of chivalry, and recorded the usages sanctioned by custom and practical considerations in a treatise on tournaments written about 1434.[11] Tournaments were an aristocratic privilege. René set the limit at the rank of knight-banneret, that is, a knight able to equip a small retinue in warfare. Anyone under that rank, unless he were a rich merchant and therefore beyond the pale, was unlikely to be able to afford the vast expense that tournaments now entailed. Instead of the brief three or four weeks' notice that had usually prevailed in the thirteenth century, preparations now began three or four months ahead, especially for a major tournament. The first step was to issue the challenge, which, until the mid-fourteenth century, might well have been a general invitation to any interested knight to meet at a certain place and date. René would have none of this: his tournament was fought between challenger and defendant, and entries were by their invitation. Even before a formal challenge was sent, an acceptance had to be negotiated in secret between the respective kings of arms, or chief heralds, of the parties concerned.

The next step was to appoint six or twelve judges to fix the time and place. They and the kings of arms were responsible for the running of events from then on, and the kings of arms were instructed to announce the details at the courts of the two opponents, the royal court, and anywhere else that was deemed suitable. They were to bear with them rolls of arms of all those concerned, including the arms of would-be tourneyers entered on the rolls at their own request. The anouncement also included the requirements as to armour and any special regulations to be observed, as well as details of the prizes offered.

For a fortnight or more before the tournament itself, the retinues of the princes, barons and knights taking part would converge on the appointed place. It was expected that all the entrants would be present four days before the tournament, which would normally begin on a Monday. This was in accordance with long tradition: English records show Monday and Tuesday as the most popular days, because

175

the jousts could then continue until Thursday without interruption. Friday, Saturday and Sunday were subject to the *treuga Dei* (truce of God), an agreement obtained by the Church in the eleventh century, whereby no fighting took place from Thursday evening to Monday morning, or on saints' days and church festivals. Tournaments, though the Church was unable to ban them entirely, were at any rate regarded as tantamount to war.

Hence Monday became the normal day for the lists to open, but the four preceding days were far from idle: on Thursday evening there would be a dance, at which details of the requirements for the display of arms on the next day would be announced. This ceremony usually took place in a cloister, where the spectators and knights could conveniently inspect the arms of those taking part. This served the dual purpose of enabling them to identify the knights later in the heat of the fight, and also of allowing any miscreant knights to be ejected: any lady who had cause to complain of a knight, or indeed anyone else with such grounds, could state her case, and his errors could be investigated. If proved, he was to be ejected from the tournament with ignominy. In addition to the reasons mentioned earlier, René d'Anjou gives three main grounds for exclusion: perjury or breaking a word of honour, usury, and marriage below one's status. In each case, the knight was to be beaten and held prisoner; in the first two instances, his horse was to be confiscated and his spurs cut off. Another dance would be held on the Friday, as on each succeeding evening. On the Sunday, oaths to keep the peace would be taken and a 'knight of honour' chosen by the ladies to open the tournament.

The climax of these elaborate preliminaries came on the Monday. At ten in the morning, the ladies would take their place in the stands. The lists were suitably imposing for the occasion, and in some places were permanent, although the materials of which they were made were usually the perquisite of the kings of arms after the event. An area one quarter longer than broad, probably about 200 by 160 feet, was surrounded by a stout fence six feet high with entrance and exit points. This in turn was encircled by another fence twelve feet high, the space between the two serving as a refuge for squires and knights. Beyond this would be the stands, richly draped and covered, for the judges and, almost more important, the ladies.

In due course the two teams would assemble behind two cords stretched across the lists. The heralds would give warning about foul blows, and about fighting after retreat had been blown at the end of the day, both of which offences were penalised by instant disqualification. The knight of honour then cut the cords, and the long-awaited *mêlée* would begin with the cry 'Laissez aller!' After the first shock of the charge with lances, the knights would draw their swords, rebated and blunted as agreed, and the greater part of the contest would be fought with these. Squires were allowed, and indeed required, to go into the lists to help their masters, should they fall or otherwise get into difficulties, but they were only allowed to wear defensive armour for this purpose, lest they should be tempted to join in the fighting. Knights could retire into the inner palisade to recover as they wished, and the contest would continue from about one o'clock until dusk, or later if the lists were lit with flambeaux. At the appointed hour of ending, the heralds would sound retreat, and the knights would disperse to their lodgings to nurse their wounds, and, if in a fit state, to prepare for the dance that evening, at which the prizes for the best performance in the lists that day were awarded. Details of the jousting to be held on the following day would be announced, and the teams arranged.

The second day's sport would be much on the pattern of the first, starting about midday and occupying most of the afternoon. For the jousts, the knights would be in two teams of from six to twelve knights, jousts for all comers being very unusual in these circumstances. Towards the middle of the fifteenth century, the jousts might be 'at the tilt', that is with a wooden barrier dividing the lists and separating the combatants. This had developed because an accidental or intentional collision was often very dangerous to both steed and rider, despite the vast straw mattresses and armour on the horses; and the knights of the fifteenth century were less careless of life and limb than their predecessors had been. There was also less danger of foul blows if the two knights were compelled to run parallel courses, although it seems that they often completely missed each other. A variation which followed about fifty years later was swordplay at the barriers, either on foot with a low barrier, or on horseback with the normal height of tilt, and combats with halberds appeared in the sixteenth century.

The jousting over, a great feast and dance concluded the ceremonies. Prizes, often of considerable value, would be given, and the company said their farewells before dispersing on the following day. Such an event, requiring considerable preparation, and very costly for the host, was not an everyday occurrence; indeed, only the richest lords could afford it. But the tournament of the fourteenth and fifteenth centuries in this form is practically a festival of chivalry itself, embodying all its best and most alluring attributes: skill in arms, glory in the field, and the winning of honour through devotion to a lady. If the skill was none too practical, the glory momentary, and the devotion either too empty or all too strong, the ideal tournament was at the same time civilised, pleasing and exciting.

The real enthusiast, however, was not satisfied with a mere two days' jousting at intervals. He demanded a month or more of daily execution of the sport, at which real heroic feats of endurance and prodigious totals of encounters might be achieved. From this desire arose a typically exuberant institution, the *pas d'armes*. Its basis was that the most ardent jousters proclaimed their intention of 'holding' a place for a given length of time, whether the holder were a single knight or a team of several. Ulrich's 'journeys' were forerunners of this, but the important distinction of a *pas d'armes* was that it was restricted to a single spot. They first became popular in the latter half of the fourteenth century, and underline the increasing emphasis on individual prowess. Their ancestry is very much part of the ideal of a hero, and goes back to Horatius on the bridge or the hand to hand fighting of the Scandinavian Sagas, though it also owes much to the romances, where we find knights who challenge all comers at a ford or some other natural passage. Malory's *Tale of Sir Gareth of Orkeney* is a succession of such combats. In some *pas d'armes*, the imitation went yet further; at Sandricourt in 1493, the knights assembled there rode forth at the end of the formal proceedings as knights-errants, jousting at random with whomsoever they chanced to meet, in the style of the heroes of the romances, who 'rode forth for to seek adventures'.

The terms of a *pas d'armes* were published in the same way as those of a tournament, except that there was no question of a challenge to a specific lord. One of the most famous examples was that at St Inglevert, largely organised by Boucicaut, who in 1389 with two other French knights challenged all foreign knights and squires to joust five courses near Calais.[12] The weapons were to be either *à outrance* or rebated, and the choice was to be indicated by striking a white or black shield outside the challengers' tents on arrival. The *venant* could choose which of the *tenants* he wished to joust with; and the whole proceeding was to last thirty days. It was a great success; knights came from England, Spain and Germany, and the *tenants* were well occupied. Boucicaut himself is reputed to have come through all his encounters without injury, fighting four or five knights each day. It was a dangerous amusement, for many of the jousts were with pointed spears; and indeed one of the chief objects

178

was to continue under a peaceful guise the fighting between England and France, then subject to a three years' truce. It was also expensive, since all *venants* were entertained in due style by the *tenants*.

The *pas d'armes* was also very popular in Spain. In 1428 there was a great *pas d'armes* 'de la Fuerte Ventura' at Valladolid, and in 1434 at the bridge of Orbigo, on the borders of the old kingdom of Leon, one of the best documented events of this kind, the *Passo Honroso*. Ten knights, led by Suero de Quinones (a favourite of Alvaro de Luna, at the time effective ruler of Castile), defended the bridge for a month, from 10 July to 9 August: there were sixty-eight challengers, including one knight from Germany, one from Italy and two from Portugal. Suero de Quinones had originally vowed to wear an iron collar every Thursday until he had held a *pas d'armes* at which 300 lances were broken, but although 727 courses were run, the final total was only 177. Although the judges of the jousts declared that he had accomplished his vow, Suero refused to accept this, and it was some time before he could be persuaded to agree. He himself had been badly injured early in the jousting, and had only fought four challengers. However, the standard of jousting was generally high, and the event was regarded as a great success.

The affiliations of the *pas d'armes* with the romances was not in evidence at St Inglevert or Orbigo. In later years, however, the particular form of fancy dress chosen seemed to exercise the knights as much as the actual outcome. Not only knightly romances, but also pastoral poetry and erotic allegory, and at the opposite extreme historical sieges, provided the background for the event. A sixteenth-century example used the last-named formula. A mock fortress formed the centrepiece, entrusted to four maidens, who chose fifteen knights and a captain to defend it; there were to be four kinds of sport: jousts at the tilt, swordplay on horseback, swordplay at the barriers, and finally a mock assault on the castle. The whole proceedings were to last for the month of December, occupying six hours a day. The result must have been more of a spectacle than a true tournament; pageantry was beginning to take over from the tournament proper.

More typical is the *pas d'armes de la bergière*, organised by King René of Naples at Tarascon in 1449 in honour of his Mistress Jeanne Laval.[13] She played the part of the shepherdess, sitting among her sheep at the centre of the festivities, while two knights fought on her behalf. He of the black shield, representing *tristesse* or discontent, challenged those who were content in love, while those who were amorous but despondent of their chances were to joust with the knight representing *liesse* or happiness, bearing a white shield. The jousts lasted for three days, with Philippe de Lenoncourt and Philibert de l'Aigne as the defendants. A total of about twenty jousts took place, three spears being broken in each. A relatively small affair, it involved only the knights of King René's acquaintance, and was more distinguished by its setting and background than by the quality of the sport. Many such events must have been held each year, though the tournament proper, with its spectacular *mêlées*, was always more popular than this rather esoteric version, whose symbolic overtones and involved settings show that they appealed to a more literary circle. Indeed, it was sometimes difficult to get opponents for a *pas d'armes*, as at St Omer in 1446, when after elaborate preparations only one middle-aged knight from Germany appeared.

From the *pas d'armes* to the duel was but a short step. It was a natural consequence of the quest for glory that individual knights should issue specific challenges to other renowned champions, or even general challenges to all comers to fight in single combat wherever they wished. It was under conditions of war that duels flourished, as the pages of Froissart bear witness; hardly a year passes without some record of a single combat. These fights usually conformed to the normal rules of jousting prevalent at the time, but they occurred in some curious places. The most notable was the episode in the siege of Melun in 1420. In a mediaeval siege, it was the practice to dig under the walls of a town, supporting the subterranean passage with massive timbers. When the appropriate point was reached the beams would be set on fire with the hope of bringing down the fortifications as the passage caved in. Counter-mines might be laid by the besieged to harass the enemy and drive back the miners, and these often made contact. It was in such an underground theatre that a series of combats took place, apparently on horseback; and Henry v himself is reputed to have taken part.

In times of peace such challenges, often to prove a point of honour, such as whose lady was more beautiful, were frequent from the end of the fourteenth century. Political motives occasionally occur, as in a duel fought over Edward iii's right to the French throne; but more usually they are pure challenges, such as that of Sir David Lindsay and the Lord Wells in London on 6 May 1390. From 1401 onwards a series of such challenges was fought out in Smithfield, where special lists would be erected. These were often held by royal licence and in the king's presence, at whose expense the enclosures and stands were put up, as for the duel between Peter de Vasques and Richard Wy-devyle in 1445, when the sheriffs of London were ordered to undertake the work. Three years earlier, there had been a notable duel there between Sir John Astley and Philip Boyle. The latter had travelled from Aragon in search of an opponent, but without previous success. The exact terms of his challenge have been preserved, and run as follows:

I, Philip Boyle, knight of the kingdom of Aragon, was set the task of fighting a knight or squire especially to serve my lord the king of Aragon and Sicily. Furthermore, I was unable to carry out this task for default of challengers in the realm of France. So I have come to the kingdom of England and into the court and presence of the king of England and France; and by supplication and special mercy I have to bear a device in this noble court by means of of which I may be delivered of my task, as set out in the following articles:

We shall fight on horseback, both armed as we please with the usual weapons of battle, namely spears, swords and daggers, and with such equipment as either of us wish, without any trickery.

He to whom God gives the victory shall have the other's sword and helm or other head-armour.

If the said battle does not end in the same day, we shall complete it on foot with the armour and weapons left to us the following day, without any repairs or replacements.

Wrestling with legs and feet, arms and hands, shall be allowed.

Because my horse and harness are in Flanders, the said battle shall take place eight days after I receive them; if I am unable to get them within a reasonable time, then the battle shall be on foot, both of us armed as we wish and allowed axe, spear, sword and dagger as above.[14]

By the latter years of the fifteenth century, the old tournament had divided into duel and pageant. The duel survived longest of the two; the later developments of the joust and *mêlée* were fantastic, and the flamboyant taste to which they appealed disappeared in northern Europe at the beginning of the seventeenth century; only spiritless cavalcades lingered on elsewhere. It might be argued with some justification that the jousts of the sixteenth century were conscious attempts to revive a dying sport. Forms such as the German *Kolbenturnier*, in which heavy polygonal shafts were used to demolish the opponent's crest, and the ordinary jousts as practised by Maximilian proceeded at a slow canter, if not a gentle amble because of immense armour; they involved some skill, but of such a specialised kind as to be doomed to rapid extinction. The knight was firmly held in his saddle, and his lance rested equally firmly in a rest on his armour, so that only aim and quality of armour really counted. The most distinctive feature of the dying years of the tournament, from 1500 onwards, is the incredible complexity of the armour, and the virtuosity displayed by the armourers. The almost impersonal fighting machines which resulted could not perpetuate an essentially personal and skilful sport, whose true *raison d'être* was not ingenuity but the search for glory in physical feats.

I I

The Tournament and Politics

The close association of the tournament with warfare proper gave it considerable political possibilities. From the earliest days it was the subject of political controversy and governmental interference. The reason for its influence in this unlikely sphere was simple. A tournament which got out of hand became a miniature war, and one which might involve men of great personal standing. Hence it could either lead to feuds or could be used for the settling of scores, and one of the real advantages which the tournament as a social institution possessed, its role as a substitute for baronial wars, would be lost. Most central governments would have preferred neither wars nor tournaments among their barons, but accepted the latter as the lesser of two evils. Only very occasionally did they consider that its value as a training for war outweighed these disadvantages.

Hence it was England, the country with the strongest central government at the time, which was the first to impose a ban on tournaments. The exact date and nature of the ban is not recorded, and in the early twelfth century it may have been ignorance or dislike of tournaments among the English knights that kept such events out of England. But the fact that no tournaments were held there in Henry II's reign is definitely recorded by the chroniclers as due to a royal ban, since there had been some under Stephen's weaker rule. Indeed, the ban would seem to be part of the measures taken to prevent a continuation of the disturbances of the previous reign. If such was the case, it lasted for forty years before a limited repeal was effected, and tournaments remained technically subject to royal control until their disappearance. No other government was able to exercise such control, and this, combined with the wealth of records that survive, makes England the best example for the study of the tournament's political role.

It was Richard I, needing money for his crusading debts and the costs of his French wars, who created the first system of licensed tourneying. In a letter to the archbishop of Canterbury on 22 August

1194, in his capacity as head of the English government, Richard requested him to license jousts in England.[1] If the king was also thinking of the value of practice in the lists as a means of improving the calibre of his knights, money was certainly uppermost in his mind, for he imposed a system of licence fees: 20 marks for an earl (presumably including his retinue), 10 marks for a baron, and either 4 or 2 marks for a knight, depending on whether he held any land. To collect this tax, the king limited the tournaments to five specified places in England: Salisbury, Stamford, Warwick, Brackley and Blyth. He also set up a commission to regulate such events, consisting of the earls of Salisbury, Clare and Warenne. All three were great landowners and men of personal influence, as well as ardent tourneyers themselves: their descendants' names echo, both tragically and heroically, through the records of English jousts to the very last days. Responsible to them were all who entered the lists and, more directly, those in charge of organising the jousts: two knights and two clerks were to be present on each occasion, to administer an oath to keep the peace and to collect the revenue. Tournaments not licensed by the king were liable to be banned by a royal writ which, even if it did not arrive in time to put a stop to proceedings, put the knights concerned at the king's mercy. Records of the workings of this system are scarce, but pardons and fines are not uncommon, and the evidence seems to be that the effect of the writs was largely to give the king a weapon against potentially rebellious or dissident barons, which was of much greater use than the mere stopping of the tournament.

There is no parallel for this edict anywhere else; though bans on tourneying occurred, there was no real attempt to regulate. Indeed, when the tournament acquired particularly strong political connotations this sprang partly from the regulations themselves: illicit tournaments became associated with revolt against the crown's authority. After the repressions of Philip iv's reign in France, the leaguers opposing his successor made the right to tourney at will one of their demands. In England, where the repression was almost permanent, there were episodes of illicit tourneying after any baronial disturbance or during any quarrel with royal favourites. After Runnymede we find the barons planning a great tournament, which had to be postponed lest the king's party should take advantage of their preoccupation to seize London; and after the battle of Evesham, similar outbreaks occurred.

In these two cases the jousting was an appendage of, rather than an element in, the struggle for power. More serious were the tournaments where the participants divided into the French party of the court and the English party of the barons. A series of these took place from 1232, the gravest incidents being in 1241, 1248 and 1257, when they became a civil war in all but name. In 1241 a tournament with *armes à outrance*, which implied a danger of mortal injuries, was arranged between Peter of Savoy, the French leader, and the followers of Hugh Bigod, earl of Norfolk. The political implications were all too clear, and the event was proscribed by the king. The possible results which the royal officers feared on this occasion were underlined very sharply in another tournament in June of the same year, at Hertford, where Gilbert, earl of Pembroke – through no fault of his opponents, but from his own inexperience – was thrown from his horse and killed; whereupon his followers rioted and sought revenge and booty at random. It may have been this that made the king particularly anxious over a proposed tournament at York two years later: it was banned with bell, book and candle 'because they [the knights taking part] are all bound to keep the peace and the more especially so during the king's absence from the kingdom; and their tournament might cause no small disturbance'. The Master of the Knights Templar and two sheriffs were sent to enforce the ban.[2]

Despite such prohibitions, popular demand for tourneying remained strong. Already in 1230–2, the royal mandates had to be supplemented by excuses – such as that the king was about to go abroad – and by promises 'to speak with the council regarding tournaments'[3] or 'to provide for tournaments'.[4] Henry III managed to scotch five attempted jousts between 1243 and 1248, two on the part of the powerful earl Richard of Gloucester; but at least two illicit tournaments were serious enough to be punished by heavy fines, and many more must have escaped either unnoticed or unpunished. When at last the king relented, his forebodings were amply justified, at the expense of the leader of the French faction, his half-brother William de Valence, who had persuaded him to allow a tournament at Newbury on 4 March 1248. There were no disturbances outside the lists, but William was unhorsed and given a sound beating by the squires of his opponents, as was the custom in England. It was not long before he and his French knights sought and found his revenge at Brackley, when Richard of Clare unexpectedly changed sides and joined William's party, but rancour was increased by an unfair attack by William on an English knight. Tempers still had not cooled in 1257, when in a tournament at Rochester on 8 December the French were soundly defeated in the lists, and found themselves pursued into the town by the squires and other camp followers, who added insult to injury by thrashing them again.

185

It was not until after the explosion into real civil war at Evesham that tourneying found royal favour again, largely at the insistence of Henry's sons; the future Edward I was a keen exponent of the art and had started his career in France in 1256. Only in the last years of Henry's reign, and the first eighteen months after Edward's accession, were writs of prohibition issued again in the thirteenth century; and when they recurred in the next century, the reasons behind them were the same: the king's absence either overseas or on campaign. The writs of November 1272 to April 1274 were issued by the regency awaiting Edward's return from Sicily; the prohibitions of 1288–9 corresponded with the king's absence abroad; and those of 1299 to 1307 were the result of Edward's Scottish wars. The first of the series, issued on 30 December 1299, was a warning of what was to follow: a general ban for the duration of the Scottish war was proclaimed, and anyone found in readiness for a tournament was to be arrested at once.

But such tournaments as were held under Edward's rule were subject to new and stringent regulations. Edward had not been involved in the really bitter contests in the 1240s and 1250s, but he was anxious to improve the sport, to make it less dangerous both to the participants and to the cause of orderly government. This resulted in a statute drawn up in 1267, the *Statuta Armorum*,[5] in which measures were taken to root out the causes of the rioting that was liable to make disagreements into major feuds. As few as possible of the onlookers and assistants were to be armed, only squires, knights and heralds being allowed swords. Cadets and standard-bearers were allowed protective armour, and anyone else wearing armour or carrying arms was liable to up to seven years' imprisonment. Pointed swords, knives, sticks and clubs were entirely banned, and all followers had to wear their lord's colours or devices. The implications of what must have gone before are rather terrifying: armed mobs of hangers-on interfering as they pleased in the *mêlée*, and carrying on the battle long after the lists had closed. On the Continent, where there was no such legislation, and where the equivalent of the German *turnier mit kipper* was frequent, this being virtually a free-for-all, it is hardly surprising that the more controllable individual joust should have replaced the *mêlée* so quickly.

Despite these regulations, the old pattern of bans returned under Edward II, corresponding with the periods of royal insecurity and baronial unrest, at the beginning of the reign and from 1320–2. In 1323, tournaments were banned unless the king licensed them specifically, and in that year, two licences, for jousts at Lincoln and

Northampton, were issued. With Edward's downfall, his opponents thought it advisable to reimpose restrictions, and the Scottish wars prolonged the currency of such measures for the next ten years.

In view of the consistency with which bans were imposed from the early thirteenth century until the outbreak of the Hundred Years' War in 1338, the virtual disappearance of them during the next sixteen years is remarkable. The last writ, on the Close Rolls, is dated 1354. Under similar political conditions at any earlier time, there would have been repeated general and individual bans; and so radical a change in policy must have corresponded to a change in the knights' attitudes to tournaments, and in the nature of the tournaments themselves. The tournament from 1200 to 1340 was regarded as a potential cause of political trouble, a safety valve perhaps, but one to be used with great caution, especially when the political temperature was running high or the central authority had other problems on its hands. It provides an incidental demonstration of the dependence of mediaeval government on the monarch in that such measures were frequent when the king was abroad, even for peaceful reasons; and some part in the lifting of such prohibitions may have been due to the increasing confidence of the king's officers in their own powers.

A much more important coincidence, however, is with the change in the tactics of warfare. Edward III's new strategy at Halidon Hill (1333) and Crécy thirteen years later demoted the orthodox knight from the main asset of an army to almost a liability, relying instead on dismounted cavalry to withstand charges and on archers to act as an offensive force. The skills of the tournament had no practical relevance in this new order; and the lance as a weapon of war was obsolete. If rebellion should arise in England, it would not gain anything by organising or using tournaments as seedbeds of discontent; the cavalry trained and gathered there would be overwhelmed by archers and knights on foot. The progress of the new tactics was so rapid that the last major mediaeval cavalry battle was fought at Grunwald only sixty-four years after Crécy, and no cavalry victory of any size is recorded after Crécy itself.

The political significance of the tournament abroad was of a rather different nature. In Germany it became an instrument of imperial or princely prestige, and the various rulers vied with each other in acting as patrons, with the result that the sport had a much more official status. The prince would often take over tournaments started on private initiative, as with the tournaments at Friesach in 1224, and at Vienna in 1240, which were set in motion by Ulrich von

187

Lichtenstein as part of his knightly journeys. On the latter occasion, Frederick II stopped the proceedings, probably for political reasons.

As the standing of the princes declined, the control and organisation of tournaments was taken over by *Turniergesellschaften*, the tournament societies, under whom the formal element in the proceedings increased. The four great societies in Bavaria, Swabia, Franconia and the Rhineland became a form of exclusive aristocratic club, and *Turnierfähigkeit*, the social qualification to take part in tournaments, became the ultimate test of noble status. This close organisation made of tourneying a ritual affair of prestige, controlled by the officers of the societies, and while it avoided the feuds of earlier years, it eliminated the romantic fantasy of the French *pas d'armes*.

In the Low Countries, the feud became the chief danger during the twelfth and thirteenth centuries. In 1170 Baldwin of Flanders had met his rival Godfrey of Louvain in a tournament, and the affair had turned into a battle, in which Baldwin was victorious.[6] And on several occasions when someone was killed, charges of treachery were raised, as with Floris IV in 1234[7] and William of Dampierre in 1251.[8] This led to prohibitions by the Church, and the sport declined until the appearance of John I of Brabant, who after being knighted in 1276 was a great frequenter of tournaments. He survived an attempt by his enemies to assassinate him in a tournament near Liège only to meet his death in an accident while jousting in 1294.

Another way in which tournaments could affect the course of political events was through the accidental death of an important person. The element of danger remained to the end; indeed, the most spectacular accident was the death of Henri II of France in 1559, when a splinter from the Constable de Montgomeri's lance penetrated his vizor, the Constable having failed to drop the broken butt-end as he should have done. Deaths in the later years were rare; but the sport had once taken a heavy toll. Its reputed originator was supposed to have met his end in the sport he invented. Leopold VI of Austria died in a tournament in 1194. Three successive earls of Salisbury were killed in the early thirteenth century. William Marshal's protégé, Geoffrey of Brittany, was trampled to death in 1186. Floris III of Holland was killed in 1223, Floris IV in 1234; John, margrave of Brandenburg in 1268 and John I of Brabant in 1294 were other distinguished victims. Over sixty lesser knights are reported to have died, admittedly for the most part from suffocation in dust, at a single tournament at Neuss in 1241. Older and wiser men saw it as a

188

dangerous and foolhardy occupation: Philip Augustus enjoined his sons not to take part in tournaments, and as late as 1370 two knights charged with the transport of royal money from London to Bordeaux were required to refrain from entering the lists until their mission was accomplished.

As the dangers of the tournament decreased, it became a kind of substitute for real war, given the right circumstances. This was particularly true of the Hundred Years' War. When a truce or even a lull in the fighting occurred, there was often a tournament or *pas d'armes* to occupy the interval, whose sole object was to continue the war in another guise. We have already described the jousts at St Inglevert; but the origins of the convention are much older. It can be traced back to episodes such as the famous Little Battle of Chalons in 1274, when Edward I challenged a hostile count to a tournament. In the course of it he himself fought a joust with the count, who, finding that Edward was getting the better of him, tried to drag him off his horse by clasping him round the body, which was a flagrant breach of the accepted rules. At this a riot developed, and several knights were killed on both sides. In 1341 Edward III's Scottish campaign ended in jousts of this semi-hostile type, and one Scottish and two English knights were killed.

In contrast, such episodes in the Hundred Years' War were usually harmless though still hostile. But they fell into a larger pattern which runs through the warfare of these years, the perpetual desire of the knights to perform individual feats of valour. Most of these undertakings, which Froissart recorded with such delight, were pure bravado, spectacular rather than dangerous. On the other hand, Marshal Boucicaut's duels with Peter Courteney and Thomas Clifford in 1386, and the series of jousts held in England for the French knights captive there after Poitiers, continued the political alignments outside the immediate context of the war, while showing how little difference there was between real and mock fighting for most of the knights; the attitude to opponents and the likelihood of injury were scarcely greater on the battlefield than in the tournament.

With the end of the Hundred Years' War, the tournament had lost the last connections with current tactical thinking, and by 1450 became purely a sport and social diversion, a pageant to decorate political occasions which required due pomp and circumstance. It also became more expensive and exclusive, developing into a private diversion for the richest lords only, as the cost of equipment, which now had to be specially made, increased to a much higher level than that of ordinary field armour. Tournaments ceased to play any part in internal politics, and the passion and enthusiasm of the contestants for the sport itself diminished correspondingly.

The Church, unlike the secular princes, maintained a consistent attitude towards tournaments. Some of the earliest evidence for the existence of tournaments consists of documents showing the Church's official disapproval of the new sport, as we have already seen. This attitude was maintained throughout most of the tournament's existence, but the edicts which resulted gradually became a dead letter. The thunder of the popes against the budding sport continued unabated during the twelfth century; Alexander III at the Third Lateran Council of 1179, renewed the anathemas. Yet fourteen years later, Celestine III's edict in the same vein was almost immediately followed by Richard I's licensing of the tournament in England. Without the secular arm, the Church was largely powerless; its ban on church burial for knights killed in tourneys was often avoided by those who survived long enough to put on a monk's habit, as in the case of one Eustace de Calquille in 1193. Only serious misdemeanours, such as a German tournament of 1175 when seventeen knights were killed, drew the technically automatic sentence of excommunication. Although the edict imposing this punishment was repeated at the Lateran Synod of 1215, such sentences were applied in the same way as the royal prosecutions in England for illicit tourneying: the offender so punished had usually committed some other crime more difficult to prove and punish, or was a known enemy of Church or king as the case might be. The ban was continued by Gregory IX in 1228 and Innocent IV in 1245 in the same terms as their predecessors had used; and the Church's attitude seemed to be becoming traditional and set.

But in the course of the latter part of the thirteenth century there was a change of heart, and instead of developing into a set opposition, the Church grew less obdurate. Nicholas III's repetition of earlier bulls in 1279 was revoked by Martin IV in 1281, although the principle of opposition remained. There were certainly divergent opinions in the Church, for some counter-propaganda favourable to the tournament survives, such as the story of the knight en route for a tournament who stopped at a church to hear mass. Being devout, he stopped to hear as many masses as the priest might say, despite his squire's impatience. As they left the church, the knight was surprised to meet a group of his friends coming away from the tournament, which had already ended, who congratulated him on his success. It was only when the squire supported his story that they believed his insistence that he had not been there, attributing his success to the

Blessed Virgin's having fought in his place. Although the main point of the story is that devout men have their reward, the story is at odds with the official fulminations against jousting, and is clearly sympathetic to the sport.

When in 1281 there seemed a chance of a more co-operative attitude from both Church and king, Philip IV of France imposed a series of writs against the jousters, which took the place of the ecclesiastical censures; and yet tourneying still continued on a considerable scale. It is therefore curious to find Philip's chief publicist, Pierre du Bois, defending tournaments against papal attack in 1313. Clement V, in his bull *Passiones miserabiles*, had condemned them on account of the forthcoming crusade, to which all good Christians should be devoting their whole energies, and Cardinal de Fréauville had banned them in France in October 1313. Repeating the old objections, unchanged for nearly 200 years, tournaments were branded as an invitation to commit the seven deadly sins; the chief dangers being vainglory, the settling of private quarrels by violence, and the temptation of lechery because of the women present. For the secular arm, Philip's royal clerks had seen them until now as a waste of men and resources. Against this, Dubois raises some interesting arguments: tournaments gave general pleasure, and provided an honest living for heralds and other attendants; they were a useful training ground for crusaders, and should perhaps be made a privilege of those who intended to go on crusade; and finally, any ban was more likely to be honoured in the breach than in the observance. It was therefore better to allow them in a limited form.

Dubois achieved his immediate object, for behind the fine phrases and generalisations, his treatise was probably aimed at obtaining a temporary suspension of the ban for the occasion of the knighting of Philip's sons in Lent 1314. But his specious reasoning also marked the moment of the larger change of attitude on the Church's part. Under Clement VI the papal court at Avignon became almost a secular prince's entourage, and tournaments, as part of the normal and becoming festivities of such a place, were on several occasions held there. By 1471 they appeared in St Peter's Square itself, and in 1565 the chief feature of the celebrations to mark the completion of the Vatican Belvedere was a great tournament. In view of this it is less surprising to find the bans on tourneying virtually disappearing by 1350; especially since monarchs had begun to give them official approval, as at the Garter feast and tourney of 1344 (See p. 303 below).

One prohibition seems to have remained unbroken, that against clergy taking part in jousts, first promulgated at Würzburg in 1287. The fact that clergy were not supposed to shed blood had not deterred Norman bishops from going into battle armed with maces alongside their sword-wielding secular brethren, but there were no such apparitions in cope and armour to be found in the lists.

The later fourteenth and fifteenth centuries produced the reverse side of the coin. The decline of chivalry and crusading enthusiasm was seen by religious writers as stemming from lack of exercise in arms. The cry was now for more tournaments of the old kind, the contemporary ones being cesspits of display and vainglory: thus Philippe de Mézières. The satirists who deflated chivalry also saw the tournament as a potential means of restoring it to its old status; Eustace Deschamps attacks the laziness and lack of skill of the knights of his day, and is eager to see them in the lists again. But other critics preach a Spartan discipline, greater loyalty and obedience, and the subservience of individual effort to the general end; and such writers have no time for tournaments, which encourage only rashness and insubordination, and in which individual knights are especially singled out for praise and honours. The French defeats of the fourteenth century inspired such feelings in men like Jean Gerson, chancellor of the university of Paris and the patriotic poet Alain Chartier; and in Italy, Petrarch saw the tournament as lacking in the ancient virtues; who had heard of Cato and Scipio jousting? Their assessment of the situation was nearer to the mark than that of those who hankered after the golden age of the past. The tournament had become irrelevant to anything outside the gilded pomp of the great courts, and papal bulls would have been laughable against this least of the indulgences which the fifteenth century permitted itself. Luxury and licence prevailed in the papal court as well; until in the new atmosphere of the Reformation and the heat of greater issues which moved all religious men, there was no breath to spare to denounce the harlequin ghosts of another age.

I Ulrich von Lichtenstein, minnesinger and knight-errant.
An early fourteenth-century miniature

II Making a knight. The girding on of the sword was the early form of the ceremony, and goes back to the Germanic rites for initiating a warrior. France, thirteenth century

III A joglar, or jongleur, fore-runner of the troubadour. He both composed and performed his songs, which might be either lyric or epic. A Spanish miniature of the tenth century

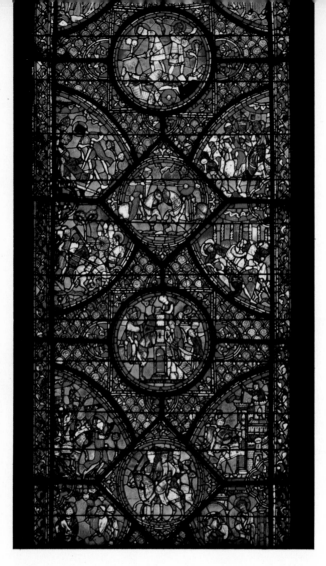

IV Scenes from the *Chanson de Roland* on a thirteenth-century
stained glass window at Chartres. From foot: departure for
Spain (centre) Charlemagne prays for victory at Pamplona
(right) and (left) captures the town, building a church there
(centre); a battle against the Saracens (right) is followed by
the miracle of the flowering lances. Roland fights Ferragut
(centre) and kills him (right). The army departs from Spain
(left). Roland sounds his horn and tries to break Durendal
(centre)

V The knight takes leave of his lady, departing for war or
crusade. France, fifteenth century

VI A fifteenth-century tournament. The ladies sit among rich
hangings, the armour is ornate with crests on the helmets,
and the form of combat is the joust. Note the attending
pages, ready to assist their masters

VII The burning of the Templar Grand Master, Jacques de
Molay, at Paris in 1313. He had protested against a sentence
of perpetual imprisonment, and was condemned to the
stake by Philip the Fair's council, the last of the Order to
die as a result of the trials.

Gil goncales

John guillem

VIII Knights of the Order of Santiago. These portraits
belong to the fifteenth century, and represent an already
romantic idea of the Order's early days

I2

Warfare

Real war and tournaments are never very far apart throughout the history of chivalry. Tournaments begin as mimic wars in the twelfth century; wars take on the appearance of mimic tournaments in the pages of Froissart in the fourteenth century. In both, the knight seems to be the sole protagonist, deciding the outcome of the day in a series of charges, against which infantry are powerless, and in hand to hand combats. Deaths are rare, the same rules seem to apply; and the knights, living for warfare, have made even this real warfare a kind of exciting, unreal game.

Mediaeval warfare was in fact a very much rougher and bloodier business than Froissart would have us believe, and much more complex than the pages of the chroniclers, themselves unskilled in its arts, would lead us to think. There is nothing quite so difficult to portray accurately as a mediaeval battle. First of all, the numbers are invariably exaggerated. The greatest armies of classical times are estimated at about 35,000 men; Caesar at the height of his career may have had this number at Pharsalia in 48BC. With the fragmentation of the Empire, the numbers involved grow less and less, though reliable estimates are impossible until the twelfth century. When numbers can once again be reckoned, the mediaeval army appears as a force of between 7,000 and 10,000 men though there is no definite instance of the latter number being engaged in a single battle. If we set these figures, based on the study of royal accounts, and occasionally of the terrain of the battlefield itself, against the reports of the chroniclers, the unreliability of their figures, and indeed of their whole reports, becomes evident. To take a single instance: at Bouvines in 1214, when Philip Augustus of France defeated the combined Angevin and Imperial army, the chroniclers record up to 9,000 knights and 50,000 infantry on the French side, the real figure being a little over one-tenth of these; and a Scottish chronicle succeeds in attributing nearly quarter of a million men to the opposing army, which may have numbered 10,000.

The accounts of the course of the battles themselves are equally suspect in some respects. While the broad details may be accurate, the writers are never interested in the minutiae. So every battle becomes a cavalry action in which the infantry are mere bystanders, unless some exceptional reversal of fortune occurs. The idea of mediaeval tactics as consisting of a vast *mêlée* of charges by heavily armed knights, invariably on horseback, captures the imagination all too easily: and the shadow of this attractive over-simplification still hangs over the history of mediaeval warfare.

The apparent improvisation and lack of theoretical manuals which are the chief features of mediaeval tactics belie the true nature of the warfare of the period. Selection of terrain, disposition of forces, and the manœuvres during the battle were as important as the strength of the cavalry force and their fighting skill; the slow evolution of new ideas meant that the individual skill of the commander was at a premium, and that it was the quality of the troops rather than possession of the latest weapons that decided the day. The basic dispositions remained the same throughout the Middle Ages. Cavalry formed the attacking force, with infantry as supporting and defensive troops. Even the introduction of the longbow and the successes of the Hussite infantry, using fortified *laagers*, did nothing to alter this. In the twelfth century, the infantry part was necessarily smaller, since the crossbow was a slow and difficult weapon to handle. If there were no crossbowmen, the battle would open without a preliminary volley, in skirmishes between outriders, as the two armies manœuvred and each tried to persuade the other side to charge. A first charge rarely succeeded, and if the enemy could be persuaded to commit himself too heavily to his initial effort, the chances of an effective counter charge before he could recover were increased. There are innumerable examples of battles being lost by an impulsive opening attack by over-eager knights, a problem to which we shall return.

Equally, the two armies might confront each other for days before battle was joined, as at Las Navas de Tolosa in 1212, where the Christians refused to be drawn by the Muslim armies for two days, while they encamped and rested, despite exchanges between archers and light horsemen. Again, in Henry II's wars against his French overlord, a pitched battle never occurred, though the armies came face to face in 1173 near Conches and in 1174 after the siege of Rouen. The number of actual battles in the twelfth century is also very small: Tinchebray in 1106, Northallerton in 1138, Lincoln in 1141, Fornham in 1173, Alarcos in 1195. Of these, Lincoln and Fornham were on a very small scale, scarcely bigger than the skirmish at

Courcelles in 1198 in which Richard defeated Philip Augustus and proudly announced in his letter reporting the victory that 90 French knights were captured, 200 had been drowned, and that he had taken 200 horses. The basic unit was a group of about thirty to forty knights around their leader's banner. In the twelfth and thirteenth centuries, these groups probably fought in tournaments in similar formation; the Brabançon mercenaries of the twelfth century came from an area where the tournament was almost a national sport. The 'battle' was composed of a number of these units, in close formation, and two or three such battles would probably be deployed, one sometimes being left in reserve or in ambush if a feigned retreat (as at Hastings) was to be used.

Sieges were the main ingredient of any twelfth-century campaign, and the real object of military manœuvres was a kind of chessboard tactic designed to deprive the enemy of his fortresses and hence of control of the countryside. Henry II's successes were largely due to his skill in siegecraft and use of mercenaries who were prepared to sit out a long siege, unlike the feudal levies who were liable to go home at the end of their allotted time, regardless of the state of the campaign. If one could take a stronghold like Castillon in Gascony as swiftly as Henry did in 1161, reducing the local lords to a state of terror and amazement, none of the latter were likely to risk a pitched battle. Siege warfare and machinery lay outside the knight's province; experts were employed from a very early date, mercenaries recruited for the purpose on a similar footing to the Genoese crossbowmen. Only a commander of some standing was likely to have to direct a siege. On the other hand, knights were often to be found as defenders, either because castle-guard was one of their feudal duties, or as a professional garrison. By the early thirteenth century, castle-guard was almost always commuted by payments, and the professional garrison took over. Nonetheless, the ordinary knight was likely to see more of sieges than of battles in his military service, and after the arts of the engineers had effected a breach with mangonels, battering rams or mines, the knights formed the assault troops who actually stormed the citadel. At the siege of Ascalon in 1153 the Templars were so eager to gain the glory of capturing the town that when a breach was accidentally made in the part of the wall opposite their encampment, a small body of forty knights went through it to come to grips with the defenders, while their fellows prevented other Christian troops from entering. They paid dearly for their pride, however, and were overwhelmed.

In the West sieges were rarely pursued with such energy; it was very unusual for a major town to be taken by assault. Even in Spain, the Moorish cities fell by intrigue rather than open warfare; Valencia, where the exiled Cid established himself, came into the famous warrior's hands after a series of diplomatic manœuvres in which the strength of his army was only one factor. His final victory over the Valencians, who twice rebelled against him or his allies, was the exception: after a siege of nineteen months he succeeded in starving the city out in June 1094, and only then became full sovereign of it.

The pattern of warfare changed very little in the thirteenth century. Edward 1's Scottish wars were fought on entirely orthodox lines, and there was very little difference in the tactics or proportion of foot to horse between Bouvines in 1214 and Falkirk in 1298, though the Welsh archers' part in the latter battle was an omen for the future. From a tactical point of view, there seems to have been very little coordination on either side at Bouvines; and only the action of a Templar, Guérin, ensured that the French drew up in such a way that they could not be outflanked. His evidently greater experience underlines the amateur nature of the feudal levies when compared with the more permanent armies in the East.

A knight who did not go on crusade had little hope of seeing more than intermittent warfare; and however well trained he might be in the individual skills of arms, the idea of discipline and its importance could only be instilled on the battlefield. Its value was clearly realised: in an apocryphal speech of Henry the Fowler to his troops before a battle against the Hungarians (written in the twelfth century) he is made to say: 'Let no one try to pass his companions because his horse is swifter. But, using your shields as cover, take their first arrows on them; then charge them quickly and violently so that they cannot fire again before you have wounded them.'[1] Yet discipline was the weakest point of the mediaeval army, and especially of the knights.

The emphasis on individual glory (or in the case of the Military Orders, the glory of the order) was so strong that even experienced knights were unable to argue reasonably against it. In the East it was the downfall of the Frankish troops time and again. At Mansourah in 1250 Robert d'Artois nearly brought disaster on the entire army by disobeying specific instructions not to attack. True, he succeeded in surprising the Egyptians with the vanguard he commanded, but his initial success was too much for him, and he swept on into the town, and into an improvised ambush. The counter-attack almost swept the rest of the crusading army back into the canal they had just so laboriously crossed. Repeatedly in the Frankish councils of war the barons urged attacks against unfavourable odds, or against strong positions, because they were so eager for battle and glory. The Templar Gerard of Ridfort was one of the most impetuous: at Cresson in 1187 he attacked a large Muslim force with a hundred or so knights and was one of only three survivors. When the entire resources of the kingdom were perhaps 1,500 knights, this was a disaster of the first order: and that the attack should have been made against saner counsels simply because Gerard had taunted the knights with cowardice was sheer folly. Tactics which involved use of a strong defensive position were often impossible to carry out, or were overruled by the opinions of such knights: at Gaza in 1244, the wiser heads among the Christian army, and particularly their Muslim allies, urged that their strong position should be held; if they had, the Egyptian armies would either have been defeated or would have withdrawn, but the temptation to try and overwhelm their opponents was too much for the count of Jaffa. In the event it was the Christians who, moving out into the plain, were massacred. The lesson of order was only learnt in the bitter days of defeat.

The knight's role in the actual fighting was strongly influenced by the development of armour. To some extent, armour evolved to meet the knight's needs, but the lure of greater protection at the expense of mobility proved too strong. The chain mail of the eleventh to thirteenth centuries allowed great freedom of movement, and was comparatively light. On the other hand, it might not stop the sword's edge or the lance's point. A quilted undergarment came to be used as a shock absorber in the twelfth century, but the force of the blow might still produce a fairly serious wound. Made from a series of forged or riveted rings, chain mail (or mail) could easily break, and it was very difficult to keep clean and free from rust. Attempts at making a more effective yet reasonably light defence began with hardened leather garments to shield the trunk; and at about the same time in the early thirteenth century plate-armour proper appeared. At first the mail coat was reinforced with small patches of solid metal plate at vital places, on the knees and elbows especially; then a construction of jointed plates on a leather base was used to cover the trunk. The progress of the new ideas was largely limited by the armourer's technical skill: it was not until the end of the century that gauntlets made on the same principle, which needed much closer fitting and accurate work, appeared. It was at this point that the armourer's craft moves from the local workers, who were little more than skilled blacksmiths, to the great international centres: the north Italian armourers established themselves at this time, and dominated the trade until its decline.

Armour reached its most complex point in the days of early plate-armour, about 1330, in that it was made up of a large number of individual pieces, often forming several layers, with complex lacing to hold each in its proper place. The length of time needed to don this equipment was underlined by the occasions when an army was taken by surprise. Later armour, being closely tailored to the body, was probably no easier to put on, but its construction was simpler and stronger. The breastplate, which seems such an essential part of the knight's equipment, did not in fact appear until the late fourteenth century, and the complete body armour of polished steel (al-white armour) in which the Pre-Raphaelite painters clad Tennyson's heroes is of the mid-fifteenth century.

Nonetheless, the knight of the fourteenth century was sufficiently impregnable on his armoured horse to resist almost anything a foot-soldier could do; only the Flemish pikemen at Courtrai in 1302, forebears of the Swiss companies of the fifteenth century, and the Turkish horse at Nicopolis in 1396 – the latter vastly superior in numbers – were able to inflict serious defeats on them. However, the dismounted knight, who had played an effective part in battles such as Northallerton in 1138, was now at a disadvantage; unable to move swiftly, less because of the weight of the armour than because armour was not designed for movement on foot, he was an easy prey to the dagger of a lightly armed soldier thrust between the joints of his carapace. The classic example of this was the experience of the French at Poitiers in 1356, when their first charge failed to break through the English archers who lined both sides of the road leading to the main body of the enemy, because their horses were shot beneath them, and both they and the dismounted second wave were cut down or killed by the English arrows used at short range.

The development of this elaborate defensive armour was not paralleled by a similar development in the knight's aggressive weapons. His usefulness in the field was dependent on the same skills in the fifteenth century as in the twelfth, and his weapons had scarcely changed; the lance might be of better wood, the sword of keener metal, but all the great advances were in the field of ballistics. For the knight was essentially conservative in his attitude to new modes of warfare, which he was apt to declare unknightly. No knight would have dreamt of using a bow; with some reason, for a horseman would have great difficulty in handling six feet of yew, and the short eastern bow was no match for the longbow. Both longbow and crossbow were introduced after cavalry warfare had become the universal pattern of warfare. The crossbow seems to have been invented in north Italy in the eleventh century, and became a speciality of the Genoese. It is a powerful but slow-firing weapon: on the later types, the tension is produced by a ratchet and screw, and experiments in 1894 showed that in order to load it, the archer's hand had to travel thirty feet in a circular motion as he wound back the cord.[2] Two shots a minute would be a good rate of fire, though this could be overcome by using one archer as a loader while the other aimed and fired, as at Jaffa in 1192. The squat bolt, known as a quarrel, made up for this slow delivery by its power when launched; it was still effective at 300 yards to the extent of piercing armour easily. Its devastating impact on warfare when it first appeared is reflected in Innocent II's condemnation of it at the Lateran Council in 1139: 'The deadly art, hated of God, of crossbowmen and archers should not be used against Christians and Catholics on pain of anathema.'[3]

The Genoese had a virtual monopoly both of manufacture and use of the crossbow, probably because it required a very high degree of training; and this meant that relatively few crossbowmen were available at any one time. The cost of employing them was accordingly high, and like all mercenaries their loyalties were at best uncertain. It never became a general weapon, but was used principally in sieges.

The longbow, on the other hand, was a weapon which required much less training for efficient use, and was relatively easy to manufacture. It first appears in South Wales in the twelfth century, (in North Wales the lance was the prevalent weapon: thus Giraldus, at least) though similar, shorter bows had been used since Roman days, and appear on the Bayeux tapestry. Giraldus Cambrensis has this to say of the men of Gwent in South Wales about this time 'This people ... very accustomed to warlike ways, and most renowned for their powers, are also the most skilled archers among the Welsh.'[4] He claims that their arrows can penetrate an oak door for a hand's breadth, and that they have been known to transfix both knight and horse with a single arrow. Modern writers estimate the arrow's penetrating power as equal to that of a rifle bullet, as elephant hunters have shown: but its penetration is cleaner, and it kills only if used accurately, since it lacks the effect of the bullet, which produces shock and bruising as well. With a rate of fire over six times that of the crossbow, it rapidly achieved a predominant role in warfare after Edward I's conquest of Wales. The bodies of archers from Wales and the border counties first began to play an important part in Edward's Scottish campaigns at the end of the thirteenth century; the battle of

Falkirk in 1298 is a good example. Their full tactical potential was only realised under Edward III, at Dupplin Moor (1332) and Halidon Hill (1333); and from then until the end of the next century, they were the key to the defensive tactics which brought the English armies such success.

There was no question of the knights adopting either crossbow or longbow for their own use. Apart from the impossibility of handling them on horseback, they were both supporting weapons, which required an offensive squadron to press home the advantage. It was not merely the knightly disdain for such servile weapons — the longbowmen were English peasants, the crossbowmen Italian mercenaries — which the *chanson de geste* of Girart de Viane forcefully expresses: 'Cursed be the first man who became an archer: he was afraid and did not dare approach.'[5] There were also sound tactical requirements which ensured that neither innovation dislodged the knight from his position as the mainstay of the army. Nor did either weapon appreciably increase the number of deaths on the battlefield; only a very small percentage of the missiles fired inflicted mortal wounds.

For similar reasons the knight was not interested in learning the skills of firearms, especially since gunpowder and artillery were until 1400 little more than a curiosity, like Greek fire, with very specialised uses. It was only well after the knight had ceased to be master of the battlefield for quite other reasons that the musket and arquebus appeared as practical infantry weapons, and examples of knights being killed by cannon are rare: the most famous to perish in this way was Jacques de Lalain in 1453, at the siege of Poucques, though Talbot at Castillon in 1435 had been thrown from his horse by a shot from the strong position he was trying to storm, which had been entrenched and provided with artillery; and the earl of Salisbury was killed by a stone from a veuglaire at the siege of Orléans in 1428. It was only in the closing stages of the Hundred Years' War that artillery played any serious part, and the difficulty of transporting it meant that it was confined to sieges. The giant cannon known as bombards which appeared in the 1380s were so inefficient that they were superseded by smaller weapons by 1450. In that year a chronicler records of Charles VII setting out for Normandy that 'he had the greatest number and variety of battering cannon and bombards, veuglaires, serpentines, crapaudines, culverines and ribaudequins that had ever been collected in the memory of man'.[6]

It is the variety, not the sheer size of the pieces, that is now important: veuglaires and serpentines are smaller pieces which we should call cannon pure and simple; crapaudines are a kind of mortar; and the culverines and ribaudequins are hand-firearms. Even so, the technical development of firearms was still in its infancy. James I of Scotland was killed at a test-firing of a new cannon in 1437 when the barrel burst. Hand-firearms, which appear from 1369 onwards, also had their problems. Two men were needed to operate a culverine, one to aim and support it, the other to fire. Despite the appearance of the shoulder-butt in the 1420s, the bow still retained its ancient pre-eminence; at Rupelmonde in 1452, 'the Ghent men made good use of their culverines; but they could not withstand the arrows of the Picards, and, turning about, fled'.[7] And in 1471, first of many such episodes, a band of 300 Flemish mercenaries armed with handguns were put out of action by a storm which extinguished their matches and damped their powder.

Siegecraft likewise was an art which lay outside the knight's ken. It was only when a breach was made or a siege-tower built that the knights would see action again: it was regarded as a great honour to be among the first into a beleaguered city. Generally, however, the knights found the long inactivity of the siege irksome, and sought diversions to while away the time. Challenges between garrison and besiegers were quite common, usually for a skirmish at the barriers. Froissart describes one of these at Noya (in Galicia) in 1387. The French are already in position:

> [The besiegers] gave their horses to the pages and servants, and marched in a compact body, each knight and squire with his spear in hand, towards the barriers: every six paces they halted, to dress themselves without opening their ranks. To say the truth, it was a beautiful sight. When they were come as far as they wished, they halted for a short time, and then advanced their front to begin the action. They were gallantly received; and, I believe, had the two parties been in the plain, many more bold actions would have taken place than it was possible to find an opportunity for where they were; for the barriers being closely shut, prevented them from touching each other. . . . So every man had his match; and when they were fatigued or heated, they retired and other fresh knights and squires renewed the skirmish.[8]

The most famous of siege combats was that of the 'Combat of the Thirty' in 1351, when the commanders of two Breton castles arranged a joust to the death between thirty of their men on each side, in the open field. Initially, a contest of three knights on each side armed with daggers was offered and declined as too dangerous, but the final casualties, nine English and Germans and six Frenchmen killed, were very high. Jean Le Bel, who records the episode, is full of admiration: 'I never heard tell of such an enterprise taking place save this. And the survivors of this battle should be all the more honoured for it, wherever they go.'[9]

When a brief spell of peace intervened, these challenges became jousts. Miles Windsor, in the service of the king of Portugal, finding to his dismay on his arrival 'that as peace was concluded, there would not be any engagement, he determined not to quit Spain without doing something to be talked of', and arranged a joust against Sir Tristan de Roye, a Frenchman in Spanish service. The jousts of St Inglevert are another example; on this occasion, no passions were aroused and the atmosphere remained friendly; but such meetings of old enemies could prove dangerous. The 'Combat of the Thirty' had been arranged 'for the love of their ladies'; but with fifteen out of sixty knights killed, and a castle captured as a result, it looked more like real war, and the 'Little War of Châlons' in 1278 was another example of a supposedly friendly meeting that became earnest.

This persistence of hostilities in times of official peace leads us to the deeper question of the knight's attitude to war. The modern attitude is to regard peace as normal, war as the exception, and as immoral and evil. Mediaeval attitudes were very different. The knight regarded war as the normal state of mankind, partly through dim memories of days when this had been true, and his services as defender of society had been essential, and partly because war was so strongly in his financial interest if he were a fighting man and not a merely titular knight. And at the most abstract level, that of the Roman lawyers and political theorists, war was part of the established order of things. In the fifteenth century, Honoré Bonet, in his *Tree of Battles*, drawn largely from earlier writers, declares:

> War is not an evil thing, but good and virtuous; for war, by its very nature, seeks nothing other than to set wrong right, and turn dissension to peace, in accordance with Scripture. And if in war many evil things are done, they never come from the nature of war, but from false usage.[10]

The right to make private war was another complication in knights' attitudes to warfare. By the fourteenth century, examples of *guerre couverte* were rare in France, but the legal right remained. Formal defiance had to be made, and due cause given, and burning and ravaging were technically forbidden. In practice, the greater struggle between England and France provided cover for any number of private feuds and raids. In Germany the right to private war was jealously guarded by the nobility. Even in Charles iv's Golden Bull of 1356 private war is acknowledged as legal provided due notice of three days is given, and it is only unjust war, and other such disorders, that are prohibited. War was a perfectly normal method of settling a dispute in the knight's view; the enthusiasm of the Church for endless parleys and negotiated settlements only gained ground among the lay nobles in the fifteenth century, and the idea that assemblies could make peace as well as war was first tested at the Congress of Arras in 1435. Even then pacifism remained the mark of the bourgeois whose trade was disturbed, or the peasant whose crops were burnt.

If private war was gradually limited by the kings, the Church and the common people had at one time managed to impose considerable restrictions on normal warfare. War to the death was normally reserved for battles against the infidel, though the French at Crécy displayed the oriflamme before the battle, which was normally the signal that no quarter was to be given and all prisoners killed. In 'open war', where quarter and ransoms were allowed, the combatants escaped lightly, and it was the non-combatants who suffered most, from the fire and sword of an army ravaging the countryside. Most of the campaigns of the Hundred Years' War consist of devastations rather than sieges and skirmishes: the Black Prince's expedition of 1355–7, for example, was intended to be no more than an armed raid for the purpose of economic warfare, and the battle at Poitiers only came about because the prince had made such an effective nuisance of himself that a drastic response became necessary. The pillaging and burning may have seemed wanton and merely designed to demoralise the population and persuade them that their French masters were broken reeds as protectors; but there were other, shrewder reasons as well: the prince's steward, Sir John Wengfeld, wrote:

And my lord rode against his enemies eight whole weeks, and sojourned not in all these places save eleven days. And know for certain that, since this war began against the king of France, there was never such loss nor such destruction as hath been in this raid. For the lands and the good towns which are destroyed in this raid found for the king of France each year more to maintain his war than did the half of his kingdom, not reckoning the exchange which he hath made each year of his money and of the profit and custom which he taketh of them of Poitou, as I could show you by good records which were found in divers towns in the houses of receivers.[11]

While knights were expected to uphold the standards of chivalry in such warfare, it was an open question as to how far they should try to restrain their men, and even then they were often powerless. Neither the Black Prince in 1355 nor his father in 1346 were able to prevent the burning of Church property; at Carcassonne, explicit orders that it was to be spared were ignored.

The taking of a town by siege was likewise governed by legal provisions. If a siege had been properly declared by a herald, the besieged could make terms at any point until the actual storming of the walls. If they remained adamant, the town lay at the besiegers' mercy. Churches and clergy were immune, in theory, but the inhabitants were regarded as rebels and their goods as forfeit. Plunder and slaughter might be carried out in cold blood, after formal possession had been taken and the victorious general had made his entry. It is the idea that rapine is a legal remedy for defiance that underlies the incredible cruelties of mediaeval sieges. A horrifying example had been set by the knights of the First Crusade, when they avenged themselves not only for the agonies of a month encamped in the desert, but for centuries of Muslim 'desecration' of the Holy Places, in the blood bath at Jerusalem in 1099:

> The Crusaders, maddened by so great a victory after such suffering, rushed through the streets and into the houses and mosques killing all that they met, men, women and children alike. All that afternoon and all through the night the massacre continued. Tancred's banner was no protection to the refugees in the mosque of al-Aqsa. Early next morning a band of Crusaders forced an entry into the mosque and slew everyone. When Raymond of Aguilers later that morning went to visit the Temple area, he had to pick his way through corpses and blood that reached up to his knees.[12]

If they can be excused in some measure as an army of fanatics, whipped into fervour by their preachers, their example was followed in all too many cases where there was no such excuse. When the Bishop of Limoges, a close ally of the Black Prince, went over to the French in 1370, the latter, already a sick man, vowed to take vengeance for this treason: and when a breach was made, his men went in with instructions to spare no one.

> You would have then seen pillagers, active to do mischief, running through the town, slaying men, women and children, according to their orders. It was a most melancholy business; for all ranks, ages and sexes cast themselves on their knees before the prince, begging for mercy; but he was so inflamed with passion and revenge that he listened to none, but all were put to the sword, wherever they could be found, even those who were not guilty; for I know not why the poor were not spared, who could not have had any part in this treason; but they suffered for it. ... Upwards of three thousand men, women and children were put to death that day.[13]

Froissart does not deny the Black Prince's right in such deeds when he suggests that mercy would have been well placed.

Parallels for the sack of Limoges are by no means rare: some are intentional warnings to other towns of the wrath that will fall upon them; in other cases, the commander has been unable to control his men. In the narrow streets of the mediaeval town, there was little a handful of knights could do, even when they did try, to stop a massacre. Only dire threats before the assault began were likely to have much effect, backed up by an occasional example after the event.

At the siege of Dinant in 1342, Louis d'Espagne was so angered by the burning of churches by pillagers that 'he immediately ordered twenty-four of the most active to be hanged and strangled upon the spot'.[14] The common soldier might not be sure to whom he owed obedience, and as devastation was part of the normal business of a raid into enemy territory, and loot the only pay he was likely to get, it was difficult to restrain him. The problem was aggravated by the general pardons issued to criminals and outlaws if they would serve in France, which meant that the English armies had a certain element of troublemakers from the outset; and the free companies were largely self-formed bands of such men, though a strict captain like Perrot le Béarnois could protect the inhabitants of towns to some extent. Even knights on the opposing side might find themselves in danger, like the garrison at Caen in 1346, who shut themselves in a tower and made such defence as they could, until Thomas Holland arrived, whom they knew from crusades made with him to Prussia and Granada.

The horrors of the fate of the common people contrast sharply with the treatment of noble prisoners. It was extremely rare for captives of any standing to be killed, because of the very lucrative systems of ransoms. Chivalry became a question of business. Froissart sorrowfully recorded that the English and Portuguese, fearing a reverse of fortune at the battle of Aljubarota, were forced to slay their prisoners, 'for whom they might otherwise have had ransoms of 400,000 francs'.[15]

The custom of ransoming goes back to classical times; but it was in some degree forgotten during the ninth and tenth centuries. Guibert de Nogent says of William the Conqueror that it was his custom never to hold his prisoners to ransom, but to condemn them to lifelong captivity. As the practice grew, however, the agreement to ransom came to imply slightly more than merely buying one's way out of imprisonment. The prisoner had to be protected from other members of the opposing army, and he could not be severely treated while in prison; irons were permitted but very rarely used, but threats of death or blackmail to make him do something dishonourable voided the agreement and he was then at liberty to escape.

These conditions were by no means universal: the Spanish and the Germans had a bad name for their treatment of prisoners. When the earl of Pembroke was captured in Spain in 1372, 'they conducted their prisoners to a strong castle and fastened them with iron chains according to their usual custom; for the Spaniards know not how to show courtesy to their prisoners'. Froissart contrasts the French and German usage thus:

> They neither shut them up in prison, nor put on shackles and fetters, as the Germans do in order to obtain a heavier ransom. Curses on them for it! These people are without pity or honour, and they ought never to receive quarter. The French entertained their prisoners well, and ransomed them courteously without being too hard on them.[16]

Though there was a tacit understanding that a ransom should be related to a knight's estate, and should not ruin him financially to such an extent that he could no longer live as a knight should, ransoms occasionally reached huge proportions. At the head of the list stand the 'king's ransoms' demanded after Poitiers for John the Good, and that paid by Richard Cœur de Lion. Below this, princes of the blood royal such as Charles d'Orléans were held for very high sums; and Charles languished in the Tower, bewailing his lost youth in some of the loveliest of French poetry, for twenty-five years until Philip the Good of Burgundy ransomed him for his own political ends. Edward III received about £268,000 for three major ransoms in the period 1360–70. A great captain like du Guesclin was also highly valued; indeed, when he was captured in Spain, the Black Prince was reluctant to let him go at all, and finally asked du Guesclin what ransom he ought to pay. Du Guesclin named the impossible figure of 100,000 francs, at which the prince remitted half of it, and sent him to raise the remainder. The story that he distributed all the money he had been given by his friends in Brittany to ransom his old comrades-at-arms whom he met on the road is probably apocryphal; in any event, the sum was paid by the king of France, Louis of Anjou, and Henry of Trastamare (in whose service he had been when captured). At the very humblest end of the scale a sum of a few crowns might well suffice if the prisoner were a mere man-at-arms, or the captor might settle for a suit of armour or a horse. So episodes such as the incident at Tournay in 1339 when Raymond, nephew to Pope Clement, 'was killed for the sake of his beautiful armour after he had surrendered, which made many good men angry'[17] were fortunately rare, as the armour could easily have been made part of his ransom. The custom was so generally accepted that it spread even to tournaments, and we have seen how the vanquished knight's horse and armour fell to the victor.

War, like tournaments, had become a matter of business. When a simple squire like one Croquart in the count of Holland's household in 1347 could make 40,000 écus and thirty or forty good horses in a very short time in Brittany, the monetary side became very important. War had long been almost an economic necessity for the poorer knights, whose small fiefs could hardly support them. Bertran de Born's *sirventes* in praise of war brushes aside the idea that war is fought for anything but sheer love of fighting; but from the eleventh to the fifteenth century there were always knights who had to find employment for their swords. In the *Life of the Emperor Henry IV* the German knights of the early twelfth century are vigorously attacked for destroying the prosperity of the country, when the emperor's successful enforcement of peace led to a conspiracy in 1104:

> When the lords and their accomplices had been restrained by this law for some years, displeased that they could not practise their misdeeds, they began to murmur against the emperor. What wrong had the emperor done? Only this: he had prevented crimes, restored peace and justice, so that robbers no longer lorded it on the highways and bandits no longer lurked in the forests, so that merchants and sailors could go their various ways freely, so that robbers starved while robbery was forbidden. Why, I adjure you, can you only live by robbery? Give the men back to the fields, whom you took away for war; keep as many followers as your means allow, buy back your estates that you probably squandered in order to hire as many warriors as you could, and your boards and cellars will groan with plenty; and you will no longer need to take other people's goods, having more than enough of your own. Then you will no longer need to mutter against the king, and the Empire will have peace. You will have what you need for your body, and, best of all, will save your souls. But my words are vain; I am asking the ass to play the lute; evil ways are rarely forsaken.[18]

When these words were written, it was only half a century since the Normans had conquered two kingdoms by the sword, Sicily and England, and in the process many individual fortunes had been made. The same impulse lay behind some of the crusaders' zeal: in the East it was possible both to win wide lands and save one's soul. As opportunities of this kind diminished, so the mercenary appeared on a humbler, non-knightly level, and ordinary war became a matter of business contracts as well as the clash of arms.

By the fourteenth century, fortunes could be made, not only from a fortunate capture, but also from loot: the increasing prosperity of the towns of France provided both English and French troops with ample opportunities, for if a town was taken by assault, it was regarded as being 'at mercy', and only churches and clergy were immune. And such plundering could be done not only in the heat of the moment, but also systematically after the victorious commander had made his formal entry, because the town was technically forfeit for having rebelled against its lawful lord. The notorious sack of Limoges by the Black Prince's troops was a case in point. The spoils so taken were usually divided in a fixed proportion, which was usually one-third to the soldiers, one-third to the commanders, and one-third to the crown. At the sack of Constantinople in 1204, churches were used to store the booty, which was then divided up: 'one mounted serjeant received as much as two serjeants on foot, one knight as much as two mounted serjeants'.[19]

In the indentures of war of the 1360s and 1370s which mark the final development of the system, and put the conduct of war on to an entirely commercial basis, the captain has to surrender the most important castles and lands to the king, and any prisoners whom the king regards as influential in return for a reasonable reward. Any other spoil was to be divided between the captain and the crown, the latter usually taking one-third. So far as the ordinary soldier was concerned, the Ordinances of Durham of 1385 laid down that he was to surrender one-third to his commander, who then surrendered one-third of this to the crown. Hence it was the successful commander who stood to make the greatest amount; and quite apart from the mercenary captains who rarely surrendered any of their spoils, such eminent figures as du Guesclin, Sir John Chandos, and Sir Hugh Calverley founded their fortunes in this way.

On the other hand, sieges were not all that frequent, and many were unsuccessful; and in the lean periods there might be very little to live on, and no pay forthcoming. Spoils of war were probably deducted from pay, so a rich haul of booty might well prove to be nothing more than a year's wages in advance. The author of the *Boke of Noblesse*, addressed to Edward IV before his expedition to France in 1475, attributes the excesses of previous campaigns to lack of proper and regular pay. One means of dealing with the problem was by an agreement to share spoils with another knight, the 'brotherhood in arms' whose high-sounding title conceals a very practical arrangement. For instance, in the contract between Nicholas Molyneux and John Winter signed at Harfleur in 1421, all gains in war were to be sent to London to be banked, and each is responsible for raising the first £1,000 of the other's ransom in the event of capture, and we have already noticed William Marshal's partnership with Roger de Gaugi in the tournaments of 1177–9, the earliest appearance of such an arrangement. Brothers-in-arms would also inherit the other's military fortune on his death.

Yet, despite the financial basis of such agreements, brotherhood-in-arms acquired a veneer of idealism. Its deepest roots may go back to the primitive oath of blood-brotherhood, in which blood was mingled in a cup. At its highest, it was a bond of alliance second only to those of family and liege homage, and acquired a special mystique of its own. Brothers-in-arms were supposedly 'bound to one another in such a way, that each will stand by the other to the death if need be, saving his honour,' in both counsel and action, and such a bond could sometimes be forged without a formal oath. The curious custom of fighting in mines – dug at a siege to bring down the wall of a fortress – was one such occasion. If a mine and countermine met, a skirmish would often ensue; and this often became a form of tournament. Knights who fought in such a combat became brothers-in-arms by the mere fact of having taken part, even though on opposing sides. At Melun Henry v himself is supposed to have taken part in such a combat, on horseback and with the mine lit by torches. At Limoges, John of Gaunt fought Jean de Villemur in a mine; and Jean was one of the few knights spared when the town was taken. More usually, the agreement was drawn up in proper legal form, and could be a form of alliance. Between princes, it became an important diplomatic weapon; but it was practised by the lowest kind of soldiers as well, including the mercenary captains. Froissart tells of one Louis Raimbaut, who left his mistress with his brother-in-arms, Limousin, only to find that he had taken too good care of her, and had obtained every favour from her. Raimbaut revenged himself by flogging his brother-in-arms out of the town; but Limousin betrayed him to a neighbouring lord, and he was ambushed and executed. Like homage and liege homage, which promised an exclusive bond when first introduced, brotherhood-in-arms became adulterated, and could be extended to more than one knight, but it remained the strongest of the various ties between man and man.

A byproduct of the idea of brotherhood is the various small confraternities of knights which appear at the end of the fourteenth century. These are apparently small orders of knighthood, with insignia and chapters. Instead of being an honorific institution, however, they are practical: the 'Pomme d'Or' in Auvergne, the 'St George' in Rougemont and the 'Tiercelet' in Poitou are a mixture between fighting companies, mutual protection associations and commercial organisations, but with an element of idealism as well. The statutes of the 'Tiercelet' provide for two special kinds of insignia, both for those who have been to Prussia to help the Teutonic knights; one is for those who have not been in action, and one for those who have actually fought the heathen. At the other extreme, the members are expected to help each other in lawsuits, and warn each other of any action likely to be taken against them.

The confraternities sum up the chivalrous attitude to war; beneath the high idealism of chivalric honour, war continues much as before, as cruel, atrocious and thoughtless as ever. Knighthood becomes a kind of guild of warriors, who may put the ordinary soldier and the civilian to the sword, but who rarely kill each other intentionally on the battlefield, and who see to it that military enterprises have a suitable financial reward. The occasional feat of arms is a diversion from the more serious business of pillage and destruction, and chivalry owes more to the pen than the sword. The glowing words of Froissart's preamble to his chronicles, 'that the honourable enterprises, noble adventures and deeds of arms, performed in the wars between England and France, may be properly related, and held in perpetual remembrance – to the end that brave men taking example from them may be encouraged in their well doing',[20] cast a golden spell of chivalry over the black harshness of war, an illusion in which the knights themselves believed, but which was nonetheless unreal.

PART IV

Chivalry and Religion

13

The Church, Warfare and Crusades

The traditions of the primitive Christian Church were wholly opposed to warfare of any kind, in sharp contrast to the *djihad* or holy war which played so great a part in the early history of Islam. Indeed, the early fathers questioned whether any part in warfare, however slight, was lawful for a Christian. It was not until Constantine's adoption of Christianity in 313 that practical considerations forced a change in this attitude, and thereafter the traditions of Eastern and Western Christendom divided. The East rapidly went over to a militaristic cult, complete with soldier-saints, of whom St George was one, and emphasised the image of St Paul, portraying the Christian life as that of a soldier in God's wars, as justification for this. The Roman church, less immediately involved in imperial politics, continued to regard war with suspicion, and when Augustine came to write on the subject, he could still insist that war was always evil, qualifying this very slightly by allowing that one side might have just cause for war; he also absolved the individual soldier who took part in an unjust war without being able to judge the rights and wrongs of the case.

Yet even as Augustine wrote, the Eastern emperors were engaged in suppressing by force the Donatist heresy in his native North Africa. By the end of the sixth century, the idea that heretics and infidels could legitimately be converted by force appears in one of Gregory the Great's letters: 'Wars are to be sought for the sake of spreading the republic in which we perceive God to be revered ... inasmuch as the name of Christ may be spread throughout the peoples thus made subject by the preaching of the faith.'[1]

It was not until the eighth century that such wars became politically possible. The Carolingian wars against the Saxons had a definitive political objective, but were presented as religious exercises. A mission to the soldiers first appeared in the West about this time. Mass was said before battle, and saints' relics were carried with the troops. This change was in some degree due to the Germanic element in Frankish civilisation: the old heroic ethics had been adapted rather than completely suppressed, and the German cult of warfare was so fervent that it was impossible to expect a complete change in ways of thought and feeling. Hence the idea of the 'soldiers of Christ' led by St Michael is brought in to replace the old warrior paganism with Wotan as its deity, and the *militia Christi* of St Paul are no longer the meek and spiritual martyrs, but the all too earthly soldiers of Charlemagne's armies. Charlemagne's opponents were those German tribes who had remained unconverted, and hence the Church had few qualms of conscience about giving its blessing, and indeed its encouragement. If conversion had sometimes been part of a political settlement at the end of a war, it now became one of the avowed aims at the outset of the campaign.

The Church's growing material wealth and involvement in secular affairs helped to assist this change of attitude. Bishops and abbots invested with lay fiefs, born into and brought up in an aristocratic warrior world, were quite liable to decide to take up arms, both in their own defence or in the king's service, despite the edicts of the fourth century against the clergy bearing weapons. The popes themselves accompanied armies raised to fight the Muslim pirates at the mouth of the Tiber; Leo IX in 849, and John X in 915 both did so. The defence of the Church against heathens and robbers in the troubled times of the ninth and tenth centuries became a sacred duty, and the reward for those who fell in such battles was eternal life. The liturgy included prayers not only for the destruction of enemies, but also that the Roman emperor might subject the heathen.

With the Cluniac reform of the monastic movement, and the insistence that the Church must take a greater part in everyday life, the warrior came to be regarded as one of the many professions of secular existence. His activities were blessed by the Church so long as they conformed with the Christian ideal, though penance might still be exacted for actual killing in battle if a general absolution had not previously been issued. So along with prayers for the harvest and for the fishermen's catches, that seed and nets might produce a plentiful reward, prayers were said over the knight's sword, prayers which later became the service of knighthood. The army on campaign was provided with sacred banners bearing a saint's image, which quickly became the subject of miraculous tales; these were sometimes carried by the clergy, witness the deaths of a priest and deacon acting as standard-bearers in battles against the Slavs in 992.

Yet the Church's attitude was still guarded: it encouraged knighthood, but only in order to control and tame the warrior instinct. Even in the tenth century the life of St Edmund, martyred by the Danes in 870, portrays him as a passive martyr, not a soldier dying bravely against great odds. The general lawlessness of the tenth century provoked a strong reaction among people and clergy, as did the menace of unrestricted warfare. At the council of Charroux in 989 it was suggested that the Church should act as the protector of the poor, and laws from Carolingian capitularies were adopted as Church law to this end. At the council of Le Puy in 990 and at other synods of the Church in southern France the idea was taken up, and was put into a solemn declaration at Poitiers in 1000, to which not only William of Aquitaine but also the French king subscribed. Quarrels were no longer to be settled by force of arms, but in the courts of justice, and the threat of excommunication was levelled at those inclined to think otherwise. By the second decade of the eleventh century, the movement had spread to northern France, despite some opposition from those who, like the bishop of Cambrai in 1023, objected that this was a matter for the temporal powers.

The protection under this peace movement extended in the first place to churches and clerics, and secondly to those liable to oppression, the merchants and peasants. Lords were not to destroy the peasants' livelihood; mills, vines and cattle were to be immune, though certain exceptions to the last were made. More important, however, was the general peace or 'truce of God' to be observed on certain days. This began with the Carolingian ban on private warfare on Sundays, and was revived in 1027 in southern France. Eventually the great festivals and the period from sunset on Wednesday to dawn on Monday, regarded as the vigil for Sunday, were included, and there was less time for war than peace'.[2]

Perhaps the movement might have had greater success if less had been demanded. As it was, from the council of Narbonne in 1054 onwards, the Church regarded these days of peace as sacrosanct, until the end of the Middle Ages. Yet in practice the First Crusade attacked Constantinople on Thursday of Holy Week, and it is hard to find a single instance where a battle was postponed because of the day. However, the rules were apparently observed during sieges, where they were less of an obstacle to military success: for instance, at Rouen in 1174 a one-day truce was declared on St Lawrence's Day,

215

10 August, during a siege by Louis VII, though the latter broke it with a surprise attack which was only just repulsed.

Popular enthusiasm for the truce of God was such, and the breaches of the laws of protection and peace-days so flagrant, that the idea of a militia to enforce the idea was soon mooted. At Bourges in 1038 such a confederation was formed by administering an oath to maintain order to all men over fifteen, but it became such a potential menace to public order with its own burning of castles (which were the strongholds of lawlessness in popular eyes) that Odo de Déols massacred its members after it had burnt an entire village. The objection to such movements was that the peasants and clergy were usurping functions which did not belong to them, and setting themselves up as arbiters of justice. Properly directed, and armed with royal authority, some degree of success might have been possible, but the peace armies resembled social revolution too closely to be tolerated.

On the borders of Christendom greater matters were afoot than the petty maraudings of feudal barons, matters which affected the whole Christian world. From the third century onwards, through all the vicissitudes of Roman, Byzantine and Muslim rule, pilgrims had gone to Jerusalem to worship at the Holy Places of Christendom. The custom had grown to considerable proportions in the tenth century as trade routes reopened and contacts with the east renewed, and had become a recognised form of penance for crimes. Pilgrimages were no longer purely matters of private enterprise, as the monks had begun to organise the means of travel, and pilgrims came from all corners of Europe, from Iceland to Sicily.

The journey to Jerusalem had always been difficult and dangerous, but the problems were those of any long journey at the time: brigands and bad roads, disease and famine. Though the Muslims had held Jerusalem since 638, they tolerated Christian visitors and even encouraged them. It is true that there was a brief interlude of persecution under the Caliph Hakim in the early eleventh century: the reasons for this change of policy are obscure, but as Hakim was a megalomaniac who finally declared himself divine, it seems to have been a purely personal action. His destruction of the Church of the Holy Sepulchre in 1009 had alarmed Christians everywhere, but they were reassured by his change of heart five years later. In 1020 he restored the damaged churches, and the numbers of pilgrims began to increase rapidly. By the mid-eleventh century, we hear of parties as large as 7,000 under the leadership of a German bishop. Such a large body evidently contained some kind of armed guard, for when they were attacked by Muslims, they fought a defensive action

216

lasting several days. Such attacks were by no means unknown, and in general there was no great change in conditions of pilgrimage. What was changing, however, was the attitude of the Papacy. The reformed Papacy of the eleventh century was now an aggressive temporal power as well, seeing itself as arbiter of Italy's affairs. It was thus by no means illogical for Leo IX to invoke war as a means of defence against his spiritual opponent, Benedict IX, and against the invading Normans in southern Italy in 1053. He led his troops in person on the latter expedition, and was defeated and captured at Cività, a fate which more orthodox contemporaries saw as a divine retribution, less for taking part in war at all than for using war as a means to temporal ends, though Leo had been careful to portray his campaign as being designed 'to liberate Christendom'. Those who fell at Cività were regarded by the Pope as martyrs, and a cult was instituted.

Hence papal sponsorship of the expedition against the Muslims in Spain in 1063 was by no means surprising. Any hint of early Christian pacifism had long since been eradicated from the strategy of the Curia; and the international force that was led by William Montreuil, 'Captain of the Cavalry of Rome' as a Muslim historian calls him, probably had a papal banner, and its members certainly enjoyed papal absolution in advance – as well they might, for their massacre of prisoners at Barbastro and subsequent lascivious existence, 'utter abandonment ... to the pleasures of the harem',[3] was hardly the behaviour expected.

The papal blessing on military expeditions was likewise used to political ends. By placing the later stages of the Norman conquest of Italy under its protection, and encouraging the Norman invasion of England (a papal banner was carried at Hastings), the Papacy obtained a nominal overlordship and tribute from both countries. Gregory VII used the same methods to support the commune of Milan in its early days, and transferred the *militia Christi* completely from the spiritual to the material world, raising armies of papal troops among his vassals and among mercenaries, by means of both financial and spiritual rewards. This scheme did not meet with any great success: yet the idea of the Pope as a summoner of armies and as a leader in warfare was established. Gregory VII attempted to use it in 1074 to further his favourite project of a union between the Orthodox and Catholic Churches, and appealed to 'all those who wish to defend the Christian faith'.[4] The response was small: only William of Aquitaine, who had fought in Spain in 1064, answered favourably, and the problems of Italian politics intervened before any definite plans could be made.

The idea of a holy war in itself, despite the great attraction of the East for pilgrims, was not enough to lure ordinary knights to undertake such lengthy and dangerous expeditions merely for the sake of adventure. Recent studies in economic history have suggested that there were more practical reasons for the eagerness of many knights to enlist for distant parts with only a slender chance of tangible reward. We have already come across the wandering, landless younger sons of knights: and it was precisely they who were becoming more numerous during the eleventh century. Rather than eke out an uncertain existence at home, they were ready to gamble on such expeditions, since the possible prizes, if they were ever achieved, were mouthwatering. This would explain the behaviour of the French army at Barbastro: whatever the motives of their leaders, booty was what interested their followers. The same dichotomy of attitude is a recurrent theme in later crusades: we shall find it in the Frankish troops revelling in Eastern pleasures on the Third Crusade, the diversion of the Fourth Crusade to Constantinople, and the sack of Alexandria by a crusade in 1365. The Papacy saw the crusades as a way of harnessing the concept of knighthood to spiritual ends: the knights saw them as a solution to earthly ills, with the promise of absolution and heavenly reward as well. Furthermore, by removing the discontented knights from their homes in the west, the popes believed that they would bring peace to Europe as well as helping their fellow-Christians in Palestine and Byzantium.

For help was needed urgently in the East. Hakim's whims had shown that the Christians in Jerusalem were at the mercy of their secular rulers. Though Muslim rule was comfortable enough, there was always a possibility of change, and with the advent of the Seljuk Turks the old ease of access disappeared, not because of religious hostility but from bad government, brigandage and extortionate taxation. The defeat of the armies of Byzantium at Manzikert in 1071 and the Seljuk capture of the great cities of Asia Minor along the pilgrim route meant that little help was likely to come from Eastern Christendom: and indeed both the emperors Michael VII and Alexius had appealed to the West for help against the invader. Urban II, who had in some measure re-established the papal position at home, had maintained friendly relations with Alexius; when the latter's envoys appealed for troops at the Council of Piacenza in March 1095, his own ideas on the Eastern problem had turned in the same direction. At the Council of Clermont in November 1095, he appealed for a crusading force. His exact words are lost, though we know that his speech was eloquent and aroused immense enthusiasm:

218

It seems that he began his speech by telling his hearers of the necessity for aiding their brethren in the East. Eastern Christendom had appealed for help; for the Turks were advancing into the heart of Christian lands, maltreating the inhabitants and desecrating their shrines. But it was not only of Romania [which is Byzantium] that he spoke. He stressed the special holiness of Jerusalem and described the sufferings of the pilgrims that journeyed there. Having painted the sombre picture, he made his great appeal. Let western Christendom march to the rescue of the East. Rich and poor alike should go. They should leave off slaying each other and fight instead a righteous war, doing the work of God: and God would lead them. For those that died in battle there would be absolution and the remission of sins. Life was miserable and evil here, with men wearing themselves out to the ruin of their bodies and their souls. Here they were poor and unhappy; there they would be joyful and prosperous and true friends of God. There must be no delay. Let them be ready to set out when the summer had come, with God to be their guide.[5]

His hearers, crying 'Deus le volt' (God wills it), crowded round him at the end of his speech, begging to be allowed to take part in the great expedition. But much planning was still needed, and though a series of resolutions were passed concerned with the administration of the crusade it was now a question of obtaining lay support. Those who wished to go were to vow not to turn back before Jerusalem, and in token of this to wear a red cross on their shoulders. They were to be ready to leave by August 1096. Constantinople was to be the place of assembly for the army so raised, and Byzantine support was expected. Adhémar, bishop of Le Puy, was named as leader and papal legate, for this was a holy expedition.

The secular response was overwhelming. Members of many of the leading families of France, the Low Countries and Italy, took the crusading vows, including Raymond of Toulouse and Bohemond of Taranto, the dukes of Flanders and Normandy, and Godfrey of Bouillon. Sermons by bishops and itinerant preachers brought in immense crowds of the common people, and one Peter the Hermit became the leader of what was a second, unofficial movement among the peasants, who may have understood him to promise to lead them out of their misery to a visionary Jerusalem of plenty. It was this expedition that departed first, a purely religious movement with little or no military pretensions; and it seriously hampered the real crusade, which followed some three months later, by its indiscipline at Constantinople. It finally came to a disastrous end on the coast just across from Constantinople, the peasants massacred in a Turkish ambush.

The leaders of the crusade proper were more cautious: for them God was indeed on their side, but they did not expect him to cause the obstacles that beset their path to crumble away like the walls of Jericho. The religious enthusiasm that had attended their original vows was nonetheless the mainstay of their morale, and remained so throughout. At the blackest moment of the whole expedition, when it seemed that, having taken Antioch, they would be starved into surrender by a relief force which was in turn besieging them, it was the finding of the Holy Lance, said to have pierced Christ's side at the Crucifixion, that restored their wavering faith: they made a successful sortie and drove off their besiegers. Whether the find was genuine or not, and there is strong evidence to suggest that it was invented by a cleric, the belief was what mattered. Those who doubted (including the Pope's deputy, Adhémar, bishop of Le Puy) held their tongues, seeing the value of miracles in a dispirited army. God favoured them once more, it seemed, and the discovery reassured them that they were indeed fighting for an invincible cause.

Again, the capture of Jerusalem in little under four weeks, with an army weary from its long journey, short of provisions, ill-equipped, and not large enough to encircle the city completely, was a remarkable feat. That it was accomplished at all was once more due to a revival of the enthusiasm which had originally launched the crusade. Though the garrison was small, the great danger was the arrival of a relieving force from Egypt. Hence it was realised from the beginning that action would have to be swift, and a general assault was attempted within five days of arrival, but failed for lack of siege-ladders. The arrival of the materials needed for siege-towers improved the situation, and two huge siege-castles were begun. As time ran out, the army grew exhausted and dispirited in the great heat; but once again a vision came to their aid. A three-day fast was enjoined, and a solemn procession round the walls ended with three sermons from the finest preachers in the army. The old fire was rekindled, and with victory so near, the great towers were completed in two days. The general assault, which began on the night of 13 July, ended on the afternoon of the 15th, and the triumphant crusaders poured into Jerusalem.

It was a triumph marred in the very hour of its achievement. Knowing that all Christians had been expelled from the city before the siege began, the Franks repeated the horrors they had already perpetrated earlier, at Antioch, on a grander scale: almost all the inhabitants were slaughtered by the Christian soldiers, whose enthusiasm had turned to fanaticism. It was a moment of folly and bloodthirstiness which was to be repaid in full by an enemy whose instincts might otherwise have been far more civilised.

For as the crusade had made its weary way across Europe and Asia Minor, it had become clear that even the highest and holiest of wars was still much the same as other wars, and that an army dedicated to God's service was as sinful as any other. It is true that there had been no scenes of complete riot such as the massacres of Jews in Germany for which the wilder elements of the people's crusade had been responsible. There was, on the other hand, no lack of quarrels between leaders and indiscipline among the troops, perhaps because there were a number of minor princes but no one great figure in overall command. In Byzantine territory, towns had been plundered, and the Emperor, Alexius Comnenus, had had to put a heavy escort on guard in order to prevent such excesses. His well-founded doubts as to the army's good behaviour had been confirmed by an attack on Constantinople itself on Maundy Thursday, which was partly a political move by the less responsible leaders, and partly a protest by the troops against what they considered to be the inhospitality of the Greeks.

The very nature of the crusading enterprise tended to attract those men who were least amenable to discipline: the adventurers and the landless, lawless younger sons outnumbered the devout lords of settled estates who had come only at the dictates of their belief. Even Godfrey of Bouillon, whom later ages transformed into a golden hero, had some political reasons for setting out. Added to the temptations of adventure itself, was the possibility of winning great estates in the East, and men who might not have been interested in mere soldiering came because there were hopes of a fortune to be won. On the other hand, this provided the Frankish kingdom of Jerusalem with its original settlers, and meant that the moment of triumph could be turned into a material achievement: without these men, there would have been no permanent Christian state in the East.

Again, the crusade might have been inspired by religious ideals, but it moved among political realities. The problems of the crusaders at Constantinople were greatly complicated by the Byzantine claims to overlordship of the Holy Land, and the oaths of loyalty which Alexius demanded in order to safeguard that title. And it proved impossible to reconcile religion and politics either in the organisation of the crusade or in the structure of the new state. The leadership came from secular princes, with secular aims: Baldwin of Boulogne saw his opportunity at Edessa, and founded a principality there, while Bohemond claimed Antioch as his own. Only at Jerusalem itself did idealism briefly prevail. Godfrey of Bouillon ruled there not as king, but as 'advocate of the Holy Sepulchre', refusing to wear a royal crown

221

in the city where Christ had been crowned with thorns. But there was no ecclesiastical figure of sufficient stature either to assume leadership of the crusade or to control the barons of the new state. Adhémar of Le Puy provided wise counsel, but was unable to assert his authority against the headstrong lords; and with his death at Antioch, the ecclesiastical element lost much of its influence. Baldwin of Edessa was crowned king of Jerusalem on Godfrey's death, despite the latter's wish that the Patriarch of the city should be ruler of the Franks in Palestine. Visions had yielded to the needs of the moment: the knights who had settled in the East understood only the familiar forms of government.

And so in times of peace the Frankish settlements of Outremer (Overseas), as it came to be called, were no different from their European counterparts; their institutions were closely modelled on those of their homelands, and normal relations began to be established with the surrounding, infidel, states. It was only in times of distress that the crusading cry was raised, when the forces of the new state were inadequate against the greater resources of their Muslim foes. The crusading ideal was a state of permanent war against the heathen which was far beyond the resources of the settlers, and which would have made the establishment of a settled Christian state well nigh impossible. In practice, as the First Crusade had shown, it resulted in a mixture of petty jealousies, bad organisation and credulousness on the one hand, and immense resolve and real religious enthusiasm on the other. The discipline of the time was not strong enough to contain the zeal aroused by crusading; in the hour of triumph, religion was seen to have provided abundant fervour, but all too few moral qualities. The balance between ideal and reality remained unachieved.

The First Crusade had been conceived as an expedition which would settle once and for all the control of the Holy Places. Its triumph echoed through Europe, and in the confidence it engendered the disasters which overtook those crusaders who had set out after the main expedition went unnoticed. Annihilated by the Turkish armies of Kilij Arslan in Asia Minor, very few escaped with their lives, let alone reached Palestine. Because these reverses were ignored, the realisation that the victory of 1099 was not a permanent one did not penetrate men's minds until the third decade of the twelfth century. The newly formed Military Orders and the resources of Outremer seemed sufficient, until in 1146 Antioch was threatened by a Muslim army which had already overpowered Edessa. The weakness of the Frankish position now became evident, and an appeal went out to the West.

The Second Crusade set out when the memory of the First was still fresh in men's minds, and the response it aroused was great. Its failure to take Damascus and subsequent ignominious retreat seriously damaged the philosophy behind the crusade, because much of the morale of the crusader depended on his conviction that he was invincible, protected by the God for whom he was fighting. The reverses might be attributed to sinfulness on the part of those involved, but such excuses wore thin as expedition after expedition failed to achieve its objectives. The problems facing crusades were persistently underestimated for the same reason; to an age which was convinced that God gave the victory to the righteous in secular battles, His help seemed certain in so holy a cause.

The Second Crusade had set out in response to a specific crisis; after the disaster at Hattin in 1187, when the army of the kingdom of Jerusalem was annihilated, King Guy was captured, and the Holy Cross fell into infidel hands, the state of crisis was to remain almost permanent, especially as Jerusalem was now under Muslim rule again, and remained so except for a brief interval from 1229–44. The crusader could once more hope to achieve the glory of reconquering the Holy Places. Within two years of the disaster, the Third Crusade reached Outremer, and even though the Emperor Frederick Barbarossa had been drowned en route, two kings, Philip Augustus of France and Richard Cœur de Lion, were its leaders. The response had been universal, exceeding even that for the First Crusade, among the knights of the West; it was well organised and equipped, lacking only an overall commander. With the departure of Philip owing to a quarrel with Richard which had developed en route, the latter was left in sole command; and only Saladin's astuteness as a diplomat and skill as a general was sufficient to prevent him from achieving the recapture of Jerusalem. The eventual failure of the Third Crusade was even more damaging, in a different way, than that of the Second: the greatest princes of the West had made common cause, and had still failed to attain their goal.

Worse was still to come, with the Fourth Crusade's attack on Byzantium. At the beginning of the First Crusade, the West was not politically involved in the Mediterranean beyond Sicily; but increasing attention was paid to the possibilities of diplomatic manœuvres which would strengthen the position of the Frankish kingdom, and trading interests in the area had been built up by the Italians. Venetian hopes of commercial gain, the presence of a pretender to the Byzantine throne, and, more distantly, papal dreams of a reunion of the Roman and Orthodox Churches combined to divert the crusade

223

from its original objective, Egypt, to the destruction of the Greek empire. This was disastrous both in its tangible effects on the balance of power in the East and its impact on the crusading ideal. Europe was treated to the spectacle of an entire crusade being excommunicated, while Byzantium never recovered from the blow. The Latin empire which was established there was too concerned with maintaining its own precarious power to assist future crusades. It is only fair to say that the Venetians duped and blackmailed the crusaders at every turn, exploiting their shortage of money, and to this extent poor organisation was to blame. It was extremely difficult to raise a crusading tithe without the full royal support which the Third Crusade had enjoyed. Nor was there a leader of sufficient stature to resist the Venetian demands, though some crusaders, to their credit, left the expedition before its raids on Christian territory, and sailed straight for Palestine.

It was only with the Sixth Crusade in 1249 that a capable leader again appeared at the head of an army in the East. St Louis was the most remarkable of all crusaders. His stern devotion to religion and justice had something of the puritan in it; he refused at first to entertain any approaches from the infidel, showed no mercy to those who broke his laws, and lived an austere life in an age when monarchy and ostentation were usually synonymous. That such a man should respond to the appeal for a crusade after the second fall of Jerusalem was only to be expected. The interval between his taking the crusading vows in December 1244 and his departure in August 1248 was occupied by elaborate preparations, and a large number of the French nobility joined the expedition. There were very few contingents from other countries, a symptom of the rising national feeling within Europe. But even Louis failed to overcome the vast problems that now beset any attempt at a large-scale campaign in the East. He took Damietta, and could have exchanged it for Jerusalem, only to be betrayed by the indiscipline of his brother at Mansourah when a great victory was almost within the crusaders' grasp. What had begun triumphantly ended in dark defeat: Louis and his whole army were captured, and the price in lives and ransom was enormous. Even the years of his wise government of Outremer after his release could not repair the damage.

And yet, despite popular murmurings in the West, the crusade was not discredited, nor the crusaders discouraged. The theory behind the crusades began to take a different shape. The crusading movement had to some extent originated in the Papacy's attempts to wield secular power against its enemies, and had always included a certain number of expeditions of this type, whether directly instigated by or merely approved by the Pope. A crusade could be used to suppress a dissident monarch: Innocent iv had appealed for an attack on the heir of Frederick ii in 1251; or it could be used against heretics, as in the blood-thirsty Albigensian crusade of 1209–12. The political and religious reasons which led to the destruction of the counts of Provence and the laying waste of the fertile lands of the south were complex, and to call a crusade against heretics whose preaching against early corruption had won much sympathy seemed to be making such campaigns a means of doing the Church's work rather than God's. The success of Frederick ii's expedition in 1228–9, when he negotiated the return of Jerusalem while still excommunicate, did little to strengthen men's faith.

The later crusades, with the exception of St Louis' attempt to convert the Emir of Tunis by a show of arms in 1270, begin to look like an extension of the search for *gloire*, renown. Knightly conduct was above all governed by tradition, and tradition decreed that crusading was one of the great knightly activities. Henceforward it was to be either younger men who became crusaders, men who had not yet come into their inheritance, as though an expedition to the East was part of their training for high estate; or men who had never lost their youthful vision of knightly fame. The secular knights who in all earnestness regarded the crusade as a holy war – and they had once been legion – dwindled to a mere handful, and those who had once gone on crusade in the hope of making their fortune realised that the East offered little prospect of riches. Both types of knight had a real cause for which to fight; they were replaced by men whose incentives were less powerful.

Nor were conditions in the East growing more favourable to the success of the crusades. Egypt and the lands to the east of Palestine had been weak and internally divided at the time of the First Crusade; there had been dissensions since then, but the passage of time had seen the rise of a formidable kingdom in Egypt which finally destroyed the Frankish kingdom of Jerusalem in 1291, and without a foothold in the Holy Land, the last real impetus of the crusading movement faded into dreams and visions.

14

The Military Orders in Palestine

Once the initial impetus which had carried the First Crusade into Jerusalem and established the Frankish kingdom in Palestine began to wane, the problems raised by a Christian state dependent on the West in such remote lands began to appear. The Holy War gave way to pilgrimages again; and instead of the crusading forces, lightly armed bands of pilgrims began to make their way through Asia Minor to Jerusalem. What the Frankish knights needed were either settlers or reinforcements, not this added liability; they existed uneasily with the indifferent support or downright hostility of the native population on whom they depended for the daily necessities of life. The crusade had been launched to recover the Holy Places for Christendom; but Western Christendom had never possessed them before, and was unwilling to face the problems of maintaining them: the Eastern Empire was not disposed to support the intruders to any extent.

The Kingdom of Jerusalem had arisen in the absence of any planned alternative; and in these first decades it was chiefly concerned with preserving its own existence, rather than with the function of guardian of the Holy Places with which it found itself endowed. Yet pilgrims could not be turned away; they had therefore to be protected. In the absence of official action, it was left to a small group of knights to act. Under one Hugh de Payens, they banded together to protect pilgrims on passage and to guard and keep open the public roads. Soon after their pact was made, in 1118, King Baldwin granted them a royal house near the Temple as their residence; the association became formal when they took a vow before the Patriarch of Jerusalem, in the usual monastic form of poverty, obedience and chastity. It seems most probable, in the absence of all records of these early years, that the idea of an association to protect pilgrims must have preceded that of a monastic vow. The latter was the means of giving the group a coherent form: and it was probably chosen to underline the devotional nature of the undertaking. For the idea of an order at once military and religious would have been almost unthinkable anywhere except in Palestine. 'He that liveth by the sword shall perish by the sword', had been the Church's teaching since time immemorial; and the preaching of a Holy War was a revolutionary enough idea, invoked only in order to recover Jerusalem. To combine monasticism and war was to make a temporary departure from scriptural teaching into a permanent change of attitude.

But the 'poor knights of Christ', as they called themselves, were too urgently needed for anyone to raise objections; and once they turned from merely defending pilgrims to a more general war to keep the infidel at bay and preserve the whole Frankish kingdom, active support began to increase. Fulk of Anjou gave the knights £30 in silver in 1120; and their riches soon began to accumulate. By 1126 the knights were too influential to remain a merely local arrangement between king, patriarch and members; and a rule on the lines of those granted to the normal monastic orders was sought from the Pope.

The rule of the Templars and their status in relation to the rest of the Church was determined by two documents: the rule granted at the Council of Troyes in 1128, and the bull *Omne datum optimum* of Innocent II in 1139. The original precepts which the brothers followed had been simply those of the Augustinian canons, with the three vows of chastity, poverty and obedience. But something more specific was needed for a body whose importance and wealth were rapidly increasing, and Baldwin III enlisted for the purpose one of the great figures of the Christian West, Bernard of Clairvaux. Bernard had been the chief instrument in the spread of the new Cistercian rule and the revival of monasticism; and in some ways the military Orders were very much part of this movement. He had been a vigorous supporter of the Temple when its existence was still uncertain, and had written a pamphlet in support of their ideals, *De laude novae militiae* (In praise of the new soldiery)[1] in which he contrasts the luxury and indolence of secular knights with the poverty and zeal that the Templars ought to possess. The rule of the Templars, which served as model for that of the Hospitallers, was largely the work of Bernard and Hugh de Payens; and it in turn is largely based on the Cistercian rule.[2]

The hierarchy of the Order was carefully defined. The Grand Master, or more simply, the Master, enjoyed wide powers, but there were severe restrictions nonetheless. He could dispose of minor matters as he wished, and was even allowed his own treasury. If, however, the question of a gift of the Order's land, alteration of a decree of the Grand Chapter, or admission of a candidate came up, he had to refer it to the Grand Chapter of the Order. Any diplomatic problem had to be decided by them, such as the signing of treaties or declaring of war; the military undertakings such as sieges required their approval. The Grand Chapter consisted of high officers and seems to have varied with the subject to be discussed; it was paralleled by lower chapters with jurisdiction over a single province, who could be summoned by the local master. Besides the Master, the central officers consisted of the Seneschal, the Master's deputy; and the Marshal, who was responsible for the direction of military affairs. The commanders of provinces made up the remainder of the senior hierarchy. The commander of the land and Kingdom of Jerusalem acted as treasurer, the commander of the city of Jerusalem as hospitaller was responsible for the welfare of pilgrims; while the nine remaining commanders, of Tripoli, Antioch, France, England, Poitou, Aragon, Portugal, Apulia and Hungary, had no special tasks beyond those entailed by the care of their respective provinces. The provinces were divided into houses, each again with its commander, and the houses were controlled by the knights-commander acting as the latter's lieutenant. The organisation was thus equally well adapted for monastic and military discipline: in war, the divisions of command in the field corresponded to the administrative ranks.

The everyday administration and discipline of the Order was in the hands of the ordinary Chapters, at which all Knights were bound to attend. The disciplinary assemblies followed a strict formula. The president, usually the commander of the house, would give a brief address; and any brother who felt he had committed a breach of the Order's rules would then kneel and confess. Minor matters could be dealt with on the spot; major offences would be reserved for higher judgment. The list of crimes and penalties gives some idea of the strictness of the Order's life and the chief problems of discipline. Since members of the Order owed no secular allegiance, all the cases covered by the normal communal code fell within the scope of the rule. The severest penalty, expulsion from the Order, was reserved for only one of the usual criminal cases, murder; but eight offences which injured the Order were punished in this way. These included treason and desertion, heresy, purchasing entry into the Order, plotting among the brothers, revelation of the Order's secrets. The most unusual entry is that of 'absence without leave', 'quitting the house other than by the main door', and being away from the house for more than two nights if more than the bare essentials of clothing had been taken. Offenders against these laws were to be sent at once to an even stricter order, preferably Benedictine or Augustine in rule, to expiate their sins. For men trained to fighting and action, the peace of a monastery must have been punishment indeed. Lesser offences, such as disobedience, consorting with women, and attempting to escape from the Order, were punished by the loss of privileges for a year, which meant living with the Order's slaves, deprived of horse, arms and habit. Really serious cases of any of these crimes could lead to imprisonment, sometimes perpetual, in one of the Order's castles.

Some of the knights went to the other extreme, and pursued their religious avocation too far, though this was the exception rather than the rule. Jacques de Vitry, bishop of Acre from 1216, tells of an amusing incident in one of his homilies addressed to the Order. One of the brethren was so assiduous about fasting, being more interested in piety than valour, that when he rode into battle, he was unhorsed by the first blow he received. Another knight, at some risk to his own life, picked him up and put him back on his horse; whereupon he fell off again as soon as he received another blow. As he was remounted for the second time, the knight who had helped him said: 'If you fall off again, Sir Bread-and-Water, it won't be me who picks you up.'[3]

The desired rule was granted at the Council of Troyes in 1128, and the increased prestige confirmed by becoming an Order was at once reflected in increased numbers and riches. The first gift of land to the knights, now known as Templars from their residence near the Temple in Jerusalem, was in Portugal in the same year. Hugh de Payens travelled throughout Europe seeking men and money for the Order of which he was now Master. He was well received everywhere. Provinces of the Order arose in Portugal, Aragon, Castile, England and France. These in turn were divided into preceptories, whose object was to administer the gifts made to the Templars, whether land or money, and to furnish the warriors in Palestine with recruits and financial support. Besides gifts, the Order recruited some notable figures, including Raymond Berenger III, count of Barcelona, in 1130.

The first offensive action in which the Templars took part was Baldwin's expedition to Antioch, after Hugh de Payens' return to Palestine in 1130 with some 300 knights recruited for the crusade. Ironically, this was against rebellious barons within the kingdom; and it was not until 1147, with the arrival of the Second Crusade, that they saw real operations against the infidel. The intervening years must have seen skirmishes, but nothing that the chroniclers deemed worthy of record. A lack of men prevented the Franks from planning offensives in these years; the combined strength of the Temple and such feudal forces as could be raised was overawed by the might of Islam, drawn from a much wider area. As long as the Christians remained on the defensive, these forces were disunited, interested in their own internal squabbles; but an offensive campaign had to reckon with the possibility of a united resistance. That the Templars fought during this period is shown by their use of a battle-cry, 'Beauséant', after their black-and-white battle standard. But the decade was primarily one of consolidation, the acquisition of new land, and their gradual acceptance as one of the stable forces in the eminently unstable kingdom.

The great privileges of the Order date from the bull of Innocent II, *Omne datum optimum*, probably granted in 1139. For the Order owed no secular allegiance; and this bull, originally designed to provide for the spiritual needs of the Order by giving it its own clergy and churches, freed it from the only immediate rulers it had, the bishops. It could appoint priests and build places of prayer without reference to anyone; and above all it was exempted from tithes, a privilege it shared with the Cistercians alone. Even if this last right was not at once exploited to the full, the Order was exercising it at the end of the twelfth century, and the bishops of Palestine never forgave them for it; their anger still thunders in the pages of William of Tyre and his followers, from whom the history of Palestine must largely be written. Perhaps that is why we hear so much more of Templar treachery than of Templar bravery, a suspicion that is confirmed when we find another conflict with the local clergy between 1198 and 1212: Innocent III had to reprove the latter for their hostility towards the Templars over their right to an annual appeal for alms in every parish.

The efforts of the Templars had not gone unnoticed among the brethren of the Hospital of St John the Baptist, who had long cared for the pilgrims visiting Jerusalem. This establishment, an offshoot of the monastery of St Mary of the Latins, had come into being after some merchants from Amalfi had been given land in Jerusalem by one of the Egyptian caliphs, which they had used for these pious purposes. The monks had come from Italy and were Benedictines; they had already been caring for visitors to Jerusalem for nearly half a century when Hugh de Payens formed his band of knights. With the coming of Frankish rule, they had benefited greatly from the charity of the foreign knights, and from the new rulers of the Church. They also enjoyed royal patronage, and Baldwin I confirmed their already wide lands in a charter of 1112 witnessed by the new Patriarch of Jerusalem, Arnulf.

These newly acquired riches, and donations made to it in Europe, enabled the Hospital, as it was usually known, to set up an international organisation for the care of pilgrims, with hospices strategically sited throughout the pilgrim ports of France and Italy. Under its governor, Gerard, it became an Order in its own right, and this was confirmed in a bull of 1113. Its independence was recognised, and it was taken under papal protection, giving the Master a standing equal to that of a secular prince or an archbishop. The impetus of these early years was maintained under the two succeeding masters, especially in terms of the lands acquired, and the development of the rule. In a document of the 1130s, the Augustinian rule was adopted, with additions emphasising the duty to the poor and the sick, and disciplinary regulations which enjoin that all brothers shall wear the cross, thus identifying them with the crusaders proper.

In all this there is no word of military activity. Both the date and reasons for the change from charity to the sword, and hence the appearance of the Hospitallers as the second of the great military orders, are obscure. The care of pilgrims might easily be extended to include their defence from attack; and parties going on pilgrimage very rarely went without some kind of armament. Likewise, the whole of Frankish Palestine remained throughout its existence to a lesser or greater degree in a state of war, and any gift of property was bound to entail the possibility that it might have to be defended. For both these activities, hired troops may have been used. The first references to the Hospitallers' involvement in warfare all imply the assumption of defensive responsibilities without saying how these were carried out, and even in the 1170s a traveller could write of the Order 'which sustains many persons in its castles, instructed in all arts of war, for the defence of the lands of the Christians against the incursions of the Saracens'.[4]

The gifts received in the early years were free from direct military obligations, and the first recorded acquisition of a castle is in 1136, when Fulk built the key fortress of Bethgibelin in the south, on the Hospital's land, and then gave it to the Order with the idea that the latter's rich revenues could be made to contribute to the costs of defence. That this arrangement was successful is implied by the gift eight years later of a very much larger responsibility in the north, in the principality of Tripoli, on terms which were entirely in the Hospitallers' hands; and other donations which followed were in the same pattern of great privileges in return for the defence of dangerous and difficult positions. By 1150 these new duties were almost certainly reflected within the Order by the appearance of a small class of knights serving as lay brothers, though the duties of these were probably strictly limited. Even in the 1180s, the Hospital was primarily a charitable order and only incidentally a feudal force.

Nonetheless, the military side had greatly increased between 1150 and 1180. In 1168 we find it raising 500 knights and a number of native mercenaries at its own expense, for an ill-starred expedition to Egypt. If the venture had succeeded, the Order was to have received lands in return for its expenses, so its motives were not entirely altruistic; and it entered into similar agreements at Antioch, where it was given borderlands which had long since been in Saracen hands. Certainly its knights, whether actual members of the Order, knights holding fiefs from the Hospital, or merely hired troops acting in its name, had acquired a reputation as early as 1157, when a column relieving one of the Hospitaller castles was ambushed, and Nur-ed-Din gave orders for all prisoners to be executed, a measure which was repeated on later occasions when the Order had definitely become a military organisation. That attempts to increase its military element were afoot is shown by the admonishments of Alexander III, in a bull of about 1179, that they should not depart from their original objectives.

It was only after the disaster at Hattin, and the accession of Lucius III, that a change in the papal attitude took place. It seems to have been a recognition of a *de facto* situation rather than active encouragement, but without the approval of the Pope as the Order's ultimate ruler, any continued activity would have been impossible. At all events, the development of the official military institutions of the Hospital was very rapid from this period, and it is hard to see how, in such a warlike state, any other solution would have been possible. Their wealth made them politically influential; and politics were largely concerned with war policies. Besides, the increasing disarray of the secular barons now left the Orders as one of the chief stable forces in the kingdom, and any move to reduce their power would reduce both the chances of internal peace and the strength of Palestine's defences, which had now come to rest largely on the quasi-military gifts to the Hospital and Temple. The burden was such that it had already brought the Hospital near to financial disaster in the 1160s.

Had a strong king emerged in Jerusalem in the latter part of the twelfth century, it is possible that the growth of the Hospital's military power might have been checked, or at least taken a different course; but Guy of Lusignan and his successors were either too weak or were thwarted by events beyond their control, and the loss of Jerusalem demoralised the laymen even more than the Orders, who could make fresh appeals for men and money from the West.

Yet the Hospitallers still remained an officially ecclesiastical institution. It was not until 1206, some sixty years after the establishment of the Knights Templar that the statutes were revised to provide for military brethren at an assembly at Margat. Until that time only the presence of lay brothers was laid down in the rule and the Statutes of Margat are not an amendment to the original foundation, though they were regarded as almost equally binding. That the brothers of the Hospital themselves had fought the Saracens since the 1140s seems almost certain: but they did so unofficially, even if it was in defence of the Order's estates. The Marshal, who first appears in the 1160s, was probably responsible for the levying of mercenary troops at first, but had become a military commander by the Egyptian expedition of 1168. At Margat, this situation was embodied as part of the Order's institution, and a military force which had grown up haphazardly, partly as a practical measure, partly at the behest of the barons who had wearied of border warfare, and partly at least in emulation of the Templars, at last received recognition. The previous existence of the Temple meant that its rules were bound to be based in large measure on theirs; and there were the same restrictions as to entry, that a man must be qualified for secular knighthood before entering the Order. The qualification, however, was not formally set out until 1262, when the test of legitimate noble birth appears. Those who could not join as knights were admitted as sergeants, though they could very occasionally attain knighthood later; and no distinction of dress was made between them and the knights, despite attempts to introduce different garments after the Templar practice.

The military organisation of the Hospital rapidly overtook its charitable counterpart in prestige. By the end of the thirteenth century all the important offices were in the hands of the knights, and the Marshal ranked second only to the Grand Master in authority. He was concerned as much with supply as organisation, and the difficulties of obtaining equipment and especially horses meant that stringent rules had to be laid down. In this the strict discipline of the order was of great assistance, and increased the superiority of the Hospitallers as troops over their secular brethren. We know little about the details of the military discipline imposed, and it is to the Rule of the Templars that we must turn for a picture of life within the Orders. For the Hospitallers, only scraps survive to give us a glimpse of what went on; and it does not seem to have differed greatly from the Templar way of life. The address to the candidate who wished to enter the Order shows many of its characteristics:

> Good friend, you desire the company of the House and you are right in this, for many gentlemen earnestly request the reception of their children or their friends and are most joyful when they can place them in this Order. And if you are willing to be in so excellent and so honourable a company and in so holy an Order as that of the Hospital, you are right in this. But if it is because you see us well clothed, riding on great chargers and having everything for our comfort, then you are misled, for when you would desire to eat, it will be necessary for you to fast, and when you would wish to fast, you will have to eat. And when you would desire to sleep, it will be necessary for you to keep watch, and when you would like to stand on watch, you will have to sleep. And you will be sent this side of the sea and beyond, into places which will not please you, and you will have to go there. It will be necessary for you therefore to abandon all your desires to fulfil those of another and to endure other hardships in the Order, more than I can describe to you.[5]

The total establishment of the Hospitallers in Palestine remained small despite their great influence. Recent estimates put the figure as low as three hundred in all, since when Hospitaller casualties after a battle were counted these very often included knights serving for pay or feudal service. To lose forty knights, as at Tripoli in 1289, meant that recruits had to be found from the West as a matter of urgency. Hence the exceptional power of the Order stemmed less from its resources of men within its own ranks, than from its military and financial organising ability, and its knowledge of the country. Yet it was not in command of unlimited resources, and many of the hesitations and political errors which mar its record are due to a realisation of the weakness of the Order in relation to the task with which it found itself entrusted. Despite its wide estates in Europe, it was always difficult not only to raise enough surplus cash for Palestine but also to arrange for its safe and rapid transport: the tangible results of an urgent appeal to the prior of the Order in England or Spain would not reach the East for a year or more.

The lesson had to be learnt by experience. For the moment it was war to the death: no Templar was ever ransomed, and both Templar and Hospitaller prisoners were often killed by their captors. Losses could be enormous: about four hundred knights were killed in one ambush in 1156. Though this includes mercenary and other troops, it must have seriously reduced the actual Templar establishment of about five hundred knights. Replacement was slow, since the news took between two and six months to reach Europe, and the recruits had then to be found and equipped. As with financial appeals, it might take a year or more to restore even part of the number.

As the Orders grew more powerful their interests did not always coincide with those of the kingdom of Jerusalem as a whole. The Frankish settlement was small compared with the great powers of the East: it could only hope to survive by presenting a united front and by exploiting the frequent dissensions among the Muslims to the utmost. Instead, the various parties within the kingdom tended to pursue their own ends, and even to bring in Muslim help if they could see a way of doing so. And in addition to the king, the barons, and the Church within the state, the Orders also had to work with frequent crusades and papal interventions.

The weakness of the royal power in Outremer arose partly from the constitution, which did not provide sufficient authority over unruly barons, but in the main it was the character of the kings themselves that destroyed any hope of leadership from that quarter. The bravest and most able of the rulers, Baldwin IV, was a leper; and none of the succeeding kings was as capable as Baldwin I, the founder of the kingdom. Indeed, it is not difficult to see the history of Outremer as a steady decline from the strength of the state that he ruled. The problem was complicated by a lack of direct descendants, with all the multiplicity of claimants and intrigues for the throne that this entailed. The Orders never played a very respectable part in such affairs. They were too independent to welcome strong rule wholeheartedly; and in any case the Hospitallers were supporters of royal authority, the Templars advocating a strong barony instead, even when they were not each trying to secure the accession of a favoured candidate. As the Orders' power increased, it became more and more difficult for the kings to challenge their authority when they misused it. Even by 1170, the Templars often acted independently of royal officers, and opposed royal foreign policy. They argued fiercely against an Egyptian expedition in 1169, and four years later resisted a royal treaty with the Assassin sect, whose fanatical members were more concerned with the internal politics of Islam than with the Christians. This potentially valuable alliance was prevented when the Templars ambushed and killed the Assassin ambassadors, probably because the treaty would have meant the loss of the tribute which the Assassins had paid to the Templars. Nor would the Grand Master surrender the culprits to the king, claiming that he was responsible to the Pope alone.

This independence of action was accentuated by the rivalry between the two Orders. It is rare to find Templars and Hospitallers agreeing on important issues, despite much valuable co-operation at lesser levels, and it sometimes seems as though one Order's approval of a project meant that the other was bound to oppose it. Only in the difficult days after Saladin's invasion and almost complete conquest of the kingdom in 1195 did they work together in the political field: in 1219, on the Fifth Crusade, both Masters opposed the offer of the return of a defenceless Jerusalem as being a military burden which they could not shoulder, and in 1229 they both boycotted Frederick II when he won back Jerusalem, supporting the papal sentence of excommunication which had been pronounced on him for his intolerable delays in setting out on crusade. But these cases were still to prove exceptions. In the years following 1240, the Templars' and Hospitallers' diplomatic and political moves were aimed less against the infidel than against each other. One Order made peace with Damascus, the other with Egypt; one supported the baronial faction, the other Frederick II's viceroy, to the extent that Christendom was treated to the sight of Templars and Hospitallers shedding each other's blood in the streets of Acre. Only disasters such as that at La Forbie in 1244, when the Egyptians and their allies overwhelmed the entire Frankish army, taught them that co-operation was imperative. In 1258, a treaty was drawn up to govern the settlement of quarrels between them, but by now the pressure from Egypt was too great, and the most superhuman efforts would have been wasted.

At worst, the Orders' independence of action became mere rashness and pride in their own power. The Templars could be as heedless of consequences as their wilder baronial allies, like Reynald of Chatillon, whose persistent breach of truces became a byword. What Reynald did for gain, men like Gerard de Ridfort did for glory. As early as 1153, Templar indiscipline at the siege of Ascalon had nearly brought about the failure of the entire operation; a fortunate chance (the burning of a siege-machine by the defenders) caused a breach in the section of the wall opposite the Templar encampment. So determined were they to have the glory of the victory that a band of forty men entered the city while others prevented the rest of the army from following. The result was a massacre of the knights within the walls which almost caused the abandonment of the siege, though in the event the town fell at the next assault. Gerard de Ridfort's activities in 1187 as Grand Master of the Templars were far more serious

236

in their consequences. He first attacked a vastly superior Muslim force, although warned of its size, with a mere handful of knights of whom only three, including Gerard, survived. Since the four hundred or so who fell were all members or auxiliaries of the Order, this was a serious blow to its strength; but when Gerard tried to seek revenge, an overwhelming disaster ensued. Saladin had assembled a vast army, and King Guy was persuaded not to risk battle. Gerard, however, crept to his tent at night, and obtained the order to advance. The defeat that ensued (Battle of Hattin, 1189), led to the fall of Jerusalem, and indeed of the whole kingdom save only the fortress at Tyre. The lesson was learnt, albeit late, and under the new Grand Master, Robert du Sablé, caution prevailed: we find him, together with the Hospitaller Grand Master, counselling that saddest of all retreats, the withdrawal from Jerusalem in 1191 when Richard Cœur de Lion's generalship had brought the Third Crusade so near its goal. Only in the dying days of the kingdom did the fighting spirit of the Orders show to best advantage, in the series of desperate resistances put up by isolated garrisons against the Egyptians' vastly superior forces in the 1270s and 1280s.

Similarly, neither of the Orders found it easy to co-operate with crusaders coming from the West. There were good reasons for this. The Orders were deeply involved in the affairs of Outremer, which was their home, and did not welcome the inexpert counsel of eager crusaders, who hoped to solve in a year the problems which the Orders had wrestled with for decades. When the crusaders were safely home, it was they who would be left with the crusade's legacy of untenable fortresses won or patiently earned goodwill squandered. It was such long term views that accounted for their discouraging attitude towards the terms proposed on the Fifth Crusade which would have given them a Jerusalem which they could not defend. Besides this, the inevitable arguments over leadership emerged in the motley armies which set out on campaign: while the Orders were ready to provide generous contingents, they were also reluctant to obey commanders newly arrived from the West. And men who had crossed the Mediterranean to fight the infidel were usually reluctant to listen to diplomatic arguments; they had come to destroy Islam with the sword, and all too often only bitter experience taught them what the Orders already knew: that Outremer was merely a small, relatively weak, state trying to survive among powerful neighbours, and diplomacy was frequently the only possible weapon. The Franks had at all costs to prevent the Muslim princes from uniting: and military operations always tended to drive their opponents into alliances.

Furthermore, the Orders found difficulty in organising both their defensive garrisons, which were essential to protect the country if a campaign was going badly, and a field army to mount the attack. Even for a small raid in 1187, the Templars had to empty one castle of its entire garrison to find enough troops. They came to rely on Turcopoles, lightly armed local troops, who were naturally less reliable under difficult conditions, or on the intermittent presence of crusading armies from the west, and this tendency merely increased their defensive, cautious attitude.

The Orders had begun to develop good relations with the Muslims as early as the 1140s, and cultural interchanges became frequent. The Arab historian Ousama ibn Mounkidh relates that Franks and Saracens used to travel together, telling each other stories to while away the journey. Again, despite the apparent insensitivity of Templar politics at the time, the story of his visit to Jerusalem in 1144 shows that as individuals they respected the Muslims. Ibn Mounkidh made friends with the Templars and was allowed to pray to Allah in a church which had once been a mosque, but now belonged to the Order. One day, as he was in the middle of his prayers, facing south towards Mecca, a Frankish knight seized him and faced him to the east, saying 'That's the way you should pray'. The Templars expelled the knight from the church, but he crept in again, and repeated his action. The Templars dealt with him and apologised to ibn Mounkidh, saying that the offender had only just arrived in Palestine and had never seen anyone pray towards Mecca before. Similarly, the friendly exchanges between Richard I and Saladin encouraged an attitude of tolerance, though it was by no means an unquestioning one: the frequency with which the Orders had broken their truces had led Saladin, after the battle of Hattin, to have all the Templar and Hospitaller prisoners executed by their Muslim equivalents, the *sufis*. The better relations between the two religions in the early thirteenth century were also due to the lack of open warfare in Palestine during this period: the crusades centred on Egypt, while the Orders carried out a quiet reconstruction of their strength in Palestine.

By the period of the Sixth Crusade (1248–54), Outremer had become a land with little real existence as a secular state. The continuing Arab successes had fallen heaviest on the feudal lords, who could ill afford to keep their castles on a permanent war footing, and who therefore sold them to the Orders. And the kingdom itself was in no better shape. Dominated by the Orders and their castles, its feudal and economic structure was not capable of sustaining the immense costs of warfare, whether defensive or offensive. The previous decades had seen the great consolidation of Templar and Hospitaller castles. Castle Pilgrim at Athlit was built on the southern frontier of the kingdom to guard the coast road. Safed and Tortosa were rebuilt in the following decades. The style of Templar military architecture is now recognised to be basically that of western Europe, but it was influenced by the requirements of the country and by Byzantine fortresses. A European castle was also a residence: a Templar castle was closer to a barracks, and concessions to gracious living were few and far between. T. E. Lawrence, in his study of crusader castles, strongly criticised the design of Athlit, finding it too massive and unsubtle: 'Such a place is as much a prison for its defenders as a refuge: in fact a stupidity.'[6]

However unsubtle such castles were, they were usually very capable of resisting sieges. In 1220 Athlit was under attack for six months, and in 1265 it resisted Sultan Baibars; it was only surrendered in 1291 because, as at Tortosa, there were insufficient men to garrison it until help could be sent. The Hospitallers' great edifices at Margat and Crac des Chevaliers rivalled anything that the Templars produced: Crac is the most imposing of the ruins of the castles of the Orders, and its vast mass, built from 1144 onwards in concentric form, was only taken in 1272 when the garrison, once a constant menace to the Muslims of the neighbourhood, was much reduced by lack of money and men.

For as the crusading spirit waned in the West, so the Orders themselves had begun to decline in morale. The endless appeals which grew annually larger as the resources available from Outremer itself diminished, were viewed with increasing hostility by the Templars and Hospitallers in Europe. The Orders' wealth and power had led them to become organisations with very different interests from those originally intended. There was a danger of attracting administrators into the Order, whose skill in financial matters was balanced by a lack of zeal for the Orders' religious and military objectives. Furthermore, it was impossible, even with the immense resources at the Orders' disposal, to supply men and provisions for an entire kingdom from across the Mediterranean; and as the knights were driven back into their garrisons, this was virtually the task that faced the Orders in the third quarter of the thirteenth century.

Nor did other circumstances improve the situation. Even as late as 1282, when Egyptian pressure on the kingdom was already intense, the Templars were involved in civil war with Bohemond of Tripoli (a quarrel which only ended when the discontented vassal who had incited the war was captured and buried up to his neck in sand). The crown itself was disputed between Charles of Anjou and Hugh of Lusignan. With the disappearance of Charles' power in 1282 after the 'Sicilian Vespers' and Hugh's death in 1284, the last hope of effective leadership by a strong king vanished. The Muslim respect for the Franks as soldiers had long since been tempered by scorn for their generalship and amazement at their obstinacy in quarrelling among themselves; and the campaigns against Palestine were renewed in earnest until, with the fall of Tripoli in 1289, Acre was the only remaining Frankish city. Two years later, Acre in turn was besieged, and despite an heroic resistance of eight weeks, was taken by a well-equipped Egyptian army. The Egyptians, having once realised their complete military dominance, had decided that there was no need to tolerate the existence of Christian fortresses; and the Orders proved powerless against them.

So ended the kingdom of Jerusalem, a state whose own internal contradictions had almost predetermined its doom. Henceforward both the Orders and the Crusaders were to dream of a glorious return; but the fire of zeal which had inspired the men of the First Crusade to their goal was burning low, and the lustre that had so long surrounded the name of Templar and Hospitaller proved to be much tarnished. The Church, scarcely able to rule its own affairs in Europe, offered precious little hope of being able to rebuild the Eastern kingdom which its fervour had once created. The ideal of a Christian Jerusalem won by the sword endured only as a vision in zealous minds; and the Orders found that a more worldly fate awaited them.

15

The Templars in Exile

At the end of 1306, fifteen years after the loss of Acre, the Pope summoned the Grand Master of the Templars, Jacques de Molay, to Rome to discuss plans for a union of the two Orders and for a new crusade. De Molay, in a rather naïve reply, opposed the scheme of union; among his reasons were that the rivalry between the two Orders had been one of the chief spurs to glory, and that the new Order would be far too powerful! His objections to the new crusade, which was to be mounted from Armenia and Cyprus, were more sensible; but the Pope does not seem to have been in a mood for such unco-operative answers.

De Molay was probably unaware that the tide of popular feeling was beginning to run against the Templars. He had been in the East for most of his career, and the criticisms levelled against the Orders for losing the Holy Land and for lack of action since then may not have reached him. Since their arrival in Cyprus, the Templars had done little more than mount some unsuccessful raids on the Syrian and Egyptian coasts. The abuses of Templar privileges of exemption from royal justice, already a problem when he left for the East, had grown worse; and those who had envied for many years the Order's vast possessions had new reasons for attacking it, now that it seemed to have lost its purpose. Counter-proposals were needed, not refusals, especially since rumours that the Order had secular political ambitions in the West were circulating.

How and why Philip the Fair of France came to be the leader of the attack on the Order has never been satisfactorily explained. Greed for the Order's lands and money (he was certainly desperate for both), fear of their ambitions within France, dislike of everything combining ecclesiastical and secular power, his own enthusiasm for a combined Order under his leadership, and even genuine belief in the charges against them, have all been advanced as reasons. The financial and political reasons seem the soundest, but it also seems likely that he hoped for some settlement with the Pope before the Order was utterly destroyed.

What is certain is that when specific charges were made against the Templars the accuser found a willing audience at Philip's court. Esquiu de Floyrian, a renegade from the Order, had first laid information against the knights at the court of Jaime II of Aragon, but, meeting with a cold reception, repeated the charges in France. The crimes of which the Templars were accused centred round the admission ceremony, which, like all other chapters of the Order, was held in secret. The candidate was said to have to make a triple denial of Christ, spit three times on a crucifix, and give a triple kiss to the officer who admitted him, at the base of the spine, on the stomach, and on the mouth. He was also told that knights must not refuse their bodies to each other; and idols were produced and worshipped at this and other ceremonies. Philip and his councillors turned these into a formal indictment, and gathered other evidence from spies and other renegades. The Pope, Clement V, a creature of Philip's but not entirely in the latter's power, was informed of the charges in 1305, and the summons to de Molay may have been designed to bring him back to answer the accusations. It was not until immediately after his return that the charges were really pressed by Philip, in April and May 1307. Clement saw that something must be done, and on 24 August agreed to hold an inquiry.

Philip had other ideas. Either the Templars had got wind of his intentions, and were preparing to leave France, or the speed at which the Pope acted was not swift enough. On 14 September he sent sealed instructions for the seizure of all members of the Order and their property throughout France, to be carried out on 13 October. The coup was carried out with incredible efficiency: only thirteen Templars seem to have escaped. The rest were thrown into prison and charged with the crimes already listed. In the confusion and under the threats of the royal officers all save three admitted them in some degree – including de Molay himself, who repeated his admission before the University of Paris on 25 October. The Pope remonstrated with Philip for his hasty action; but, because of the admissions and de Molay's letter recommending the other Templars to confess, he could not intervene on the Order's behalf, and on 22 November issued a bull commanding the other Christian princes to arrest the Templars.

If Philip thought he had gained his victory already, he was to be sadly disillusioned. He had made careful preparations to ensure that the trial was damning; but he had not reckoned with the resilience of both Pope and Order. Philip could not refuse to hand over the prisoners to the papal delegates, and once this was done, de Molay retracted his confession, and advised the other Templars to follow him. The Pope realised that Philip's clearcut case was not all that it might seem, and reserved the matter for his own judgment.

This put a very different complexion on the situation. It was most unlikely that more than a reprimand would be issued if Philip allowed the Pope to have his way, so the king moved to propaganda. His brilliant publicist, Pierre Dubois, produced pamphlets on de Molay's confession and drafted an appeal from the people of France, which was approved by an assembly in the spring of 1308. Armed with these, negotiations were opened with the Pope as to the best method of procedure. Philip gained his point: early in July, Clement delegated the conduct of the trial to the bishop in each diocese, and followed this with the setting up of commissions to investigate the conduct of the Order as a body. The work began in 1309, and the Templars had meanwhile prepared their defence, which rested mainly on two points. All the original evidence had been given by renegades, who could not be trusted, and any confessions made in prison had been extracted under duress. None of the tribunals outside France found sufficient reason for condemnation, but in France, the situation was drastically altered by the presence of Philip's minions. Seeing that the Templars were not going to co-operate, the archbishop of Sens declared all the witnesses who appeared before the tribunal and withdrew their confessions to be relapsed heretics, and had them burnt at the stake.

Under this threat, very few knights were prepared to come forward in the Order's defence, though Aimery de Villiers-le-Duc, the day after he had seen fifty-four of his fellow-knights burnt to death, came before the commissioners in terror of his life, and denied all the charges, saying that the confessions were extracted under torture; 'but he begged and adjured the Commissioners and notaries present not to reveal what he had said to the King's men or his wardens, because he feared a like fate'.[1]

When in June 1311 the commission finished its work in France, it had heard a very small number of witnesses, none openly denying the charges. Yet the Order still had hopes that all was not lost; at the papal council at Vienne in October it was agreed that the knights should be allowed to put forward their defence, and large numbers of Templars gathered for this purpose. It was only by diplomacy that Philip finally gained part of his object in April 1312. The Order was suppressed and its wealth was to go to the Hospitallers. In 1313 the four chief officers of the Temple held at Paris were condemned to perpetual imprisonment; de Molay and another protested, and the King's council sentenced them to the stake.

Such, in its bare outline, was the incredible web of intrigue, double-dealing and mystery that surrounded the end of the great Order. Philip had had a more difficult passage than he might have hoped, but the Pope, whether his creature or not, was fully conscious of his position, and of the fact that the Templars, corrupt or otherwise, were a considerable pillar of the Church. Hence Philip had to use pressure to avoid a light sentence and secure the suppression as opposed to admonishment of the Order. He is believed to have dropped his demand for a denunciation of his dead arch-enemy Boniface VIII, who had condemned his high-handed dealings with the Church, in return for the suppression of the Templars, and he certainly had armed followers present during the last stages of the negotiations.

Even though Clement V could never have condemned a completely blameless Order, his reasons for the suppression were by his own admission inadequate for a condemnation by the normal course of justice: 'Since we cannot do it by law in the light of the inquisition already held, we have effected it by way of a provision or Apostolic order, a sanction against which there is no appeal and which is perpetually valid.'[2]

The problem of guilt or innocence remains. The confessions can be set aside as inconclusive. They were made after the charges were known, and the torturers asked leading questions. Evidence from countries outside France is totally inconsistent, consisting chiefly of hearsay and rumour. In England, where Edward II had no special love for the Templars, and was delighted to have their estates – the Hospitallers had great difficulty in obtaining anything – it is surprising that only three fugitives from the Order had any accusations to make. All of them spoke of the spitting on the cross and renunciation of Christ. In Italy some confessions were obtained. But where the Order still had work to do, the charges were completely denied. In Cyprus all the brethren defended the Order, and lay witnesses gave evidence of their courage and honesty. In Spain there was armed resistance, and the knights were eventually acquitted at Tarragona in 1312.

The real truth seems to be that the Order was not so much innocent or guilty, but at a low ebb in its fortunes; above all, its morale was low, and it was not especially popular. The loss of the Holy Land had been a shattering blow, and decisive leadership was badly needed. The élite of the Order had been lost; de Molay was not equal to the situation, and never showed any signs of being equal to the responsibilities of the mastership. The brothers were idle; they could not collect funds for an expedition until a new crusade was preached, and the sense of purpose essential to the Order was lacking. Nor did the decline date merely from the fall of Acre; disillusionment with crusading had been evident since the failure of St Louis' Crusade in Egypt. Until then the sins of the crusaders had been held to account for the failures of the Holy War; but when a man so widely esteemed for his holy life as St Louis came to grief, men began to lose faith in the righteousness of their cause. Since the whole idea of the military Orders rested on this implied divine assistance, they suffered accordingly. The quality of the recruits was lower during the thirteenth century; too many of the members joined it for the security it offered, especially in its richest province, France, with little intention of going to Palestine if they could avoid it. When such men were faced with the terrors of the Inquisition, it is hardly surprising that they failed to put up a united resistance in the absence of leaders, and union and firm denial were the only hope for the Order against Philip's propagandists.

For propaganda is almost certainly the key to the nature of the charges against the Templars. The renunciation of Christ and spitting on the Cross may have crept into the admission ceremony as symbols of absolute obedience to the Order, but the bulk of the charges were drawn by Philip's chief adviser, Guillaume de Nogaret, and his assistants from the standard cases of heresy of the last two or three centuries. Some of the details can be traced back to the late eleventh century, while the charges made against a group of German heretics in 1233 by Pope Gregory ix are very similar to those used against the Templars. De Nogaret used this technique of defamatory propaganda based on heresy against other enemies of his master, and had always been successful. Indeed, the case of the Templars was the only one in which he failed to obtain a final verdict of guilty, because Clement avoided the issue by suppressing the Order. In the face of de Nogaret's record, it would be easy to assume that the Templars were entirely innocent: but it is also possible that the French court had learnt of some real heresy among the Templars and was merely pressing home its advantage by using the accepted descriptions of heretical practice. So the final verdict must be 'not proven' with a strong hint that they may have been innocent in view of the source of the evidence against them.

That the chief problem in the Order was the knight who had

gained admittance purely for the sake of the privileges it offered is borne out by the ceremony of admission. The questions asked of the knight were largely to see that there was no impediment to his joining, such as marriage, debt or chronic illness, illegitimate birth, or membership of the clergy. The greater part of the proceedings were taken up with repeated warnings as to the hardship of life in the Order, and the need for absolute obedience; and the candidate could withdraw after hearing of these discomforts.[3] In addition to the triple vow, he swore to submit to the Rule, to help in the conquest of the Holy Land, never to desert the Order without permission, and never to suffer injustice to be done to a Christian. There was no need to set out the greatness of the Order and the glory of being a member; the emphasis was entirely on the duties and responsibilities, never on the rewards.

For the Order offered many rewards. The Templar was respected and trusted wherever he went; and within its organisation every kind of talent could find a satisfying outlet; the warrior in crusades, the financier in its banking operations, the administrator in the care of its European possessions, the diplomat in its international dealings. The Order offered security in an insecure world; the knights might not know luxury, but they would never starve, and they were immune from the whims of secular and ecclesiastical princes alike. In later days, the laws regarding poverty fell into neglect, and an ambitious knight might hope for rich apparel and costly horses as well; of the other delights of secular knighthood, tournaments and hunting, he would learn little, for tournaments were strictly forbidden to the Orders, and the Templars were only allowed to hunt lions.

The wealth of the Order was the cause of much jealousy. Leaving aside the question of how far the rule of poverty was disregarded by the individual brothers, the size of the Templar estates throughout Europe gave rise to unfavourable comment. They were particularly strong in France and in Aragon; the lands in the latter had come to them in settlement of their claim to the succession to the kingdom in 1141. Their total value and extent has not yet been properly studied; all we know for certain is that the largest single landowner in Europe was the Church, and that the two Orders followed it. Gifts which had once flowed to it for pious reasons began in later years to come for other motives. The secular power of the Temple was considerable, and bribes to obtain its support grew in frequency. We can see the changing position of the Order in its relations with the Plantagenet dynasty. Fulk of Anjou had given the knights at Jerusalem £30 a year as a charitable act towards the new foundation. His grandson, Henry II, also made them large gifts, but in return he obtained the release of two castles which they held in custody as the dowry of his daughter-in-law, and he made extensive use of the services of two leading English Templars, Richard of Hastings and Tostes de Saint-Omer, as diplomats and royal officials. John, fifty years later, attempted to enlist the Order's support in his purely secular struggle with his barons. The Order's treasuries benefited in each case, but its ideals were becoming perverted.

In the disposal of its wealth, the same change of attitude appeared. The object of the great network of Temple preceptories throughout Europe was to provide men and money for the East. As the war against the infidel went from disaster to disaster, many of the Western officers began to regard money sent out to Palestine as a waste of resources better employed in consolidating the power of the Temple in the West, and hence increasing their own standing. The practice of maintaining retinues spread, and the laws about clothing being of a simple nature were increasingly ignored; the resistance to the requests of the Visitors-General, who were the Master's deputies responsible for the transfer of men and money to the East, grew stronger in proportion. Appeals for reinforcements were more and more frequent in the last years of the Frankish rule in Palestine, and complaints about the lack of response equally numerous; the commanders in the field said that they could only raise three hundred knights where they used to send out a thousand. The castle at Tortosa alone had a garrison of 1,700 in normal times, increased to 2,200 in war, and all of them were supported at the Temple's expense. When the initial cost of the building works is added (about twenty times the annual expenses) and the whole figure is multiplied for the dozen major fortresses in Palestine, some idea of the huge costs involved emerges.

A further reason for the reluctance to send out money to the Order in the East was the Order's use of these funds to finance its banking operations. From a very early date, the Order had lent money. Louis VII in 1148 borrowed from them when he ran into difficulties on the Second Crusade. These simple advances developed into a banking network unrivalled in Europe. Sums could be transferred by payment at one Temple preceptory and the issue of a letter authorising withdrawal elsewhere. Although there was a good deal of movement of bullion, and the Order had to send its own money physically to the East, an ordinary pilgrim or crusader could arrange for payments to him during his visit to Palestine by a similar transfer. Nor, despite the theoretical prohibition on the lending of money on usury, did the

Temple hesitate to charge interest. The transaction would often consist of the advance purchase of a certain rent for so many years, and such long-term finance, sometimes involving thousands of pounds, made heavy demands even on a treasury as well filled as that of the Templars. It might not merely seem a waste of money to send it to Palestine, where it invariably disappeared like water through a sieve, but it might also cause considerable embarrassment to the financial dealings of the Order.

The Templars specialised in medium-sized dealings, up to about £5,000, and could not compete with the Lombard merchants who raised £20,000 for Philip IV's war against England in 1295. Hence the withdrawal of large amounts to the East was all the more complicated, as it might involve the collection of numerous debts. The Orders were, however, experts in this, since they were on occasion charged with the collection of taxes; with the Hospitallers, they had gathered the 'Saladin tithe' in France and England in 1188 which helped to pay for the Third Crusade, and under Edward I they collected the capitation tax on the Jews, keeping the proceeds as a current account for the king to draw on. In Spain they levied the same type of tax on Jews and Muslims for their own benefit.

If the activities of the Temple in this field are surprising and hardly in accord with the objects for which the Order was founded, they are an indication of the powerful organisation which had sprung from the original band of poor knights. The honesty with which their dealings were conducted does them nothing but credit. Had their skill in administration been allowed free run in Palestine, the result might have been a state as strong as that of the Teutonic Knights in Prussia. But there were too many conflicting interests at work, and at moments the Templars can hardly be blamed for pursuing a self-interested course in the tangled thickets of Palestinian politics. Their real fault was to pursue self-interest too far; when a good leader appeared, they were reluctant to follow him, and when a reasonable truce was made, they were too ready to break it. Their political judgment was always poor; there are only occasional glimmerings of political sense in the later years. This was partly the fault of the division of the Order into Eastern and Western branches: the Master had to reside in Jerusalem, and tended to be a purely military leader, not a diplomat or statesman.

We no longer value moral zeal in the same way as our forebears of the twelfth and thirteenth centuries, and in conjunction with a delight in war it is gravely suspect to us. So any judgment on the Templars is bound to be coloured; against their failings we can only put qualities which are now devalued. They must stand accused of pride, avarice, and to a lesser degree love of luxury; of an independent pride in spiritual matters; and of misusing their privileges. Pride was the chief of their faults; their efforts in Palestine were largely ruined by it, and it led them to outright treachery at times.

By and large their record in the history of the Kingdom of Jerusalem was politically disastrous, diplomatically inexcusable and militarily incompetent. If they died gallantly for the faith, it was all too often the result of their own foolhardiness. In Europe they were perhaps more successful. They administered well and carefully, and their honesty was beyond doubt; if they were parasites on both Church and state, draining money better used for other ends, it was excused by the universal acceptance of the crusades as a worthy cause.

Yet there was something drastically wrong with an Order which could organise so brilliantly in Europe, and make such mistakes in the East. It was perhaps this: the Knights in Palestine were too concerned with the righteousness of their cause, too convinced that one day God would *give* them the victory, to pursue a steady policy designed at recovering and retaining the Holy places. They had the sense to recognise the immediate military needs and problems, to build castles and to reject offers they could not maintain, such as those made during the Fifth Crusade of the restoration of an indefensible Jerusalem. Against this, there was no consistency in their policy, no clear plan for uniting the ailing kingdom or dealing with its enemies in diplomacy. As a military Order, it was all too prone to fight at the wrong moments, and all too scornful of peaceful pursuits: the Teutonic Knights were far greater as an organisation.

But here we come to the heart of the matter. The Templars are part of the ideals of chivalry; the Teutonic Knights belong to the history of mediaeval statesmanship and government. The bitter conclusion must be that religious chivalry was no principle by which to conduct everyday affairs. An admirable rallying cry in times of stress, it was an unsure guide in times of peace; and the history of the Templars points the moral exactly.

16

The Hospitallers at Rhodes and Malta

A year after the taking of Acre, the new headquarters of the Hospitallers was fixed in Cyprus. They had possessed estates there for some time, though these were small; but Cyprus was now the outpost of Christendom in the East. They had also had a fleet of some kind since the early thirteenth century, and a few brothers were in effect sea-captains in charge of a transport fleet. Therefore operations against the infidel could still continue, despite the very slight chances of such a purely seaborne operation against a mainland entirely in hostile hands being successful. The proportion of seamen to knights was also far too small, and from the beginning of their stay in Cyprus, knights had to be dissuaded or prevented from coming East, a complete reversal of the position while Palestine was still being defended.

Fortunately, the possibilities of a Hospitaller fleet in the eastern Mediterranean were quickly realised, and the first attempt to organise it was made within months of their arrival in Cyprus. However, the objectives against which it was to be used were far from clear, and no major operations ensued until the spring of 1306. Meanwhile although both the Hospitallers and Templars had both become involved in the internal politics of the island, they were not permitted to increase their holdings of land. King Henry of Cyprus, a descendant of the kings of Jerusalem, remembered the great power which gifts had brought to the Orders in Palestine, and was unwilling to see his own monarchy similarly threatened. Hence their attachment to Cyprus was by no means strong, either in terms of land or influence.

The projects for reform which contributed to the downfall of the Templars had a very different effect on the Hospitallers' fortune. The Hospitallers did not make any official reply to the idea of uniting the two Orders, and their memorandum on the possibility of a new crusade, prepared by Fulk de Villaret, was much more detailed and constructive than that of the Templar Master. When a much smaller expedition was finally launched in 1308, it was under the command of the Master of the Hospital, and the Hospitallers were never in danger of incurring papal disfavour, despite the fact that some of the charges levelled at the Templars could have applied equally to them. When the Templars were finally suppressed in 1312, the whole of their estates were supposed to fall to the Hospital except in Spain and Portugal, and even though much of the Templar lands and treasure found its way elsewhere, especially in England, an immense amount of wealth came to the Order at a point when, with the loss of Syria, its resources were seriously depleted. And it was now the single crusading Order in the East, the projected union having in effect come about. Against this, the proceedings against the Templars had brought the whole idea of the military Orders into some disrepute, and the crusade of 1310 was a mere shadow of the grand design set out two years earlier. The Order's survival was not in question, but its power and influence certainly were.

The Hospitallers soon realised that conditions in Cyprus offered very little chance for the recovery of their military strength, due to the suspicion of both king and barons; and it was decided in 1310, apparently on the initiative of the Grand Master, Fulk de Villaret, to establish the Order's headquarters in the newly acquired island of Rhodes. From here it could play a part in the affairs of Constantinople, now once more in Greek hands, whose reconquest was usually advocated as the necessary preliminary to any successful crusade; and it would become a sovereign and independent state, like the Teutonic Knights in Prussia, free from the difficulties of domestic politics which had hampered or distracted it since its foundation. From here also it could pursue the Muslim corsairs who dominated the seas, and who were from now on its chief enemies.

However, freedom from secular sovereignty did not mean that the Order was able to pursue its ends without political problems. Much depended on the character of the Grand Master, who was now more powerful than ever; an autocratic Master tended to arouse enmity within the Order, while a weaker character would be unable to wage war effectively on the Order's enemies. Furthermore, the whole fighting force of the Order was now concentrated in the island, apart from the occasional mainland garrison in Greece or Asia Minor; and while revolt had been difficult in the scattered fortresses of Outremer, here it was only too easy for the dissident knights to band together. As early as 1317, open rebellion had broken out against

Fulk de Villaret's rule, and a rival Master was elected. De Villaret, despite his great work for the Order, was forced to resign in 1319.

The ultimate judge of the Order was the Pope himself, and John XXII not only played a large part in finding a solution to the difficulties of 1317–19, but also summoned the great chapter-general at Montpellier in 1331 which provided a new framework for the Order. The knights of the various nations from which the Order drew its recruits had habitually grouped themselves by their place of origin; this division into 'langues' was now made official, and certain posts allocated to each langue in order to guarantee the balance of power. Again, Innocent VI played an active part in the Order's affairs, sending a commissioner (Jean Fernandez de Hérédia, later to become one of the Order's greatest masters) to Rhodes in 1354, and holding a reforming assembly at Avignon in 1356. The internal reforms were continued in 1368 and 1370, a sign that the problem of the Order's government was not an easy one. Nor were matters simplified by the Great Schism, which began in 1378; the defeated party in an internal quarrel could always transfer its allegiance to the anti-pope, though the latter only succeeded in appointing a rival Grand Master in the last years of the schism.

The Hospitallers were now the focal point of all crusading projects in the East, and remained so until crusading zeal was quite extinct. Even as Acre fell, Pope Nicholas IV had been actively campaigning for a crusade. He had collected advice from men with experience of the East, and one book written for him, Fidenzio of Padua's *Book on the Recovery of the Holy Land*, contained much practical advice. Unfortunately, it was not to be the precursor of a crusade, but of a series of such projects, all ably argued and largely realistic. It is these books which show how real the idea of a crusade remained, even if the dream was never accomplished. They were not the work of isolated eccentrics, but of men with a sound knowledge of affairs, and who well understood the difficulties involved. However, the schemes were not always quite what they purported to be. Pierre Dubois' tract entitled *The Recovery of the Holy Land*,[1] like his other works, was propaganda aimed at enhancing the prestige of Philip the Fair, and its appearance in 1306 coincided with the campaign against the Templars. Their possessions were to be confiscated to pay for the expedition, and the Order abolished or merged with the Hospitallers. When we also find a memoir from de Nogaret, another of Philip's close advisers, written four years later, which advocates the diversion of the revenues of *both* Orders into a treasury to be controlled by the French king, the real purpose of the schemes becomes apparent. Like so many previous crusading taxes, little of this would have found its way to the East.

About the same time as Dubois' tract, Raimon Llull, whose theories on secular chivalry we have already noticed, produced a scheme for a crusade which was a thorough study of the theoretical aspects of the problem. It was typical of the change that was beginning to appear in European attitudes that he felt it necessary to start the work with a tract against the infidels. His remarks on the waging of the crusade are well thought out, and his proposed 'dominus bellator rex', a single commander of royal blood chosen by the Pope with jurisdiction over a united military order, shows that he had realised the dangers of divided leadership. As to the route of the crusade, he advocates an invasion of Moorish Spain and a gradual conquest of North Africa, to be supported by naval action in the Mediterranean and a trade blockade against the Muslims. But Llull's schemes ignored the realities of European politics just as those of Dubois and Nogaret had been all too down-to-earth; Llull died at Tunis in 1316 not as a conquering crusader but as a martyred missionary.

It was not until the middle years of the century that any tangible results came from all these exhortations. A raid on Smyrna in 1345 by a small papal and Hospitaller force had resulted in the town's capture and new enthusiasm for the crusading ideal, but there was now a distinct change of emphasis in the objectives involved. The recovery of the Holy Land remained the ultimate objective: meanwhile, any expedition against the Turks, even if only to relieve pressure on Smyrna, was dignified with the name of crusade, in sharp contrast to the grandiose expeditions envisaged by propagandists. Such was Humbert de Viennois' crusade in 1345–7; Amedeus vi of Savoy went to the rescue of his cousin John v Palaeologos in 1366 wearing the cross; and following the example of St Louis in 1270, Louis de Bourbon crusaded against Tunis in 1390. And even the promising expedition of 1365, largely supported by the Cypriots under Pierre i de Lusignan and the Hospitallers, with small Italian contingents, achieved no more than its initial success at Alexandria, where the booty was so great – greater even than the massacre of the inhabitants – that the majority of the crusaders refused to continue, and the fleet returned to Cyprus, having merely added another black page of bloodthirstiness to the history of the crusades, and having burnt the great library there, with its priceless collection of ancient manuscripts.

Yet among these failures, the vision persisted. Philippe de Mézières, chancellor of Cyprus from 1360, had been at Smyrna with

Humbert de Viennois in 1346, and with the Carmelite friar Pierre Thomas had been deeply involved in Pierre I's crusade. At Alexandria, Philippe had seen that it was not the fervour that Pierre Thomas had so ardently preached that was lacking, but discipline. Pierre I did not launch another expedition before his death in 1369, and Philippe returned to France. Here he led a life of literary activity. His great ideal was to create a new military order, 'The Order of the Passion of Our Lord Jesus Christ'; and he worked out a detailed scheme for this; but he also saw that reforms were needed in the whole of Christian society before the West would be ready to launch a successful crusade. The evils of the world in which he lived were analysed in his polemic work, *The Dream of the Old Pilgrim*, an appeal for the launching of a new crusade addressed to Charles VI of France. Philippe's experience, sincerity and power as a writer command respect, and of all the great schemes put forward, his is the most impressive.

His requirements were too great, however, to be put into effect; instead his preaching produced in 1396 exactly the kind of expedition he wished to avoid, under the youthful duke of Nevers, heir to the duchy of Burgundy, consisting of the chivalry of Burgundy and France. It was bent on the pursuit of glory rather than the waging of scientific warfare, and above all lacked discipline, despite the presence of leaders such as Marshal Boucicaut.

When the army went into action at Nicopolis on the Danube, the blockade of the town was scarcely taken seriously. Feasts and jousts were the order of the day, and rumours of Bajazet's approach to relieve the town were not seriously heeded. When battle became inevitable, divided counsels prevailed. The French refused to take Sigismund's advice and place those of his local allies whose loyalty was dubious in the vanguard, so that they could not desert; the van, they said, was the place of honour, and theirs of right. Nor did they understand the Turkish tactics, which relied on light-armed horsemen who could wheel round and take up their formation again if their line was broken. Sigismund wanted to wait until the Turks had worn themselves out against the solid line of the Christian forces, but the French charged first, breaking the Turkish line, only to find a line of stakes. As they dismounted and made their way through, the archers kept up a constant fire, and the light horsemen regrouped; when they reached the crest of the hill, these and the reserve troops put them to flight, and the local Hungarian allies deserted. The arrival of more reinforcements under a Christian prince in Bajazet's service turned the rout into a massacre. Bajazet had all Christian prisoners except the most important killed, and a mere handful of the leaders were able to return to the West on payment of immense ransoms. Yet such was the magic of the crusading ideal and the aura attached to those who had been on crusade that John of Nevers was able to make a triumphal progress through Flanders on his return.

The crusade of Nicopolis was the last great expedition to set out for the East, not because the crusading spirit died with the disaster that overtook it, but because that spirit belonged to another page of a united Church and Christendom. The weakness of the Papacy during the period of the Great Schism and the conciliar movement meant that there was no strong appeal from that quarter for a renewal of the crusade. Nationalism had undermined the possibility of concerted, international action; chivalry might transcend national feeling at times, but practical politics offered too many obstacles. The balance of power was too delicate for such a major military undertaking to be agreed upon; national suspicions had become too strong. On the other hand, the rise of international trade militated strongly against the crusade. The Italian ports were prepared to engage in almost any kind of mercantile operation so long as it was profitable, selling Christians into slavery or even armaments to the Turks in return for the luxury goods of the East; and the immediate effect of the success of the crusade at Alexandria in 1365 was a vast increase in the price of spices because supplies were cut off. Finally, the great shield of Byzantium to the north and west of the Holy Land had been slowly disintegrating over the centuries, until only the Tartar victory at Angora in 1402 saved Byzantium itself from the Turks, while the Muslim states went from strength to strength. The crusade had been a difficult enough undertaking in the twelfth century, with a divided Muslim world and the Byzantine imperial power a real presence; now the odds had become impossible.

Throughout these expeditions, the Hospitallers had largely contributed by sending small contingents of galleys. There were now a small naval power, aggressive and skilled seamen, who harried the Turkish shipping along the coast of Asia Minor; and all efforts to expand their territories beyond Rhodes had failed. Even the able mind of Jean Fernandez de Hérédia had had to abandon his dream of a Hospitaller base in southern Greece, having spent much energy and money on it. Indeed, it was all he could do to keep the Order intact, and during the Great Schism it had been deprived of its revenues in Italy, Bohemia and England, which no longer came to Rhodes. Nonetheless, the Order remained powerful enough to attract the hostile attention of the Egyptian and Ottoman sultans in turn, as the other Christian powers in the East decayed or disappeared.

In 1435 the Sultan of Egypt, Baybars, having overrun Cyprus, and reduced it to the status of a vassal state, turned his attention to the Hospitallers, whose opposition was hindering his projects. The alarm at Rhodes was considerable, and reinforcements of 500 knights were raised, leaving very few able-bodied men in the West. This energetic reaction gained the knights a breathing-space, but no more than that. The defeat of a squadron of Egyptian galleys in 1440 provoked a furious reaction from Baybars's successor. Four years later a huge Egyptian fleet appeared off Rhodes, and landed a very large Mameluke force. The island was overrun, and the town of Rhodes itself besieged for a month or more; it was only by a daring counter-attack that the Mameluke camp was overrun and the Egyptians put to flight.

When the usual problem of replenishing the treasury from the West arose, a new difficulty presented itself, in that the commanders there had become reluctant to part with the funds which provided them with an easy existence. Had it not been for the vigorous action of de Lastic, the Grand Master, the Order might well have found itself in the same disrepute as the Templars, one of whose chief crimes had been just this luxury. Novices who had taken preliminary vows and then used the order's good name to lead a vagrant life without proceeding further in its ranks had also caused scandal, and had had to be disciplined; and it was only a keen sense of the Order's good name among the council at Rhodes that enabled it to survive in a far from favourable period.

The Hospitallers had now become the chief obsession of the Muslim rulers of the Eastern Mediterranean. With the fall of Constantinople in 1453, they were the one defiant outpost of Christianity in the East; and the Ottoman Sultan Muhammad II had demanded tribute from them, only to be met with a curt refusal. After a series of uneasy truces, in 1480 he equipped an even greater force than that of the Egyptians in 1444, under Palaeologos Pasha. Two assaults, preceded by heavy bombardments, were beaten off by the defenders of the fort at the mouth of the harbour, and a third attack, launched against the main town, was thwarted only after a desperate struggle, in which the Hospitallers finally drove back the Turks in disorder and sacked their camp. The arrival of relief ships and the poor state of his troops led Palaeologos to abandon the siege after three months, on 18 August.

Nonetheless, the Order's days in the East were numbered: fresh triumphs had brought the Turks deeper and deeper into Europe, and it was only their preoccupation in the Balkans that delayed the final settlement. The minor successes of their fleet along the coast of Asia Minor only served as an irritant to the Turkish ambitions. The force that sailed for Rhodes in 1522 was the greatest yet mounted against the knights. With all the resources he could muster, Villiers de l'Isle Adam, the Grand Master, had a bare five thousand men, of whom six hundred were members of the Order. The siege was protracted. After the Turks had at first met with strong opposition, doubts about the enterprise began to be felt, and Sulayman the Magnificent himself was summoned to head his army. The undertaking was a formidable one: if the armies were unequal in terms of men, the Hospitallers had made of Rhodes one of the great fortresses of the world. After the previous sieges increasing amounts of money had been spent on its defences, particularly by Pierre d'Aubusson, Master at the time of the siege of 1480. The harbour, with its twin forts at the mouth and heavy ramparts on each side provided good shelter from any besieging army for relief vessels; and the artillery was as fine as any to be found in Europe.

It was on the landward side that the brunt of the attack fell, in particular on the sections of the wall defended by the knights of England and Aragon, where the natural defences were weakest. It nonetheless took two months of bombardment and mining to effect the first breach, which was successfully defended by the English knights on 4 September and again on 17 September. In the general assault on 24 September which followed these two reverses, the Turks were once more repulsed, though the Order's losses were by now heavy and no reinforcements had appeared, despite appeals throughout Europe for men. Sulayman dismissed Mustafa, his general until now, and replaced him by an engineer, Ahmad. A corresponding change in tactics followed. Mustafa, personally brave but not a brilliant strategist, preferred the idea of taking the city by storm. Ahmad changed these plans to a war of attrition, and in this he was helped by the complete failure of all the Order's attempts to break the blockade, despite the supplies which had been gathered at Messina. On 20 December de l'Isle Adam had no alternative but to surrender or face a general assault which he had no hope of resisting, and as Sulayman's terms were magnanimous, he chose to accept. The knights had been in Rhodes for over two centuries when they departed; and with them there disappeared the last impression of the crusading spirit on the Eastern Mediterranean.

Once again, the Order was homeless, and it was typical of the changes that had come about since its last exile that its new home was acquired not by force of arms but by diplomacy. Charles v was prevailed upon to allow the knights to settle in Malta, an island whose strategic value he realised, but which his strained resources did not allow him to use properly. The bargain was not an easy one, since the knights were obliged to take on the defence of Tripoli in North Africa as well, a liability in that its position was far from simple to defend; they were almost glad to lose it when it was captured by the Turks in 1551. Besides this they had great difficulty in avoiding more than nominal allegiance to Spain.

With the move to a new theatre of operations, the Knights of Malta, as they were now generally called, were faced with new enemies, the corsairs of the Barbary coast centred on Algeria. These pirates, supported by their fellow-Muslims in the East, had seriously threatened all Mediterranean trade, and carried out daring raids into Italy and Spain in the manner of their predecessors of the tenth century. Once it became apparent that there was no question of reconquering Rhodes, the knights devoted all their energies and experience to turning Malta from a defenceless barren rock into a rich fortress to rival or even surpass their last home, with its splendid castle and the spacious halls of the various tongues. Their position in Europe was not improved by the loss of their English possessions in the wake of the Reformation, which even de l'Isle Adam's diplomatic skill had been unable to prevent, and the German branch, too, was much weakened. It was the French, Spanish and Italian knights who now contributed almost all the Order's members.

The knights had been seaborne for two centuries, but their methods changed to keep pace with the corsair menace. Though they had indeed harried merchant shipping before now, their chief method of attack had been to effect a landing on the mainland and pillage the nearest port. Now the knights formed small raiding fleets, between whom and the corsairs no quarter was asked or given, to attack the shipping of the Levant; and the names of their commanders were as feared in the East as those of the corsair captains in the West.

The measure of their success was a renewed determination on the part of Sulayman to destroy the Order's fortress. By 1565, both sides had made their preparations, Sulayman with a fleet of 180 vessels and perhaps 30,000 men: the Grand Master, La Valette, with reinforcements from every commandery in Europe and a general appeal to the sovereigns of Europe, which, however, produced no more than a handful of troops from Spain and a papal gift of 10,000 crowns.

The Turkish fleet appeared at the end of May, and began by attacking the fort of St Elmo, guarding the entrance to Grand Harbour, with massive artillery. This quickly reduced its walls, and with the capture of an outpost, the fort became almost untenable. Despite the garrison's insistence that resistance was impossible, La Valette was obstinate that it should be held, and a general assault on 16 June was beaten off. However, the Turks succeeded in isolating the fort completely and took it on 23 June; the garrison was slaughtered, and their mutilated bodies were thrown into the harbour, to be washed ashore below the main fort. From now on, no mercy was shown on either side: in horrible reprisal, the Turkish prisoners in the main fort were executed, and their heads fired by cannon into the enemy camp.

As the Grand Master pointed out, 'poor, weak, insignificant St Elmo was able to withstand his [the Turk's] most powerful efforts for upwards of a month',[2] and the enemy losses had been out of proportion to those of the knights. Yet the Turks now had the upper hand and, on 15 July, were able to deliver a general assault by land and sea, which, though beaten off, came dangerously near to success. A mine dug through solid rock to the north of the fortress resulted in a great breach on 7 August, at which only La Valette's personal courage averted disaster; and the Turks launched two more great assaults on 19 and 23 August, after prolonged bombardments, for the last of which every man capable of moving, even though wounded, had to be employed. The breaches had been repaired, however, and two months' work by the Turkish forces had produced little result. The besiegers in their camp were less at ease in the summer heat than the knights in their beleaguered but spacious quarters. By the time belated reinforcements under the Viceroy of Sicily appeared on 7 September, there was little spirit left in the Turkish army, and their arrival was the signal for a general retreat. The Order had lost 7,000 men to as many as 20,000 on the Turkish side; but Sulayman had failed to dislodge the knights for a second time.

No enemy as powerful as Sulayman was to reappear in the remaining years of the Order's existence to rouse it to heroic deeds again. Perhaps because of the weakening of Turkish naval power after Lepanto in 1571, and certainly because of the increasing Christian commercial interests in the East, the knights rarely found an opportunity worthy of their prowess. Their alliance with Venice, despite the heroic opportunities it gave them in defence of Candia, in Crete, against the Turks, meant that commercial interests now carried great weight in their counsels.

Activity was essential to the morale of the Order; and though after three great sieges in less than a century the mentality that turned Valetta into a monumental impregnable fortress is understandable, this too proved more of a hindrance than a help to a revival in the Order's strength. The only recruits they were likely to attract were soldiers of fortune, eager for action; and instead they were offered a ceremonial, disciplined life of relative ease in a castle that was slowly becoming a palace. Added to this, the Spanish and French political rivalry of the seventeenth century was reflected within the Order, and incessant quarrels distracted the knights. Nor were they effective rulers of Malta or of themselves. The Maltese groaned under heavy taxes, and the knights grew lax in morals, until the island was no more than a despotism in the worst eighteenth-century manner. It was no irony that the seizure of its estates during the French Revolution was to prove its deathblow. Deprived of their resources, divided among themselves, lacking strong leadership, the knights surrendered Malta to Napoleon after a siege lasting only two days. They had become part of the old political hierarchy, unable to find an outlet for their energy in a world which had long forgotten the ideals to which they still subscribed.

17

The Teutonic Knights

The Templars and Hospitallers had had their roots in Jerusalem. Their life was geared to that of the Kingdom of Jerusalem, and when the tide of Muslim conquest flowed back over the ruins of that state, their best hour was past. The Templars never found a new role: lords without dominion, they paid the price of political pride all too quickly. The Hospital became a minor but heroic Mediterranean power, able by skill in war and management to continue to defy the Muslim banners. Both Orders had aimed at great power, and their failure had been sealed by the loss of Jerusalem. The Order that was to achieve their goal was only formed after the Holy City had been finally lost, and was to become the strangest of the many strange governments of Europe: an Order of warrior-monks ruling a commercial empire with a rod of iron.

The beginnings of the story can be briefly told. During the Fourth Crusade, at the Siege of Acre in 1190, German citizens had set up a small hospital to tend the wounded and sick. As the eight-month blockade dragged on, what had been a temporary relief became an institution to the crusading army. Towards the year's end, the leader of the German crusaders arranged that it should be subject to the rules of the Hospitallers. It was recognised by the Church as a small independent Order in 1191, and when Acre fell, was given quarters within the walls. By 1196 it had several branches in the remaining Christian territories in the East, and gained its full status as an Order from Pope Celestine III in that year. It might well have remained a charitable Order but, given the time and place, it was hardly surprising that two years later the assembled leaders of a new German crusade took steps to transform it into an Order of knights. This was done early in 1198, under the Templars' auspices; their rule was to be followed by the knights, priests and other brothers, while serving men and lay brothers were to remain under the Hospitallers' ordinances. Heinrich Walpoto, the first Master, was invested with a Templar mantle, and the first brothers enrolled.

The times might favour the creation of a knightly Order, but growth was another matter. The next decade saw steady but scarcely rapid development. Thirteen scattered houses in Palestine, Greece, Italy and Germany were as nothing beside the wealth of Temple and Hospital. Yet the Teutonic Order was fortunate in that its small size made it more flexible than its greater predecessors, and still more fortunate in finding a remarkable leader to guide that flexibility. Hermann von Salza was the greatest of all the Masters of the Orders, of whatever denomination; not in wealth or power, but in statesmanship and foresight. Largely on his own judgment, he shaped the new and fruitful path of the Teutonic knights, whose Master he became in 1210. Throughout Frederick II's quarrels with the Pope he seems to have retained the confidence of both sides; and in St Louis' ill-fated Egyptian crusade he was one of the few leaders to emerge with some credit. During his mastership, from about 1218 onwards, rich gifts began to fall to the Order's portion, and it was soon able to mount its own campaigns.

This was not of itself remarkable, as the older Orders had long been in a position to do this. But at the outset of von Salza's mastership, the King of Hungary had sent for the brothers of the Teutonic Order to help him against the heathen of Burzenland. They had fought the campaign largely at their own expense, but when the object was achieved and the king cheated them of their reward, they were not powerful enough to wrest it from him. Their eyes had turned to the pagans of Eastern Europe, however, and other lands could be found, for their leader and others among the brethren had seen here a new objective, fully in accordance with their statutes and likely to offer much richer prizes than the intrigues and disappointments of crusading in Palestine. A new crusade, against the pagans of the north, could justify the Order's existence, and it would win glory by making converts with the sword.

This method of conversion lay at the basis of the Spanish crusade, and was the *raison d'être* of the native Spanish Orders of knights. But in Spain the monarchy held a tight rein on the Orders, and gradually assumed direct control. In Prussia the secular arm had hardly ventured into the field, and the Emperor was in no position to assert his rights. Lip-service was paid to the imperial court when it suited the Order, but the very absence of real imperial control gave the Prussian crusade its peculiar features. The other acknowledged suzerain was the Pope, whose mandate was weak enough in such distant parts, and counted for little more than that of the Emperor. When the project was first mooted both Pope and Emperor hoped to control the impulse of the new crusade and reap the benefits; in the space between their ambition and their real power, the Order created its own state.

Prussia was not new territory for the Church. Missions had been active there since the tenth century, but their scale and success had been slight until the early thirteenth century under Bishop Christian. It was he who had invoked the protection of crusaders for his converts, in 1217; and it seems that the missionary activities had aroused a heathen reaction. For the Prussians had proved the most obdurate of unbelievers and their resistance increased with each renewed effort to convert them. Recruits were sought in Poland and Germany and the first Prussian crusade took place in 1221. All it produced was a massive retaliation, and by 1224 Duke Conrad of Masovia was in negotiation with the Teutonic knights for help. Hermann von Salza, however, was not going to find himself betrayed again as in Hungary, and it was not until 1230 that the Order was ready to set out. The terms were harsh enough: the duke had to surrender all rights to Kulmerland, including his jurisdiction and patronage. But Hermann had acted wisely, for without a secure and undisputed base the Prussian campaign could not hope to succeed. On the basis of the earlier stages of the negotiations he had already obtained the necessary grant from the Emperor and he already enjoyed the Pope's full blessing. The work could now begin.

The first castle on the Elbe had been built by envoys of the knights in 1228, at Vogelsang. This was the base for the first operations: the securing of Kulmerland, and the building of the first great fortresses of Thorn, Kulm and Marienwerder. These and the later strongholds that rose out of the heaths and pine forests on natural and artificial eminences made real the hold of the Order on the land; like islands above the flood, they endured against the tide of the Prussian counter-attacks, as the Orders in Palestine had held the desert from Crac and Banyas; but the latter had been confronted with an enemy equally capable of using fortifications. Remembering their experience in the East, even in the first years of easy success, the knights built well and often, a precaution that paid well in leaner years. The system was well adapted to dealing with an enemy numerically superior but not technically skilled: the knights could retire into their fastnesses and safely watch fire and sword go through the land. As long as their provisions were good, only the remotest and weakest ports fell to the enemy. By 1239, the year of Hermann von Salza's death, the knights had reached the coast, and the key fortress of Elbing between the Baltic and the Drausensee had been built.

Cistercian missionaries had been active in Livonia, the area which now comprises Estonia, Lithuania and Latvia, from about 1150 onwards. By 1167 there was a Cistercian bishop of Estonia: and heathen raids on Sweden, where a Cistercian was bishop at Uppsala, gave an added reason for pressing on with their conversion. The difficulties were such, however, that a crusade was called in 1171 by Alexander III, which ended about 1177 without having put a stop to the continued skirmishes with the pagans. The next decade saw a revival of hopes, and a bishopric was established at Üxküll; but a reaction from 1193 onwards led to the abandonment of the bishopric. It was not until the appearance of Albert of Bekeshovede in 1201 with a large expedition that tangible results were achieved, and the city of Riga founded. Albert developed the policy of colonisation which the Teutonic knights were later to follow; and either he or the colonists founded in about 1202 the Order *Fratres militiae Christi* for the defence of the colony, known from their badge as the Brethren of the Sword.

There were perhaps ten members in the first year, rising to fifty knights and a hundred serving brothers within two years. Most of them came from a small area in central Germany, and the Brethren never built up the network of possessions and contacts in Germany and elsewhere that the great Orders relied upon for support in difficulty. Their resources were small, and largely drawn from the land they conquered. A military defeat was liable to mean not only crippling losses in terms of men, but also impoverishment because the source of revenue was lost. Within Livonia, however, they were the greatest power after the bishop, and after 1208 rarely owned less than one-third of the converted lands. The first decade was one of great success: they reached the eastern limits of their conquests, the edge of the Russian territories, very quickly, and their later fighting was largely concerned with the Lithuanians, except for the conquest of the Island of Ösel in 1227. Their chief setbacks were the rebellions of 1212 in Latvia and of 1223 in Estonia, when one-third of the Order's members were killed in a concerted rising on 29 January.

Their real problems were internal feuds with the bishops of Riga and external quarrels with the Danes, who had sent missions to Estonia before the arrival of the Germans. The question of the relationship between Bishop Albert and the Brethren of the Sword occupied the energies of both sides for twenty years, and that of their relationship to the papal legates was only settled on their union with the Teutonic Order. These were diplomatic problems, and the Brethren had no men of the stature of Hermann von Salza: indeed, their rivals almost always had the diplomatic advantage. A series of plans for the division of Livonia and the reduction of the Order's standing were only averted by renewed attacks from Russia or the Lithuanians, in which the Brethren showed how indispensable they were. But neither the Brethren nor the bishop could create a unitary state, and the conquered territories were fragmented in the usual feudal way, being held by natives, settlers and monasteries, and only occasionally directly administered by either of the central powers. In a land at peace this would have caused little stress; but where the loyalty of each native and the provision of proper armed service by each settler was vitally important, it increased the problems of defence enormously. Their opponents were reasonably well organised, capable of learning by imitation and copying captured siege-machines and of taking concerted and carefully planned action, as in the Estonian revolt of 1223. This made the division of power a double handicap. Only with the appearance of the papal legate in 1225 did the position begin to favour the Brethren. New bishoprics were created and endowed and the rights of the town of Riga were increased, at the expense of the bishop's position; and when the Brethren made a formal alliance with the townsmen in April 1226, they controlled two-thirds of Livonia.

But the prosperity was only temporary. A new vice-legate, Baldwin of Alna, put forward a scheme for the creation of a papal state in the eastern Baltic, by which the Order's status would be reduced to that of a mere bishop's army. This was to be on the lines of the Order of Dobrin, which Bishop Christian of Kujawia had founded (on the model of the Brethren of the Sword), and which only survived five years before becoming part of the Teutonic Order. The Pope confirmed this scheme in 1232, whereupon the Brethren invoked the aid of Frederick II and prepared for armed resistance. The battle of the Domberg at Riga led to the vice-legate's defeat, and diplomatic moves at Rome to his withdrawal in 1234. Meanwhile, another diplomatic battle over the Danish claim to Estonia was being fought; and the Brethren of the Sword had begun to look longingly at the power and influence of the Teutonic Order, which had just appeared in Prussia. Negotiations for union had begun in 1230, but the unresolved problems of the Livonian order meant that progress was almost non-existent.

Baldwin of Alna had not yet finished with the Brethren of the Sword. On his recall to Rome, he laid a list of complaints before the Pope, alleging a series of malpractices in the exercise of their power, and in February 1236 the Order was tried. The Pope found Baldwin partially justified, and condemned the Brethren to surrender two-fifths of their territory. This was a bitter blow to the Order, but before it could be implemented, worse had befallen. A new crusading army had arrived in Riga in September 1236, and against the advice of Volkwin, the High Master, they and the Brethren had set out on an autumn campaign. Volkwin, knowing the country, had advised the newcomers to wait until winter, an unorthodox procedure in the rest of Europe, where campaigns were usually fought between April and October, but correct enough in the north, where the marshes were only passable in the grip of winter's ice. So when a Lithuanian army trapped the force on a marshy island near Saulen in central Latvia, the cavalry could not be used, and about half the Order, including Volkwin, were killed.

The news did not reach the West until spring 1237. Baldwin's papal state had no chance of success in the face of this disaster, and the only practical solution, the long-mooted union with the Teutonic Order, was rapidly completed. The inheritance of the Brethren of the Sword was an equivocal one. On the one hand, there were the loyal lands in Latvia and Estonia, which brought in good revenues and were little trouble; on the other hand, the Teutonic Order was now inevitably faced with a collision with the Lithuanians, whose lands were bordered on three sides by theirs, and inherited old quarrels with the Danes and Livonian bishops. Amalgamation was, however, the only solution to the problem of the smaller Order: unequal in resources to the task it had begun, it would have sunk into oblivion, like the lesser Spanish Orders.

With the implementing of Gregory ix's bull of union of May 1237, the pattern of the Teutonic Order's activities was now set; but two major reverses in 1242 destroyed much of the earlier success and shattered dreams of empire for them meanwhile. The lesser disaster was the defeat of the Livonian brethren at Peipussee in 1242 by Alexander Nevsky, which meant that the larger possibilities of a coastal empire to the north west were ruled out by the Russian preponderance there. All the Livonians' efforts now went into the consolidation of their rule and into joining with their Prussian counterparts by conquering the south eastward coast. However, the knights there were in no case to make a reciprocal effort, for a greater cataclysm, a major rising of the Prussians, had razed almost all trace of their twelve years' work. Svantepolk of Pomerania, formerly an ally of the Order, had become their enemy in the course of a dispute over an inheritance. He had allied himself with the heathens in Prussia itself, and organised a concerted and general uprising against the Order. Hard-pressed months and years of heroism and rashness followed alternately, and each triumph was liable to have its counterpart in folly. This first uprising took seven years to suppress; and even then the intervention of Rome was needed before peace was made. The treaty which resulted, in 1249, established the legal basis of the state. We shall return to the implications of this later: its immediate effect was to leave the knights free for new campaigns to the east.

The obvious target for attack was now Samland, lying between Eastern Prussia and Livonia, on the coast. A great crusade in 1253 led to the foundation of Königsburg, and a succession of victories, both military and diplomatic, led to the total subjection of the east Baltic coastlands by 1260. But these wide lands were held by a mere handful of men, and a single major defeat in the field could undermine the whole tenuous structure. In a great campaign against the inhabitants of Samland in 1260, a chain of unlucky circumstances led to a massive slaughter of the knights at Durben. The work of the previous decade soon evaporated. The Lithuanian king, Mindaugas, repudiated his allegiance, and the Prussians rose against their masters again, reducing many of the lesser castles. Only massive efforts from outside saved the Order. Urban iv issued twenty-two bulls calling for crusades between 1261 and 1264, and in 1272 the results began to be evident. By 1290 the last outposts of rebellion had been stilled, and the Order's lords enjoyed peace once more. The years of conquest were closed.

The following years were a period of consolidation. One important change came about in 1309. The Order, though centred in Prussia, had retained its official role in the East, and the High Masters of the Order as a whole had lived in Acre until the fall of that city in 1291. It was some time before the decision to move the headquarters to Prussia was made, for there was a certain reluctance to admit that a return to Palestine was unlikely: hence the first choice of Venice in the intervening years, before Marienburg was named as the residence of the High Master. In September 1309 he made his entry into the town. Here a stately gothic castle and church rose in subsequent years – eighteenth-century engravings indicate something of its magnificence – whose ruins were reconstructed by Hitler and finally razed in the fighting of 1945.

The Order was now faced with the problem which had ultimately baffled the Frankish settlers in the East: the administration of its conquest. Palestine had proved too poor a land, and its conquerors too jealous and ambitious, for an adequate army and stable government to be established. Any mediaeval army was directly related to the wealth of the country; troops had to be paid, in cash or in land, and here the Teutonic Knights in Prussia were at an advantage. With proper management the forest could be made to yield an adequate return as cultivated land, and it was never so intensely farmed during their rule as to bring on the evils of dust and drought. The political status of the Order was also much more favourable than that of the Eastern counterparts – the great importance of the imperial bull of 1226 and the ducal deed of gift in 1230 lay in the complete freedom given to the knights. Sovereigns in their own right, they had no vacillating or overbearing kings to contend with, and turned their energies wholeheartedly to the business of creating order out of chaos. In contrast, in Livonia, where the Order was merely one of the ruling powers, much of its energy was diverted into political intrigue.

The material they had to manage was intractable enough. The Prussians had already shown their independent mettle in the previous fifty years; they were also among the most backward races of northern Europe. Their agriculture was of the most primitive nomadic kind, the year's crop being raised on newly cleared forest land, which was abandoned immediately after harvest. They had few settled centres, and were loath to give up their wandering life. Their paganism, in peacetime relatively harmless, being a nature cult of grove and spring similar to that of the Norse peoples, grew ferocious in war. If their temper was aroused, the captured knights were often sacrificed to propitiate the gods; for the outlying garrisons deep in the forests, battle, despite impossible odds, must have seemed preferable to capture and the risk of torture and death. The efforts of the missionaries had not been successful, and the number of genuine converts was very small; the majority of so-called Christians were liable to revert all too quickly to their fathers' ways. Few of the knights can have spoken their language, and very little is recorded of their beliefs and customs. This lack of communication, in such contrast with relations between Christian and Muslim in the later years of the Kingdom of Jerusalem, increased mutual fear and suspicion, and must account for much of the bloodthirstiness of the campaigns.

The kingdom of Lithuania created by Mindaugas was revived by Gedymin about 1310. From now on the leaders of this state were the Order's chief antagonists, for besides being the last heathen remaining in the area they were also pursuing a conflicting course of conquest.

268

From 1300 to 1380 the Order's armies marched against them as many as eight times a year; but the Lithuanians were as stubborn as the Prussians had been, and the fortunes of war remained even. They were skilled riders and daring warriors, moving swiftly across the country, however wild, elusive in retreat and dangerous in victory. Nor were they to be trusted in peacetime. Both skilful and treacherous as diplomats, they outwitted the cleverest minds of the Order on several occasions. By themselves, however, they were not powerful enough to impose their own terms.

Indeed, the Order reached its zenith at this time, under Winrich von Kniprode, a High Master second only in resourcefulness to Hermann von Salza. The achievements of his time were many, but the greatest was undoubtedly the acquisition of Estonia from the Danes, which sufficiently extended the Order's territories in the Baltic provinces to overshadow any remaining local dissidence.

On the other hand, the Order had made diplomatic enemies in the south as its strength and status grew. The most serious of these was Poland, which allied itself with Hungary to keep the knights in check. As the two great Catholic monarchies of Eastern Europe, they regarded the order as intruders, and were jealous of its stable government and accumulating wealth. Hungary was a nominal rather than effective opponent, and the Polish intrigues came to very little until in a black moment for the Order the Grand Duke of Lithuania, Jagiello, married the Queen-regnant of Poland, Jadwiga, in 1386, and brought together the Order's two closest rivals. The bitterest blow lay in the conditions of the settlement: Jagiello and his people were to accept Christianity. What the Order had failed all these long years to achieve, and what had remained its official *raison d'être* until now, was at one stroke accomplished, and the religious aspect of its wars swept away. Without the clarion call to the crusade, its influence was bound to decline; and the knights found themselves as no more than a secular power struggling for political ends against their fellow-Christians.

That they had legitimate grounds enough for war against the Polish-Lithuanian union in the years that followed cannot be denied, once they had made the initial mistake of meddling in the internal power struggles of the new state. Accustomed to regarding the Lithuanians as their traditional enemy, they could not see that their one hope was to stand aside and let the fragile bonds dissolve of their own accord. They became involved in a quicksand of allegiances, treacheries and double-dealings, in which most of the deceit was on the Lithuanian and Polish side. A series of skirmishes punctuated these manœuvres, and a major encounter could not be held off for ever. When it finally came, in the summer of 1410, it found the Order apparently as strong as ever. The knights were confident of their own superior skill: and it was a century and a half since their last serious reverse at Durben. On the other hand, Jagiello was determined to settle matters once and for all; and his mobilisation of perhaps 10,000 troops in a month was a major feat. Once assembled, the army was organised as little as possible, and this very lack of a formal hierarchy and reliance on a central authority was the secret of his success. There were no quarrels as to precedence, no problems of foraging; the only common aim was the destruction of the Teutonic Knights as swiftly as possible. Tartars, Russians and as many other patrons and princes as could be roused formed the larger part of the army: and with this motley array, ranging from the future Khan of the Golden Horde to knights in the strictest European tradition, Jagiello invaded the Order's territory in July. Despite the refusal of the Livonian Master to join in a war begun without his knowledge, the knights were still confident, for the Order's commanders had not been idle.

Pomerania, which had long been coveted by the Poles, was guarded by a small force who could hold off the invader until help came, and the main body of the army was in the centre of the border with Poland. Contact was quickly made and the Grand Master, Ulrich von Jungingen, decided for immediate action. Although reinforcements were at hand, and he could have delayed until German mercenaries of the Pomeranian army reached him, he chose to strike quickly, relying on his own strength. The strategy used on previous occasions, of withdrawing into the Order's fortresses, no longer seemed profitable: the land was rich and able to support a besieging army well enough, and the Poles were now capable of handling siege-engines successfully. Nevertheless, a retreat into the castles might well have brought in the Livonian branch of the Order, and the vast Polish and Lithuanian army would not have stayed together in a protracted campaign. So there are some grounds for finding von Jungingen's tactics rash: they stem too nearly from the Order's own high opinion of itself. He had little to gain, as defender, from a quick encounter, but on the first intelligence of Jagiello's invasion, he ordered an immediate march towards the enemy.

When, at midday on 15th July the army of the Order halted, after a march of fifteen miles, among the rolling wooded hills round Grunwald, they found Poles and Lithuanians already encamped in the forest. This was the first blow to the Order: the heavy cavalry on which they relied was vastly more effective on open plains than in the forest, and hence their action had to be defensive. Both sides were reluctant to make the first move, and there was some hope of a parley, until the knights' herald bore two swords to Witold of Lithuania. A general advance ensued, and the shock of the knights' first attack broke the Lithuanian wing. The centre and Polish left stood firm, however, and the over-eager pursuers on the left were met by Russian squadrons and fresh Polish troops who held them in check. Neither side could make headway, and the Grand Master was forced to advance with his remaining reserves in a bid to break the Polish line. This decided the battle, but decided it against him. The line held firm, and he and the potentates of the Order were surrounded and killed. The rest of the army tried valiantly to retrieve the lost battle, but when the remnant fled, two hundred of the Order's knights lay dead on the field, and the Order's lands lay open to Jagiello, victor of one of the most spectacular, yet most meaningless, of chivalry's battles.

The truth of the matter was that the Order could not have benefited from a victory. It was neither justified in, nor capable of, conquest of Christian states; relying as it did on a religious impetus, it could not afford to behave like a secular state. The remaining story of its declining years is punctuated by no such dramatic moments as Grunwald; the knights, prudent after the event, avoided a headlong encounter in the second and third northern wars, but were nevertheless forced to conclude disadvantageous peaces both in 1422 and 1435.

Other forces were at work against the outmoded disposition of the Order. The towns and guilds, the small squires and farmers, resented its foreign and exclusive rule, which, while the pagan were still at their doors, they had accepted as a necessary price for protection. Prussians were actually debarred from joining the Order, and the result was not unlike British rule in India in the early twentieth century: an essentially well-meaning administration which grew progressively less able to adapt itself to the realities of political feeling among the people it governed. The situation was aggravated by the knights' increasing use of mercenaries, and a general raising of the taxes as the treasury grew empty. At a time when the Order needed good administrators above all, the falling off in the standard and number of recruits began. The Order's own standards, too, had fallen from the days when they were 'good monks in the cloister and stern soldiers in the field'.[1]

In the mid-fourteenth century Heinrich der Teichner had complained that knights only went to Prussia to waste money and gain glory, while things went from bad to worse at home; and the knights were accused in 1343 of not converting the conquered heathen because they could tax them more heavily, though Philippe de Mézières, at the end of the same century, surveying Europe from a crusader's point of view, found the knights the embodiment of his ideal of Christian discipline.

Roger Bacon complained that 'the Christian princes who labour for their conversion (i.e. of the heathen), and especially the brothers of the Teutonic Order, desire to reduce them to servitude, as the Dominicans and Franciscans and other good men throughout all Germany and Poland are aware. For this reason they offer opposition: hence they are resisting oppression, not the arguments of a superior religion'.[2] By 1430 the complaints were more general. To oppression was added worldly show, and breach of all three vows; but the Carthusians had been accused in similar terms in 1427, and some of the enormities were magnified by the general growth of anti-monastic feeling. By 1454 the old Prussian League which had been a potential focus for such discontent since its formation in 1240 had become a formidable union of guilds and local nobles, which, supported and financed by Poland, staged a well-timed revolt against the Order. Despite a clever victory at Konitz, where the Order's mercenaries held the Poles and Leaguers at bay until the Marshal overwhelmed them from the rear, the war went against the Order. To pay the mercenaries, it had to give them Prussian towns in pledge, which they then sold to the Poles. By 1466 both the League proper and the Order were exhausted; only the Poles could take advantage of the situation. So, in the Peace of Thorn, Casimir IV accomplished what his forebears had begun to work for before the Grand Master had even settled in Prussia a century and a half earlier. He took West Prussia for the Polish crown, and forced the Grand Master to rule the rest as a Polish vassal.

If the Order's star had set, a faint reflection of its old glory lingered in Livonia and elsewhere. The Livonian branch had recovered from the defeat of Vilkomir in 1435 and was in better shape than that in Prussia when faced with new dangers, this time from Russia. Its independent standing had saved it from inclusion in the humiliation at Thorn. In Walter von Plettenberg, it produced the last great statesman of the Order, and in the victory at Pskow in 1502, the last great hour of the Order. Within twenty years the Reformation had undermined the remnants of the Prussian Order, and in 1525 Albrecht von Brandenburg converted it into a secular duchy as a Polish vassal. The Livonian branch survived until 1591, when a similar fate befell it.

What remained was a postscript, though the tradition died hard. The Order very nearly revived, like the Hospitallers, to fight the Turk. In the Peloponnese they had resisted Turkish attacks in the late fifteenth century; and in Austria, where the Order remained strong after its decline in Germany proper, the knights found themselves matched against the infidel from 1529 onwards. The attacks of Sulayman the Magnificent, and a century later those which culminated in the siege of Vienna in 1683, found in the Order a mainstay of the defenders. Their part was admittedly not to lead, as in Prussia and Livonia, but they could provide a full regiment. In any case the majority of their lands were in the troubled borderlands, and had to be defended. The last major field action involving the Order took place in 1697 at Zenta; and it is only with the passing of the menace of Islam from Europe – a menace which was already 400 years old when the Order was born – that its part in military affairs finally became a thing of the past. The Order survived into the world of the Renaissance but this was a world where diplomacy counted for more than zeal, and treaties for more than an Order's vows and aims. The Order counted for no more than the sum of the individual prowess of its members.

The historical reputation of the Order has suffered no less from its zealous supporters than from its enemies; German and Slav historians respectively have seen in it the apotheosis of knighthood, and the nadir of piracy in the name of idealism. To the Prussian Treitschke they were 'conquerors, endowed with the triple pride of Christians, Knights and Germans';[3] to Latvian and Lithuanian historians, the murderers of the infant national spirit of their peoples. But their heritage cannot be evaluated in terms of nineteenth-century nationalism nor in the context of a controversy on the ethics of religious war. On its own terms the Order's achievement was remarkable. Its tradition of diplomacy, from the days of Hermann von Salza, would alone assure its reputation. Of Hermann's own skill as diplomat there is no greater proof than his position of trust as the only acceptable intermediary between the excommunicate Frederick II and Gregory IX. He alone of the Masters of the Orders stood at Frederick's side on the forbidden crusade to Jerusalem in 1228; and yet he retained the Pope's confidence. Both Emperor and Pope encouraged his Prussian schemes, and gave him practical support at a time when their feud was at its height. He brought about the union with the Brothers of the Sword, despite their embattled position. Here, for once, Hermann cut the Gordian knot to achieve his end: he agreed to yield over a dispute with Denmark which the Brethren of the Sword obstinately refused to do, and to accept the remaining lands. Having arranged this, he then had the two negotiators from the other Order brought to Gregory IX, where they were told that the union had been agreed, and given cloaks of the Teutonic Order to put on. Only afterwards were the terms of the union revealed, and they could no longer argue with von Salza, to whom they now owed obedience.

Hermann's successors maintained this skill, though perhaps without earning the same degree of respect. The Order became a byword for cunning, and a German proverb ran: 'If you're so clever, go and deceive the lords of Prussia.'[4] The lords of Prussia succeeded in securing the support of the dominant side in the conflict of Pope and Emperor, changing their real allegiance as necessary. They maintained a system of diplomacy as far afield as England, Sicily and Hungary to gain support for their ends, and such efforts repaid the Order many times over in periods of stress; after Grunwald, it was support from their old enemy Hungary that helped them to recover, and diplomatic skill meant that the Peace of Thorn was far from unfavourable, considering that a bare handful of castles was all that had been left. It was this, rather than the old fighting spirit, that enabled the Order to survive in some form until the end of the fifteenth century; military reverses were followed by diplomatic recoveries. On the other hand, no amount of diplomacy could resolve the rival aims of the order and her neighbours, once the latter became Christian and the Order's role became secular.

The internal structure of the Order was supremely important to its success. While the other great Orders were assailed on grounds of immorality and luxury, the Teutonic Knights largely avoided such complaints until the very end of their time. Recruitment was limited to sons of knightly parents of German origin, born within the Empire. This avoided the clashes that occurred between the various *langues* of the Hospitallers, drawn from different nations; and it prevented the Order from becoming the pawn of local knights, since no one from the Order's lands could be admitted. On the other hand this led to an aloofness from local pressures that proved dangerous in the last years; without a local assembly co-operation was difficult to obtain, and grievances were liable to go unheard.

As in other Orders, the individual knight was subject to his local priory; the priories were in turn adminstered by the bailiwicks or *Balleien;* and these were answerable to the central administration of the Order, at first in Acre, later in Venice, and finally in Marienburg. Prussia and Livonia were far from being the exclusive habitat of the knights; as with the Templars and Hospitallers, the establishments of the Order ranged from Cyprus, Greece and Calabria through the Tirol to the Rhine, Saxony and the Netherlands. The extreme outposts of the Order's activities were the Holy Land, Spain, Flanders, Gotland, Estonia and Hungary, a circle round the edges of Christendom. But the great reserves of the Order lay in its possessions and ties in Germany. It was the strength of its basis in Germany that prevented it from succumbing to the almost mortal reverses it met with in the course of its crusades, as the Brethren of the Sword had almost succumbed after the battle of Saulen. Indeed, the chief reason for the union in the eyes of the Brethren of the Sword was in order to tap the reserves of manpower and wealth at the Teutonic Order's disposal.

The higher administration consisted of a general chapter of representatives from each bailiwick, the five great officers, and the High Master himself. The High Master and the great officers decided the day-to-day policy of the Order, but were answerable to the general chapter for their actions; and the High Master, as in the case of von Plauen, in 1413, could be deposed by the general chapter. The election of the High Master was carried out by an electoral college, which was formed by the nomination of one knight as 'election leader'. He would then name another knight to join him, and the two would then choose a third, and so on until thirteen knights were chosen and approved by the Marienburg knights and officers. These thirteen had to be as widely representative of the Order as possible: and their choices were, on the whole, remarkably farsighted, even in the darkest years. Even von Plauen's election was undoubtedly the right choice, while his subsequent deposition has been much debated.

On this administrative system the Order's success depended. It was outstandingly successful, and probably unrivalled by any other mediaeval state. Cases of malpractice were almost unknown, and detailed financial organisation went hand-in-hand with frugal habits for many years. The main aim of the financial machinery was to provide for the expenses of the campaigns; a year rarely passed without a major expedition setting out, and while this constant drain remained, there was little money to spare for misuse on personal comfort. Since the campaigns were undertaken to protect lands which were a major source of revenue, there was no temptation to withhold funds, as with the Templars. Only towards the end of the fourteenth century do signs of heavy expenditure on luxuries appear, and some of this was certainly due to entertainment of secular visitors, for as a secular prince the High Master had to show these outward signs of power by which men of the time distinguished a great prince from a lesser one. The nature of their estates made the knights into men of commerce, trading corn, hides and wood; and their relations with the north German towns of the Hanse were dictated by both policy and trade. At its height, the Prussian trade carried on by the Order and the merchants of the towns included not only the staple products of the land but a flourishing market in wares brought overland from the Levant and Rumania.

The growth of this trade and the great wealth of Prussia were not only due to financial skill. Since its earliest days, the Order had pursued a deliberate policy of development and colonisation. In this it was fortunately placed, for the great weakness of Frankish Palestine had been its lack of settlers and of manpower, partly due to the distance and climate, but mostly to lack of any concept of colonisation. The Order was near to Germany and the land was favourable; but without encouragement, the colonists would never have come, and the all-important substructure of the state would have depended on the unreliable descendants of the old pagan races. The settlers were given wide privileges, equivalent to the most liberal prevailing in the German towns; and these privileges were codified within three years of the Order's acquisition of Kulmerland in the Kulmer Handfeste of 1233. In return for a large measure of freedom in their own affairs, the settlers had to acknowledge the Order's lordship and basic rights and the Order was careful never to grant large estates to individuals; but the Order also waived its rights to many kinds of taxation and made the military service required as light as possible. Trade was made easier by the adoption of a standard coin, replaced over ten years at a set rate of exchange, and the absence of tolls. Nor did the Order's work stop here. Regulations as to the building and layout of houses were laid down, so that there was as little danger as possible of overcrowding or fire, and the best defensive arrangements could be made. A minumum area for each building site was laid down, as well as the basic ground plan for each town; and brick was preferred to wood, tiles to straw.[5]

The Order could only carry out farsighted schemes such as this in Prussia, where it was undisputed master. No bishops could contend with it there, though they were technically masters of nearly a quarter of the land; and the local nobility, despite the Polish-inspired Prussian League of 1240, feared the pagans more than the Order. Most of the disaffected nobles were either killed or deprived of their rank during the rebellion of 1260. Furthermore, the Order actively pursued a policy of buying out their lands and granting them in smaller lots to peasants. In Livonia the Order inherited the quarrels of the Brothers of the Sword with the bishops and the Danish kings, though the terms of union had poured some oil on these troubled waters. Fortunately the pressure of external politics alleviated the risk of internal troubles, but Livonia never prospered in the same way as the older territories.

The Teutonic Order was chivalry at its most practical. The Order's faults were the faults of chivalry in real life, and nowhere does the tinge of unreality appear. Its virtues, however, were curiously un-chivalric, the virtues of practical wisdom carefully applied. They cannot be claimed as being of the essence of chivalry, but belonged rather to the science of good government. Behind the skilled diplo-mats, administrators and warriors, the driving force nevertheless re-mained that of religious chivalry: the defence and furtherance of the faith by discipline and the sword. This ideal never became irrelevant to the Order's existence; indeed, its downfall came when, in attack-ing Christian states, it betrayed that ideal, and showed the inherent danger of building a secular state on active idealism: for its purpose had gone and only the outward trappings were left. In its declining days the Teutonic Order did not refuse to fight the infidel, but it made no effort to do so when the infidel was no longer to be found on its doorstep; for the temper of the fifteenth century was very different from that of the thirteenth. Once the crusading ideal had died, conversion into a secular state was inevitable, for chivalry had never envisaged itself as a means of ruling the world; far rather, as a means to right the wrongs perpetrated by the world's rulers. While chivalry made the secular achievements of the Teutonic Order pos-sible by providing the internal discipline and driving force, it had very little impact on the nature of those achievements.

Hand-in-hand with this idealism went a practical machinery which enabled it to continue in its work long after the former had died away. Yet the basis of the Order was not very different from that of the Templars. Indeed, from 1198 to 1245 the Order followed the Templar rules, but following a dispensation in a papal bull of 1244 to change the rules in any details which needed alteration, a revision was undertaken in the light of fifty years' experience. The statutes have come down to us in this later form. They fall into three parts: rules, laws and customs. The rules were the kernel of the Order's life and their first commands were: 'eternal chastity; renunciation of one's own wishes, that is, obedience unto death; and the third is a vow of poverty . . .'[6] Not even the Master could exempt a member from these rules. All property had to be held in the name of the Order, and brethren were not even allowed separate places, such as chests, in which private belongings of any kind might be kept. The habit of the Order was specified in detail: all brothers wore the black cross on their over-tunics, which were always white from 1244 onwards. No brother could possess more than the stipulated number of clothes, and any divergence in favour of worldly splendour was strictly forbidden.

The laws laid strong emphasis on the role of the Order as Christ's warriors, and especially on the need for Christian conduct towards their fellow Christians. They also prescribe the ways in which the brothers had to avoid temptation, especially where women were concerned; and anyone guilty of homosexual practice was to be ejected from the Order at once. Possession of money and the exchange of anything issued to the brothers for personal use were not allowed. Penalties for infringements ranged from three days' penance to what was in effect a year's hard labour, working with the servants and deprived of the insignia of the Order. A second year's sentence or even perpetual imprisonment might follow serious offences. Since the Order was exempt from all royal judges and bishops' courts, it had to have powers of punishment adequate for the most serious crime; and in extreme cases, such as that of the Prussian Master who burnt two rebellious brothers alive, the Order appealed to the Pope for sentence.

This discipline was equally adapted for both fighting men and a governing élite. The Order was – and this is one of the most remarkable things about it – very small by our standards: in 1400 there were no more than 1,600 members. Hence its greatest asset was a strong corporate spirit, and this feeling of exclusiveness contributed greatly to its internal stability and the high degree of discipline. By 1350 the only serious problems were the use of money and fugitives from the Order. The religious element in the Order was strengthened by two other factors not found in the Templars and Hospitallers: the parochial work of the priest-brothers in the Order's lands in Germany, and the cult of the Virgin Mary, which seems to have been very strong in the Order. The *Officium Marianum* was to be said daily, besides the usual church services; the longest and one of the most important of the rare works of literature produced by the Order, *The Passional*, begins with a life of the Virgin, and contains anecdotes of the Virgin's miracles; and on the Church of the great castle of the Order, named Marienburg in her honour, there stood a twenty-foot high golden mosaic in half-relief of her. With so few literary remains, it is hard to tell how far this cult went beyond the ordinary worship of a patron saint; but it seems more than likely that the mariolatry current among poets and knights elsewhere reached the Teutonic Order too.

The moral decline of the Order only began to become a serious subject for complaint after the disaster of Grunwald. The crimes complained of seem to imply a feeling of fatalism, that the Order's days were numbered, but the same complaints were echoed elsewhere against knights both secular and religious, and Orders both military and monastic: dicing, drinking, impiety and breach of the three vows. The special charges against the Order were those of worldly show, levelled against the Templars a century earlier, and, most particularly, of oppression. We have considered the Order's government in Prussia already. If there was oppression, it was mild compared with that of other European rulers, and the real cause of irritation was the alien birth of the knights. The ambitious merchants of Danzig could justifiably protest against their exclusion from power; ambition and half-forgotten episodes from the days of conquest, when a civil war was raged by both sides, led to a picture of the knights as sadistic tyrants which lingers in nationalist histories today. In fact, they misused their power very little; their real sin was to be a reactionary institution with little ground for continued existence in times which were increasingly critical of the *status quo*. They had not entirely maintained their early standards: their hospitals had been reduced in number, mercenaries were used from about 1300 onwards, and the criticisms of pomp and pleasure were sometimes more than justified. Yet if the Order's faults were those of other institutions of chivalry as well, its achievements were entirely its own.

18

The Spanish Orders

The third corner of Christendom at which believer and pagan met on the battlefield was Spain. Here the Muslim invaders had been established much longer, since the beginning of the eighth century, but they had replaced a Visigothic kingdom with Roman traditions. Its scattered heirs remembered the days when all Spain had been Christian, and regarded the infidel as an intruder. In the north, the Germans were the invaders, and the Eastern crusaders lacked the clearly defined territorial aims of the Spanish knights. The *reconquista* in Spain, which began in earnest under Sancho 1 of León in the tenth century, was the only fully successful military operation in the holy wars of Christendom, and hence assumed a special character. On the other hand, the military Orders appeared on the scene relatively late, after the first triumphs of the *reconquista* were past, and their part was less than in the East and in Prussia: the war was between two groups of feudal kingdoms in alliance, and the Orders became a component of the Christian feudal host. Their place is less in the history of chivalry than in the internal history of Spain; but their institutions and career illustrate the relation of chivalry to the practical politics of feudalism.

The *reconquista* had begun as a largely political movement, stemming from the growth in power and influence of the Christian kingdoms of northern Spain as the Umayyad caliphate of Cordoba, which ruled half the Muslim world, fell into decline. It was exemplified in its early stages by the Cid, whose heroic figure showed what Christian warriors could do; yet even he was either in revolt against his lord or actually in infidel service for much of his career. Moor and Christian had lived side by side for too long for religious differences to count for much, and there were no Holy Places as the goal of the struggle. It was only with the increasing intervention of the Church in secular affairs that the war became a question of beliefs, and mutual intolerance, a necessary prelude to a holy war, appeared.

The papal expedition which produced the triumph and disaster at

Barbastro in 1063–5 had been followed by a succession of smaller forays from France, largely organised by Gascons, whose lords had strong political ties with the kingdoms beyond the Pyrenees. But the response to recruiting for these expeditions had been inspired less by the call to a sacred task than by ties of alliance or even friendship, and the hope of booty from the wealthy Moorish kingdoms, whose riches were exaggerated to fantastic proportions. Even the successes in Palestine did not discourage the Spanish expeditions; indeed, they seem to have added new impetus. However, the stout resistance of the southern kingdoms made the struggle a protracted one. The first crusade to be preached as such in Spain was that which led up to the great victory over the Almohades at Las Navas de Tolosa in 1212 (if we discount the crusading absolution given to the Portuguese in 1197 to fight a Christian monarch, Alfonso x of León). However, the success of this expedition was not due to the crusaders, who quarrelled with the Spanish and departed before the battle, leaving the latter to win a victory which halted the last great Moorish offensive against the north. In 1215 Innocent III cancelled the absolutions offered for fighting in Spain on the grounds that the Holy Land required the attention of all available knights. Indeed the crusading idea in Spain was largely local, royal and unofficial. The great thirteenth-century conquests in Aragon and Portugal, which ended the Porguese *reconquista,* were partly fought with the banners of a papal crusade, and the crusading ideal lingered on in Iberia longer than anywhere else in Europe: the last campaign of the Catholic kings in 1492 and even Sebastian of Portugal's suicidal African raid of 1578 were widely regarded as crusades. But the form of these crusades differed from those in the East in that they were really politically inspired, and the papal blessing was not essential to their success. If it was not forthcoming, there were no drastic consequences such as befell Frederick II in Palestine.

Yet there was enough religious inspiration in the *reconquista* for the Templars and Hospitallers to be eagerly welcomed as a possible source of assistance. By 1136, their fame was such that Alfonso the Warrior tried to leave the kingdom of Aragon to them on his death. The scheme was obviously unworkable, and was rejected by his heirs; the Hospitallers acquired their first real foothold in Cataluña in 1143; the Templars were well established in 1146. But though they held some of the frontier forts, their greater preoccupations lay elsewhere. They were more interested in acquiring possessions outside the Holy Land which supported their endeavours there by providing revenue rather than involving an extra drain on their resources. The abandonment of a castle at Calatrava, which led to the foundation of the Order of that name, was not cowardice but a recognition that they could not undertake another major front in their war against the infidel.

The rise of the native Orders is mainly due to the reluctance of those from Palestine to commit themselves fully to Spanish adventures. Later nationalist historians found precursors of purely Spanish origin but dubious authenticity, and the idea of the Orders as being at once military and religious is undoubtedly derived from the Templars and Hospitallers. On the other hand, it is possible that the institutions known as *ribats* may have contributed something. These small frontier stations were found throughout Islam, and to build one was accounted a good work, as was the manning of it; both furthered the cause of the *djihad* or holy war. However, the defenders were not members of any organisation, but citizens who spent limited periods in prayer and fighting in these quasi-religious retreats. It is possible that himilar defence associations were found among the Spanish knights, and that these had something to do with the secular structure of the Order of Santiago.

The atmosphere of the Spanish wars did not encourage the zeal with which the Templars and Hospitallers fought in the East. Conditions in the two halves of Spain were too similar and contracts with Moorish civilisation too frequent. Both sides suffered from a proliferation of kingdoms and interminable quarrels among themselves. The advantage, to a much greater degree than in Palestine, went to whichever side was temporarily at one with itself. The humane element of Moorish civilisation had influenced the Christians as well, and the wars were conducted with considerable humanity, slaughter of prisoners being generally frowned upon, even if the terms of imprisonment were harsh. There was surprisingly little attempt at conversion or at religious repression in conquered territories. The worst excesses of the Palestine crusades do not appear; relations between Moor and Christian show the respect bred by familiarity which was so often disturbed in Palestine by new recruits from Western Europe, for whom an infidel was beneath contempt.

The oldest and greatest of the Spanish orders was that of Calatrava. Its foundation came in a period of frustration after the great successes of the Cid and of Alfonso vi, and was partly due to a failure on the part of the Palestinian orders to devote enough energy to the *reconquista*. The Templars had been given the royal fortress of Calatrava in 1147, on what was then the frontier with Islam. This dangerous outpost was no sinecure; and when the next major Moorish counter-attack was mounted, they resigned it to Sancho of Castile, on the grounds that it was untenable. In desperation Sancho offered it to anyone who was prepared to hold it, with sufficient territory to maintain the costs of defence. The story goes that the heralds offered it three times, and received no reply, whereupon a Cistercian monk, Fray Diego Velazquez, who was at the royal court in attendance on his abbot, Raymond of Fitero, persuaded the latter that this was Christ's cause and the castle could not be abandoned. Velazquez, an old soldier, must have known the perils of the enterprise; he may also have realised that in Raymond, a brilliant organiser but unexperienced in war, he had found the right man. Within the year, by the end of 1158, Raymond was in Calatrava as Captain-General of a group of knights and monks; Diego had cleared the area of raiders; and the surrounding fields were being cultivated again.

The immediate problem that arose was the status of this new enterprise. Fitero's mother-house, Escaledieu, was opposed to the whole scheme. Fitero had been emptied of its able-bodied monks and its abbot. The king intervened just as Raymond seemed liable to be disciplined, pacifying the abbot of Escaledieu, and Calatrava was established as a new house, obeying the Cistercian rule but with special provisos in view of its military role. Under this dispensation, the knights were able to place colonies in nearby strongholds to form a system of defence for the region by the middle of the following decade. But relations within the monastery were not easy: for on the death of the abbot Raymond, a dual election took place, the monks favouring one candidate, the knights another. The monks returned to Fitero, which left the knights as a purely military group. This was not what they had wanted, and it was decided to admit priest-brothers, and to apply for a special rule to govern their conventual life, on the lines of those given to the existing orders. So, by a bull of Alexander III at Sens, the order of Calatrava was formally created, as an independent body responsible only to the Pope. Within twenty-five years, however, the Order returned to the fold of the Cistercians (on whom its institutions were based): because in the absence of an accessible court of appeal, there had been unresolved arguments within the Order, culminating in a disputed deposition of the Master himself.

Hence in its final form, Calatrava owed its first allegiance to kingdom and knighthood, to crusading and Cistercians only when these qualities did not conflict with politics and war. As long as pressure from the Moors was strong, all the forces within the Order worked magnificently together; when internal dissensions divided the Spanish kingdoms, the Order too was divided. Until 1240 the Order's energy, if not rewarded by unbroken successes, was at least directed to the right ends. Indeed, the invasion of the Almohades in 1195 and the defeat at Alarcos made the Order homeless for a while; Calatrava fell, and only after dissensions with the Aragonese members was a new home found at Salvatierra, again on the frontier. This, too, fell soon after the quarrel within the Order had been settled; and it was not until the great crusade of 1212 when the revenge for Alarcos was found in the triumph of Las Navas de Tolosa that the Order was again in possession of Calatrava. Its next home was Calatrava la Nueva, near Salvatierra, chosen because the original fortress was in too unhealthy a site and too far from the frontier. Later a great palace-fortress was built nearby at Almagro.

The idea of 'brotherhoods' of knights, operating together against the Muslims and choosing their own leader, was not uncommon in Spain, but most such companionships were temporary. On the frontier of León, one such brotherhood, recorded from 1170 onwards, became by 1176 the Order of Alcantara, and in 1183 the first master was recognised by Pope Lucius III. But such a small body as Alcantara seems to have needed support from a more powerful organisation in order to survive, and soon afterwards Alcantara placed itself under Calatrava's protection, eventually becoming little more than a minor branch of the latter. Likewise, the Portuguese order of Evora, founded in the 1160s, came under Calatrava's jurisdiction, and after the reverses of the early thirteenth century was refounded as the Order of Aviz. Aviz became independent of Calatrava after 1238 and flourished where Evora had failed: it eventually provided Portugal with its ruling dynasty when the Master, Joao, gained the throne in 1384. On the suppression of the Templars, another Portuguese order was founded, that of the Knights of Christ. Under the leadership of their Master, Henry the Navigator, they fitted out expeditions to the Azores and to Africa, beginning with the siege and capture of the Moorish stronghold of Ceuta in 1414. Despite the early successes of the adventurers in the caravels with the red cross on their sails, the explorations never developed into a new missionary crusade, the orders themselves had become part of the past, and merchants, not crusaders, opened up Africa for Europe.

The most important of the Spanish orders, the Order of Santiago, has its own version of its foundation in its statutes. At a time when the Moorish peril was at its height, and the kings of Spain persisted in fighting each other instead of uniting against the common enemy, thirteen knights adopted the badge of a sword with a cross at the hilt, and swore never to injure a Christian, but, renouncing earthly vanities and ordering their life according to Holy Writ, vowed to fight no one but the heathen. Later tradition placed these events as early as the eleventh century, but the accepted date of formation is that of the first evidence of the Order in 1170, when a group of knights was associated with the canons at Loyo. In 1175 a bull of Alexander III confirmed the Order's statutes. The traditional version of the early days is borne out by the bull; for the Knights of Santiago were the most unorthodox of the religious orders. Their rule stems from a secular warrior fraternity and from the early influence of the Augustinian canons. They were, strictly speaking, not a monastic order, for although they tended to live in community in their castles, members could marry and have possessions. However, on the death of a knight his family was cared for by the Order, which inherited all his wealth; and there were restrictions on the knight's power to act as a private individual. This similarity to a charitable association was increased by the Order's activities in redeeming prisoners. By 1184 two *casas de merced* had been established for the exchange of captives, and this good work continued throughout its history. On the other hand, the rules made the Order wealthy and discipline difficult, and in 1310 a chapter-general at Merida revised them lest the Order should suffer the Templars' fate, which had largely come about from excessive riches and inattention to their true purpose.

For the primary object of the Order was military, despite these other activities; and Santiago's services were as valuable as those of Calatrava. Its knights were prominent at Las Navas de Tolosa in 1212, where the Master was standard-bearer, and they maintained an unceasing frontier war in the Order's early years, disregarding royal truces with the Moors, which they did not regard as binding. By mid-century its fame was such that Baldwin of Constantinople invited the knights to assist the Latin Empire, promising wide lands in Asia Minor; but the knights were too few in number for such an extensive undertaking, and the scheme came to nothing. Santiago, with its married knights and hence stronger domestic ties, was in any case a purely Spanish institution, while Calatrava, which resembled the international orders very closely, might have mounted such an expedition with less difficulty.

Like the other Orders, in particular Calatrava, the knights of Santiago were also landowners on a vast scale, controlling the settlement and farming of great tracts of land on the frontier. Since they were responsible for the safety of the frontier, they evolved a pattern of life which not only ensured that land newly won from the Moors continued to be farmed, but also that any Moorish raids could be beaten off without too much damage. Settlements therefore consisted of tightly grouped villages dominated by defensive walls and often quarters for a small garrison, and a wide area would be cultivated from each of these, in contrast to the more loosely knit communities elsewhere in Spain. Gradually a pattern of ranch-style farming emerged, which was to have considerable influence on the shape of later agriculture, both in Spain and in the New World. This involvement with farming also meant that the Order never relied simply on castles for its defensive system, but rather on fortified towns and castles integrated with villages, in contrast to the desert strongholds of the Palestinian Orders.

Just as the Orders in Palestine had failed to establish a satisfactory relationship with the secular authorities, so a similar weakness soon appeared in the Spanish Orders. Being more open to secular influence, this took the form of internal quarrels over elections and discipline. In 1175, a former knight of Santiago had founded the Order of Montjoie in protest against the admission of married knights to Santiago, but it foundered for lack of support, and was merged into the Templars after 1196. More serious than the problem of discipline was that of obedience, particularly over elections. A dissident section of the order of Montjoie resisted the union of 1196 until well into the thirteenth century, and disputed elections were becoming all too frequent in the other Orders. In 1240, this weakness was aggravated by royal intervention in the choice of a new Master of Calatrava. The Spanish Orders lacked the international prestige which had saved the Templars and Hospitallers from local interference: Calatrava was primarily Castilian, and one of the most wealthy and powerful bodies within that kingdom, as well as its only form of standing army. By 1318 Calatrava included not only Alcantara, but also the newly formed order of Montesa, among its dependents, Montesa having been endowed with the confiscated Templar lands. So royal interest was excusable, and the knights certainly did not regard themselves as above politics, especially since the *reconquista* had lost its impetus in the thirteenth century in face of increasing Moorish resistance.

By 1259 Santiago was insisting on noble birth for anyone wishing to become a knight, and quarrels over rank and points of privilege increased. Calatrava introduced a similar condition soon afterwards, and with this insistence on noble birth the connection with the royal court, and hence the possibilities for royal interference, increased. From 1254 the king expected to have a say in elections, and the arguments grew more and more frequent. In 1326 the Master was deposed for retreating in face of the enemy; the abbot of Morimond, which had been Calatrava's mother-house since 1275, reinstated him, only to find that a new royal candidate had taken power meanwhile: the situation was complicated by a schism with the Alcañiz branch of the Order. No sooner was the last breach healed than a new royal outrage created worse storms. In 1342 the king's gift of the mastership of Santiago to Don Fadrique, his seven-year-old bastard, led to protests from the Master of Alcantara. When challenged to appear at court he shut himself up in his castle, and was beheaded when royal troops took it by storm. Soon afterwards the Master of Calatrava fell to the assassins of Pedro the Cruel for plotting against his favourite, Doña Maria de Padilla; and Don Fadrique met a similar fate at Seville for suspected treason, as did the next Master of Calatrava.

Yet the old spark remained as long as the Orders' objective and *raison d'être*, the Moorish kingdoms established in Andalucia, remained undisturbed. The last flowering of the *reconquista* in the fifteenth century finds the two sides of their character in evidence at once. Alvaro de Luna, as constable of Santiago, won a great victory at Higuera in 1431; but, elected as John II's favourite, he fell in a palace revolution in 1453. Enrique IV's illegitimate son, Rodriguez Tellez-Giron, was appointed Master at the age of eight, and supported Queen Isabella's rival in the dispute for the throne; yet he was the last great heroic figure of the Order, serving the Catholic kings well after his reconciliation with Isabella, and dying before Loja during its siege in 1482. Under the leadership of the Catholic kings the last embers flickered into flame again at the taking of Granada, the emotional climax of Spain's medieval history: the acting governor of Calatrava, Diego Garcia de Castillo, hoisted the Spanish flag over the Alhambra on the morning of 2 January 1492, marking the end of the efforts of 500 years to dislodge the Moors from Spain.

The Catholic kings had already seen the danger of a rich and idle Order brawling among themselves for want of better work, and in 1485 they had declared their intention of reserving the mastership to the Crown. In 1487, on the death of the incumbent Master, the election was left to the Pope, as had been agreed; and Hadrian VI, some thirty years later, annexed it to the crown of Castile, making Charles V and his successors its masters.

Of the two Orders, Calatrava's constitution was more liable to lead to dissent over elections, and its real influence was less despite greater fame. Santiago, as the single example of an Order where members could marry, has its place in the history of chivalry, if only to prove that marriage seemed to be no deterrent to deeds of arms. Nonetheless, it was usual for the Master to remain unmarried, a custom which was not broken until 1350, in order to avoid the danger of the mastership becoming hereditary (though nephews of previous masters were twice chosen). The religious element was never very strong, and the Order of Santiago in its later years is best seen as a kind of defensive organisation combined with a standing army. Individuals might pursue the war against the heathen wholeheartedly, but the knights as a body grew content to leave the initiative to others.

The Spanish Orders were from the start hampered by too close a relationship with the secular state. While the Orders in Palestine were a mainstay of the Frankish kingdom in the absence of an adequate feudal army, it is tempting to wonder how different the Spanish *reconquista* would have been without the Orders. Drawn largely from the knightly class they supplemented, their contribution was more one of spiritual than of physical reinforcement. Once their spiritual nature became openly subordinated to political pressures the only remaining advantage was that of their special constitution as a kind of standing army, unpaid yet always on the watch. Their value is shown by their survival until the end of the *reconquista*, although fighting was irregular and occasional for the last forty years. Only when Granada had finally fallen did the Catholic kings put into effect arrangements they had made in 1487 to incorporate the Orders into the royal power. They remain no more than a large footnote to the pages of Spanish history, a kind of symbol of the spirit of Spain during those years: high aims and chivalry corrupted by petty ambitions and pride, yet in the end victorious.

PART V
Chivalry and the State

19

The Prince and Chivalry

Just as the Church had viewed the rise of chivalry with a dubious eye, and had only come to accept it and turn it to religious ends despite itself, so monarchs were doubtful of the new spirit abroad among their knights. The knights were, after all, their army, or the most effective part of it, and to have them always hankering after adventures abroad, whether in the lists or on crusade, meant that the kingdom's military resources were depleted. William I remarked of one of his subjects that he would be a much better knight if only he was not always going off on pilgrimage; and by 'a much better knight' he meant a knight more useful to himself. The insistence on individual honour set chivalry and good discipline in the field at loggerheads, as we have seen; the tournament could be both a graveyard of good fighters and a meeting-place for rebels; and the right to make knights could be used to conjure up an armed force. Hence royal opposition to chivalry in its early stages is scarcely surprising: it took the form of the restrictions on tournaments in England and elsewhere and the attempts to make the conferring of knighthood a ceremony hedged round by strict regulations.

For the knight was also a baron, or at least a small landowner, and as such ranked immediately below the king in the social hierarchy. The royal interest demanded that such men should be taught obedience and discipline before the code of individual heroics which chivalry preached. As long as the game of power politics was played between the barons and the king, chivalry was a subversive force, for it reflected the barons' aspirations of independence. As soon as other forces, the townsmen and merchants, threatened the hegemony of the lords, chivalry became a bond between king and lords against the upstarts. Hence the edicts against tournaments gradually disappeared and were replaced by the attitude of the German *Turnier-gesellschaften*, whose determination to exclude all those not properly qualified was encouraged by the various princes of the Empire, including the Emperor himself. Royal decrees on knighting became less concerned, as in Frederick I's laws, with the possibility that a peasant rabble might be given knightly arms, than with the social aspirations of the bourgeois families.

Yet from the beginning the king or prince had also been a knight. The earliest records we have of knighting ceremonies of any kind involve Charlemagne's descendants, and it had always been of the utmost importance in primitive warrior societies that the chieftain should be seen as a warrior *par excellence*. Hence if policy dictated a course unfavourable to the aspirations of knighthood, the king personally could share those aspirations at the same time, being a knight himself and brought up in knightly society. When Richard Cœur de Lion relaxed the ban on tournaments in England, a variety of motives urged this step: a means of raising money, increasing English proficiency in arms to the level of the French, a method of controlling a sport already practised illicitly. But to all these we must add that Richard himself loved tournaments and had fought in them in France.

The knighting ceremony itself had chivalric implications by the thirteenth century, and as the knighting of a prince had to be attended by suitable pomp such occasions became festivals of chivalry. From 1250 onwards there are few state investitures of this kind of which the chroniclers do not record that two or three days of jousting ensued, and that the great chivalric virtue of largesse was suitably honoured. By 1313 Philip the Fair was prepared to employ his publicist, Pierre Dubois, to write a treatise setting out the virtues of tournaments, in order to persuade Clement V, who had just condemned that very spot in his bull *Passiones miserabiles*, to lift his ban for three days at the knighting of the royal princes. In it Dubois makes the point that any royal edicts against tournaments had been instigated by clerks in the king's entourage, rather than by earlier monarchs themselves, who had enjoyed tournaments.

Edward I was an excellent example of this contradiction. He himself was a great participant in and patron of tournaments: at his knighting there had been a tournament, and he went abroad in 1260 to tourney in France, where he lost horses and armour, was badly beaten and injured, and still remained an enthusiast. Yet during his reign at least twenty-eight bans on tournaments are to be found in public records. And the paradox increases when we find the end of the campaigning in Wales in 1284 being celebrated by a great tournament, a Round Table tournament at Falkirk during the Scottish campaign of 1302, and an Arthurian festival which may have been a tournament as well at his wedding to Margaret of France in 1299. Tournaments were now treated as something which could be invidious to the national war effort – most of the bans derived from the critical period of the Scottish wars at the end of Edward's reign – but which were a perfectly respectable royal occupation at others. And their appearance during or after campaigns suggests that they were being used as an inducement or reward to knights on active service, while the events at Edward's marriage were designed to recall his achievements in the field.

That some of this stemmed from Edward's own enthusiasm is shown by the lack of other examples of royal tournaments associated with campaigns. On the other hand, most of the increasingly elaborate tournaments of the fourteenth and fifteenth centuries occurred at either knightings, marriages or, more rarely, triumphal entries. Royal pageantry, designed to impress the subject with the awe of kingly pomp, adopted the tournament as one means of doing this; but it had a second, subtler, design as well: the strengthening of the links between the lords and the crown through their vocation of knighthood. This is in essence the one object of royal concern with chivalry. The mass knightings, such as that at Edward II's knighting in 1306, were another way of producing links between the sovereign and his knights, though these had been practised from as early as 1125, when Adalbert of Austria is said to have had more than a hundred companions. Now the chivalric vows and the idea of knighthood as an order were used to reinforce the feeling of brotherhood. The later knighting ceremonies contain a prayer that the new knight may use his weapons faithfully in the service of the kingdom of France, or England, or Castile, as the case may be; so the international ideal is not emphasised, and the brotherhood is first and foremost composed of the knights of one nation under their ruler.

Hence the king became the chief patron of chivalry. In the twelfth century even such a model of chivalry as Richard Cœur de Lion had not pretended to this position, but left such frivolous matters to lesser princes such as the counts of Hainault, and no chronicler ever saw their fondness for tournaments as anything other than youthful folly. On the other hand, the Angevin court under that most practical of monarchs, Henry II, had become a centre for the literature of chivalry, and no monarch felt offended by the dedication of a poem or romance. And from the king as a patron of chivalric literature to becoming the patron of chivalry itself was but a short step. Much of Edward I's enthusiasm seems to have been for that kind of chivalry which based itself on literature, and in the fourteenth and fifteenth centuries the same literary basis underlay most of the royal pageantry.

293

Richard Cœur de Lion and St Louis set examples of the king as crusading knight, an ideal which touched the sceptical Frederick II as well, and which almost every monarch of the later Middle Ages aspired to but could never find opportunity to accomplish. The king as secular knight was another matter. Crusading vows could be a useful way to find favour with the Church, and no one dared criticise a Christian king for such an undertaking. Secular chivalry, on the other hand, was all too liable to scathing attacks from the Church or from popular poets: the chivalry and generosity of John the Good at Poitiers and afterwards nearly ruined France. The English kings were more careful: undoubtedly the chief motives for Edward III's exploits as a knight were personal. He enjoyed the adventure of fighting at Calais incognito under Sir Walter Manny's leadership in 1348, and also did honour to one of his finest commanders. However, when we find the dukes of Burgundy taking part in tournaments, it is as part of a political design to unite the leaders of their disparate realms, and to find 'a harmless outlet for the violent instincts of the nobles'.[1]

Maximilian I was heir to this tradition, combining it with that of the German tournament, while for Francis I chivalry became the outward trapping of imperial dreams in Italy. The knightly quest for *gloire* and an aggressive military policy merged into one until in the words of his famous motto, *Tout est perdu fors l'honneur*, 'All is lost save honour', at Pavia in 1525. On a lesser level, royal jousters still appeared in the lists in the sixteenth and seventeenth centuries; though in France the death of Henri II in 1589 put an end to this, in England James I rode in the Accession Day tilts of 1612.

It was as organiser of tournaments and jousts that the ruler played his chief part as patron of chivalry. In William Marshal's day, it was usually the lesser rulers and the royal princes who were the instigators of such events. Even the tournament of Ham in 1278 was under the patronage of Robert II, Count of Artois, though Marie de Brabant, the French queen, was present. This is the first 'romantic' tournament of which we have a detailed account, and was the forerunner of many such pageants in the Low Countries. At a tournament already arranged at Ham, a damsel arrived with a tale of distress; and a knight playing the part of Kay, King Arthur's sharp-tongued seneschal, received her rudely. She was followed by seven knights from the castle of a lord who had been invited to the tournament. This lord had detained the damsels sent to request his company, who had had to be rescued by the Knight of the Lion, Yvain, another Arthurian character. The seven knights were sent as his prisoners to do homage to Guinevere, Arthur's queen, and at their arrival, the jousts began. One more adventure closed the proceedings: a knight arrived with a dwarf, who derided Arthur's court, and beat the first damsel in distress for calling Guinevere's knights the best in the world. The knight was duly defeated and asked pardon for his servant's behaviour, and the company turned to feasting and dancing.

This was a private entertainment, but had obviously been very carefully staged, as witness the defeat in the lists of the Mocking Knight. Hence the element of danger had been reduced, and discipline could be imposed; and the adventures could easily be given a political meaning redounding to the glory of a prince or ruling house. During the fourteenth century this gradually begins to happen. We shall return to the great festival held at Windsor in 1344 by Edward III in another connection. In France, the state entry into Paris of Charles VI's bride Isabella in 1389 set the pattern for many such occasions over the next century and a half. An allegorical pageant unfolded as the royal couple rode into the city, with triumphal arches erected for the occasion. Four days of jousting ensued, between thirty knights bearing the device of the Golden Sun, and Charles VI was awarded the prize on the first day. Perhaps because these jousts were somewhat marred by dust – two hundred water-carriers were employed and 'there was still a sufficiency of dust'[2] – the knights ended the proceedings by tilting in the hall where the feast was held.

If Charles VI and his court loved such spectacles for their own sake, his brother, Philip the Bold of Burgundy, saw in them a means of soothing political discord and strengthening the tenuous connections between his domains. Besides occupying warlike nobles in a peaceful way, entries and tournaments provided entertainment for the townspeople of the Low Countries, and impressed their leaders with his might. His own wedding to Margaret of Flanders in June 1369 was 'the first of that series of glittering and elaborate ceremonies which punctuated the history of Valois Burgundy and enhanced the prestige of its rulers'.[3] The marriage of his son William to Margaret of Hainault at Easter 1385 was likewise occasion for high festival, and Froissart, an eyewitness, said of it: 'This tournament was very handsome; the tilts were well performed and lasted a considerable time.'[4] And in the intervening years, there had been a series of tournaments at Ghent and Bruges in which the flower of Europe's knights had taken part. In 1376 we find the dukes of Lancaster, Brittany, Anjou and Brabant, Count Louis of Mâle, and Albert of Bavaria, ruler of Hainault-Holland, assembled for one series of jousts; all these were not only accomplished jousters but also figures of great importance in Philip's political calculations, whom he was eager to impress by the splendour of the proceedings.

Nor was the diplomatic purpose of such occasions unrecognised at the time. In September 1390 Richard II held a tournament in London avowedly inspired by those at Queen Isabella's entry into Paris in the previous year, at which sixty knights held the lists against all comers. To this came William of Hainault, an ally of the French king, and carried off the prize; and on being offered the Order of the Garter, he accepted. On his return, however, he found that the French regarded the whole expedition as a diplomatic affront, and it was with difficulty that he succeeded in making his peace with Charles VI.

Another attempt to use chivalry as a diplomatic weapon was the idea that a war could be settled by a single combat between the two leaders of the opposite sides. Such challenges appear at intervals from the twelfth century onwards but there is a spate of them in Froissart. None of them came to fruition, though Philip the Good's challenge to Humphrey Duke of Gloucester in 1425 was taken by the former with the utmost seriousness. Philip went into training, took fencing lessons, and had all the arms and pavilions made, but diplomacy prevailed in the end.

As the festivals of the fifteenth century grew more elaborate, so such events in France and England became very rare. The political use of chivalry, for the moment, was the preserve of the Burgundian dukes, emphasising their claim to the status of sovereign princes, though they had their imitators in the Italian cities, where a revival of chivalry had begun about 1400, and at the Castilian court under John II; the 'Paso Honroso' of 1434 was a feat to rival any of the Burgundian festivals.

In Burgundy itself, the 'entry' of the prince into the capital of one of his territories, whether after his coronation or marriage, or merely on the occasion of a general chapter of his personal order of knighthood, was the signal for a carefully staged pageant centred on his person. Though disguisings and elaborate dress had been used at tournaments since the mid-fourteenth century, there had been no attempt to use a single theme throughout the proceedings. Now, a subject was chosen or a story devised, perhaps classical, perhaps allegorical, perhaps in the old tradition of chivalric romance. The letters announcing the tournament became part of this convention, sometimes purporting to be an appeal from a lady in distress; the earliest surviving examples are those for a tournament at Eltham in 1401. By the 1450s, marvellous statues and set pieces, arches and columns were erected, poets composed odes in the prince's praise, the finest artists were employed to paint frescoes or design tapestries. We find Ronsard and du Bellay writing for the French kings' entries into Paris in the sixteenth century, Poliziano writing a poem on the Medici jousts; Roger van der Weyden painted for the entry of Charles the Rash into Bruges in 1450. Entertainments were presented by professional actors, ranging from grandiose declamations to interludes with jugglers, acrobats and equestrian ballets; and the great composers of the day, Okeghem, Josquin des Pres and Fayrfax, contributed canzonets and motets in their gayest secular manner.

If the great princes of Burgundy and Italy alone could afford pageants and tournaments on this lavish scale, where chivalry was but one element in the festivities, the lesser rulers nonetheless continued to be patrons of knighthood. The greatest single arbiter of chivalry in the fifteenth century was René, Duke of Anjou and erstwhile King of Sicily and Naples. His rules for tournaments and the pastoral *pas d'armes de la bergière* held by him in honour of his mistress, and his Order of the Crescent are mentioned elsewhere (see page 179 above); but he also took part in many other tournaments during a period of relative tranquillity in his affairs between 1446 and 1455, including his own *pas d'armes de la joyeuse Garde* of which the centrepiece was a castle modelled on that in Arthurian romance. The knights who took part had all fought in a previous tournament called the *emprise de la gueule au dragon*, which Gaston IV of Foix had held near Chinon in 1446, where René himself had carried off the prize.

Gaston IV was another enthusiastic jouster, and had won the prize at the jousts held by Charles the Rash at Nancy for the marriage of Margaret of Anjou to Henry VI. At this festival, Charles VII of France had ridden three courses; and one Pierre de Brézé, having unhelmed him, was 'blamed for riding so hard against the king',[5] a comment which implies that a little flattery was in order in the lists as well as in the royal halls, and that jousts were now becoming a sport whose result could be prearranged if the occasion so demanded. Equally, they were more and more a public display. Philip the Good's tournaments in Flanders entertained the urban populace, and Gaston IV's popularity was in no small measure due to his lavish display at tournaments where he appeared on rare Apulian, Sicilian and Andalusian horses bedecked with gold and jewel-studded chamfrons, and to his reputation as a skilled jouster. As Castiglione says: 'So now as far as sports are concerned, there are some which are hardly ever performed except in public, including jousting, tourneying and volleying, and all the rest in which weapons are used.'[6] Though there had always been a ready audience for tournaments, in the fifteenth century they had definitely become public spectacles, and Castiglione can warn his ideal courtier that 'next he should give full consideration to the kind of audience present and to who his companions are; for it would be unbecoming for a gentleman to honour by his personal appearance some country show'.[7]

With the collapse of the Burgundian empire in 1477, the remnants of Charles the Rash's lands found their way into the lands of Maximilian I of Germany. Maximilian was already an enthusiastic horseman and jouster, and adopted the Burgundian tradition readily enough. The *pas de l'Arbre d'or* at Charles the Rash's wedding in 1468 had shown that there was still great enthusiasm for jousting and the trappings of chivalry; indeed, there had been some difficulty in parting the contestants at the end of the general tournament, and the duke himself had had to enter the lists before they would desist. Maximilian was reputed to be 'so skilled with the lance that no opponent of equal birth was to be found in Germany or elsewhere',[8] and he was known to joust with men-at-arms of humble origin in order to find a match for his dexterity.

The old type of tournament had fallen into neglect in Germany, and for his festivals Maximilian invented new kinds of jousts, the most extreme involving mechanical horses, while another variation was to give one knight a shield with a hidden mechanism which made it fly apart if struck on the right spot. His opponent was armed with a lance, and the object was to manœuvre the shield so that it struck the lance in the correct spot. Such devices, however, did not outlive their inventor and rule-giver, and the magnificent German tournament books, painted for such princes as Johann Friederich of Saxony, who fought 146 courses between 1521 and 1535, show that almost all the normal tournaments of the time used the simple *Stechen* and *Rennen* rules. The decline is marked sharply by the record of Johann Friederich's successor, August, who only fought thirty-four courses between 1543 and 1566, as compared with an average of between six and ten a year for the comparable periods of his two predecessors' careers.

Maximilian turned his enthusiasm for chivalry to political ends as well: the 'romances' of *Theuerdank, Der Weisskünig* and *Freydal* which represent his career in fictional terms were conceived as both propaganda and as an artistic monument. *Theuerdank* was a romance in verse portraying his skill in the chase; *Freydal*, the most lavish of the three, was to deal with his prowess in the lists; while *Der Weisskünig* made a historical prose romance out of his political career. Each was written at the emperor's dictation, that is, the outline was provided by him, and his secretaries produced a polished narrative, which the greatest exponents of the art of wood-engraving then illustrated. Dürer and Burgkmair were responsible for many of the blocks. These witnesses to the imperial glory could thus reach a far wider audience than manuscripts or paintings had enjoyed in the days before printing; and the whole enterprise would have been a skilful piece of public relations, pandering to the universal taste for romances and using the latest technical methods, if it had come to fruition. As it was, at the emperor's death in 1519, only the woodblocks and a manuscript for *Der Weisskünig* and for *Freydal* survived, and only a few copies of *Theuerdank* were printed.

The diplomatic uses of chivalry had now moved to a very much higher level; and the last great festivals of chivalry, such as the Field of the Cloth of Gold, have been described as an attempt to bring about an international rapprochement on the basis of chivalry. Certainly both monarchs involved, Francis I and Henry VIII, fancied their reputation as jousters, Henry had spent over £4,000 on the tournament at Westminster in 1511 to celebrate the birth of Prince Arthur, compared with £2,300 for the greatest ship of his navy, the *Great Elizabeth*. The preparations in 1515 were on a suitably grand scale, 600 two-handed swords, 100 heavy swords for use on horseback and 400 for use on foot being provided, together with 3,000 lances, as compared with 1,000 lances used at the jousts at John the Fearless' wedding in 1385. In the event, wind and rain spoilt the tilting, and national rivalry was more apparent than chivalric harmony, a rivalry largely expressed in magnificence of dress and the complex mottoes taken by the various knights. A parallel attempt to use pageants for diplomatic ends was that of Catherine de' Medici in 1565 at Bayonne, where she attempted to reconcile Catholics and Huguenots at the splendid festivities recorded in the Valois tapestries.

Even in Italy, where there had been no tourneying tradition, jousting flourished from 1400 onwards. After the initial enthusiasm had passed, in which jousts were held by all and sundry (for instance, the public officials, lords and private individuals who formed the Compagnia del Sasso at Perugia in the 1420s) the lists were patronised as in Burgundy and elsewhere by the princes, seeking to add to the renown of their line. The Italian tournaments were particularly rich in literary devices and allusions, ransacking classical myth as well as both old and new romances for plots and for the mottoes known as *imprese*, a kind of heraldic motto adapted for the circumstances.

A series of magnificent wedding feasts at Bologna under the

Bentivoglio family culminated in that of 1487 when Francesco Gonzaga of Mantua, who carried off the prize, appeared at the head of a squadron of horsemen dressed in oriental fashion, bearing round shields, scimitars and lances which they brandished as they went. Gonzaga himself held splendid jousts in 1462 and 1478, and Lorenzo di Medici was responsible for jousts at Florence in 1469. Florence seems to have provided an especially enthusiastic group of jousters, as thirteen such events are recorded between 1463 and 1478, many at private expense, and the same devotion to the sport reappears in Padua, where a number of tournaments are recorded from 1524 until as late as 1643, though it seems likely that these may have been displays of horsemanship or *carroselli*, without actual tilting or swordplay.

With the religious differences that divided Europe in the sixteenth century, the international ideal of chivalry disappeared. It was carried on as a more parochial tradition, surviving longest in Italy and England. In Italy it survived in literature while its festivals degenerated into popular sideshows; in Spain it disappeared almost entirely except as a literary tradition; in Germany and France it succumbed to the pressure of high politics. Only in the Protestant England of Elizabeth did it survive, as part of the ritual surrounding the Virgin Queen. The full panoply of allegorical romance and martial display was used to this end in a series of tilts from 1581 onwards, held on the day of her accession to the throne. Though such events were supposed to have been held annually from 1559, and the rules of jousting were revived in 1562, that of 1581 is the first recorded, and it seems curious that no trace of the twenty or so previous ones should have survived when the rest are so well documented. Tilting had certainly been in abeyance from the 1520s, as Edward's Puritan and Mary's Catholic courts had both viewed it with an austere eye, until early in Elizabeth's reign. It is possible that the prototype of the idea was the entertainment mounted by Sir Henry Lee for the Queen on her visit to Ditchley in 1575, an occasion in the best Burgundian style, not unlike the elaborate romance prepared for the visit of Philip of Spain to Flanders in 1549. Then the framework had been a chivalric tale, complete with knights errant, enchanters, and a magic sword in a stone copied from that in Arthurian legend, which had to be drawn before the adventures, a carefully managed series of stage effects, could come to an end. The successful drawer of the sword and liberator of the 'prisoners' in the castle was naturally Philip himself.

At Ditchley in 1575 the setting was different. Renaissance learning and the pastoral came to the fore, and the central characters belong to the world of Elizabethan poetry, Sidney's *Arcadia* rather than *Amadis de Gaula*: the 'Faery Queen' makes her first appearance here. That this is indeed the prototype for the later Accession Day tilts is proved by the reappearance of many of the characters in these festivals.

As in other aspects of Elizabethan culture, the Italian influence is strong. Castiglione might be describing Sidney in his guise of a shepherd-knight when he writes of 'when a knight dresses up as a country shepherd, but rides a beautiful horse and wears a handsome and appropriate costume'.[9] The Italian fashion for *imprese* or allegorical devices was adopted so enthusiastically that Sir Henry Wotton was moved to comment on the 'bare *imprese*, whereof some were so dark that their meaning is not yet understood, unless perchance that were their meaning not to be understood'.[10] And for the Accession Day tilt of 1613, the Earl of Rutland employed Shakespeare to do his *impresa*.

The literary influence went much further than in Italy, where actual jousts are only occasionally reflected in poetry: in 1587 booklets explaining the symbolism were distributed to spectators, and many poets described the champions in their verses. Sylvester, translating from the French of du Bartas, inserts into his great poem on the creation a simile comparing Sir Henry Lee to the sun; George Peele in his *Polyhymnia* describes the tilts of 1596, with the appearance of Essex mourning Sir Philip Sidney, and the theme always reverts to the glory of the central figure, Elizabeth herself. Now that the old ecclesiastical pageants were no more, this new secular pomp was set up as an improvement on 'the Pope's holidays', a strongly political phrase. The tilts were popular enough to continue into James I's reign, and in January 1612 Henry Prince of Wales was jousting almost every day. With his death in that year, enthusiasm diminished somewhat, and the last occasion on which they were held was in 1621.

By the seventeenth century chivalry had been kept alive in too artificial a world for too long. It had had no place on the battlefield for almost a century, and its magic was beginning to grow weak. The ideals of knighthood had no place in royal courts where Castiglione and Machiavelli were admired, and where gentlemen and diplomats took precedence over mere rude soldiers. So royal patronage of chivalry disappears, and new means of propaganda are sought in an increasingly literate age. The taste for the spectacular abates; and only at the end of the century does it reappear at Versailles. Between the last Renaissance festival and the first of the Sun King, classicism has beaten down the old romantic literature. Arthur is back among the Breton fables, a classical restraint is the order of the day, not fantasy; and the pageantry of the tournament has been transmuted into theatrical spectacles, ballet and opera. Only in the secular orders of knighthood does a trace of chivalry's glory remain.

20

The Secular Orders

The idea of knighthood both as a universal order of society and as specialised groups within that order had been the monopoly of the Church, in spite of its initial reservations, until the beginning of the fourteenth century. The trial and downfall of the Templars and the failure of the Church to relieve the Holy Land by a crusade, combined with the crisis within the ranks of the Hospitallers had led to disaffection among secular knights with the ideals set up by the religious Orders. They turned from the crusading epics to the romances, and the Arthurian court became increasingly the focus for the dreams. Here the institution of the Round Table represented a kind of secular Order, an equal fellowship of knights chosen for their merit. And in a romance outside the Arthurian cycle, an Order for knights who have shed their vices, and especially the vice of pride, was set up.

When the secular Orders appeared, they were both nationalist and personal to the monarch. They had much in common with the retinues at tournaments, where a group of knights would wear the same device given to them by their leader. Indeed, the first tangible evidence for the idea of a purely secular Order was Edward 1's proposal at a great feast at Windsor in January 1344 for an Order of the Round Table. In the course of a 'Round Table' tournament, he vowed to found an Order with that name with 300 members, and commissioned a building to house its assemblies. It is true that earlier dates of foundation are claimed for other Orders, but none of these will stand up to close examination: such accounts date from a period when nationalist historians were keen to claim the greatest possible antiquity for their own particular candidates. (The only possible exception is the Castilian Order of the *Banda* or Sash; this is examined in detail in Appendix 1.)

The possibility of such an idea was quickly realised, for John the Good of France submitted a proposal to the Pope soon afterwards, which Clement VI approved in six bulls dated 5 June 1344. This

Order of the Star was to consist of 200 knights and a college of canons, under the patronage of the Virgin and St. George, on whose feast days the knights were to assemble for a religious ceremony, jousting being specifically excluded. However, the disaster at Crécy two years later seems to have prevented any such scheme from being carried out at that moment.

It was therefore the Order of the Garter which was the first true secular order to come into existence. When this body was formed in 1348, it owed more to John the Good's scheme than to the ideas of 1344 (Froissart's confusion of the two festivals suggested a closer link between the two events than actually existed). Although we have no exact date for its inauguration, by November of that year the Order had grown to twenty-four knights, and its first full meeting was on St. George's Day 1349.

Whether the traditional story of its foundation related by Tudor chroniclers had any part in this change or in the famous motto we cannot say for certain, though recent research makes the story much more probable. It must have been about August 1347, at a feast at Calais to celebrate the recent capture of the town, that Edward danced with the young countess of Salisbury, Joan of Kent. Froissart tells of his love for her in terms that make it an example of courtly love at its highest, though he has suppressed some very discreditable tales which Jean le Bel, from whom he got the story, has to tell of Edward's behaviour. As they danced, one of Joan's garters fell to the floor; and as she blushed at the mishap, Edward stooped and bound it on his own knee. Hearing the bystanders' whispered comments on the presence there of the blue ribbon, the king rebuked them with the words '*Honi soit qui mal y pense*', 'Shame on him who thinks this shameful', and declared that the garter should soon be held in the highest esteem.

The select band of twenty-six knights who became its members did indeed make of the Garter a great honour. But there are other intentions with which the motto and colours are more likely to be associated. The motto could well apply to critics of Edwards' claim to the French throne, and the colours of the robes are those of France, blue and gold. And the statutes, in all except the number of knights, follow John the Good's scheme of 1344 with remarkable fidelity. Underlining Edward's pretensions in France, the Order as a whole has a much more serious basis than an institution which derived purely from an amorous interlude would be expected to have. Yet the first reference to it is an entry in the Exchequer Rolls recording payments for tunics at the tournament held at Eltham in 1348: the king had a

14 (*right*) Siege, from an early fourteenth-century manuscript, showing the weapons and methods of the period.

15 (*below*) Fifteenth-century siege, from a manuscript of the *Chronique d'Angleterre* by Jean de Wavrin

16 Christ as leader of
the crusading host,
from a
thirteenth-century
Apocalypse

17 Two Templars on
one horse. Matthew
Paris' drawing
symbolises the poverty
which was the Order's
original ideal

Florente g ordic rt humilitate pperante

18 Schloss Marienburg in Prussia, head-quarters of the Teutonic Order, as restored under the Nazi regime. It was razed to the ground by the Russians in 1945

19 Crac des Chevaliers, the greatest of the Hospitaller fortresses in northern Syria

20 (*above*) Gift of the castle of Uclès to the Order of Santiago. The standard of the Order waves over the castle, while the Master, Don Ferrando, is shown receiving the charter from King Alfonso X, and a brother looks on at the right

21 (*left*) The Hospitallers prepare to defend Rhodes against the Turks in 1480

22 (*above*) The chapel at
Marienburg in the eighteenth
century, with the huge image of
the Madonna, patron saint of
the Order

23 (*right*) The old hermit
instructs a squire: from the
introduction to Raimon Llull's
Book of the Ordre of Chyvalry

24 Design by Inigo Jones for the *Barriers* of 1610, at which Prince Henry
made his first appearance in arms. Henry, like his namesake the Young King
four centuries earlier, was hailed as Chivalry's deliverer; the figure at the
right is Chivalry himself who appeared to greet him

25 Knight in insignia of the Golden Fleece. Although the collar was
relatively simple, knights were supposed to wear it the whole time

26 The romantic vision of chivalry: *The Death of Arthur* by James Archer

mantle, hood and surcoat decorated with garters, and his companion knights each bore a blue garter with the words *Honi soit qui mal y pense*. The whole is a skilful interweaving of politics and chivalry, and the brilliant success of the idea is largely due to the presence of elements which appealed to the knights, especially the Order's association with tournaments, and a diplomatic usefulness which gave the sovereign an interest in keeping it alive, whether to reward his military commanders or honour his allies.

The terms of the foundation, which were strictly adhered to and are the basis of the modern order, were that the Order should consist of the sovereign and twenty-five knights. This was a very small group, and the order owed much of its reputation to the fact that the temptation to increase the number was resisted until the seventeenth century. Associated with these knightly members was an equal number of priests, and twenty-six poor knights maintained at the Order's expense. So, like the mediaeval guilds, it combined with its main purpose, the furtherance of chivalry, those of religion and charity. The nature of the chivalric obligations involved shows it to have had a strongly practical military aspect. Knights were not to bear arms against one another unless in obedience to different liege lords or in settlement of just quarrels, and they were to form a military élite, whom the sovereign was to 'prefer' in any warlike expedition. The numbers were to be chosen 'among those most profitable to the crown and Kingdom',[1] and of the original twenty-five knights named to the Order, all except the youthful Sir Hugh Courtenay, had held commands of some kind in Edward's French wars. Many of them had been among the defendants at the 1344 jousts. All save two were English, one of these being the Captal de Buch, a Gascon lord who had twice been imprisoned by the French and had each time refused an offer of liberty in return for a vow not to oppose French interests. Three members were of the royal family, but their loyalty, in a period when kinsmen were often the most dangerous of enemies, was as necessary as that of the great lords.

This pattern continued up to the Civil War, with one important change. Of the knights elected to replace deceased or (very rarely) degraded members up to 1600 only six are foreigners of no more than knightly standing. However, in the same period fifty-one foreign sovereign princes were offered or accepted the order. The diplomatic purpose behind this is clear. By associating them with an English order, it was hoped that they would prove favourable to the English interest, and such elections are particularly noticeable during Henry IV's diplomatic manœuvres after his usurpation of the throne in

1399. Philip the Good, though friendly to England, refused the Order apparently for this very reason, that he was not prepared to enter into such a commitment, when offered it in 1422. Apart from this, the bulk of the knights of the Garter were military officers of the English crown. Military distinction was the only qualification for the admission of an English subject not of royal blood, until with the rise of the Tudor civil service Thomas Cromwell became the first purely secular member. Two of the three original reasons for which a knight could be degraded were military: treason and flight in battle (heresy being the third), though wasteful living was later added. There are several examples of degradation during this period, though it is unlikely that any of the Garter knights suffered a ceremonial as elaborate as the degradation from ordinary knighthood inflicted on Sir Ralph Grey in 1464. The latter was convicted of treason, and sentenced to have his spurs hacked off, his coat of arms torn from his body, another surcoat bearing his arms reversed put on, and his armour broken up, a sentence which, with the exception of the reversing of the arms which the king excused, was duly carried out.

The Order of the Garter's 600 years of continuous existence is in sharp contrast to almost all other chivalric orders. Its French counterpart, the Ordre de L'Etoile (Order of the Star), finally saw the light in 1351–2. It was a much larger institution; the original 200 knights proposed in 1344 had been increased to 500. Other alterations had been made in view of the Garter's existence: St George was no longer a patron, and Our Lady was the Order's sole protector. There is no hint of frivolity about the enterprise: its emblem, a star, bears the motto *Monstrant regibus astra viam*, 'The stars show the way to kings'. Its objectives were more idealistic than those of the Garter, the furtherance of chivalry and the increase of honour, though any ordinance of 1352 adds a military purpose: it is to further the unity and accord of the knights of the realm and animate their prowess in order to ensure its security and peace. All deeds related at the *Table d'Honneur* were to be deeds of war, and no member could hold another order, a regulation aimed at those knights who might aspire to the Garter as well, and which shows the nationalist character of both Orders.

While the Garter's prestige was enhanced by the English victories, the Order of the Star was virtually annihilated at Poitiers, having held only one general chapter in 1352, and having reached a strength of only 140 knights out of a possible 500. Jean le Bel attributes this to a vow taken by the knights never to retreat more than a quarter of a mile in battle, and says that eighty-nine knights of the Order were killed in an ambush in Brittany in 1353 because of this; but even if the vow is true, his figure would seem to be exaggerated. Poitiers is a more likely cause of its destruction; with the capture of John the Good only four years after its foundation, the Order of the Star never really became active, and the gift of its house at St-Ouen to Isabella of Bavaria in 1407 marked the end of all possibility of revival.

If the Garter and the Star belonged to the sphere of international politics, the rivalries within France and England gave rise to a series of lesser orders. The royal ducal houses of Bourbon, Orléans and Brittany each had their own badge and Order. Louis II of Bourbon's Escu d'or (Golden Shield) was short lived, but the Porc-Epic (Porcupine) of Orléans was widely distributed in the decade following 1430, and the Hermine (Ermine) of John IV of Brittany was still in use in 1532. All of them, however, showed the inherent difficulty of any secular Order, that it relied for its glory entirely on the prestige of its leader, and on the patronage, both political and financial, that he could offer, though the intention was the reverse, that the Order should enhance its patron's standing.

The Order of the Golden Fleece, which belongs to the same group, bears this out. It was the wealth and energy, as well as political acumen, of the Valois dukes of Burgundy and their Imperial and Spanish heirs, that made this the greatest Order in Europe. Founded by Philip the Good on the occasion of his marriage to Isabella of Portugal in January 1430, it was a project that he had long cherished. It was modelled closely on the Garter, and had a similar number of knights, twenty-four excluding the duke, though this was almost immediately increased to thirty and later to fifty. Its avowed objects, as set out in the foundation charter, were as follows:

> To do reverence to God and to uphold the Christian faith, and to honour and increase the noble order of chivalry; and also for the three following reasons: firstly, to honour older knights whose noble and high deeds are worthy of recognition; secondly that those who are now strong and able-bodied, and exercise deeds appropriate to chivalry every day, may have cause to continue them even better than before; and thirdly, that knights and gentlemen who see this order worn ... may be moved to noble deeds themselves and lead such a life that their valiance will earn them great fame, and they will deserve to be chosen to wear the said order: my lord the Duke has undertaken and set up an order called 'La Toison d'Or'.[2]

The motives ascribed to Philip besides those set out in the statutes have been various. At some later date, a romantic legend was invented to explain the choice of the symbol of the Golden Fleece; it was in memory of a lady at Bruges whose golden hair Philip admired, despite the mockery of his courtiers at its unfashionable luxuriance in an age which liked a broad forehead with the hair drawn back on the head. Again, its links with crusading projects led contemporary chroniclers to see it as a kind of permanent crusade. Its real purpose was designed to increase the partisans of the House of Burgundy, and to enhance the prestige and independence of the ducal house: in refusing the Order of the Garter, Philip excused himself by saying that he was about to found his own Order. In Philip's diverse territories a unifying force was badly needed, and he attempted to strengthen the bonds between the nobility which had already been established at ducal festivals and tournaments. Louis XI paid tribute to the Order's success when he copied it, even in small details, for his Order of Saint Michael. Even more strongly nationalist than the Garter, it became attached to the sovereignty of Flanders when the Burgundian empire disintegrated, but until then it had drawn for its recruits on all the Valois lands. The original members included six cousins of the duke, and three members of the distinguished knightly family of de Lannoy. No foreigners were included.

The strictly Burgundian nature of the membership was due to the use of the Order as a kind of advisory council to the duke; and except for emperors, kings or dukes (a clause added later so that the gift of the Order could be used as a diplomatic weapon), no other order might be held. The chapters of 1468 and 1473 in particular aired their grievances to Charles the Rash in no uncertain terms, and reprimanded him for being over-eager to go to war; but the Order never had real political influence and there were frequent complaints that the Order's advice was not sought by the monarch. Yet the members of the Order were still represented on the governing body of the Netherlands as late as the eighteenth century. Besides this, the general chapter held an inquest on the behaviour of the other members, reproving offenders for their faults. One of the de Lalaing family was told that he was too dirty in appearance, while two other knights were accused of being too fastidious; the 1545 chapter, in a puritan mood, produced an exceptional list of sins – adultery, concubinage, drinking and bad temper – and deprived one knight of his insignia for a year. In more serious cases such as criminal offences the chapter claimed to be the only court in which members of the Order could be tried, and a clause to this effect was inserted in the Statutes of 1516. However, when the counts of Egmont and Horn stood accused of treason in 1568 and insisted on trial by the Order instead of by the Spanish authorities, they were overruled on the strength of a case of 1468 in which the court's jurisdiction had been limited to matters of honour, and no full-scale criminal trial ever occurred. The last general chapter took place in 1559, as the lengthening shadows of religious dissension darkened the Low Countries, and Philip II and his successors were loath to summon a meeting of respected figures who might have opposed their policies. Thereafter appointment to the Order remained the gift of the king, but was purely honorific; a revision of the statutes in 1631 confirmed this, and it became part of the Spanish aristocratic world, where status and precedent had come to rank before real honour or worth.

Besides these Orders of openly high intent, there is another group of Orders from the same period whose only *raison d'être* was a chivalric whim on their founders' part, rather as though the Garter had ceased to exist after the tournament at Eltham. One of the earliest of these was Amadeus VI of Savoy's Order of the Annunciation of 1362, taken from a token given to him by a lady, with which he appeared at a series of jousts. Boucicaut's *Ordre de la dame blanche à l'escu verd* (Order of the White Lady with a Green Shield), to protect defenceless and disinherited ladies, which he founded in 1399 and which lasted about five years was another courtly Order, though with charitable undertones. Varying degrees of organisation for such Orders, down to the mere wearing of a badge appropriate to the fictional theme of a *pas d'armes* led Olivier de la Marche to comment that 'when a prince gives some device to several noblemen without a number and chapters, it should not be called an Order, but only a device'.[3] The Order of the Fer de Prisonnier of John I of Bourbon, and the device of the Dragon of Jean I of Foix were such, not unlike the liveries of English retinues of the mid-fifteenth century applied on a higher level, badges of personal alliance rather than of membership of an Order.

Many of the Orders had in their statutes echoes of the military Orders and of the long awaited crusade which never materialised. One article of the Garter statutes refers to distant expeditions, which are probably crusades; and in 1454, many of the knights of the Order of the Golden Fleece took the crusading vow. In René d'Anjou's Order of the Crescent the Order could only be renounced if the knight became a monk, and in the brotherhood of arms of the 'Tiercelet' those members who had made the journey to Prussia had a special mark on their insignia, one golden spur if they had not actually seen action there, two if they had fought the heathen.

At the other extreme from the purely chivalric Orders are the practical associations, of which the 'Tiercelet' is one and the Order of the Crescent and the Order of the Golden Apple others. The object of these was that their members should band together to share the profits and hazards of war, just as brothers-in-arms did. The members of the 'Tiercelet' named one of their number as leader in war, and a deputy if needed; they contributed to each other's ransoms, shared the booty and looked after the dependents of those killed. Their annual service and insignia distinguished them from a mere mutual assurance group, even if they were a 'body' first and an 'Order' second, and there was no attempt to create a permanent institution which would outlast its original members.

The secular Orders finally degenerated into mere honorifics. Of the reasons listed in the Statutes of the Golden Fleece one came to dominate the rest; 'to honour older knights whose noble and high deeds are worthy of recognition'. The corporate existence of the Orders instituted after 1450 was minimal, and often there were no limits on the number of knights holding the honour, which was merely at the sovereign's discretion. A brief ceremony and a medal replaced that corporate spirit which briefly appeared in the great Orders, and which was the driving force behind some of the lesser ones. But the knight's idea of glory was too individual and personal for the secular Orders to become more than a series of marginal notes in the history of chivalry. It is by their later incarnation as Orders of merit rather than of knighthood that they are remembered, and their greatest age was to be in the nineteenth century, when they proliferated in every petty court of Europe, until only a handful remained that were not mere badges. In the smaller world of chivalry personal valour had needed no medals to distinguish it.

The Epic of Chivalry Revived

Most of the great pageants of the fifteenth century borrowed to some degree from the romances of chivalry, which as a result enjoyed a new flowering at this period. The demand, however, was less for novelty than for retellings and embroideries of the old tales. Nothing of importance had been produced during the fourteenth century, though the old romances were frequently copied, and remained very popular. It was only in 1388 that any new version of Arthurian romance appeared. Froissart's huge verse romance *Meliador*, which used an Arthurian framework for a series of invented adventures, was mostly centred on vast descriptions of tournaments. In a different vein, there was a prose compilation which contained a complete history of Britain up to Arthur's death as told in the romances, produced for the library of Louis II of Bourbon in 1391. The Charlemagne legends, collected from the degenerate versions of the *chansons de geste* still circulating, were fashioned into a verse cycle in the late thirteenth century, which in turn was the basis for a prose rendering in 1454, and was finally translated into English by Lord Berners as *The Boke of Duke Huon of Bordeux*. Another Arthurian compendium was produced for Jacques d'Armagnac in 1470, and there must have been others which have disappeared.

The most famous of these types of compilation is that of Sir Thomas Malory. Approaching the material from a very different angle, his eight romances each tell a single story, seven of them carefully extracted from the French prose works, whose tapestry-like interweavings he unravels to present a much clearer and sharper tale. As a group, they cover the whole history of Arthur, and it was this that enabled Caxton, when he came to print them, to present them as one book, using the title *Le Morte d'Arthur*. Even if he did not set out to make 'of this vast assemblage of stories, one story and one book',[1] Malory deliberately includes all the greatest episodes of the cycle, and covers the whole history of Arthur's rise and fall. Unlike the French scribes, he was not writing for a patron, but for 'jentylmen and jentylwymmen' of his own standing, who were eager for such reading matter: Raimon Llull's fourteenth-century work was translated as *The Book of the Ordre of Chyvalry* at the request of 'a gentyl and noble esquyer'[2] and Malory's works were printed for 'many noble and dyvers gentylmen of thys royame of England'[3] who had asked for an English version of the Arthurian legend. Writers such as Gilbert de la Haye and Henry Lovelich were busy with their own versions of the literature of chivalry, writing like Malory as enthusiastic amateurs rather than professional makers of romance.

In the course of his translations, Malory not only unravels the tales, but also makes many subtle alterations of emphasis, by omission and selection, and more rarely by addition. He sees chivalry as a secular institution with moral rather than religious associations. Thus Lancelot is his true chivalric knight, rather than the spiritual Galahad; and Arthur, from the shadowy figure of the French romances, becomes the archetype of heroic knighthood. Part of the change in Arthur's character comes from the English romance from which he derives *The Tale of the Noble King Arthur*, where Arthur is portrayed almost in the manner of a *chanson de geste* as a second Charlemagne. This in turn enhances his standing when the tragedy of his involvement with Lancelot and Guinevere reaches its climax; it is from the highest point of the Wheel of Fortune that he falls to his doom. Around Arthur, as the greatest prince of his time, the great knights gather; and they are no longer merely knights, since many of them play a part as Arthur's military commanders in the Roman wars of the second tale, especially Lancelot and Gawain, who only appear in the French romances as knights-errant. This practical view of knighthood reflects the realities of courtly life in the fourteenth and fifteenth centuries, where the great jousters and exponents of chivalry were likewise the king's right-hand men in the field.

Malory also alters the conception of the Round Table, until we would scarcely be surprised to find him inserting its statutes as an Order into the text. He imagines it as a secular company with a practical mission in the world, the keeping of order in unruly times, and derives this from the view of knighthood propounded by the Lady of the Lake in the French *Prose Lancelot*, that knights were appointed defenders of the weak and powerless in the days after the Fall when envy and covetousness began to increase. He has a much clearer view of good and evil than appears in the French romances; the wickedness of the 'false traytour knight' Breunys Sanze Pyté (the

Merciless) and a Tarquyn stands out sharply. Hence the Round Table becomes a continuation of Boucicaut's Order of the White Lady on a Green Shield and of the Order of the Golden Fleece, and represents the true fulfilment of knight-errantry. Malory selects adventures which have a high moral intent in keeping with his theme, preferring the rescue of damsels and overthrow of wicked knights in single combat to the enchantments and marvels which were one of the chief delights of his original. And such a theme would appeal strongly to his readers in the England of the Wars of the Roses.

Likewise, Malory rejects the now moribund ideal of courtly love. Lancelot is challenged by a damsel whom he has just rescued, who says: 'But one thyng, sir Knyght, methynkes we lak, ye that ar a knyght wyveles, that ye woll not love som mayden other jantylwoman', and repeats the rumour that he loves Guinevere. Lancelot, instead of protesting his single-minded adoration of his lady, defends himself on quite different grounds:

> For to be a weddyd man, I thynke hit nat, for that I muste couche with hir and leve armys and turnamentis, battellys and adventures. And as for to sey to take my pleasaunce with peramours, that woll I refuse: in prencipall for drede of God, for knyghtes that bene adventures sholde nat be advoutrers nothir lecherous, for than they be nat happy nother fortunate unto the werrys; for other they shall be overcom with a sympler knyght than they be hemself, other ellys they shall sle by unhappe and hir cursednesse bettir men than they be hemself. And so who that usyth peramours shall be unhappy, and all thynge unhappy that is about them.[4]

Knighthood is entirely practical, a vocation from which there is no respite. Love has become an obstacle on the knight's road, as Iseult points out when Tristram refuses to go without her to Arthur's court: 'For what shall be sayde of you amonge all knyghtes? "A! se how Sir Trystram huntyth and hawkyth and cowryth within a castell wyth hys lady, and forsakyth us. Alas!" shall som sey "hyt ys pyte that ever he was knyght, or ever he shulde have the love of a lady".'[5] The lady is no longer the inspiration of the knight, fount of all his prowess; intead knighthood itself urges him on. Knighthood can only survive as long as it remains the supreme ideal; the darkness of tragedy begins to descend when the knights put their personal feelings before all else; and that includes Lancelot's love for Guinevere as well as the hatred of Mordred and Gawain's loyalty to his dead brothers.

Nor does Malory require a higher motive for knighthood than good deeds in this world. Finding the Grail adventures to be an essential part of the stories he was translating, he does not abandon it, even though it sets up a greater ideal than that of the Round Table; instead, he excises the numerous diatribes on the depravity of the knights of this world wherever he can. When he comes to deal with the failure of the greatest of the secular knights, Lancelot, to achieve the quest, he emphasises his partial success, in the vision of the Grail at Carbonek. And of the problem of grace and repentance little remains. Malory accuses Lancelot of other failings, saying that he is unstable, but does not specify his sinfulness beyond this. The grave and noble pages which tell of the achievement of the quest belong to a separate world, where secular knighthood still has its representatives in the nine knights of Gaul, Ireland and Denmark, and in Sir Bors; but as Sir Bors returns to Camelot from Sarras, bearing Galahad's greeting to the court, we feel that it is the Round Table above all else that has made this achievement possible, and it is Arthur who 'made grete clerkes to com before hym, for cause they shulde cronycle of the hyghe adventures of the good knyghtes'.[6]

Malory's greatest achievement is to give us a last glimpse of the high purpose that chivalry could provide, using romantic material and writing in days when the ideas of knighthood had given way to the pomp and circumstance of ceremonial. Caxton insists rightly on his moral intent in his preface: 'For herein may be seen noble chyvalrye, curtosye, humanyté, frendlynesse, handynesse, love, frendshyp, cowardyse, murdre, hate, vertue, and synne but t'exersyse and folowe vertu . . .'[7]

Italy, like England, had not produced any great epics of chivalry before the fifteenth century. Chivalry had only become widespread after 1400 and the occasional romance of Charlemagne and the Round Table to be found before then was simply a translation from the French, like the book that led Francesca da Rimini and Paolo Malatesta to their doom in the Circle of the Lustful in Dante's *Inferno*:

> One day we read in pastime how in thrall
> Lord Lancelot lay to love, who loved the Queen:
> We were alone—we thought no harm at all.
>
> As we read on, our eyes met now and then,
> And to our cheeks the changing colour started,
> But just one moment overcame us—when
>
> We read of the smile, desired of lips long-thwarted,
> Such smile, by such a lover kissed away.
> He that may never more from me be parted

314

Dante censures the frivolous romance as much as he does the behaviour of the lovers: yet the next great epic poems in Italian after
his were to draw on that very stuff of courtly legend for their inspiration, as chivalry became the preoccupation of the Italian
princes. It was particularly at Ferrara that the epic was revived, its
beginnings being the Charlemagne romances which Barberino had
collected under the title *I Reali di Francia* (The Peers of France) at
the end of the fourteenth century. We are back in the world of the
chansons de geste: loyalty and treachery loom larger than love and
courtesy, and the basic motif is Christianity's struggle against the
pagan lords. The Florentine court found such material apter to
parody than to serious ends, and the *Morgante Maggiore* of Pulci
(1470) exaggerates the giants and marvels until they seem ridiculous.

In Ferrara under Hercules I matters were seen differently. Hercules,
a great jouster, was regarded as the type of perfect knighthood, and
under his patronage Boiardo wrote his epic *Orlando Innamorato*, in
which courtly love and the magical are borrowed from Arthurian
legend and attached to the epic of Roland. It is not an entirely serious
work, 'plesaunte to rede in' rather than instructive; action and adventures are preferred to any attempts at psychology, and the unex-
pectedness of its marvels is one of its joys. The poet himself equates
the strange and the pleasant: 'I will relate to you the strangest, most
delightful and truest thing in the world, if God gives us peace.'[9] Its
great success was probably due to just this lack of high intent in an
age which often took itself very seriously. Boiardo left it unfinished,
breaking off to lament how reality, in the shape of Charles VIII's
invasion of 1494, had disturbed the peace which the writings of romances demanded; and this lack of an ending invited attempts at
completion.

Ludovico Ariosto's poem *Orlando Furioso* is only nominally a continuation of the *Orlando Innamorato*. It starts from the same premises, with the same characters. But it regards chivalry as a serious
subject, worthy of all the ornament that art can lavish on it. The
main epic theme is overlaid with a sentimental one, the love and
madness of Roland; there is a romance attached to the history of the
ducal house of Ferrara, the story of its mythical founders Roger and
Bradamante, and subsidiary plots – the fantastic adventures of Astolpho, and the vicissitudes of three couples, two faithful, one

passionate and fickle; there are assorted episodes by way of diversions, as well as *novelle* and character studies: all this set in a world of war, love and magic. Ariosto's richness, which would appeal to the *uomo universale* of the Renaissance, tends to bewilder his modern readers, but there is no contradiction within his own terms.

Above all, he does not attempt to introduce satire, save in Astolpho's journey to the regions below the moon, and he never mocks the ideas on which his own work is founded. His chivalry may be remote from reality, but it is not the less valid for that, and adheres to the old rules: if the arquebus appears briefly, it is only so that this new-fangled threat to the knight can be destroyed by Roland. From the epic he derives the theme of loyalty to the prince, an idea well calculated to please his patron's ear; and while his main characters obey the rules of courtly love, he is prepared to show the obverse of the coin by retailing some dubious *histoires galantes* at intervals. Perhaps the most disconcerting things in Ariosto are his combats. While in Malory sword rings on sword clearly and sharply as two knights fight for their lives, and the tension of battle is present in every line, Ariosto's heroes slay the foe by the thousand, and the presence of this or that champion decides the battle. Yet there is humanity in his companions and moderation in his use of allegory.

The *Orlando Furioso* was designed to be the Aeneid of chivalry, as its bold Virgilian opening declares:

> *Ladies and knights, arms and lovers,*
> *Courteous deeds and bold I sing*[10]

Yet its style is neither that of the classical epic nor the mediaeval romance, but a new pictorial imagery, which paints in clear and vivid detail, like the intricate background of a Botticelli fresco. And it is hardly surprising that no stern clarion call to honour knighthood such as Malory works into his tales rings out from the *Orlando furioso*, where all is rich and elaborate, like some masterpiece of Renaissance armour meant for state occasions rather than real campaigns.

Ariosto's successor in the tradition of Ferrara worked in a different vein. Torquato Tasso, like Milton, took the epic to be an entirely serious occupation, and found his theme in the stories of the First Crusade. Here chivalry's purposes and accomplishments were both at their highest; and here was a theme worthy of the darker days of the Counter-Reformation which nonetheless retained the chivalric framework beloved of the court at which he worked. He had already completed a simple chivalric romance, *Rinaldo*, in which his moral earnestness and his love of the idyllic, at its purest in his lyric poems, had appeared. His reading of poetic textbooks, such as Aristotle's *Poetics* and study of classical examples before he embarked on the *Gerusalemme Liberata* (Jerusalem Freed), as well as his researches into the history of the First Crusade, showed the seriousness with which he approached the task. This was to be a work which would educate first and entertain afterwards.

In fusing the heroic epic and chivalrous romance as Ariosto had done before him he could not escape from a certain contradiction of tone, and he blends an attempted realism in his descriptions of war and of love (which he sees as an eminently human and fallible force) with a supernatural machinery deriving from classical poetry. The unity of action of classic epic and the adventures in the style of modern romances were equally at loggerheads. Hence he retains Ariosto's diversity and remains puzzling to a modern reader, though perfectly intelligible to his own contemporaries. It is his high seriousness which makes him out as the more ambitious poet: from the opening lines which half-echo Ariosto:

> The sacred armies and the godly knight
> That the great sepulchre of Christ did free,
> I sing; . . .[11]

the emphasis remains on godliness as central to chivalry. Rinaldo, after his escapade with the temptress Armida, must first repent his sins before he can once more work valiant deeds; and Tasso makes much of the historical episode of the Mass and procession before Jerusalem's walls during the seige. In contrast, the pagans find little tolerance for their ways as they 'to idols false for succour call', and only conversion redeems them.

Love, for Tasso, is a snare and entanglement. Both Rinaldo and Tancredi fall in love with pagans, Rinaldo with the beautiful but evil Armida, Tancredi with the warrior Clorinda who disdains love. Yet Rinaldo's sojourn in the enchanted garden and Tancredi's grief for his killing of Clorinda bring them to salvation in the end. There is nothing particularly courtly about their passion: Rinaldo falls above all to Armida's physical charms:

> As when the sunbeams dive through Tagus' wave
> To spy the storehouse of his springing gold,
> Love-piercing thought so through her mantle drave,
> And in her gentle bosom wander'd bold:
> It view'd the wondrous beauty virgins have,
> And all to fond desire with vantage told.[12]

317

And it is only at the last when he has her at his mercy that a nobler love, destined to end in marriage, springs up between them. Tancredi's love for Clorinda is indeed unassuaged, but only because her Amazon ways allow no room for such feelings, and even at her death she has no fond word for him other than gratitude for his baptism of her.

Chivalry is therefore a marital and religious virtue; which is not entirely unexpected in a poem on this theme. It extends further than the Crusaders, however, for Suleiman, the sultan who defends Jerusalem against them, is chivalrous in his way, and Tasso paints him as a noble, stout-hearted warrior, and others among the Saracen army are similarly courageous. Yet, lacking the Christian belief, they cannot prevail. The fulfilment of the ideal in Tancredi and Rinaldo combines the virtues of the courtier, consideration, gentleness and good manners, with bravery and vigour and a spiritual maturity. It owes little to knightly ideals, far more to the teachings of Castiglione overlaid with the new religious seriousness of the Counter-Reformation. And Tasso regards his heroes less as examples of chivalry than as representatives of physical and spiritual perfection to whom chivalry is a natural and incidental virtue, inherited from their forebears but no longer the greatest of their guiding lights, just as it was to their counterparts in real life.

As the Italian epic progresses, it grows increasingly serious. In Spain, on the other hand, fantasy is wholly absent from the *Poem of My Cid*, and reality is banished entirely in the last additions to *Amadis of Gaul*. Even in the first true romances – for the *Poem of My Cid* is a chronicle poem – the tendency to plunder all available sources to produce a dazzling confusion of episodes is apparent. The *Gran Conquista de Ultramar*, supposedly a crusading *chanson de geste*, throws in the story of Charlemagne's mother for good measure along with all the fabulous ancestors of Godfrey of Bouillon: and the earliest original Spanish work, *El cavallero Cifar*, of about 1300, used the legend of St Eustace for the first book, a didactic treatise for the next, and the Arthurian cycle for the real core of the romance in the third book. But none of the Spanish romances enjoyed wide popularity until a very much later date; even the greatest of the Hispanic works, *Amadis de Gaula*, probably written in Portugal in the late thirteenth century by one of the Lobeira family, was known to courtly circles only and did not survive in manuscript.

For it is the printing press that is the key to the revival of romance in Spain. Ariosto and Tasso went reluctantly to press, prompted by pirate editions from the manuscripts circulating among their friends.

318

Amadis was printed in 1508, and went through nine editions in the next twenty-five years; whereupon a torrent of romantic prose flooded the Spanish market, to be eagerly swallowed by all and sundry. The original four books of *Amadis*, a neat enough romance in the late Arthurian manner, with a well-organised plot, and rendered in noble Spanish prose, were not enough for a voracious and indiscriminating public. The adventures in *Amadis* revolve around the lives and loves of Amadis and Oriana whose passion is tested by a series of enchantments and adventures; the characters and the story are not wholly unconnected, and the two lovers have an ideal quality worthy of Tasso. What matters is that Amadis,

> shall be the flower of knighthood in his time; he shall cause the strongest to stoop, he shall enterprize and finish with honour that wherein others have failed, and such deeds shall he do as none would think could be begun nor ended by body of man. He shall humble the proud, and cruel of heart shall he be against those who deserve it, and he shall be the knight in the world who most loyally maintains his love, and he shall love one answerable to the high prowess.[13]

Compared with the French romances of the thirteenth and fourteenth centuries, there is a lack of logic about the adventures, which are often episodes inserted at random; and, more curiously, there is a streak of wanton cruelty which is surprising: 'In the gate-way Galaor found the first knight whom he had smote down, who was yet breathing and struggling; he trampled him under his horse's feet and then rode away.'[14] Amadis, too, can be as cruel as his brother; and violence is apparently relished purely for its own sake, not as a necessary byproduct of skill in arms.

This, however, like all the romances, is 'literature of escape'; and the demand for such relief from the tedium of everyday life was far greater than the literary skill available. Continuations of *Amadis*, in all another eight books, and their successors, concentrate on adventure; they emphasise their remoteness by high flown and archaic language, or by a new 'elegance' of style which is more euphuistic than anything the Elizabethans ever dreamt up. Here is a sunrise:

> With difficulty the rubicund father of the untutored youth Phaeton, revealing himself in the northern tropic of the lower hemisphere, advanced on swift Phlegonian chariot to clear the golden and profulgent path of the twelfth zodiac, sending from his fourth sphere to the circumference of the immovable earth most certain harbingers of his approach.[15]

Each romance becomes, not an intricate tapestry of themes as in

319

the French cycles, but an overloaded cart of words, the wheels of whose plot creak along under the burden. And yet, in an age of widening education and new leisure, the fashion caught on. Between 1508 and 1535, twenty-eight new romances (including some sequels) appeared, and numerous reprints made. It was to a new audience that they were addressed, for while the rich French or Flemish bourgeois might have run to the luxury of an occasional manuscript, books were within the reach of much humbler pockets. They aroused fanatical belief, and St Teresa of Avila is said 'to have devoted herself passionately to these books',[16] and even to have written one in her youth. Apocryphal stories of their effect abound. There is the tale of a man who returned home to find the household in a state of mourning, all weeping together, and when he asked if a son or relative had died, they answered, 'No'. 'Why then do you weep' he enquired, perplexed. 'Sir,' they said, 'Amadis is dead.' And one Simon de Silveira is said to have sworn on the Gospels that every word in *Amadis* was true; but then he was the man who, having won a lady after a lengthy courtship, took his revenge on their wedding night by asking for a candle when they retired, and reading *Palmerin of England* for so long that the lady, taking it amiss, said to him: 'Sir is that what you married for?' Whereupon he replied: 'And who told you, Madam, that marriage was anything else?'

The vogue for such works continued throughout the century, despite attacks from critics and from the Inquisition. Amadis and Palmerin and their respective clans were the leaders, and a host of lesser figures tagged along behind. Italy, France and Germany each took up the vogue. In France, the various books of *Amadis* were printed 117 times – an average of eight times for each book – between 1540 and 1577 and it was still well known in 1666, when La Fontaine referred to it; in Italy, there were several dozen printings between 1546 and 1615; only England, with a strong literary activity of its own and few links with popular culture on the Continent remained relatively aloof. In all this, little of the old ideals was left. *Amadis de Gaula* was at least reasonably respectful of chivalry, and more moral than many of its predecessors in that all its liaisons end in marriage. Later works dwelt only on the theatrical and melodramatic side of the adventures, until the once noble knights are no more than performers going through their tricks to amuse a clamouring crowd, stripped of all ideals and growing ever more fantastic in their feats. The tables are turned: chivalry has become the people's plaything.

Yet there was one more masterpiece to come, perhaps the most astonishing work in all the literature of chivalry, comic, satirical and yet deeply concerned with the values of chivalry. If the romances were already at a low ebb in 1600, Byron's famous phrase about Cervantes and his *Don Quixote*, that he 'smiled Spain's chivalry away,' has some truth in it. Like all great comedy, Cervantes keeps his comedy near to reality, and the fundamental absurdity from which his humour springs is the close juxtaposition of real life and romance.

Don Quixote seems to have derived from an anonymous play of about 1590, in which one Bartolo, bereft of his wits by reading too many chivalric ballads, sets out in Quixotic style: but Bartolo is swiftly brought to his senses after only one adventure. Given the idea, the story seems to have shaped slowly in Cervantes's mind. The first seven chapters, before Sancho Panza appears, are little more than an expanded version of Bartolo's mishap. Once the inquisition on the books of chivalry has taken place, and Sancho Panza's native wit has been brought to salt the Don's dry and elegant discourses, the theme and counterpoint of the work are complete. The object stated in the Prologue now comes to the fore: 'this book of yours aims at no more than destroying the authority and influence which books of chivalry have in the world and among the common people',[17] and remains as a guiding thread through the book. The theme reappears in the canon of Toledo's diatribe:

> I have never seen a book of chivalry with a whole body for a plot, with all its limbs complete, so that the middle corresponds to the beginning, and the end to the beginning and middle; for they are generally made up of so many limbs that they seem intended rather to form a chimaera or monster than a well-proportioned figure. What is more, their style is hard, their adventures are incredible, their love-affairs lewd, their compliments absurd, their battles long-winded, their speeches stupid, their travels preposterous and, lastly, they are devoid of all art and sense, and therefore deserve to be banished from a Christian commonwealth, as a useless tribe.[18]

And the last sentence of the second part repeats the author's avowal of his intention:

> For my sole object has been to arouse men's contempt for all fabulous and absurd stories of knight-errantry, whose credit this tale of my genuine Don Quixote has already shaken, and which will, without a doubt, soon tumble to the ground. Farewell.[19]

Don Quixote is nonetheless a romance of chivalry in all its outward appearances. It consists of a series of adventures with the obligatory diversions and inserted stories; it uses the conventional

321

language of the romances (something which no translation can ever convey); and in many ways it conforms to the ideal romance of which the canon of Toledo speaks, which under the guise of the popular formula will give the author an opportunity to display his versatility in 'the epic, the lyric, the tragic and the comic, and all the qualities contained in the most sweet and pleasing sciences of poetry and rhetoric'. It has, too, 'an ingenious plot, as close as possible to the truth', and it achieves 'the excellent purpose of such works, which is, as I have said, to instruct and delight at the same time'.[20]

It is by their heroes, however, that books of chivalry stand or fall. Cervantes has seen this; he accepts the formula, and attacks chivalry at its central point. If the hero becomes a comic figure, he seems to say, all your elaborate trappings are so much glittering tawdry; and my hero is only a little more comic than yours. Don Quixote, 'verging on fifty, of tough constitution, lean-bodied, thin-faced, a great early riser and lover of hunting',[21] is not so different from Lancelot when he sets out on the quest for the Grail, except that the romances know nothing of age, and toughness and early rising are equally un-romantic. His habits are exactly those of the knight-errant: he is careful to regulate his sleeping hours by the approved rules; each time he sleeps beneath the open sky 'it seemed to him that he was confirming his title to knighthood by a new act of possession',[22] and he is careful to do his duty as a lover: 'He spent the rest of the night in thoughts of his lady Dulcinea.'[23] All that divides Don Quixote's actions from those of the real knights-errant of romance is his awareness of correct behaviour: he always feels that this or that ought to happen to him, and makes certain that it does, while in the books from which he draws his inspiration the adventures appear of their own accord, and the knights are really sleepless for love.

This perpetual self-consciousness is sharply contrasted with Sancho Panza's natural earthiness. Don Quixote lies sleepless for love 'while Sancho Panza's sleep, as he settled down between Rosinante and his ass, was not that of a rejected lover, but of a soundly kicked human being'.[24] Cervantes subtly underlines the unnatural life of the romances, which is one of his chief objections to them: indeed, in the great burning of these volumes which Quixote 'sold many acres of cornland to buy', one of the books to escape is 'Tirant lo Blanch' because 'here the knights eat and sleep and die in their beds, and make their wills before they die, and other things as well that are left out of all other books of that kind'.[25] Whenever Quixote threatens to become too fantastic, Sancho is there at hand to bring him back to earth – or at least to somewhere near it.

Sancho, being unaffected by Don Quixote's madness, sees windmills as windmills and sheep as sheep, but if he believes his own eyes, he believes his master's interpretation of what he sees. And Don Quixote lives in a world which is almost permanently under the enchanter's spell. Windmills become giants, sheep opposing armies, a barber's basin Mambrino's helmet. But such a device palls quickly enough, and Cervantes is prepared for this. Having made his initial point about the absurdity of the romantic setting, he turns the enchantments into the key to his hero's development. In this, again, he is offering an unfavourable contrast to the romances, where a perfect knight is always a perfect knight, and like some comic-strip hero, always emerges victorious and unchanged in the end. Life is not like that; Don Quixote is a more subtle and resilient character than we at first suspect. True, he remains steadfastly convinced of the reality of knight-errantry as he imagines it; but he manages to reconcile the everyday world and his own vision to a remarkable extent. When in the second part enchantments are contrived by Samson Carrasco and by the Duke and Duchess, who have read of his adventures of the first part in print, he overcomes their ingenious attempts to mock him by a high idealism which no amount of ridicule can touch. Even when Sancho deliberately deceives him for reasons of his own, and presents 'three peasant girls . . . riding on three young asses or fillies' as Dulcinea and her attendants, and seems to have the upper hand over his master, Don Quixote goes surely on his way: and in the episode of his dream in the Cave of Montesinos he makes such an enchantment a commonplace and natural event which troubles him not one whit. He says that one of the peasant girls borrowed money of him, and by ways of thanks 'leaps two yards, by measure, into the air'; at which Sancho breaks in to demand: 'Are such things possible in the world? Can there be enchanters and enchantments so strong as to have changed my master's sound wits into this raving madness?'[26] Yet despite the author's pretended doubts as to the authenticity of this episode, it is all of a piece with Don Quixote's way of thought; and as the knight resists all attempts to shake his belief, we begin to wonder if he is not a lone sane voice in a world gone mad.

For from the enchantments, his own logic produces greater truths. When he defends himself before the Duke and Duchess, he speaks of these enchanters, and especially of Dulcinea's transformation, which is the cruellest blow of all, 'for to rob a knight-errant of his lady is to rob him of the eyes with which he sees, of the sun by which he is lighted, and of the prop by which he is sustained'.

The Duchess objects 'that your worship never saw the lady Dulcinea, and that this same lady does not exist on earth, but is a fantastic mistress, whom your worship engendered and bore in your mind, and painted with every grace and perfection you desired'. ' "There is much to say on that score," replies Don Quixote. "God knows whether Dulcinea exists on earth or no, or whether she is fantastic or not fantastic. These are not matters whose verification can be carried out to the full. I neither engendered or bore my lady, though I contemplate her in ideal form" . . .'[27] Cervantes sums up the place of the lady in chivalry perfectly.

But Cervantes also moves far outside the world of chivalric romances. Don Quixote starts out as a symbolic figure of folly with human traits added, and ends stripped of his symbolism as an entirely living character, vindicated in his apparent folly. Sancho grows in stature as his native wit takes him safely through situations beyond his experience. For Cervantes has lived up to the versatility to be found in the ideal chivalric novel of the canon of Toledo; and he has made of it something quite new as a result. If he began by satirising the mere formulae of chivalry, he ends by hinting at alternative views of life, based on his experience and reading.

He had been scholar, soldier, official, playwright and author in his day; when he wrote the last pages of *Don Quixote* he was famous without the rewards of fame. He had read the books of the Erasmian thinkers and of the Counter-Reformation, as well as Italian epics and literary theory; in short, he was a man of far wider horizons than his predecessors as writers of romance, and romance did not allow of any wider vision than its own narrow conventions. He inserts autobiographical episodes of his captivity in Moorish hands; he throws in fashionable pastoral scenes and lyrics (being particularly proud of the latter). And he can create the character of Sancho, who holds as much of our attention as Quixote himself. At a higher level, he takes the patent unreality of books of chivalry as a starting point for a subtle exploration of the nature of reality, disguising this schematic reasoning behind the vital and spontaneous surface of the book.

Like his hero, Cervantes still continued to keep some affection for and belief in the romances; the enchantment lingered on. At the end of the prologue to part two he says: 'I forgot to tell you that you may look out for *Persiles*, which I am just finishing, and the second part of *Galatea*.'[28] Of these two projects, only *Persiles* was completed: and it proved to be a romance of chivalry in which the author not only fulfils the canon of Toledo's rules as to variety, but also obeys its regulations as to the central figures, giving them 'all those attributes which constitute the perfect hero, sometimes placing them in one single man, at other times dividing them amongst many'. Classical romances as well as mediaeval and modern are laid under contribution; the geography is at once realistic and fantastic; and the whole work was the apple of its author's eye. Yet it was Don Quixote, the fallible hero, who proved immortal, like Malory's Lancelot; we are readier to sympathise with their humanity than to marvel at the gilded perfection of a Perceval or Persiles.

Don Quixote had an immediate success; a spurious second part was published before Cervantes provided his own, and translations were quickly made. It is the last major work to be inspired by the ideals of chivalry, partly because its satire was all too effective, and even the most traditional courtier could hardly take his disguise in a tournament seriously after reading it, and partly because the age of chivalry was near its close. In any case, the Spanish romances had been a very late and unreal flowering. But in Cervantes' pages there is more true insight into chivalry's real meanings than in many far more serious works; and for all his comic ways, the lean and lonely figure of the Knight of the Sad Countenance on the dusty Spanish roads is no unworthy tailpiece to the procession of knighthood.

Critics of Chivalry and
Advocates of Reform

men turned soft

* Chivalry was an ideal which aimed to soften the rough ways of the soldier, and substitute a controlled and disciplined way of life for the old heroic frenzy. Its critics from the very earliest days accused it of failing to find the golden mean of an effective but civilised knighthood; and if Eberhard's criticism of the over-warlike barons of Germany in the eleventh century is one side of the picture, the other is represented in the mid-twelfth century by Peter of Blois, who complains that not only does military discipline no longer exist, but that soldiers going to war 'take wine instead of swords, cheeses instead of lances; bottles instead of blades, spits instead of spurs'. The newly made knights at once go off to break their vows, 'oppressing the poor subjects of Christ, and miserably and unmercifully afflicting the wretched, in order to sate their illicit lusts and extraordinary desires in the sorrows of others'.[1] He compares these so-called Christian knights unfavourably with the soldiers of ancient Rome, brave and virtuous despite their paganism. The preamble to the Rule of the Templars, written about 1130, says of the early members of the order of knighthood in general that 'they despised the love of justice, which belonged to their duties, and did not do as they ought, that is defend poor men, widows, orphans and the Church: but instead they competed to rape, despoil, and murder.' And Urban II, launching the First Crusade, was reported to have made similar criticisms, saying that knighthood (*militia*) was now falsehood (*malitia*). Other writers accuse thirteenth-century knights of going to war 'all dressed up like a knight going to the Round Table' or of going 'to war dressed for a wedding'.[2]

But the chief attack on chivalry was from those preachers who supported the Church's execration of tournaments, 'detestable fairs'. All sensible men recognised them as folly, so ran one line of argument, despite their value as military training, because of the excesses which they bring in their train: thus Humbert des Romans in the thirteenth century, speaking of the 'insensate prodigality of the nobles' in pursuit of glory, of the use made by some 'who take advantage of tournaments in order to settle private feuds',[3] and of the debauchery to which they are exposed. If only knights would use them as occasions for the practice of arms and nothing more, tournaments might be tolerable. Jacques de Vitry takes a sterner line, proving that all the seven deadly sins are involved, a theme taken up and repeated by the poets. Most dramatic of all, however, are the legends woven around real episodes and designed to put fear of God into the erring knights. The tournament at Neuss, where the soberest authorities give a figure of forty-two dead (which may well be exaggerated even so), became the basis of Thomas of Cantimpré's lurid warning in his book of miracles:

> Hear what happened in our time, as all Germany knows. In the year of our Lord 1243 near the noble town of Neuss on the Rhine, many nobles, dukes counts, barons and knights gathered for a tournament. A certain brother Bernard of the order of Preachers arrived with a companion, and pleaded with them, almost in tears, to spare each other and desist from their foolish plan, and to have pity on Christianity and the Church in her affliction, which was being ravaged even then in Hungary, Slovakia and Poland by the Tartars. When many would have willingly desisted as he asked them, a certain count of Castris mocked the friar, and those who agreed with him; and when the squadrons of knights assembled, the miserable man began that wicked tournament. Early in the morning of the same day, so many said, a great cloud appeared like a clod of earth with birds like crows croaking, and hovering around it. And I am convinced that these were demons which foreshadowed coming ills. And soon, when the tournament was in progress both knights and their attendants fell in such heaps and in such numbers, some dead, some driven mad, some permanently disabled, that no one would doubt that this seemed to be the sport not so much of men, but, by divine vengeance, of demons. The total of dead was reckoned at 367. Among whom the first to die was said to be the Count of Castris who had obstinately opposed the friar. On the night after this had happened, demons in the shape of armed men were seen to gather near Isscha in Brabant, as the priest of that village says: and I believe that they were rejoicing over such evil deeds.[4]

Thomas goes on to relate the horrifying torments that await those killed in tournaments, including armour covered with spikes on the inside (in the manner of an Iron Maiden), baths of flames, beds of red-hot iron, and the embraces of a huge and horrible toad, the latter punishments because the knight in question had been wont to take a bath after a tournament and then have himself put in bed with a young girl, to whom he would make love. Similar terrors were in store for those who killed knights in tournaments: their victims' ghost might appear and warn them of their approaching fate. As

Caesarius of Heisterbach says in another book of miracles, 'As to these who die in tournaments, there is no doubt that they go to hell, unless they are helped by repentance,'[5] unlike those who die in a just war, to whom no blame is attached.

But this is propaganda rather than criticism, propaganda based on the Church's inflexible opposition to tournaments. As that opposition begins to weaken, so does the attack: and later detractors of chivalry turned to more general themes. Though complaints such as Jacques de Vitry's that knights did nothing but pillage and rob are not unusual in the twelfth and thirteenth centuries, it is only with the succession of French defeats in the Hundred Years' War that serious attacks are made on the idea of chivalry as a whole. Here was a court acknowledged to contain the flower of Europe's knights and to be unsurpassed in matters of chivalric taste, defeated twice in ten years, and the bitter years of disorder that followed showed that the knights did not practise what they preached but were just as eager to make their fortune from booty as the rest of the men-at-arms. Froissart records frequent changes of loyalty without a qualm; and he hardly troubles to distinguish between *routiers* and true knights. Eustace d'Aubrecicourt, of whom he makes much, had lived off the land with an armed band in Champagne for many years; and yet Froissart says at the end, 'God has his soul, for he was a very valiant knight in his day.'[6] It is only correct behaviour towards other members of the knightly class that counts; the sufferings of the common people go unnoticed.

It is from the people that the complaints against knighthood are most serious. In England an anonymous poet had written a biting satire directed against the renewal of the war in France in 1337, based on the so-called *Vows of the Heron*. It was a custom of the time that knightly vows should be made on the bird which was the centre of the feast. Edward I had vowed by the swans to conquer Robert Bruce in 1306, and Philip of Burgundy was to take the crusading 'vow of the pheasant' in 1454. The poet, however, exaggerates the vows until they become ridiculous or brutal, and makes the whole episode a grim, almost humourless satire on enthusiasm for war and the custom which epitomised it.

In France, Eustace Deschamps, writing at the same time as Froissart, uses the common theme of the contrast between the knights of old and the knights of today in his *Lay de Vaillance*.[7] Once knights used to be properly trained, spending eight or ten years in the profession of arms before they were actually knighted. They were courteous, godly, restrained in speech, not miserly, and 'their hearts were not stolen away by soft beds'. Nowadays the knights sleep until the sun is high in the sky, and when they wake up their first thought is where to find some good wine. They are lazy wastrels, fond of dressing up in fine clothes; but what can be expected of men who have been knights since they were ten or twelve years old, and were never properly trained?

Yet for all this Deschamps sees chivalry as something of value, worth rescuing from its present pass. His remedy is sometimes austere: the nobles should disdain wealth, refrain from marrying too soon, if at all; and sometimes not entirely unattractive to the knights, as when he advocates more jousts and tournaments as a means of training for them. And some of the blame attaches to their commanders, who failed to maintain discipline and to plan adequately.

Alain Chartier, writing after Agincourt, is not so convinced of the value of chivalry itself. He sees it as a decoration for tournaments and feasts, best left to heralds and masters of ceremonies, and when in the *Livre des quatre dames* he attacks the French knights it is for their lack of martial virtues, a theme which he takes up again in the *Quadrilogue invectif* of 1422. He sees love of luxury as the chief reason for the defeat of French knighthood, an accusation already made by Honoré Bonet in his *Tree of Battles*. Not only did the knights lead a life of ease, but they regarded war as a means of obtaining wealth, in which robbery and pillage were more important than fighting the enemy, and their mercenary nature is underlined. Besides this, he has no time for the international aspects of chivalry: a knight's job is to fight his country's foes, not fraternise with them, and patriotism is one of his greatest virtues. He sums up by blaming lack of loyalty, inadequate spending on military matters and lack of good counsel as the causes of the disaster.

The same ideas are the basis of Jean de Bueil's manual of knighthood in the mid-fifteenth century, *Le Jouvencel*. The knight is to be a professional soldier above all else; de Bueil's own experience has taught him this. Training is all-important, and the greater a man's rank, the greater his pride in his profession should be, and the less he should object to being put under a skilled captain despite the latter's inferior social standing. Even though he allows the value of an almost chivalric comradeship-in-arms, the hard school of the camp is the only way to make a good soldier. He would not have approved of Monsieur de Croy encamped before Neuss sighing for 'the ladies to entertain us, to admonish us to bear ourselves well, to give us tokens, devices, veils or wimples'.[8] War is much too practical a matter for such courtesies, though ransoming is a good commercial proposition. De Bueil is much more interested in cannon and siege-machines, in strategy and tactics, than in honour and glory. And for this reason he is flatly opposed to jousting, which is not only a waste of time but all too often of men as well:

> First, those who do it wish to take someone else's property, namely their honour, in order to gain a vainglory of little worth; and in doing so, he does service to no one, spends his money, risks his body to take life or honour from his opponent, and little profit comes his way; while he is occupied thus, he abandons war, the king's service, and the general good; and no one should risk his life except in worthwhile activities.[9]

De Bueil expounds a completely modern view of warfare, where the efficiency of the soldier ranks above all other considerations; and though the veneer of chivalry survived into Francis I's Italian campaigns, the realities of warfare after the defeat of the Bohemian chivalry by the Hussites and of Charles the Rash at Nancy by the Swiss pikemen were on de Bueil's side. The knight could only justify his presence in the warfare of the following century by his skill as a commander.

Other writers had reached the conclusion that chivalry had had its day on the battlefield without being able to make such practical suggestions for the new mode of warfare as de Bueil. Philippe de Mézières, enthusiast for the crusading ideal, saw that ideal come to grief in the disaster at Nicopolis, and found his worst fears as to chivalry's military value confirmed. From his participation in the crusade of 1346, he had realised that the Turks were a formidable and capable enemy, and that chivalry, instead of being an advantage to the Christian army, had become a positive hindrance. In his scheme for a new and disciplined Order of religious knighthood, the Order of the Passion of our Lord Jesus Christ, he attacks crusaders who followed only one of 'the great ladies of this world',[10] vainglory, in such expeditions. But chivalry itself is not at fault; it is only that knights forget that obedience is also a knightly virtue. His Order is to be a secular revival of the old military Orders, designed to set out as a single great crusade of 21,000 men, under strict discipline; and the details of transport and organisation are carefully set out. Mézières's insistence on the practical aspects of warfare shows that he had realised some of the faults of the earlier attempts at crusades, yet the idealists who might have been attracted by his project would probably have brushed all this aside: the contradiction at the heart of his scheme remains. Even so practical a man as Jean Gerson failed to see

330

that chivalry called for self-discipline according to its ideals, and offered in return a reward in terms of personal glory, while warfare needed corporate discipline imposed in order to gain a corporate end.

Other aspects of chivalry besides its military failings came in for criticism in the fifteenth and sixteenth centuries. Its pomp and pageantry were not the only targets for attacks by the Puritans. Roger Ascham found its literature as well to be subversive, 'as one for example, *Morte Arthure*: the whole pleasure of which booke standeth in two speciall poyntes, in open mans slaughter, and bold bawdrye: In which booke these be counted the noblest Knightes, that do kill most men without any quarell, and commit fowlest aduoulteries by sutlest shiftes.'[11] And the main impetus of that literature, courtly love, had long ago been a target for criticism. The reaction begins not with the preachers, one of whom even agrees that 'a knight is only brave if he is in love', but with secular writers who champion the woman's cause and see it as a mere masculine deception. The Chevalier de la Tour Landry, instructing his daughters in about 1371, tells a story of Marshal Boucicaut's father. Three ladies discovered that he had sworn true love to them all within the past year, and when challenged, he merely replied that he had been sincere on each occasion. And when he advocates 'love paramours', saying 'For in certayne me semeth that in good love and trewe maye be but welthe and honour, and also the lover is better therefore, and more gay and holy; and also the more encouraged to exercyse hym selfe more ofte in armes, and taketh therefore better maner in al estates, forto please unto his lady or love,' a classic statement of chivalric love, his wife gives him short shrift: 'These wordes are but sport and esbatement of lordes and felawes in a language much comyn.'[12] Christine de Pisan, writing in fifteenth-century Burgundy, likewise distrusts the flattering intentions of the knight, whose supposed chivalry she would prefer to see replaced by real military ardour.

In the love poems of the fourteenth and fifteenth centuries a similar change takes place. Realism is the hallmark of the criticism of chivalry here: courtly love bears no relation to what actually goes on. The *Cent Ballades* of Jean le Seneschal reflect this neatly. When the author has finished his description of 'the code of the perfect knight and perfect lover, able to resist the seduction of passing love, and desirous of giving himself solely to his lady',[13] he asks for opinions on whether fidelity is better than change in love. Of thirteen replies some prefer constancy, some prefer change, some are evasive: but the bastard de Coucy sums it up nicely:

> Most honoured lady, your splendour fair
> Has overwhelmed me, and I am yours.
> I shall not waver, I yield me quite:
> Thus say they all; and yet it's never so.[14]

And the Duc de Berry advocates this kind of behaviour quite openly: swear constancy, seek change.

At the other extreme, the tradition of the *novella* or short story, best known in Boccaccio, has little sympathy for either knight or bourgeois in its plots, where both alike are cuckolded. It is in this manner that Antoine de la Salé's *Le Petit Jehan de Saintré* ends when Saintré is abandoned for a muscular abbot with hairy thighs who beats him in a wrestling match. For de la Salé, love is a distraction for chivalry and is a danger to its true glory:

> Ah, false, wicked and traitorous love, must you be ever like unto Hell, that was never yet surfeited with swallowing-up of souls? Will you likewise never be sated with tormenting and wounding of hearts? ... you have taken captive the hearts of some and have dealt full falsely and evilly therewith, and then left them all confounded, so that you are answerable for the loss of their souls and their lives (unless God have mercy upon them), and their honour.[15]

Here is the counterpart to de Bueil's realistic view of war in *Le Jouvencel*, a realistic view of misdirected passionate love, which rewards not with an ethereal bliss but with frustration and waste of energy.

By the end of the fifteenth century there was little enough real substance in chivalry for moralists to regard it seriously. The spate of romances in the early sixteenth century provided a new and much easier target for their attacks. Here were the peacock feathers of knighthood, its vain adventures, with no possible claim to moral worth. Juan Luis Vives, like Ascham an educationalist, attacked them in 1529 as being 'written and made by such as were ydle and knew nothinge. These bokes do hurt both man and woman, for they make them wylye and craftye, they kyndle and styr up covetousnes, inflame angre, and all beastly and filthy desyre.'[16]

Yet the Inquisition, which might have been expected to take a very dim view of such trifles, never placed a single chivalric romance on the *Index Expurgatorius*. Indeed, the humanist critics may be suspected of trying to divert attention from their favourite classical and philosophical reading, which was often seen as much more subtle and dangerous. There were bans on the import of romances into the Spanish colonies in the New World in 1531 and 1553, on the grounds that they might hinder the spread of Christianity there, though shipments continued nonetheless. In Spain the story of a priest who believed all the romances to be true because they bore on the title-pages the state's licence to print them aroused bitter comment; but there was no real effort to take measurements against the books of chivalry, which might corrupt morals but preached no heresies.

So the inheritance of chivalry was divided: the knight at war became the professional soldier, the knight in love either a poet whose delicate conceits were the sum of his longings or an honest married man, and the knight of romance a scarecrow mocked by all and sundry. And so the knight at court became something else as well, the courtier and gentleman. The new men of the Renaissance were by no means a sudden phenomenon: the duties of a knight had become more and more complex as each successive moralist or teacher of manners added his views. From the simple restraints on the misuse of a warrior's power, the duties enjoined on a knight had come to include all the social graces. He was expected, if he was to be thought fully chivalrous, to be courtly as well as heroic, to know the intricacies of the dance floor as well as the finer points of the lists, and to be good company on all occasions.

To the Renaissance mind this was not enough. Any hail-fellow-well-met character could pass off as a man about court, however small his mind and however wearying his tales of his latest feats of arms. The Italians, arbiters of taste to Europe for the next three centuries, who had come late to chivalry and borrowed only its plumage for their pageants, now set up a new model of behaviour to supersede the knight. If it owed only marginal flourishes to chivalry, it was because the fully fledged knight had been absent from Italy; and yet because the court was as important there as it had been in Aquitaine or France or Burgundy, there are many points in common.

The knight had lost the feudal basis of his existence in the course of the fourteenth and fifteenth centuries. Though many knights remained landowners, it was no longer essential for the younger son to win his lands, and he could make his way in the world as soldier or administrator. Hence the court had grown considerably in importance, as many of its members regarded it as their home rather than some distant castle; and the courts of the early Middle Ages with their incessant peregrinations round the countryside are a far cry from the settled establishments of the Italian princes. The knight was now just as much a courtier as a warrior, and even that was changing as soldiers grew more and more professional: the military aspect of his existence was no longer his chief pride.

With the advent of printing and the great increase in secular education that followed in its wake, the old chivalric habits, which had done well enough for the fifteenth century, became outmoded. Della Casa's *Galatea*, with its insistence on the outward forms of behaviour, good manners, points the way. New ideas and fashions, new entertainments and arguments, could be spread quickly; where there had been one manuscript, there were twenty books for each man to read and form his own opinion. The intellectual ferment that resulted was almost entirely artistic and secular. What marks off the gentleman from the knight is above all his critical appreciative attitude towards both politics and art, an attitude which permeates Castiglione's study of the new man, *The Courtier*. In these dialogues ascribed to his fellow-courtiers at Urbino, the new ideals are set out for the first time – if one can call them ideals: qualities would be a more appropriate word. The courtier is opportunist where the knight was loyal; he is more concerned with cutting a good figure than with real skill in war or tournament; he will admire chaste women, and yet take his *amours* as he finds them; and above all he will seek his own fortune. But against this he will value learning and appreciate the painter's and sculptor's work, and will at least be gracious and well-mannered. Castiglione tells an anecdote against those who have only one purpose in life. A lady asked a man to dance with her, and was told

that such frivolities were not his business. And when at length the lady asked what his business was, he answered with a scowl: 'Fighting ...' 'Well then,' the lady retorted, 'I should think that since you aren't at war at the moment and you are not engaged in fighting, it would be a good thing if you were to have yourself well greased and stowed away in a cupboard with your fighting equipment, so that you avoid getting rustier than you are already.'[17]

At first sight, Castiglione's motto seems to be moderation in all things; but we find it is a purposeful moderation. Affectation in dress draws unfavourable comment, as does boasting or drunkenness; and it is not the principle of moderation, but other men's opinions that are important. The courtier at war should

accomplish the bold and notable exploits he has to perform in as small a company as possible and in view of all the noblest and most eminent men of the army, and, above all, in the presence, or if possible under the very eyes, of the prince he is serving. For it is certainly right to exploit the things one does well.[18]

This is a world of career-seeking which contrasts sharply with the idle glory of chivalry; and if it is more practical, it is scarcely an attractive ideal. And the condition and connoisseurship of the courtier is, we feel, bent to the same end: to shine in his prince's eyes by finding the right words to praise the latest masque or painting. It is a more polished world, but its daggers are polished too, and the competition for favour is as intense as the financial rewards are necessary to the courtiers' existence.

Nonetheless, the love of art is genuine, and love itself is taken seriously. Castiglione's discourse on love is full of noble ideas, and its philosophical heights are explored enthusiastically by his audience. When he equates goodness and beauty he expresses the new hedonism perfectly, and if the courtier-gentleman has to know how to make his way into the prince's favour, he will also know how to enjoy his reward.

Castiglione's influence was wide. Published in 1528, *The Book of the Courtier* met with wide approval, from England to Spain, and became the model for many later works on the education of a gentleman. More important, it coloured the thought and manners of Europe in a way that the previous courtesy books, with their insistence on form and behaviour without giving thought to the inward attitude of mind, could never have succeeded in doing. It came at a moment when the organisation of the state was assuming increasing importance, and when a career in the state's service was as high a calling as arms had once been. The old paths to renown on the battlefield and in the lists were no longer open; Castiglione showed the new way of intellectual and physical grace.

EPILOGUE

The ideals of chivalry appeal to the emotions, and they flourish best in a gothic and romantic climate; neoclassicism appeals to reason and to the sense of order. When the seeds sown by the Renaissance humanists became the classical movement of seventeeth-century France, chivalry was driven from the land which had for so long been its chief refuge. In England its last flourish coincided with Inigo Jones' revival of the Gothic; but puritanism was as ardently on the side of order and restraint as the advocates of neoclassicism. Milton, seeking for a noble theme for his epic aspirations, rejected the Arthurian tales as too fantastic. When fantasy returned, the Restoration court preferred to follow continental fashions.

It was only when antiquarian interest turned towards the mediaeval period in the eighteenth century that chivalry was once again studied; and just as it had gone out with a dying gothic movement, so it reappeared in the revival, and was soon in literary favour once more in England and Germany. Hurd's *Letters on Chivalry and Romance* of 1762 were the beginnings of a flood of reprintings of old texts, studies of the trappings of chivalry, and recreations in fiction of the Middle Ages. The fruits of antiquarian researches such as those of La Curne de Ste Palaye in France were popularised by books like Kenelm Digby's *Broad Stone of Honour* and a dozen other general outlines of chivalry, including Sir Walter Scott's *Essay on Chivalry*. The Waverley Novels aroused the enthusiasm of readers everywhere, and the baronial gothic which succeeded the lighter, more imaginative style of the eighteenth century was in large part inspired by them.

The literary inheritance of the Middle Ages was so rich that English writers were able to explore it for nearly a century before it palled. But it was only in the stability of Victorian England that the cult could survive so long, and could produce such strange manifestations as the great tournament at Eglinton in 1839, where the enthusiasm of a few noblemen led them to spend a fortune in re-creating a fifteenth-century joust. Even in England such nostalgia for the past had its political overtones. The Eglinton tournament arose out of the reduction in pageantry at the coronation of William IV, and the radical press had a field day at the participants' expense. Nor, despite the gentle golden glow of Tennyson's verse and of Pre-Raphaelite interpretations of chivalry in art, was the ideal itself without its critical opponents. Thomas Arnold saw it in the blackest of lights: 'If I were called upon to name what spirit of evil predominantly deserved the name of Anti-Christ, I should name the spirit of chivalry – the more detestable for the very guise of 'Archangel ruined' which has made it so seductive to the most generous minds.'[1]

But the champions of the new order, whether Arnold and his militant Christianity or the evangelists of radical politics on the Continent, were hardly to be expected to approve an ideal so reactionary in the enthusiasm it aroused and so individualistic in its search for perfection. Chivalry had been used for far too long as a mere escape from reality for its ideals to have any relevance to the problems of society; the themes which had once had very concrete implications for the world in which they had been developed had lost all but the remotest link with everyday life; the word itself had acquired a new meaning, that of the very courtesy and politeness which had replaced chivalry proper. All that remained of the old high dreams and visions was an empty shell, a pretty relic of the past, fit to while away an idle moment.

APPENDIX

The Order of the *Banda*

Unlike the many invented national orders of the later Middle Ages and of the Renaissance which claimed dates of foundation as early as the fourth century AD, the Castilian order of the *Banda* or sash has a serious claim to consideration as the first recorded secular order. The difficulty lies in assessing the reliability of the sources, which, as with much of mediaeval Castilian history, are unsupported by any archival evidence in the form of official records. The archives of Castile seem to have been peripatetic for longer than those of any other European court, and when in the fifteenth century they finally found a permanent resting place, a single chest contained them all. Of this chest, about half the contents were rejected in the sixteenth century. Our evidence therefore comes entirely from chronicles.

In the *Chronicle of Alfonso* XI, under the year 1330 (a misdating which should read 1332) we read:

> The king being at Vittoria, because in times past the men of his kingdoms of Castile and Leon had always practised chivalry, and he had been told that they did not do so in his day, in order that they might be more eager to practise it, he commanded that some knights and squires of his household should wear a sash on their surcoats, and he, the king, would do likewise. And being at Vittoria he sent orders to those knights and squires whom he had chosen for the purpose to wear surcoats with, on them, the sash which he had given them. And he also put on a surcoat with a sash: the first surcoats made for the purpose were white, and the sash vermilion. And from then on he gave each of these knights two surcoats with sashes each year. And the sash was as broad as a man's hand, and was worn over cloaks and other garments from the left shoulder to the waist (i.e. diagonally): and they were called the knights of the Sash (*de la Banda*) and had statutes among themselves on many good matters, all of which were knightly deeds. And when a knight was given the sash, he was made to swear and promise to keep all the things that were written in that book of statutes. And the king did this so that men, wishing to have that sash would have reason to do knightly deeds. And it happened afterwards that if a knight or squire did some feat of arms against the king's enemies, or tried to perform such a feat, the king gave him a sash and did him high honour, so that all the others wished to do good

339

knightly deeds to gain that honour and the goodwill of the king, like those who already had it.[1]

The knights of the Sash reappear on two further occasions in the Chronicle: before Alfonso's coronation at Burgos in 1334, when jousts were held at which the knights held the lists against all comers, and again in 1335 at Valladolid in a tournament at which they fought together against the challengers, the king doing great deeds on their side.

The *Chronicle of Alfonso* XI, in the absence of other sources, is generally held to be reliable, though it does seem to have been edited at some point. The most recent opinion is that a very full version, of which traces remain in two MSS of the Chronicle and in a sixteenth-century Portuguese historian's work, was the original, written about 1344. This was then condensed in about 1360–70, by order of Pedro the Cruel, Alfonso's son, to fit into the series of official chronicles, the *Cronicas de los Reyes de Castilla.* A rhymed version, the *Poema de Alfonso el Onceno,* was made during the same period: but neither the poem nor the supposed original version throw any additional light on the passage.

The only supporting document is a sixteenth-century copy of the statutes, also found in two MSS at Paris. The language and style point to a direct copy of an almost contemporary manuscript, and the prologue claims that the rules which follow were laid down by Alfonso XI at the foundation of the order in the year of his coronation, which does not agree with the Chronicle, though the discrepancy is only a minor one. The statutes proper begin with the reasons for founding the order

> 'because chivalry should be greatly honoured and advanced, and because that thing in all the world which most appertains to a knight is truth and loyalty, and which is most rewarded by God, for that reason (the king) ordered this book to be made of the Order of the Sash, which is founded on two principles: chivalry and loyalty . . .'[2]

There follow the twenty-two headings of the rules, as follows:

How the knights of the Sash should try to hear Mass each morning
What the knights of the Sash should have in the way of arms and equipment
How the knights of the Sash should avoid playing dice, especially on campaigns
The speech and clothing to be adopted by the knights of the Sash
How the knights of the Sash should behave when eating and drinking
How a knight should be invested with the sash
How a knight of the Sash should act if another knight wishes to challenge him for the sash
How a knight should act if challenged for the sash outside the Royal court

The penalty for striking or drawing a sword against another knight of the Sash

How a knight of the Sash who has a grievance against the king should proceed

What the knights of the Sash should do if any knight repudiates his homage to the king or to the king's son

How a knight of the Sash should proceed if another knight of the order is found guilty of a capital crime

The knights of the Sash to form one squadron in the royal army on campaign

Chapters of the Order to be held at least three times a year

How the knights of the Sash are to behave in jousts

What should be done if two knights of the Sash quarrel

Procedure at a knight's marriage

Procedure at a knight's death

Procedure at a tournament

How the knights of the Sash are to observe everything in this book

The organisation of tournaments

The organisation of jousts[3]

It is clear from this outline that jousts played as large a part in the order's affairs as did the conduct of war. In many ways, the statutes are reminiscent of the tournament rules which were increasingly common throughout Europe at this period, whether in the early 'round table' meetings with their pacts to use certain types of weapons, or in the later fourteenth-century oath to keep the peace enforced at major tournaments. But this element is probably accounted for by Alfonso's personal prowess as a jouster, if we may believe the chronicle on that score. More important are the provisions for loyalty to the king and avoidance of quarrels, as well as those for behaviour. All these statutes seem to aim at a distinctive *corps d'élite*, set apart both by their way of life as the most polished of courtiers and by their special oaths of loyalty, as well as their function as the royal bodyguard in war. In the words of one of the very few scholars to have studied the order:

> It is clear ... that Alfonso XI was pursuing a double goal when he founded his order of the Sash: to create a corps of gentlemen who would distinguish themselves by knightly deeds and who would prepare for war by constant physical exercise: and to group round himself and his successors an elite body whose members, bound by a special oath of loyalty and entirely devoted to the sovereign's person, would be a solid support for royal authority at a time when it was weak and ill-established.[4]

This is borne out by the terms of the oath administered to the knights when they joined the order. The king and at least six knights were to be present

> and the knight to whom the sash is to be given shall come fully armed: and they shall ask him whether he wishes to take the sash and be a member of

341

the knights of the Sash. And if he says yes, they shall say: 'You have to swear two oaths. The first is that you will serve the king all your life or will always be a vassal of the king or of one of his sons: but if it befalls that you leave the king's service or that of his sons, you shall return the sash to the king and may never ask for it to be given to you again ... And the second oath that you have to swear is that you will love the knights of the Sash as your brothers, and that you will never challenge a knight of the Sash unless it is to help your father or brother. And if two knights of the Sash quarrel or fight, you shall do everything to part them, and if you cannot part them, you shall not help either of them.'[5]

Alfonso had particular reason to value loyalty to his person and peace among his knights. He had begun his reign in 1312 at the age of a year and nine months, and a troubled regency of thirteen years had followed. Continual revolts and intrigues had seriously weakened the kingdom, particularly in the south, where much territory was lost to the Moors. Though Alfonso's first campaigns in 1327 and 1330 regained some of this, his domestic troubles continued. He had one of the former regents assassinated in 1326: but another former regent was still rebellious in 1332, and became a vassal of the king of Aragon at about this time. Nor were matters improved by Alfonso's rejection of his Portuguese queen, in favour of his mistress Leonor de Guzman, whose bastard sons later brought about civil war after their father's death. Furthermore, Alfonso's relations with the military orders of Santiago, Alcantara and Calatrava were poor, though they had not yet deteriorated to the nadir of the 1340s and the open revolt of Alcantara. So the Order of the Sash may have been an attempt to bind the nobles to personal loyalty to himself, improve the royal army for campaigns against the Moors, and provide an alternative to the existing military orders.

The later history of the Order of the Sash did not bear out these hopes. It scarcely appears in the history of Alfonso's own reign, experienced a brief revival under Pedro the Cruel, when buildings in Seville were decorated with the arms of the knights, and is last mentioned in the *Victorial* of Don Perez Nino, the 'unconquered knight', early in the fifteenth century. It was revived in the sixteenth century but even then only survived for a few years. If it arose out of a period of political turbulence, it needed a degree of political stability to survive: and Castile at this period could not offer that stability.

The most interesting question about the Order of the Sash is its relationship to the Order of the Garter. The symbol of both is an item of clothing, and some of the functions of both are similar. If we take a doubtful view of the reliability of the *Chronicle of Alfonso XI*, it would be easy to argue that the whole story was inserted at the

342

behest of Pedro the Cruel about the time of the Black Prince's alliance with him in the 1360s, as an imitation of the Garter. Yet there is no direct evidence for this, and it seems equally possible that the Garter owes something to the order of the Sash.

Diplomatically, Castile was relatively isolated during the period of Alfonso xi's minority, little visited by outsiders, though merchants travelled that way and Castilian shipping was an important element in European trade. It was only with the preliminaries of the Hundred Years' War that both England and France began to think of Castile as a potentially valuable ally, especially in view of her naval resources. England, owing to running warfare between Castilian sailors and those of her territories in Gascony, was in the weaker position, and the French enjoyed the support of the Papacy. But the traditional Anglo-Castilian links, stretching back into the previous century, still counted for something. One recent writer, surveying English diplomacy in Spain in the later fourteenth century, declared that in the early 1340s 'Spain was terra incognita to the English government. Its early agents in the peninsula had no conception of the delicate balance of power between the Christian states there.' He goes on to accuse them of making indiscriminate attempts at alliances, and of failing to identify the real sources of power. Looking at the incredible confusion of Spanish politics of the period, one is inclined to sympathise with the English envoys and to find this judgment rather harsh. Embassies had been sent at irregular intervals since 1330, in which year William Trussel and Raymond Cornhill were sent on a general mission to the kings of Aragon, Portugal, Majorca and Castile. In 1331, there was an exchange of letters with Castile, and Alfonso's help was requested by Edward iii over the buying of horses: William Trussel's letters of credence were renewed. Five years later, a more imposing embassy, led by Bernard-Ezi ii, lord of Albret, William Fitzwarin and Gerard du Puy, was sent to propose an alliance, of which the keystone was to be the marriage of Isabella, Edward's sister, to Alfonso's eldest son. They were given an evasive answer, and it was a French mission in the following year which won the support of Castile. This treaty was scarcely ratified in 1337 before the Castilians were negotiating for an alliance with England: they probably saw the alliances as non-exclusive, and were hoping for help against the Moors. When, in 1340, a truce was negotiated between England and France, the Castilians sent envoys in an effort to secure a permanent peace, so that both kings could help them against the Moors.

It was not until a visit by rather more important English envoys in

1344 that an alliance seemed really probable. Henry, Earl of Derby, and William, Earl of Salisbury, reached Castile to find that Alfonso was on campaign, besieging the Moorish stronghold of Algeciras. Though they only had a small body of men with them, they joined the besieging army: both their presence and the personal courage of the two earls much impressed the Spaniards. They had to return to England before Algeciras was taken in March but the outcome of their activities was a marriage treaty signed in March 1346, despite attempts by the French to secure a similar agreement. However, Edward's daughter Joan, whom Alfonso's heir Pedro was to have married, fell victim to the Black Death two years later at Bordeaux, on the voyage to Spain, and the alliance lapsed.

So there were considerable contacts between England and Castile just at the period when Edward was beginning to think about the creation of an order of knighthood. Both Derby and Lancaster were founder-members of the Garter: and if the list of the knights of the Sash in the statutes is to be trusted, one of their number, Alfonso Hernandez Coronel, was a negotiator both with the French and English court. Might the news of Alfonso's order of the Sash have been the decisive factor which made Edward's order not the Round Table, but the Garter? Or might it even have been the original inspiration for such an order? Spain, with its tradition of nationalist military religious orders, would seem a good candidate as the birthplace of secular orders of knighthood, but unless more tangible evidence emerges the theory must remain without adequate proof.

REFERENCES

The numbers in brackets are cross-references to the Bibliography. Where two numbers are given, the first refers to the chapter; otherwise all titles are to be found in the Bibliography for the same chapter.

1. The Knight

1. *MGH* Auctores Antiqui, xi. 361
2. *MGH* Leges Sectio 2 i. 168
3. Tacitus (7) 111–12
4. Bloch (General, 1) 151
5. *Cambridge Medieval History* ii, 134–5
6. Bloch (General, 1) 168
7. L. Genicot quoted by Duby (2) 1–2
8. Ganshof (General 2) 33
9. Ernst (3)
10. Otto (5)
11. Chrétien de Troyes (7.1) 7–8
12. Duby (2) 21
13. May McKisack, *The Fourteenth Century* (Oxford 1959) 234
14. Quoted by Lewis (4) 174
15. Waas (8) 132

2. Knighthood

1. Tacitus (1.7) 111
2. *Ibid.*
3. *Anglo-Saxon Chronicle*, s.a. 1085
4. Andrieu (1) iii. 448
5. Wilson (9) 255
6. Erben (3) 147
7. Andrieu (1) iii. 448–50
8. Barbazan (2) ll. 254–6
9. Froissart (12.3) i. 57
10. *Ibid.* i. 605
11. Pietzner (7) 27
12. Legnano (4) 235

13. John of Marmoutier in *Chroniques des Comtes d'Anjou et des seigneurs d'Amboise* ed. Louis Halphen et René Poupardin, Paris 1913, 178–80; Lambert of Ardres in *MGH* xxiv. 604
14. Réligieux de Saint Denys (8) i. 599
15. CPR s.a. 1248
16. Menhardt (5)
17. Lecoy de la Marche (22.8) 392
18. Charny (9.5)

3. The Heroic Age of Chivalry: the *Chansons de Geste*

1. Menéndez Pidal (6) 428
2. *Chanson de Roland* ll. 1070–81 (author's translations)
3. *Ibid*. l. 1107
4. *Ibid*. l. 1093
5. *Ibid*. ll. 755–8
6. *Ibid*. ll. 2360–3
7. *Ibid*. l. 3975
8. *Ibid*. ll. 1151–8
9. *Ibid*. ll. 256–7
10. *Ibid*. ll. 1999–2004
11. *Ibid*. ll. 958–62
12. Quoted in Crosland (3) 289 (author's translation)
13. tr. Kevin Crossley-Holland, *The Battle of Maldon and other Old English Poems*, London 1966, p. 38
14. *Cantar de mio Cid* (1) 219, st. 148
15. *Ibid*. 110, st. 90
16. *Ibid*. 27, st. 18
17. *Ibid*. 240, st. 152

5. The Troubadours and the Courts of Provence

1. Ordericus Vitalis (10) i. 477 ff.
2. *RHGF* xii. 450
3. *RHGF* xii. 444
4. Guillaume IX (6) 6–8 (author's translation)
5. *Ibid*. 22, ll. 13–18 (author's translation)
6. Nelli et Lavaud (9) ii. 52 (author's translation)
7. Jaeschke (7) 134
8. Berry (2) 190
9. Elias de Barjols
10. Jeanroy (8) 102
11. Berry (2) 336
12. Anglade (1) 177
13. Berry (2) 96
14. Denomy (3) 24–5
15. St Bernard quoted in Gilson (5) 14
16. Gilson (5) 37

6. The Minnesingers

1. Sayce (1) 4 (author's translations)
2. *Ibid.* 8
3. *Ibid.* 1–2
4. *Ibid.* 103–4
5. *Ibid.* 153

7. The Romances of Chivalry

1. Chrétien de Troyes (1) 1–90
2. *Ibid.* 12
3. *Ibid.* 91–179
4. *Ibid.* 103
5. *Ibid.* 131–2
6. *Ibid.* 270–359
7. *Ibid.* 180–269
8. Chrétien de Troyes (2) 11. 1632–7
9. Wolfram von Eschenbach (6) 297, 16–27
10. *Ibid.* st. 800, 1–802, 111
11. Gottfried von Strassburg (3) 263
12. *Ibid.* 43
13. Sommer (4) iii. 133–6
14. Vinaver (5) 98 ff.
15. Sommer (4) iii. 261

8. The Knight and the Clerk

1. Andreas (1)
2. *Ibid.* 100
3. *Ibid.* 136
4. *Ibid.* 81–2
5. Piaget (3)
6. Lorris et Meun (2) 1946–54
7. *Ibid.* 1295–1300
8. *Ibid.* 2132–4
9. *Penguin Book of French Verse* I, ed. Brian Woledge, London and Baltimore 1961, 158 (author's translation)

9. Chivalric Biographies and Handbooks

1. William Marshal (13) 3453–3520 (i. 124–9)
2. Chandos Herald (4) 11
3. Froissart (12.3) i. 226
4. Malory (21.4) ii. 1036
5. Philippe de Novare, quoted in Loomis (10.5), 80 (author's translation)
6. Boucicaut (3) i, iv
7. *Ibid.* i. xiii–xiv

8. Froissart (12.3) i. 108
9. *Ibid.* i. 258
10. De Gamez (6) 35
11. Mailles (9) 20
12. *Ibid.* 301
13. Llull (8) 113
14. Llull (8) 15. cf. Isidore of Seville, *Etymologiae* ix, 3.32 (Migne *PL* 82. 345)
15. Cf. p. 315 below
16. Charny (5) 409
17. *Ibid.* 399
18. *Ibid.* 396
19. William Langland, *The Vision of William concerning Piers Plowman* (ed. W. W. Skeat, Oxford 1896) (Text II 190 ff.)
20. Rice (11)
21. Ehrismann (7)
22. Malory (21.4) iii. 1259

10. The Tournament as Sport

1. Warner (8) n.p.
2. Hefele (4) 410
3. Matthew Paris, *Chronica Majora* (ed. H. R. Luard, London 1874, RS 57) ii. 650
4. William Marshal (9.13) ll. 2637–95 (tr. Powicke, EHR xxii, 1906, 40)
5. *Ibid.* 1201–1380
6. *Ibid.* 1381–1512
7. *Ibid.* 2713–72
8. *Ibid.* 2840–74
9. *Ibid.* 4457 ff.
10. Niedner (6)
11. René d'Anjou (7) ii. 1–42
12. Froissart (12.3) ii. 411 ff.
13. René d'Anjou (7) ii. 49–83
14. Dillon (3)

11. The Tournament and Politics

1. Rymer, Foedera (1816–69) 1. 65
2. CPR 3 Henry III, 23 June 1243
3. CPR 3 Henry III, 9 January 1232
4. CPR 3 Henry III, 19 November 1231
5. Denholm-Young (1) 257
6. *MGH* xxx. 224
7. Uri (2) 391
8. *MGH* xxx. 319

12. Warfare

1. Verbruggen (9) 175
2. Longman and Walrond (7) 115
3. Hefele (10.4) 441
4. Giraldus Cambrensis (4) 54
5. Hatto (5) 50
6. Monstrelet (8) ii. 158
7. *Ibid*. ii. 162
8. Froissart (3) ii. 257
9. Le Bel (6) ii. 194–7
10. Bonet (2) 125
11. Avesbury (1) 445
12. Runciman (13.2) l. 287
13. Froissart (3) i. 453
14. *Ibid*. i. 109
15. *Ibid*. ii. 123
16. *Ibid*. i. 475
17. *Ibid*. i. 64
18. *Vita Heinrici* (10) 438–41 (author's translation)
19. Villehardouin (14.3, *see* Joinville) 94
20. Froissart (3) i. 1

13. The Church, Warfare and Crusades

1. Quoted in Erdmann (1) 8
2. Bloch (General, 1) 414
3. Menéndez Pidal (3.7), 85
4. Quoted in Erdmann (1) 149
5. Runciman (2) i. 107–8

14. The Military Orders in Palestine

1. Migne, PL 182, 921–40
2. Curzon (2)
3. Lecoy de la Marche (22.8) 399
4. John of Wurzburg, quoted in Riley-Smith (5) 57
5. Riley-Smith (5) 232
6. Lawrence, T. E., *Crusader Castles* (London 1936) p. 43

15. The Templars in Exile

1. Lizerand (1) 188
2. *Magnum Bullarium Romanum* ed. L. Cherubini *et al.* (Luxembourg 1727) i. 187 (author's translation)
3. Cf. Hospitaller entry ceremonial, p. 234 above

16. The Hospitallers in Rhodes and Malta

1. Dubois (1)
2. Porter (3)

17. The Teutonic Knights

1. Bühler (1) 87
2. Roger Bacon, *Opus Maius* tr. Robert Belle Burke (Philadelphia and London 1928) ii. 797
3. Treitschke (2) 39
4. Bühler (1) 119
5. *Ibid.* 77–82
6. *Ibid.* 14

19. The Prince and Chivalry

1. Armstrong (1) 14
2. Froissart (12.3) ii. 404
3. Vaughan (6) 6
4. Froissart (12.3) ii. 28
5. Courteault (4) 116
6. Castiglione (22.2) 117
7. Castiglione (22.2) 119
8. Grünpeck (5) 56–7
9. Chambers (3) i. 148
10. Chambers (3) i. 148

20. The Secular Orders

1. Renouard (3) 292
2. Reiffenberg (2) xx
3. Lewis (1) 77

21. The Epic of Chivalry Revived

1. Saintsbury, *The English Novel* (London 1913) 25
2. Llull (9.8) 121
3. Malory (4) i. cxlii
4. *Ibid.* i. 270–1
5. *Ibid.* ii. 839–40
6. *Ibid.* ii. 1036
7. *Ibid.* i. cxlvi
8. Dante, *Inferno*, tr. Dorothy Sayers (London and Baltimore 1949) canto v, 127 ff.
9. *Orlando imnnamorato* i, i. l, quoted in Edwards
10. Ariosto (1) i, i. 1

11. Tasso (5) i. i. 1
12. *Ibid*. iv, st. xxxii
13. Lobeira (3) i. 17–18
14. *Ibid*. i. 100–1
15. Quoted in Thomas (6) 140–1
16. F. de Ribera, quoted in Thomas (6) 150
17–28. All these quotations are from Cervantes (2). The page references are as
    follows: 17–80; 18–425; 19–940; 20–426; 21–426; 22–84; 23–95; 24–95;
    25–60; 26–624; 27–680; 28–470

22. Critics of Chivalry and Advocates of Reform

1. Peter of Blois (9) 294–6
2. Lecoy de la Marche (8) 392
3. *Ibid*. 394
4. Thomas of Cantimpré (10), 444–5
5. Caesarius of Heisterbach (1) ii. 327
6. Froissart (12.3) i. 458
7. Deschamps (3) ii. 308–9
8. Quoted in Cartellieri (19.2) 87
9. Quoted in Kilgour (5) 331
10. Quoted in Iorga (16.2) 489
11. Roger Ascham, *English Works*, ed. William Aldis Wright (Cambridge
    1904) p. 231
12. La Tour Landry (7) 171–2
13. Jean le Seneschal (4) i
14. *Ibid*. 227
15. La Sale (6) 314–15
16. Quoted in Thomas (21.6) 162–3
17. Castiglione (2) 58
18. *Ibid*. 115

Epilogue

1. Thomas Arnold, *Life and Correspondence*, London 1845, i. 255

Appendix

1. *Cronicas* (2) 231–2
2. Catalan (1) *passim*
3. Villanueva (5) 553–4
4. Villanueva (5) 554 ff.
5. Daumet (3) 12–13
6. Villanueva (5) 560
7. Russell (4) 6–7

BIBLIOGRAPHY
AND SOURCES
OF QUOTATIONS

ABBREVIATIONS

AESC   *Annales Economies Sociétés Civilisations*
AHR   *American Historical Review*
BIHR   *Bulletin of the Institute of Historical Research*
CCM   *Cahiers de civilisation médiévale*
CCR   Calendar of the Close Rolls, London
CPR   Calendar of the Patent Rolls, London
Delbouille *Mélanges de linguistique romane et de philologie médiévale offerts à
            M. Maurice Delbouille*, Gembloux 1964
EcHR   *Economic History Review*
EHR   *English Historical Review*
EETS   Early English Text Society
ES   Extra Series
            Fliche, Auguste et Martin, Victor *Histoire de l'Eglise depuis les
            origines jusqu'à nos jours*, Paris 1938–56
HZ   *Historische Zeitschrift*
Jacquot   *Les Fêtes de la Renaissance*, ed. Jean Jacquot, Paris, 1956–60
Kingsley Porter *Memorial studies in memory of A. Kingsley Porter*, ed.
            William A. Koehler, Cambridge, Mass., and London 1939
Kittredge   *Anniversary papers by colleagues and pupils of George Lyman
            Kittredge*, London and Boston 1913
Lewis   *Patterns of Love and Courtesy: Essays in memory of C. S. Lewis*,
            ed. John Lawlor, London 1966
MGH   *Monumenta Germaniae Historiae*, ed. G. H. Pertz, Hanover
Migne PL   *Patrologia Latinae cursus completus*, ed. J. P. Migne, Paris
MLR   *Modern Languages Review*
MP   *Modern Philology*
MSt   *Medieval Studies*
N.S.   New Series
O.S.   Old Series
Panzer   Panzer, Friedrich *Studien zur deutschen Philologie des Mittelalters
            [Festschrift]*, ed. Richard Kienast, Heidelberg 1950
Powicke   *Studies presented to F. M. Powicke*, Manchester U.P. 1948

PMLA   *Publications of the Modern Languages Association of America*
RHGF   *Recueil des historiens des Gaules et de la France*, ed. Dom Bou-
          quet, Paris
SATF   Société des anciens textes français
SHF   Société d'histoire de France
TRHS   *Transactions of the Royal Historical Society*
Vassar   *Vassar Medieval Studies*, New Haven and Oxford 1923
Vinaver   *Medieval miscellany presented to Eugene Vinaver*, ed. F. White-
          head, A. H. Diverres and F. E. Sutcliffe, Manchester and New
          York 1965
ZfdA   *Zeitschrift für deutsches Altertum*

BIBLIOGRAPHY

Early general works on chivalry

BÜSCHING, J. G. G. *Ritterzeit und Ritterwesen*, Leipzig 1823
CAPPELLETTI, LICURGO. *Storia degli ordini cavarellereschi esistenti, soppressi ed estinti presso tutte le nazioni del mondo*, Livorno 1904
CORNISH, F. W. *Chivalry*, London 1901
GASSIER-ST AMAND, J. M. *Histoire de la chevalerie française ou recherches historiques sur la chevalerie*, Paris 1814
GAUTIER, LEON. *La chevalerie*, Paris 1891
VON GLEICHEN-RUSSWURM, A. *Der Ritterspiegel: Geschichte der vornehmen Welt im Romanischen Mittelalter* (*Geschichte der europäischen Gesellschaft II*), Stuttgart 1918
HONORÉ DE SAINTE MARIE. *Dissertations historiques et critiques sur la chevalerie*, Paris 1718
HENNE AM RHYN, OTTO. *Geschichte des Rittertums*, Leipzig n.d. (c. 1890)
HURD, BISHOP. *Letters on Chivalry and Romance*, ed. E. J. Morley, London 1911
KOTTENKAMP, FRANZ. (*Der Rittersaal*) *A History of Chivalry*, tr. A. Löwy, London 1857
LA CURNE DE SAINTE-PALAYE. *Memoires sur l'ancienne chevalerie*, Paris 1826
MELLER, WALTER CLIFFORD. *A Knight's Life in the Days of Chivalry*, London 1924
PRESTAGE, EDGAR. *Chivalry*, London 1928
SCOTT, SIR WALTER. *Essay on Chivalry*, London 1816

PART I: THE FEUDAL WARRIOR

General

(1) BLOCH, MARC. *Feudal Society*, tr. L. A. Manyon, Routledge 1961
    CALMETTE, J. *La Société féodale*, Paris 1923
(2) GANSHOF, F. L. *Feudalism*, tr. Philip Grierson, Longmans 1952; 3rd edn, 1964

1. The Knight

BACHRACH, BERNARD S. 'Charles Martel, Mounted Shock Combat, the Stirrup and Feudal Origins' *Studies in Medieval and Renaissance History*, vii, 1970, 47–76

BACHRACH, BERNARD S. *Merovingian Military Organization 481–751* Minneapolis 1972

BERLICHINGEN, GÖTZ VON. *The Autobiography of G. von B.*, ed. H. S. M. Stuart, London 1956

BIVAR, A. D. H. 'The stirrup and its origins', *Oriental Art*, N.S., i, 1955, 61–5

BIVAR, A. D. H. 'Cavalry equipment and tactics on the Euphrates frontier', *Dumbarton Oaks Papers* xxvi, 1972, 273–91

BLAIR, CLAUDE. *European Armour circa 1066 to circa 1700*, Batsford 1958

BORST, ARNO. 'Rittertum im Hochmittelalter: Idee und Wirklichkeit', *Saeculum* x, 1959, 213–31

BOUTRUCHE, ROBERT. *Seigneurie et feodalité: I. Le premier âge des liens de l'homme à l'homme*, Paris 1959

CHAYTOR, H. J. *A History of Aragon and Catalonia*, London 1933

Chroniques des Comtes d'Anjou et des seigneurs d'Amboise, ed. Louis Halphen and René Poujardin, Paris 1913

DANNENBAUER, H. *Grundlagen der mittelalterlichen Welt:* 'Königsfreie und Ministerialen' 329–53, Stuttgart 1958

DENHOLM-YOUNG, N. 'Feudal society in the thirteenth century: the knights', *History* xxix, 1944, 107–19

(1) DUBY, GEORGES. *La Société aux XIe et XIIe siècles dans la région maconnaise* (Bibliothèque générale de l'école pratique des hautes études, VIe section), Paris 1953

DUBY, GEORGES. 'The diffusion of cultural patterns in feudal society', *Past and Present*, xxxix, 1968, 3–10

(2) DUBY, GEORGES. 'Une enquête à poursuivre: la noblesse dans la France médiévale', *Revue Historique* ccxxvi, 1961, 1–22

(3) ERNST, VIKTOR. *Die Enstehung des niederen Adels* (1916) repr. Aalen 1965

GANSHOF, F. B. 'Qu'est-ce que la chevalerie?' *Revue générale belge*, Nov. 1947, 77–86

GENICOT, L. 'Noblesse, ministerialité et chevalerie en Gueldre et Zutphen', *Le moyen âge* lxxi, 1965, 109–16

GENICOT, L. 'La noblesse dans la société médiévale', *Le moyen âge* lxxi, 1965, 539–60

GUILHIERMOZ, P. *Essai sur l'origine de la noblesse en France au moyen âge*, Paris 1902

HOLMES, G. A. *The Estates of the Higher Nobility in Fourteenth Century England*, Cambridge 1957 (Cambridge Studies in Economic History)

HOLT, J. C. 'Feudalism revisited', *EcHR*, 2nd series, xiv, 1961–62, 333–40

LEFEBVRE DES NOUETTES, Comte. *L'Attelage, le cheval de selle à travers les âges*, Paris 1931

(4) LEWIS, P. S. *Later Medieval France: the polity*, London 1968

MANGOLDT-GAUDLITZ, HANS VON. *Die Reiterei in den germanischen und fränkischen Heeren bis zum Ausgang der deutscher Karolinger* (Arbeiten zur deutschen Rechtsund Verfassungsgeschichte IV), Berlin 1922

MOHL, RUTH. *The Three Estates in Medieval and Renaissance Literature*, New York 1933

MOORMAN, CHARLES. 'The first knights', *Southern Quarterly* i, 1962, 13–26

OAKESHOTT, R. EWART. *The Archaeology of Weapons*, London 1960

OTTO, EBERHARD F. *Adel und Freiheit im deutschen Staat des frühen Mittelalters: Studien über nobiles und ministeriales* (Neue deutsche Forschungen, abt. mittelalterliche Geschichte), Berlin 1937

(5) OTTO, EBERHARD F. 'Von der Abschliessung des Ritterstandes', *HZ* clxii, 1940, 19–39

POOLE, AUSTIN LANE. *Obligations of Society in the XII and XIII Centuries*, Oxford 1946

POWICKE, F. M. 'Distraint of knighthood and military obligation under Henry III', *Speculum* xxv, 1950, 465 ff.

POWICKE, MICHAEL. *Military Obligation in Medieval England: a study in liberty and duty*, Oxford 1962

(6) SANDBERGER, DIETRICH. *Studien über das Rittertum in England vornehmlich während des 14. Jahrhunderts*, Berlin 1937

SANDERS, I. J. *Feudal Military Service in England: a study of the constitutional and military powers of the barons in medieval England*, Oxford U.P. 1956.

STENTON, F. M. *The First Century of English Feudalism 1066–1166*, Oxford 1932

STENTON, F. M. 'The changing feudalism of the Middle Ages', *History* N.S. xix, 1935, 289–301

STEPHENSON, CARL. *Medieval Feudalism*, New York 1942

STEPHENSON, CARL. 'The origins and significance of feudalism', *AHR* 46, 1941, 788–812

(7) TACITUS. *On Britain and Germany*, tr. H. Mattingly, Baltimore 1948

TREHARNE, R. F. 'The knights in the period of reform and rebellion, 1258–67: a critical phase in the rise of a new class', *BIHR* xxi, 1946, 1–12

(8) WAAS, ADOLF. *Der Mensch im deutschen Mittelalter*, Graz-Köln 1964

WHITE, LYNN, Jr. *Medieval Technology and Social Change*, Oxford 1962

2. Knighthood

ACKERMAN, ROBERT W. 'The knighting ceremonies in the middle English romances', *Speculum* xix, 285–313

(1) ANDRIEU, MICHEL. *Le Pontifical Romain au moyen-âge. III: Le pontifical de Guillaume Durand* (Studi e Testi 88), Città del Vaticano 1940

(2) BARBAZAN. *Fabliaux et contes des poètes français des xi, xii, xiii, xiv, et xve siècles*, ed. Meon, i 1–82: L'ordène de chevalerie, Paris 1808

BARNES, JOSHUA. *The History of that most Victorious Monarch, Edward III^d* . . . Cambridge 1688

DUBY, GEORGES. 'Au xiie siècle: les jeunes dans la société aristocratique', *AESC* xix, 1964, 835–46

(3) ERBEN, WILHELM .'Schwertleite und Ritterschlag: Beiträge zu einer Rechtsgeschichte der Waffen', *Zeitschrift für historische Waffenkunde*, viii, 1918. 1920, 105–67

JOHN OF SALISBURY. *The Statesman's Book*, tr. John Dickinson, New York 1927

JOHN OF MARMOUTIER. *Gesta Gaufredi Ducis Andegavorum* in *Chroniques des Comtes d'Anjou*, ed. Louis Halphen and René Poupardin, Paris 1913

(4) LEGNANO, GIOVANNI DA. *Tractatus de bello, de represaliis et de duello*, ed. T. E. Holland, London and Washington 1917

(5) MENHARDT, H. 'Rittersitte: ein rheinfränkisches Lehrgedicht des 12. Jarhunderts', *ZfdA* xxx, 1931, 153–63

(6) NAUMANN, HANS. *Deutsche Kultur im Zeitalter des Rittertums: Handbuch der Kulturgeschichte*, ed. Heinz Kindermann, Potsdam 1938

(7) PIETZNER, FRITZ. *Schwerleite und Ritterschlag*, Bottrop i. W. 1934

(8) RELIGIEUX DE SAINT-DENYS. *Chronique du r. de St. D.*, ed. L. Bellagut, Paris 1839

(9) WILSON, H. A. (ed.). *Pontifical of Magdalen College*, (*Henry Bradshaw Society*, xxxix), London 1910

3. The Heroic Age of Chivalry: the *Chansons de Geste*

(1) *Cantar de mio Cid* (*The Poem of the Cid*), tr. W. S. Merwin, London 1959

(2) *Chanson de Geste und höfischer Roman: Heidelberger Kolloquium 30. Januar 1961* (Studia Romanica iv), Heidelberg 1963

La Chanson de Roland, ed. and tr. J. Bédier, Paris 1922

La Chanson de Roland, ed. and tr. René Hague (*The Song of Roland:* Text of the Oxford MS: English translation), London 1937

La Chanson de Roland (*The Song of Roland*) tr. Dorothy Sayers, London and Baltimore 1957

(3) CROSLAND, JESSIE. *The Old French Epic*, Oxford 1951

FARAL, EDMOND. *La Chanson de Roland: étude et analyse*, Paris 1934

FRINGS, THEODOR. 'Europäische Heldendichtung', *Neophilologus* xxiv, 1939, 1–30

GAUTIER, LEON. 'La chevalerie d'après les textes poétiques du moyen âge', *Revue des questions historiques* iii, 1867, 345–82

HATEM, ANOUAR. *Les poèmes épiques des croisades*, Paris 1932

HORRENT, JULES. 'Tradition poetique du *Cantar de mio Cid* au xie siècle', *CCM* vii, 1964, 451–77

(4) JONES, GEORGE FENWICK. *The Ethos of the Song of Roland*, Baltimore 1963

(5) KER, W. P. *Epic and Romance: essays on medieval literature*, London 1908

LOT, FERDINAND. 'Etudes sur les légèndes épiques françaises', *Romania* lii–liii, 1926–7. I. *Raoul de Cambrai* lii, 75–133; II, *Girard de Roussillon* lii, 251–95; III, *Encore Gormont et Isembart* liii, 325–43; IV. *Le cycle de Guillaume* liii, 449–73

(6) MENÉNDEZ PIDAL, RAMÓN. *La Chanson de Roland y el Neotradicionalismo* (*Origénes de la épica romanica*), Madrid 1959

(7) MENÉNDEZ PIDAL, RAMÓN. *The Cid and his Spain*, tr. Harold Sutherland, London 1934

MENÉNDEZ PIDAL, RAMÓN. *En torno al poema del Cid*, Barcelona and Buenos Aires, 1963

MEYER, PAUL. *Girart de Rousillon: chanson de geste*, Paris 1884

RYCHNER, JEAN. *La Chanson de geste: essai sur l'art épique des jongleurs* (Société de publications romanes et françaises LIII), Geneva and Lille 1955

357

TUFFRAU, PAUL. *La Légende de Guillaume d'Orange*, Paris 1920
WALTZ, MATTHIAS. *Rolandslied, Wilhelmslied, Alexiuslied: zur Struktur und geschichtlichen Bedeutung* (Studia Romanica 9), Heidelberg 1965
See also BLOCH (General, 1)

PART II: CHIVALRY AND LITERATURE

General

DRONKE, PETER. *The Medieval Lyric*, London 1968
HEER, FRIEDRICH. *The Medieval World: Europe 1100–1350*, London 1963
KNOWLES, DAVID. *The Evolution of Medieval Thought*, London 1962
LEWIS, C. S. *The Allegory of Love: a study in medieval tradition*, Oxford U.P. 1936
SCHULTZ, ALWIN. *Das höfische Leben zur Zeit der Minnesinger*, Leipzig 1839
See also *Chanson de geste und höfischer Roman* (3.2), KER (3.5)

4. Traditions of Love and Attitudes to Women

AHSMANN, H. P. J. M. *Le Culte de la sainte vierge et la littérature française profane du moyen âge*, Utrecht and Paris 1929
DRONKE, E. P. M. *Medieval Latin and the Rise of the European Love-Lyric*, Oxford 1965–66
LUCRETIUS. *The Nature of the Universe*, tr. R. E. Latham, London and Baltimore 1951
WADDELL, HELEN. *Mediaeval Latin Lyrics*, London and New York 1948
WEINHOLD, KARL. *Die deutsche Frauen in dem Mittelalter*, Vienna 1851
WILSON, EVELYN FAYE. *The* Stella Maris *of John of Garland*, Cambridge, Mass. 1946
See also JONES (3.4)

5. The Troubadours and the Courts of Provence

(1) ANGLADE, JOSEPH. *Anthologie des Troubadours*, Paris 1927
BELPERRON, P. *La 'Joie d'amour': contribution à l'étude des troubadours et d'amour courtois*, Paris 1948
(2) BERRY, A. *Florilège des troubadours*, Paris 1930
BEZZOLA, RETO R. 'Guillaume IX et les origines de l'amour courtois', *Romania* lxvi, 1940, 145–237
BEZZOLA, RETO R. *Les Origines et la formation de la littérature courtoise en Occident* (500–1200) (Bibliothèque de l'Ecole des Hautes Etudes), Paris 1944–63
BOUTROS GHALI, WACYF. *La tradition chevaleresque des arabes*, Paris 1919
BRIFFAULT, ROBERT. *Les Troubadours et le sentiment romanesque*, Paris 1945
CHAYTOR, H. J. *The Troubadours of Dante*, Oxford U.P. 1902

DENOMY, ALEXANDER J. 'Courtly love and courtliness', *Speculum* xxviii, 1953, 44–63

DENOMY, ALEXANDER J. 'An inquiry into the origins of courtly love', *MSt* vi, 1944, 175–260

DENOMY, ALEXANDER J. 'Fin'amors: the pure love of the troubadours, its amorality and possible source', *MSt* vii, 1945, 139–207

(3) DENOMY, ALEXANDER J. *The Heresy of Courtly Love*, New York 1947

DIEZ, FREDERIC. *Essai sur les cours d'amour*, tr. and ed. Ferdinand de Roisin, Paris 1842

DUMITRESCU, MARIA. 'Les premiers troubadours connus et les origines de la poèsie provençale', *CCM* ix, 1966, 345–54

FRAPPIER, JEAN. 'Vues sur les conceptions courtoises dans les littératures d'oc et d'oil au XIIe siècle', *CCM* ii, 1959, 135–56

(5) GILSON, ETIENNE. *La Théologie mystique de St Bernard* (*The Mystical Theology of St Bernard*), tr. A. H. C. Downes, London 1940

(6) GUILLAUME IX. *Les Chansons de G. IX, duc d'Aquitaine (1071–1127)*, ed. A. Jeanroy, Paris 1913

(7) JAESCHKE, HILDE. *Der Trobador Elias Cairel* (Romanische Studien 20), Berlin 1921

JEANROY, A. 'La première génération des troubadours', *Romania* lvi, 1930, 481–526

(8) JEANROY, A. *La Poèsie lyrique des troubadours* Toulouse and Paris 1934

KÖHLER, ERICH. 'Das *trobar clus* der Troubadours', *Romanische Forschungen* lxiv, 1952, 71–101

KÖHLER, ERICH. 'Observations historiques et sociologiques sur la poèsie des troubadours', *CCM* vii, 1964, 27–51

KOLB, HERBERT. *Der Begriff der Minne und das Entstehen der höfischen Lyrik*, Tübingen 1958

LAFITTE-HOUSSAT, JACQUES. *Troubadours et cours d'amour*, Paris 1950

LAZAR, MOSHÉ. *Bernard de Ventadour, troubadour du xiie siècle: chansons d'amour*, Paris 1966

LAZAR, MOSHÉ. 'Les éléments constitutifs de la cortezia dans la lyrique des troubadours', *Studi mediolatini e volgari* vi–vii, 1959, 67–96

MÖLK, ULRICH. *Guiraut Riquier: Las Cansos* (Studia Romanica 2), Heidelberg 1962

MOLLER, HERBERT. 'The social causation of the courtly love complex', *Comparative Studies in Society and History* i 1958, 137–63

MOLLER, HERBERT. 'The meaning of courtly love', *Journal of American Folklore*, 1960, 39–49

(9) NELLI, RENÉ and LAVAUD, RENÉ. *Les Troubadours*, Bruges 1966

NYKL, A. R. *Hispano-Arabic Poetry and its Relations with the Old Provençal Troubadours*, Baltimore 1946

(10) ORDERICUS VITALIS. *The Ecclesiastical History of England and Normandy*, tr. Thomas Forester, London 1854

SILVERSTEIN, THEODORE. 'Andreas, Plato and the Arabs: remarks on some recent accounts of courtly love', *MP* xlvii, 1949–50, 117–26

TOPSFIELD, L. T. 'Raimon de Miraval and the art of courtly love', *MLR* li, 1956, 33–48

VADET, JEAN-CLAUDE. *L'esprit courtois en orient*, Paris 1968

Troubadours, Trouvères and Minnesingers, Archiv APM 14068, 1957

Troubadour Songs, Telefunken SAWT 9567, 1971

6. The Minnesingers

BRINKMANN, HENNIG. *Enstehungsgeschichte des Minnesangs* (Deutsche Vierteljahresschrift für Literaturwissenschaft und Geistesgeschichte Buchreihe 8), Halle 1926

BURDACH, KONRAD. *Vorspiel: gesammelte Schriften zur Geschichte des deutschen Geistes* (I, 253–333: 'Über den Ursprung des mittelalterlichen Minnesangs Liebesromans und Frauendienstes'), Halle 1925

CORDES, GERHARD. 'Norddeutsches Rittertum in der deutschen Dichtung des Mittelalters', *Niedersächsisches Jahrbuch für Landesgeschichte* xxxiii, 1961, 143–58

FORQUET, J. 'La chanson chevaleresque allemande avant les influences provençales', in Delbouille ii, 155–64

FRINGS, THEODOR. *Minnesinger und Troubadours* (Deutsche Akademie der Wissenschaften zu Berlin Vorträge und Schriften 34), Berlin 1949

KUHN, HUGO. *Minnesangs Wende* (Hermaea: Germanistische Forschungen. Neue Folge 1), Tübingen 1952

MORET, A. *Les débuts du lyricisme en Allemagne (des origines à 1350)* (Travaux et mémoires de l'université de Lille 27), Lille 1951

RICHEY, MARGARET FITZGERALD. *Essays on the Medieval German Love Lyric*, Oxford 1943

SALMON, P. B. *Literature in Medieval Germany*, London 1967

(1) SAYCE, OLIVE, ed., *Poets of the Minnesang*, Oxford 1967

TAYLOR, R. J. *The Art of the Minnesinger*, Cardiff 1969

(2) WALSHE, M. O'C. *Medieval German Literature: a survey*, London 1962

Musik und ihre Zeit, Minnesong and Prosody circa 1200–1320: Telefunken SAWT 9487-A, 1966

7. The Romances of Chivalry

BARROW, SARAH F. *The Medieval Society Romances*, New York 1924

BENTON, JOHN F. 'The court of Champagne as a literary center', *Speculum* xxxvi, 1961, 551–91

BLAMIRES, DAVID. *Characterisation and Individuality in Wolfram's Parzival*, Cambridge 1966

BOGDANOW, FANNY. *The Romance of the Grail: a study of the structure and genesis of a thirteenth-century Arthurian prose romance*, Manchester 1966

BORODINE, M. *La Femme et l'amour au XIIe siècle d'après les poèmes de Chrétien de Troyes*, Paris 1909

(1) CHRÉTIEN DE TROYES. *Arthurian Romances*, tr. W. W. Comfort, London and New York 1914

(2) CHRÉTIEN DE TROYES. *Le Roman de Perceval ou le conte del Graal*, ed. W. Roach, Geneva and Lille 1956

COHEN, GUSTAVE. *Chrétien de Troyes et son œuvre*, Paris 1931

COLLAS, J. P. 'The romantic hero of the twelfth century', in Vinaver, 80–96

CROSS, TOM PEETE and NITZE, ALBERT WILLIAM. *Lancelot and Guenevere: a study on the origins of courtly love* (MP monographs), Chicago 1930

DUPIN, HENRI. *La Courtoisie au moyen âge (d'après les textes du xiie et du xiiie siècle)*, Paris 1931

FISCHER, J. H. 'Tristan and courtly adultery', *Comparative Literature* ix, 1957, 150–63

FORD, GORDON B. *The Ruodlieb: the first medieval epic of chivalry from eleventh century Germany*, Leiden 1965

FRAPPIER, JEAN. *Chrétien de Troyes: l'homme et l'œuvre*, Paris 1957

FRAPPIER, JEAN. *Etude sur la mort le roi Artu: roman du xiiie siècle, dernière partie du Lancelot en prose*, Paris 1936

FRAPPIER, JEAN. 'Le Graal et la chevalerie', *Romania* lxxv, 1954, 165–210

GOODRICH, NORMA LORRE. *The Ways of Love: eleven romances of medieval France*, London 1965

(3) GOTTFRIED VON STRASSBURG. *Tristan*, tr. A. T. Hatto, London and New York 1960

HOFER, STEFAN. *Chrétien de Troyes: Leben und Werke des altfränzosischen Epikers*, Graz and Koln, 1954

KENNEDY, ELSPETH. 'Social and Political Ideas in the French Prose Lancelot', *Medium Aevum* xxvi, 157, 90–106

KÖHLER, ERICH. *Ideal und Wirklichkeit in der höfischen Epik: Studien zur Form der frühen Artus- und Graldichtung* (Beihefte zur Zeitschrift für Romanische Philologie 97), Tübingen 1956

La Mort le roi Artu, roman du xiiie siècle, ed. Jean Frappier, Paris 1936

LANGLOIS, CH.-V. *La Vie en France au moyen âge de la fin du xiie au milieu du xive siècle*, Paris 1924–5

LODS, JEANNE. *Le roman de Perceforest* (Société des publications romanes et françaises 32), Geneva 1951

LOOMIS, ROGER SHERMAN. *Arthurian Tradition and Chrétien de Troyes*, New York 1949

LOOMIS, ROGER SHERMAN, ed. *Arthurian Literature in the Middle Ages: a collaborative history*, Oxford 1959

LOT, FERDINAND. *Etude sur le Lancelot en prose*, Paris 1918

MAURER, FRIEDRICH. *Dichtung und Sprache des Mittelalters* ('Die Welt des höfischen Epos' 11–22) (Bibliotheca Germanica 10), Bern and Munich 1963

NITZE, W. A. *Perceval and the Holy Grail: an essay on the romance of Chrétien de Troyes* (University of California Publications in Modern Philology 28, 5) Berkeley and Los Angeles 1949

PAUPHILET, ALBERT. *Etudes sur la Queste del Saint Graal*, Paris 1921

PICKFORD, CEDRIC E. *L'Evolution du roman arthurien en prose vers la fin du moyen âge*, Paris 1960

RICHEY, MARGARET FITZGERALD. *Studies of Wolfram von Eschenbach*, with translations . . ., Edinburgh 1957

SACKER, HUGH. *An Introduction to Wolfram's 'Parzival'*, Cambridge 1963

(4) SOMMER, H. OSKAR. *The Vulgate Version of the Arthurian Romances, edited from manuscripts in the British Museum*, Washington 1908–16

(5) VINAVER, EUGÈNE. *Etudes sur le 'Tristan' en prose*, Paris 1925

VINAVER, EUGÈNE. 'Un chevalier errant à la recherche du sens du monde', in Delbouille, ii, 677–85

WHITEHEAD, F. 'Lancelot's redemption', in Delbouille, ii, 729–39

(6) WOLFRAM VON ESCHENBACH. *Parzival*, tr. Helen M. Mustard and Charles E. Passage, New York 1961

See also NAUMANN (2.6), WALSHE (6.2)

8. The Knight and the Clerk

Andreae Capellani regii Francorum De Amore libri tres ed. E. Trojel, Copenhagen 1892

(1) ANDREAS CAPELLANUS. *The Art of Courtly Love*, tr. and ed. J. J. Parry (Records of Civilization: Sources and Studies xxxiii), New York 1941

COGHILL, N. K. 'Love and "Foul Delight": some contrasting attitudes', in Lewis, 141–56

GORRA, EGIDIO. *Fra drammi e poemi: saggi e ricerche* (201–302: 'La teorica dell' amore e un antico poema francese inedito'), Milan 1900

GUNN, ALAN M. F. *The Mirror of Love: a reinterpretation of 'The Romance of the Rose'*, Lubbock, Texas 1952

JACKSON, W. T. H. 'The De Amore of Andreas Capellanus and the practice of love at court', *Romantic Review* xlix, 243–51

LANGLOIS, ERNEST. *Origines et sources du roman de la Rose* (Bibliothèque des écoles françaises d'Athènes et de Rome 58), Paris 1891

(2) LORRIS, GUILLAUME DE, and MEUN, JEAN DE. *Le Roman de la Rose* ed. E. Langlois (SATF), Paris 1914–24

LORRIS, GUILLAUME DE, and MEUN, JEAN DE. *The Romance of the Rose . . .* tr. F. S. Ellis, London 1900

LORRIS, GUILLAUME DE. *Der Rosenroman*, tr. and ed. Gustav Ineichen (German, first section only), (Philologische Studien und Quellen i), Berlin 1956

NEILSON, WILLIAM ALAN. *The Origins and Sources of the Courts of Love* (Studies and Notes in Philology and Literature VI) Harvard 1899

(3) PIAGET, ARTHUR. 'La cour amoureuse dite de Charles XV', *Romania* xx, 1891, 417–54

RAJNA, PIO. *Le Corti d'amore*, Milan 1890

SCHLÖSSER, FELIX. *Andreas Capellanus: seine Minnelehre und das christliche Weltbild des 12. Jahrhunderts*, Bonn 1962

SÖDERHJELM, WERNER. *La Nouvelle française au xvᵉ siècle* (Bibliothèque du xvᵉ siècle xii), Paris 1910

TROJEL, E. *Les Cours d'amour au moyen âge*, Copenhagen 1888

9. Chivalric Biographies and Handbooks

(1) BECKER, REINHOLD. *Wahrheit und Dichtung in Ulrich von Lichtensteins Frauendienst*, Halle 1888

(2) BERNT, ALOIS. *Heinrich von Freiberg*, Halle 1906

The Boke of Noblesse addressed to King Edward the Fourth on his invasion of France in 1475, ed. John Gough Nichols, Roxburghe Club 1860

BONNECHOSE, EMILE DE. *Bertrand de Guesclin*, Paris 1884

(3) BOUCICAUT (JEAN LE MAINGRE). *Le Livre des faicts du bon messire Jean le Maingre, dit Boucicaut* in Michaud et Poujoulat, *Nouvelle collection des mémoires pour servir à l'histoire de France* ii, 205–332, Paris 1850

(4) CHANDOS, HERALD. *The Life and Feats of Arms of Edward the Black Prince*, ed. and tr. Francisque-Michel, London and Paris 1883

(5) CHARNY, GEOFFROI DE. 'Le livre Messire G. de C.', ed. Arthur Piaget, *Romania* xxvi, 1897, 394–411

CONDÉ, JEAN DE. *Dits et contes de Baudouin de Condé et de son fils J. de C.*, ed. Aug. Scheler, Brussels 1866

(6) DE GAMEZ, GUTIERREZ DIAZ. *The Unconquered Knight: a chronicle of the deeds of Don Pero Nino*, tr. Joan Evans (selection only), London 1928

(7) EHRISMANN, GUSTAV. 'Die Grundlagen der ritterlichen Tugendsystem' *ZfdA* lvi, 1919, 137–216

FROISSART see ch. 12 (3)

GEOFFREY OF MONMOUTH. *The History of the Kings of Britain*, tr. Lewis Thorpe, London and New York 1966

HÖFLER, OTTO. 'Ulrich von Lichtenstein Venusfahrt und Artusfahrt' in Panzer, 131–52

Knyghthode and Bataile: a xvth century verse paraphrase of Flavius Vegetius Renatus' treatise 'De re militari', ed. R. Dyboski and Z. M. Arend, London (EETS) 1935

LALAIN, J. DE. *Chronique de J. De L.*, in J. A. Buchon, *Collection des chroniques nationales françaises du treizième au seizième siècle*, Paris 1825

LA MARCHE, OLIVIER DE. *Mémoires* ed. Henri Beaune et J. d'Arbaumont, Paris 1883

LEFÈVRE DE SAINT REMY, JEAN. 'Epitre de Jean le Fèvre, Seigneur de Saint Remy', ed. François Morand, *Annuaire-Bulletin de la SHF* xxi, 1884, 177–239

(8) LLULL, RAIMON. (tr. William Caxton) *The Book of the Ordre of Chyvalry*, ed. A. T. P. Byles (from a French version of Llull's 'Le Libre del Orde de Cauayleria'), London (EETS O.S. 168) 1926

LOOMIS. See 10(5)

LUCE, SIMEON. *Histoire de Bertrand du Guesclin et de son époque*, Paris 1896 (vol. i only, no more published)

(9) MAILLES, JACQUES DE. *The right joyous and pleasant history of the feats, gests and prowesses of the chevalier Bayart*, tr. Sara Coleridge London 1906

MALORY. See 21(4)

MARSHAL. See WILLIAM MARSHAL (13)

MATHEW, GERVASE. 'Ideals of Knighthood in Late-Fourteenth-Century England', in Powicke, 354 ff.

MATHEW, GERVASE. *The Court of Richard II*, London 1968

NAUMANN, HANS and GUNTHER MÜLLER. *Höfische Kultur* (Deutsche Vierteljahrsschrift für Literaturwissenschaft und Geistesgeschichte, Buchreihe 17), Leipzig 1929

(10) PAINTER, SIDNEY. *William Marshal, Knight Errant, Baron and Regent of England*, Baltimore 1933

PISAN, CHRISTINE DE. *The Epistle of Othea to Hector*, ed. James D. Gordon (fifteenth century English translation), Philadelphia 1942

PISAN, CHRISTINE DE. *Le Livre des fais et bonnes meurs du sage roy Charles V*, ed. S. Solente, Paris (SHF) 1936–40

PÜTERICH VON REICHERTSHAUFEN. *Der Ehrenbrief des P. von R.*, ed. Fritz Behrend and Rudolf Wolkan, Weimar 1920

(11) RICE, W. H. 'Deux poemes sur la chevalerie: Le breviaire des nobles d'Alain Chartier et Le Psaultier des Vilains de Michault Taillevent' *Romania* lxxv, 1954, 54–97

RIQUER, MARTIN DE. *Cavalleria fra realtà e letteratura nel quattrocento* (Biblioteca di filologia romanza 14) Bari 1970

(12) TIECK, LUDWIG. *Frauendienst, oder Geschichte und Liebe des Ritters und Sängers Ulrich von Liechtenstein, von ihm selbst beschrieben*, Stuttgart und Tübingen 1812

WEST, C. B. *Courtoisie in Anglo-Norman Literature*, Oxford 1938

WHITNEY, MARIAN PARKER. 'Queen of Medieval Virtues: Largesse', in Vassar 183–215

(13) WILLIAM MARSHAL, ed. Paul Meyer, *L'histoire de Guillaume le Maréchal, comte de Striguil et de Pembroke*, Paris (SHF) 1891–1901

PART III: CHIVALRY IN ACTION

10. The Tournament as Sport

(1) CLEPHAN, R. COLTMAN. *The Tournament: its periods and phases*, London 1919

CLINE, RUTH HUFF. 'The influence of romances on the tournaments of the Middle Ages', *Speculum* xx, 1945, 204–11

(2) CRIPPS-DAY, F.H. *The History of the Tournament in England and France*, London 1918

(3) DILLON, VISCOUNT. 'On a MS collection of Ordinances of Chivalry of the Fifteenth Century', *Archaeologia* 57. i, 1900, 29–70

DUVERNOY, EMILE and HARMAND, RENÉ. *Le Tournoi de Chauvency en 1295: étude sur les moeurs chevaleresques au xiiie siècle*, Paris 1905

GISLEBERTUS. *Gisleberti Chronicon Hanoniense* ed. Georg Heinrich Pertz (*Scriptores rerum Germanicarum*), Hanover 1869

HARVEY, RUTH. *Moriz von Craun and the Chivalric World*, Oxford 1961

(4) HEFELE, C. J. *Conciliengeschichte*, V., Leipzig 1886

JUSSERAND, J. J. *Les Sports et jeux d'exercice dans l'ancienne France*, Paris 1901

LENA, PERO RODRIGUEZ DE. *Libro del passo honroso* ed. F. Juan de Pineda, Madrid 1970

(5) LOOMIS, ROGER SHERMAN. 'Chivalric and dramatic imitations of Arthurian romance', in Kingsley Porter, i, 79–100

(6) NIEDNER, FELIX. *Das Deutsche Turnier im xii und xiii Jahrhundert*, Berlin 1881

PROST, BERNARD. *Traité de la forme et devis comme on faict les tournois par Olivier de la Marche, Hardouin de la Jaille, Anthoine de la Sale*, Paris 1878

(7) RENÉ D'ANJOU. *Oeuvres complètes du roi René*, ed. Comte de Quatrebarbes, Angers 1845

RÜXNER, GEORG. *Thurnierbuch. Das ist wahrhafte eigentliche und kurze Beschreibung von Anfang, Ursachen, Ursprung und Herkommen, der Thurnier im heyligen Römischer Reich Teutscher Nation*, Frankfurt-am-Main 1578

SANDOZ, EDOUARD. 'Tourneys in the Arthurian tradition', *Speculum* xx, 1945, 389–420

SCHLAUCH, MARGARET. 'King Arthur in the Baltic Towns', *Bulletin bibliographique de la société internationale arthuriénne* ii, 1959, 75–80

STRUTT, J. *The Sports and Pastimes of the People of England*, ed. W. Hone London 1898

WAGNER, ANTHONY RICHARD. *Heralds and Heraldry in the Middle Ages: an inquiry into the growth of the armorial functions of heralds*, London 1956

(8) WARNER, G. F. and ELLIS, H. J. eds. *Facsimiles of Royal and other Charters in the British Museum*, London 1903

11. The Tournament and Politics

DENHOLM-YOUNG, N. *History and Heraldry 1254 to 1310: a study of the historical value of the rolls of arms*, London 1965

(1) DENHOLM-YOUNG, N. 'The tournament in the thirteenth century' in Powicke 240–68

TOMKINSON, A. 'Retinues at the tournament of Dunstable', *EHR* lxxiv, 1959, 70–89

(2) URI, S. P. 'Het tournooi in de 12 en 13e Eeuw', *Tijdschrift voor Geschiedenis* lxxii, 376–96

WARD, H. L. D. *Catalogue of Romances in the Department of Manuscripts in the British Museum*, ii, London 1893

See also CLEPHAN (10.1), CRIPPS-DAY (10.2), SANDBERGER (1.7)

12. Warfare

(1) AVESBURY, ROBERTUS DE. *De gestis mirabilibus regis Edwardi tertii*, ed. Edward Maunde Thompson, London (Rolls Series) 1889

BEELER, JOHN. *Warfare in England 1066–1189*, New York 1966

(2) BONET, HONORÉ. *The Tree of Battles*, tr. G. W. Copeland, Liverpool 1949

BOUSSARD, J. 'Les mercenaires au xiie siècle: Henri II Plantagenet et les origines de l'armée de métier', *Bibliothèque de l'Ecole des Chartes* cvi, 1945–46, 189–224

BURKE, EDMUND. *The History of Archery*, London 1958

CARMAN, W. Y. *A History of Firearms from Earliest Times to 1914*, London 1955

DELBRÜCK, HANS. *Geschichte der Kriegskunst im Rahmen der politischen Geschichte: iii. Das Mittelalter*, Berlin 1907

FOULKES, CHARLES. *Armour and Weapons*, Oxford 1909

FOWLER, KENNETH. *The Age of Plantagenet and Valois: the struggle for supremacy 1328–1498*, London 1967

FRAUENHOLZ, EUGEN VON. *Entwicklungsgeschichte des deutsche Heerwesens: das Heerwesen der germanischen Frühzeit, des Frankenreiches und des ritterlichen Zeitalters*, Munich 1935

FROISSART, JEAN. *Oeuvres de Froissart publiées . . . par M. le baron Kervyn de Lettenhove*, Brussels 1867–77

FROISSART, JEAN. *Chroniques*, ed., S. Luce et al. (SHF) Paris 1869–.

(3) FROISSART, JEAN. *Chronicles of England, France, Spain and the adjoining countries*, tr. Thomas Johnes, London 1855

FROISSART, JEAN. *Chronicles*, sel. and tr. Geoffrey Brereton, London 1968

FROISSART, JEAN. *Froissart's Chronicles*, ed. and tr. John Jolliffe, London 1967

GAIER, CLAUD. 'Analysis of military forces in the principality of Liège and the county of Looz from the twelfth to the fifteenth century', *Studies in Medieval and Renaissance History* (Nebraska) ii, 1965, 210–59

(4) GIRALDUS CAMBRENSIS. *Opera*, ed. J. F. Dimock vi: *Itinerarium Kambriae et Descriptio Cambriae*, London (Rolls Series) 1868

(5) HATTO, A. T. 'Archery and Chivalry: A Noble Prejudice', *Modern Language Review* xxxv, 1940, 40–54

HAY, DENYS. 'The division of the spoils of war in fourteenth-century England', *TRHS* iv, 1954, 91–109

HEWITT, H. J. *The Black Prince's Expedition of 1355–1357*, Manchester 1958

HEWITT, H. J. *The Organisation of War under Edward III,* Manchester 1966

HOLLISTER, C. WARREN. *The Military Organisation of Norman England*, Oxford 1965

KEEN, MAURICE. 'Brotherhood in Arms', *History* xlvii, 1962, 1–17

KEEN, MAURICE. *The Laws of War in the Middle Ages*, London and Toronto 1965

(6) LE BEL, JEAN. *Chronique*, ed. Jules Viard and Eugène Déprez, Paris (SHF) 1904

(7) LONGMAN, C. J. and WALROND, H. *Archery*, London (Badminton Library) 1894

LOT, FERDINAND. *L'Art militaire et les armées au moyen âge en Europe et dans le proche Orient*, Paris 1946

MACFARLANE, K. B. 'A business-partnership in war and administration 1421–1445', *EHR* lxxviii, 1963, 290–310

(8) MONSTRELET, ENGUERRAND DE. *The Chronicles of Enguerrand de Monstrelet*, tr. Thomas Johnes, London 1840

OMAN, C. W. G. *A History of the Art of War in the Middle Ages*, London 1924

PERROY, EDOUARD. *The Hundred Years' War*, London 1951

POSTAN, M. M. 'The cost of the Hundred Years' War', *Past and Present* xxvii, 1964, 34–53

SMAIL, R. C. *Crusading Warfare (1097–1193)*, Cambridge 1967

SQUIBB, G. C. *The High Court of Chivalry*, Oxford 1959

(9) VERBRUGGEN, J. F. 'La tactique militaire des armées de chevaliers', *Revue du Nord* xxix, 1947, 161–80

(10) *Vita Heinrici IV imperatoris*, in SCHMALE, FRANZ-JOSEPH, *Quellen zur Geschichte Kaiser Heinrichs IV (Ausgewählten Quellen zur deutschen Geschichte des Mittelalters)*, Berlin 1963

See also *Boke of Noblesse* (9.2)

PART IV: CHIVALRY AND RELIGION

13. The Church, Warfare and Crusades

(1) ERDMANN, CARL. *Die Entstehung des Kreuzzugsgedankens* (Forschungen zur Kirchen und Geistesgeschichte 6), Stuttgart 1935

FOREVILLE, RAYMONDE and ROUSSET DE PINA, JEAN. 'Du premier concile du Latran à l'avènement d'Innocent III' in Fliche et Martin (9.ii)

MAYER, HANS EBERHARD. *The Crusades* tr. John Gillingham, Oxford 1972

(2) RUNCIMAN, STEVEN. *A History of the Crusades*, Cambridge 1951

SETTON, K. M. (ed.) *A History of the Crusades*, Pennsylvania 1955, 1962 (Vols. I & II only)

(3) SEWARD, DESMOND. *The Monks of War*, London 1972

WAAS, ADOLF. *Geschichte der Kreuzzüge*, Frieburg 1956

See also BLOCH (General, 1)

14. The Military Orders in Palestine

BERNARD OF CLAIRVAUX. *De laude novae militiae* in Migne *PL* clxxxii, 922–39

(1) CAMPBELL, G. A. *The Knights Templars: their rise and fall*, London 1957

(2) CURZON, H. DE. *Règle du Temple*, Paris (SHF) 1886

DELAVILLE LE ROULX, J. *Les Hospitaliers en Terre Sainte et à Chypre (1100–1310)*, Paris 1904

DONOVAN, JOSEPH P. *Pelagius and the Fifth Crusade*, London and Philadelphia 1950

(3) JOINVILLE. *Life of St Louis* (with Villehardouin: *Conquest of Constantinople*), tr. M. R. B. Shaw, London and Baltimore 1963

LE CLERCQ, J. 'Un document sur les débuts des Templiers', *Revue d'histoire ecclésiastique* lii, 1957, pt. i, 81–90

MELVILLE, MARION. *La Vie des Templiers*, Paris 1951

PIQUET, JULES. *Des Banquiers au moyen âge: les Templiers*, Paris 1939

PRAWER, JOSHUA. *The Latin Kingdom of Jerusalem*, London 1972

(4) PRUTZ, HANS. *Die geistliche Ritterorden*, Berlin 1908

(5) RILEY-SMITH, JONATHAN. *The Knights of St John in Jerusalem and Cyprus c. 1050–1310 (A history of the order of the Hospital of St John of Jerusalem*, i, ed. Lionel Butler), London 1967

SIMON, EDITH. *The Piebald Standard: a biography of the Knights Templars* London 1959

SMAIL, R. C. *Crusading Warfare (1097–1193)*, Cambridge 1956

See also RUNCIMAN (13.2)

15. The Templars in Exile

BARBER, MALCOLM. 'Propaganda in the Middle Ages: the charges against the Templars', *Nottingham Medieval Studies* 1973, 42–57

CHENEY, C. R. 'The downfall of the Templars and a letter in their defence', in Vinaver 65–79

FINKE, HEINRICH. *Papsttum und Untergang des Templerordens*, Münster 1907

(1) LIZERAND, GEORGES. *Le Dossier de l'affaire des Templiers*, Paris 1923

MARTIN, E. J. *The Trial of the Templars*, London 1928

See also CAMPBELL (14.1), PRUTZ (14.4), RUNCIMAN (13.2)

16. The Hospitallers in Rhodes and Malta

ATIYA, AZIZ SURYAL. *The Crusade in the Later Middle Ages*, London 1938

ATIYA, AZIZ SURYAL. *The Crusade of Nicopolis*, London 1934

BRADFORD, ERNLE. *The Great Siege of Malta*, London 1961

BROCKMAN, ERIC. *The Two Sieges of Rhodes 1480–1522*, London 1969

COHEN, R. *Knights of Malta 1523–1798* (Helps for Students of History 41), London and New York 1920

DELAVILLE LE ROULX, J. *Les Hospitaliers à Rhodes jusqu' à la mort de Philibert de Naillac (1310–1421)*, Paris 1913

(1) DUBOIS, PIERRE. *The Recovery of the Holy Land*, tr. Walther I. Brandt, New York 1956

ENGEL, CLAIRE-ELIANE. *Histoire de l'Ordre de Malte*, Paris and Geneva 1968

(2) IORGA, NICOLAI. *Philippe de Mézières 1327–1405 et la croisade au xive siècle* (Bibliothèque de l'école des hautes études 110), Paris 1896

MÉZIÈRES, PHILIPPE DE. *Le Songe du vieil Pelerin*, ed. G. W. Coopland, Cambridge 1969

(3) PORTER, WHITWORTH. *A History of the Knights of Malta or the Order of the Hospital of St John of Jerusalem*, London 1858

See also PRUTZ (14.4), RUNCIMAN (13.2)

17. The Teutonic Knights

BARNES, A. S. 'The Teutonic knights and the kingdom of Prussia', *Dublin Review*, Oct. 1915, 272–83

BENNINGHOVEN, FRIEDRICH. *Der Orden der Schwertbrüder: Fratres Milicie Christi de Livonia*, Graz and Köln 1965

(1) BÜHLER, JOHANNES. *Ordensritter und Kirchenfürsten nach zeitgenossischen Quellen*, Leipzig 1927

CARSTEN, F. L. *The Origins of Prussia*, Oxford 1954

HENRY IV. *Expeditions to Prussia and the Holy Land made by Henry earl of Derby in the years 1390–1 and 1392–3*, ed. Lucy Toulmin Smith, London (Camden Society N.S. lii) 1894

(2) TREITSCHKE, G. *Das deutsche Ordensland Preussen*, tr. E. and C. Paul as *The Origins of Prussianism*, London 1942

(3) TUMLER, P. MARIAN. *Der deutsche Orden im Werden, Wachsen und Wirken bis 1400 . . .*, Vienna 1955

WINNIG, A. *Der deutsche Ritterorden und seine Burgen*, Königstein im Taunus 1956

18. The Spanish Orders

ALCANTARA. *Difiniciones y establecimientos de la orden y cavalleria d'Alcantara*, Madrid 1609

COSTA, FR. BERNARDO DA. *Historia da militar ordem de nosso Senhor Jesus Christo*, Coimbra 1771

DEFOURNEAUX, MARCELIN. *Les français en Espagne au xie et xiie siècles*, Paris 1949

ERDMANN, CARL. 'Das Kreuzzugsgedanke in Portugal', *HZ* cxli, 1930, 23–53

FOREY, A. J. 'The Order of Mountjoy', Speculum xlvi, 1971, 250–266

GUITTON, FRANCIS. *L'ordre de Calatrave*, Paris (Commission d'histoire de l'ordre de Citeaux iv) 1955

KING, GEORGIANA GODDARD. *A Brief Account of the Military Orders in Spain*, New York 1921

LARRAGUETA, SANTOS GARCIA. 'La orden de San Juan en la crisis del imperio Hispanico del siglo xii', *Hispania* xii, 1952, 483–525

LOMAX, DEREK W. *La orden de Santiago*, *(1170–1275)*, Madrid (Consejo superior de investigaciones cientificas, escuela de estudios medievales xxxviii) 1965

MARTIN, JOSE LUIS. 'Fernando II de Leon y la Orden de Santiago (1170–1181)', *Anuario de estudios medievales (Barcelona)* i, 1964, 167–95

RADES Y ANDRADA, FRANCISCO DE. *Chronica de las tres ordenes y cavallerias de Santiago, Calatrava y Alcantara*, Madrid 1664

See also SEWARD (13.3)

PART V: CHIVALRY AND THE STATE

19. The Prince and Chivalry

ANGLO, SYDNEY (ed.). *The Great Tournament Roll of Westminster*, Oxford 1968

ANGLO, SYDNEY. *Spectacle, Pageantry and Early Tudor Policy* (Oxford-Warburg Studies), Oxford 1969

ANGLO, SYDNEY. 'Le camp du drap d'or et les entrevues d'Henri VIII et de Charles Quint', in Jacquot, ii, 113–33

(1) ARMSTRONG, C. A. J. 'Had the Burgundian government a policy for the nobility?' in *Britain and the Netherlands*, ed. John S. Bromley and E. H. Kossmann, ii, 9–32, Groningen 1964

(2) CARTELLIERI, OTTO. *The Court of Burgundy*, London and New York 1929

CARTELLIERI, OTTO. 'Ritterspiele am Hofe Karls des Kühnen von Burgund (1468)', *Tijdschrift voor Geschiednis* xxxvi, 1921, 15–30

(3) CHAMBERS, E. K. *The Elizabethan Stage*, Oxford 1923

CHAMBERS, E. K. *Sir Henry Lee: an Elizabethan portrait*, Oxford 1936

(4) COURTEAULT, HENRI. *Gaston IV, comte de Foix*, Toulouse 1895

DEVOTO, DANIEL. 'Folklore et politique au Chateau Ténébreux', in Jacquot, ii, 311–28

DU COLOMBIER, PIERRE. 'Les triomphes en images de l'empereur Maximilien I', in Jacquot, ii, 99–112

(5) GRÜNPECK, I. *Die Geschichte Friedrichs III und Maximilian I*, tr. C. Ilgen (Die Geschichtsschreiber der deutschen Vorzeit: Funfzehntes Jahrhundert, iii), Leipzig 1899

HAENEL, ERICH. *Der sächsischen Kurfürsten Turnierbücher in ihren hervorragendsten Darstellungen auf vierzig Tafeln herausgegeben*, Frankfurt 1910

HUIZINGA, JOHAN. *Men and Ideas: the political and military significance of chivalric ideas in the late Middle Ages*, London 1960

HUIZINGA, JOHAN. *The Waning of the Middle Ages*, London and Baltimore 1949

IORGA, NICOLAI. *Thomas III marquis de Saluces*, Paris 1893

LANGLOIS, CH.-V. 'Une mémoire inédite de Pierre de Bois, 1313', *Revue Historique* xli, 1889, 84–91

LESCHITZER, SIMON, ed. *Der Theuerdank . . . nach der ersten Auflage vom Jahre 1517* (Jahrbuch der Kunsthistorischen Sammlungen 8) Vienna 1888

LOOMIS, ROGER SHERMAN. 'Edward I, Arthurian Enthusiast', *Speculum* xxviii, 1953, 114–27

RUSSELL, JOYCELYNE G. *The Field of the Cloth of Gold*, London 1969

SALZMAN, LOUIS F. *Edward I*, London 1968

STRONG, ROY. *The Elizabethan Image*, London 1969

STRONG, ROY. *Splendour at Court*, London 1973

TOSI, MARIO. *Il torneo di Belvedere in Vaticano e i tornei in Italia nel Cinquecento*, Rome 1946

TREITZSAUERWEIN VON EHRENTREITZ, MARX. *Der Weisskunig: nach den Dictaten und eigenhändigen Aufzeichnungen Kaiser Maximilians I zusammengestellt*, ed. Alwin Schultz (Jahrbuch der Kunsthistorischen Sammlungen 6) Vienna, 1888

TRUFFI, RICCARDO. *Giostre e cantori di giostre* Rocca S. Casciano 1911

VANUXEM, JACQUES. 'Le carrousel de 1612 sur la Place Royale et ses devises' in Jacquot i, 191–203

(6) VAUGHAN, RICHARD. *Philip the Bold: the formation of the Burgundian State*, Longmans 1962

VAUGHAN, RICHARD. *John the Fearless: the growth of Burgundian power*, Longmans 1966

WITHINGTON, ROBERT. *English Pageantry: an historical outline*, Cambridge Mass., and London 1918

YATES, FRANCES A. 'Charles Quint et l'idée d'empire', in Jacquot, ii, 57–97

YATES, FRANCES A. 'Elizabethan chivalry: the romance of the accession day tilts', in *Journal of the Warburg and Courtauld Institutes*, xx, 1957, 4–25

YATES FRANCES A. *The Valois Tapestries*, (Studies of the Warburg Institute 23), London 1959

See also CLEPHAN (10.1), CRIPPS-DAY (10.2), PIAGET (8.3)

20. The Secular Orders

ASHMOLE, ELIAS. *The Institution, Laws and Ceremonies of the Most Noble Order of the Garter*, London 1672

BELTZ, GEORGE FREDERICK. *Memorials of the Most Noble Order of the Garter*, London 1841

GALWAY, MARGARET. 'Joan of Kent and the Order of the Garter', *University of Birmingham Historical Journal*, i, 1947–48 13–50

HOMMEL, LUC. *L'histoire du noble ordre de la Toison d'or*, Brussels 1947

KERVYN DE LETTENHOVE, H. *La Toison d'Or*, Brussels 1907

(1) LEWIS, P. S. 'Une devise de chevalerie inconnue créée par un comte de Foix: le dragon?' *Annales du Midi*, lxxvi, 1964, 77–84

(2) REIFFENBERG, Baron F. A. F. T. DE. '*Histoire de l'ordre de la Toison d'Or depuis son institution jusqu'à la cessation des chapitres généraux*', Brussels 1830

(3) RENOUARD, Y. 'L'Ordre de la Jarretière et l'Ordre de l'Etoile', *Le moyen âge*, lv, 1949, 281–300

SHAW, WITHAM A. *The Knights of England*, London 1906

TERLINDEN, CHARLES. 'The order of the Golden Fleece', *Edinburgh Review* 1920 (Oct.) 307–15

VALE, M. G. A. 'A fourteenth century order of chivalry: the "Tiercelet" ' *EHR* lxxxii 1967, 332–41

VAUGHAN, RICHARD. *Philip the Good: The Apogee of Burgundy*, London 1970

21. The Epic of Chivalry Revived

(1) ARIOSTO, LUDOVICO. *Orlando Furioso in English heroical verse by John Harington*, London 1594

BERNERS, LORD (Sir John Bourchier). *The Boke of Duke Huon of Burdeux* ed. S. L. Lee, London (EETS E.S. xl, xli, xliii, I) 1882–87

BOWRA, C. M. *From Virgil to Milton*, London 1945

BRAND, CHARLES P. *Torquato Tasso: a study of the poet and of his contribution to English literature*, Cambridge 1965

(2) CERVANTES SAAVEDRA, MIGUEL DE. *The Adventures of Don Quixote* tr. J. M. Cohen, London and Baltimore 1950

CASTRO, AMÉRICO. *El pensamiento de Cervantes* (*Revista de Filologia española*: anejo vi), Madrid 1925

DAVIES R. T. 'The worshipful way in Malory', in Lewis, 157–77

EDWARDS, E. W. *The Orlando Furioso and its Predecessor*, Cambridge 1924

ENTWISTLE, WILLIAM J. *Cervantes*, Oxford 1940

FERGUSSON, ARTHUR B. *The Indian Summer of English Chivalry: studies in the decline and transformation of chivalric idealism*, Durham, North Carolina 1960

GIROUARD, MARK. *Robert Smythson and the Architecture of the Elizabethan Era*, London 1966

GREVILLE, SIR FULKE. *Life of Sir Philip Sidney*, Oxford 1907

HAUVETTE, HENRI. *L'Arioste et la poésie chevaleresque à Ferrare au début du xvie siècle*, Paris (Bibliothèque littéraire de la Renaissance, N.S. xvi) 1927

KRAUSS, WERNER. *Das tätige Leben und die Litteratur im mittelalterlichen Spanien*, Stuttgart 1929

(3) LOBEIRA, VASCO (Joham de?). *Amadis de Gaula* (*Amadis of Gaul*), tr. Robert Southey, London 1872

MADARIAGA, SALVADOR DE. *Don Quixote: an introductory essay in psychology*, The Gregynog Press 1934

(4) MALORY, SIR THOMAS. *The Works of Sir Thomas Malory*, ed. Eugene Vinaver, Oxford 1967

MIKO, STEPHEN J. 'Malory and the Chivalric Order', *Medium Aevum*, xxv, 1966, 211–30

SCHOFIELD, WILLIAM HENRY. *Chivalry in English Literature: Chaucer, Malory, Spenser and Shakespeare*, Cambridge, Mass., and London 1912

(5) TASSO, TORQUATO. *Gerusalemme Liberata* (Godfrey of Bulloigne, or, the Recovery of Jerusalem), tr. Edward Fairfax, London 1851

(6) THOMAS, HENRY. *Spanish and Portuguese Romances of Chivalry: the revival of the romance of chivalry in the Spanish peninsula and its extension and influence abroad*, Cambridge 1920

22. Critics of Chivalry and Advocates of Reform

(1) CAESARIUS OF HEISTERBACH. *Dialogus miraculorum*, ed. Joseph Strange, Cologne, Bonn and Brussels 1851

(2) CASTIGLIONE, BALDESAR. *The Book of the Courtier*, tr. George Bull, London and Baltimore 1967

COVILLE, A. *Le Petit Jehan de Saintré: recherches complémentaires*, Paris 1937

(3) DESCHAMPS, EUSTACE. *Oeuvres complètes*, ed. De Queux de Saint-Hilaire and G. Raynaud, Paris (SATF) 1878–1903

(4) JEAN LE SENESCHAL. *Les Cent Ballades*, ed. Gaston Raynaud, Paris (SATF) 1905

JONES, GEORGE FENWICK. 'The tournaments of Tottenham and Lappenhausen', *PMLA* lxvi, 1951, 1123–40

(5) KILGOUR, RAYMOND LINCOLN. *The Decline of Chivalry as Shown in the French Literature of the Late Middle Ages*, Cambridge, Mass. and London 1937

(6) LA SALE, ANTOINE DE. *Little John of Saintré*, tr. Irvine Gray, London 1931

(7) LA TOUR LANDRY, GEOFFROY DE. *The Book of the Knight of La Tour-Landry* ed. Thomas Wright, London (EETS 33) 1868

(8) LECOY DE LA MARCHE, A. *La Chaire française au moyen âge*, Paris 1886

(9) PETER OF BLOIS. *Epistolae* xciv, in Migne *PL* 216, 293–7

PETERSEN, JULIUS. *Das Rittertum in der Darstellung des Johannes Rothe* (Quellen und Forschungen zur Sprach- und Culturgeschichte cvi), Strassburg 1909

TESKE, HANS. *Thomasin von Zirclaere: der Mann und sein Werk* (Germanische Bibliothek 34), Heidelberg 1933

(10) THOMAS OF CANTIMPRÉ. *Thomae Cantipratani . . . miraculorum, et exemplorum memorabilium sui temporis libri duo*, ed. Georgius Colvenerius Duaci 1605

WHITING, B. J. 'The Vows of the Heron', *Speculum* xx, 1945, 261–78

Epilogue

ANSTRUTHER, IAN. *The Knight and the Umbrella*, London 1959

Appendix

(1) CATALAN, DIEGO. *Un cronista anonimo del siglo XIV*, Canarias 1955

(2) *Cronicas de los reyes de Castilla* (Biblioteca de autores espanoles lxvi, i) Madrid 1953

(3) DAUMET, GEORGES. 'L'ordre castillan de l'écharpe', *Bulletin hispanique* xxv, 1923 5–32

(4) RUSSELL P. E. *The English Intervention in Spain and Portugal in the time of Edward III and Richard II*, Oxford 1955

(5) VILLANUEVA, LORENZO TADEO. 'Memorial sobre la order de Caballeria de la Banda de Castilla', *Boletin de la real academia de la historia*, lxxii, 1918 436–65, 552–74

INDEX

Gurnemanz, 115, 116
Guy, King of Jerusalem, 223, 233, 237
Guy of Ponthieu, 43
Guzman, Leonor de, 342
Gwent, longbowmen of, 199

Hadrian VI, Pope, 287
Hainault, Earl of, 41
Hakim, Caliph, 216
Halidon Hill, battle of, 187; bowmen at, 200
Hastings, battle of, 217
Hattin, battle of, 223, 232, 237, 238
Hausen, Friedrich von, 97, 102
Haye, Gilbert de la, 312
Hector, 129
Heinrich VI, Emperor, knighting of, 96
Helm, 33
Helmet, 33
Henri II, King of France, 184, 296
Henry I, King of England, 39, 160, 161
Henry II, King of England, 34, 78, 86, 111, 145, 183, 194; as patron of literature, 293; his gifts to Templars, 247; his skill in siegecraft, 95
Henry III, King of England, 34, 46, 144–5, 185, 186
Henry IV, Emperor, 39
Henry IV, King of England, 305–6
Henry V, King of England, 147, 209
Henry VI, King of England, 297
Henry VIII, King of England, 299
Henry, King of Cyprus, 250
Henry of Trastmare, 206

Henry, son of Henry II, 163, 164, 165; death of, 166; revives the tournament, 163–4
Henry Stuart, Prince of Wales, 301
Henry the Fowler, 196
Henry the Navigator, 284
Heraldry, Herald, 43–4, 45
Hercules I of Ferrara, 315
Hérédia, Jean Fernandez de, 252, 255
Hermann of Thuringia, 113
Hermine (Ermine), Order of the, 307
Hildebert, Archbishop, 30
History of the Kings of Britain (Geoffrey of Monmouth), 147
Hohenfles, Burkhard von, 101
Holland, Thomas, 205
Homage, 23, 25, 27–8, 209; conflicting claims on, 28; liege, 28, 209
Homer, 50, 63
Honour, word of, 44–5, 167, 176
Horn, Count of, 308
Hospitallers *see* St John, Hospital of
Housman, A. E., 93
Hubert II, Count of Vermandois, 53
Hugh of Lusignan, 240
Hundred Years' War, 37, 106, 143, 187, 189, 328, 343; bombs in, 200; knighting on the field during, 41–2; sufferings of non-combatants, 203
Hungary, Hungarians, 18, 39, 196, 228, 254, 262, 263, 269, 274, 275, 327
Huns, as horsemen, 17–18
Huon of Bordeaux, 67
Hussites, 330; infantry of, 194

nier, 181; *ze rehter tjost*, 172–3; *see also* Tournaments

Juliers, Isabella de, 150

Jungingen, Ulrich von, 270

Justice, low and high, 28–9

Kenilworth, Dictum of, 34

Keye, 113

Kilij Arslan, 222

Knight, 17–37; armour of, 33, 197–8; attitude to war of, 202–3; becomes landowner, 27; becomes administrator, 28–9, 34–5; becomes distinct from nobility, 32; birth becomes qualification for, 26–7, 30–1; Church commandments to, 47; demoted by Edward III's military tactics, 187; dubbing of, 39–40, 42; equipment of, 18, 26, 32–3, 198–9; expenses in 13th century, 32; fall in incomes in 13th and 14th centuries, 29–30, 31–2; forbidden to engage in commerce, 45; forms 'battle' in warfare, 195; glory and, 111, 196; importance of warlike skill to, 19, 130; influenced by the troubadours, 87; in sieges, 195, 201, 204–5; knighting before a battle, 41; number in 13th century, 34; payment for war service late 13th century, 35–6; predecessors of, 17; 'robber' knights, 36–7; status in 15th century, 36; tournament entry rules for, 170; tournament techniques of, 171–3; tournaments as sport of, 161; training by

tournament of, 159; weapons used by, 198, 200; word of honour of, 44–5

Knighthood, 38–49; and the ideals of chivalry, 47–9; becomes hereditary right, 30–1; brotherhood-in-arms, 208–9; ceremony of, 38–40; Church's attitude to, 48, 214–15; class distinction in, 30; confraternities, 209–10; knighting ceremony, 32, 291–2, 293; glamour of, 45–6; in Arthurian romances, 123–4, 312–14; Langland's *Piers Plowman* on, 154; love and women and, 71–6; military orders of, 196, 209–10, 222, 226–88; Renaissance ideal of, 333–5; reward for deed of arms, 31; sale of, 31; secular orders of, 303–10

Knights of Christ, 284

Kniprode, Winrich von, 269

Knyghthode and Bataile, 147

Konigsburg, founding of, 267

Konitz, battle of, 272

Kulm, Teutonic fortress of, 263

Kürenberc, der von, 95–6

Kurvenal, 121

Kyot, 114

La Forbie, battle of, 236

La Mort le Roi Artu, 123, 129–30

Labé, Louise, 87

'Lady of the Lake', 47–8, 124, 152, 153, 312

Lalain, Jacques de, 146, 149, 150–1; killed by cannon, 200

Lambert of Ardres, 46

Lance, adoption of, 19; Holy, at Antioch, 220; Holy, in Arthu-

Lance (continued)
rian romances, 126; use in tournaments of, 169, 172; use in warfare, 198

Lancelot, 47–8, 108, 109, 111, 123–4, 127, 128, 129, 130, 144, 152, 312, 313, 314, 325; Sir Ector's lament for, 155

Las Navas de Tolosa, battle of, 194, 281, 284, 285

Lastic, de, Grand Master of Hospitallers, 256

Latvia, 264, 266, 273

Laudine, 109, 115

Laval, Jeanne, 179

Lawrence, T. E., 239

Lay de Vaillance (Eustace Deschamps), 328–9

Le Breviare des Nobles (Alain Chartier), 154–5

Le Conte del Graal see Perceval

Legnano, Giovanni da, 45

Leigni, Godefroi de, 168

Le Jouvencel (Jean de Bueil), 329–30, 332

Le Libre del Orde de Cavalleria (Llull), 153, 312

Le Livre des Tournois (René d' Anjou), 44, 45, 175, 176, 297

Le Morte d'Arthur (Malory), 155, 311–14, 331

Lenoncourt, Philippe de, 180

Le Petit Jean de Saintré (Antoine de la Sale), 332

Le Puy, Council of (990), 215

Le Tournoi de Chauvency (Bretel), 145

Lee, Sir Henry, 300, 301

L'Entrée d'Espagne, 67

Leo ix, Pope, 214, 217

Leopold vi of Austria, 188

Lepanto, battle of, 259

L'Escoufle, 132

Letters on Chivalry and Romance (Hurd), 337

Liber Recuperationis Terre Sancte (Fidenzio of Padua), 253

Lichtenstein, Ulrich von, 97, 101, 102, 148; tourneyer, 168–9, 173–4, 178, 187–8

Liège, feudal levy in, 35

Life of the Emperor Henry iv, 207

Limoges, 86, 209; sack of, 204–5, 208; school of St Martial at, 93

Limoges, Bishop of, 204

Limousin, 209

Lincoln, battle of, 194

Lindsay, Sir David, 180

Lists (in tournaments), 163, 168, 176–7

Lithuania, 264, 265, 270–1, 273; accepts Christianity, 269; crusading army destroyed in, 266; running war with Teutonic knights in, 268–9

'Little Battle of Chalons', 189, 202

Little John of Saintré, 149

Livonia, 267, 270, 274, 277; advance of Brethren of the Sword, 264–5; branch of Teutonic Knights in, 272; colonisation of, 264

Livre de Chevalerie (Geoffroi de Charny), 154

Livre des quartre dames (Alain Chartier), 329

Llull, Raimon, 40, 153, 154, 155, 312; his plan for a crusade, 153, 253

Loherangrin, 114, 118

Lombards, 18, 19

Longbow, 194, 198–9, 199–200

L'ordene de chevalerie, 40, 47, 48

Loring, Nele, 41, 42

Lorrain, Garin de, 53

Lorris, Guillaume de, 138–9, 140, 141

Louis II, Emperor, 38

Louis II of Bourbon, 307, 311

Louis VI, King of France, 39

Louis VII, King of France, 163, 216, 247

Louis VIII, King of France, 43

Louis IX, King of France, 308

Louis of Mâle, 295

Louis the Pious, Emperor, 38, 40, 41, 51, 59, 61, 62

Love, adultery and, 90; and chivalry, 77, 87; Arab view of, 92–3; Christian attitude to, 91–2; clerk's view of, 133–43; courtly, 81, 85, 90-1, 113, 313; courts of, 136–7, 138; ennobling effect of, 87–8; German views of, 95–6, 97, 98, 102–3; Italian view of, 142–3; platonic, 85, 87; tournaments and courtly, 168, 174; traditions of, 71–6; troubadours' ideal of, 81–5, 87–92, 98, 99, 133

Lovelich, Henry, 312

Low Countries (Netherlands), 219, 275, 308, 309; tournaments in, 188, 294–5

Lucan, 65

Lucius III, Pope, 232, 284

Lucretius, 73

Luna, Alvaro de, 179

Lunette, 109

Lyons, poets of, 87

Machiavelli, Nicolò, 301

Mail, 33

Mailles, Jacques de, 151

Mainz, 39; knighting of Heinrich VI at, 96; 'robber' knights at war with, 37

Malatesta, Paolo, 314

'Malehaut, lady of', 129

Malory, Sir Thomas, 104, 127, 146, 155, 178, 311–14, 316, 325; his conception of the Round Table, 312–13, 314

Malta defended against Turks, 258–9; Hospitallers move to, 258; surrendered to Napoleon, 260

Manny, Sir Walter, 44, 150, 294

Mansourah, battle of, 196, 224

Manzikert, battle of, 218

Marcabru, 83–4, 88, 90, 103

Marche, Olivier de la, 309

Margaret of Anjou, 297

Margaret of Flanders, 295

Margaret of Hainault, 295

Margaret of York, 45

Margaret, Queen of Edward I, 292

Margaris of Seville, 59–60

Margat, Hospitallers castle at, 239; Statutes of, 233

Marienburg, becomes HQ of Teutonic Knights, 267, 274

Mark, King, 104–5, 107, 119, 120–1, 127

Marseille, Folquet de, 76, 87

Marshall, William, 111, 163–4, 168, 174, 188, 294; as a tourneyer, 164–5, 166–7, 209; biography of, 144–5

Marsile, 56, 59

Martel, Charles, 24, 52

Martel, William Gros de, 79

Martin IV, Pope, 190
Mary, the Virgin, 73, 304, 306
Matfré Ermengaut, 138
Maximilian I, Emperor, 146, 149, 181, 294; as a tournament sponsor, 298–9
Maximilian II, Emperor, 160
Medici, Catherine de', 299
Medici, Lorenzo di', 300
Meistergesang, 102, 141
Meliador (Froissart), 132, 311
Mercenaries, 195, 200, 201, 234, 271, 272
Merchants, rise of, 29–30
Merovingians, 19, 22, 24, 26
Meon, Jean de, 138, 139–40, 141
Mezières, Philippe de, 192, 253–4, 272; his idea of a military order, 254, 330
Michael VII, Emperor, 218
Michelsberg, Johann von, 145
Military Orders, 209–10, 222; exile of Templars, 241–9; glory of, 196; Hospitallers at Rhodes and Malta, 250; in Palestine, 226–40; in Spain, 280–8, 344; Teutonic Knights, 261–79
Milton, John, 316, 337
Minaya Alvar Fáñez, 67
Mindaugas, King of Lithuania, 267, 268
Mines, knightly combats in, 209
Minne, 96, 97, 99, 101; theory of, 102
Minnesäng, 96, 97, 98, 99, 101, 103, 141
Minnesingers, 94–103, 121, 122, 148
Miraval, Raimon de, 72, 85
Mita, William, 79
Molay, Jacques de, Grand Master

of the Templars, 241, 242, 243, 244, 245
Molyneux, Nicholas, 208
Montanhagnol, Guillem de, 87
Montaudin, Monk of, 167
Montereau, siege of, 175–6
Montesa, military Order of, 286
Montfort, Countess of, 150
Montfort, Simon de, 34
Montglane, Garin de, 51
Montgomeri, Constable de, 188
Montjoie, Order of, 286
Montreuil, William, 217
Moors *see* Muslims
Mordred, 129, 313
Morimond, Abbot of, 287
Moritz von Craûn, 45
Morgante Maggiore (Pulci), 314
Morold, 119
Morungen, Heinrich von, 97–8
Mounkidh, Ousama Ibn, 238
Muhammad II, Sultan, 256
Muslims, 53, 64, 194, 197, 204, 222, 235, 253; growing strength of, 255; in Jerusalem, 216, 218, 223, 236, 237, 261; relations with Crusaders, 238, 282; scorn for Frankish quarrels, 240; Spanish *reconquista* and, 217, 280–8 *passim*; *sufis*, 238; *see also* Turks

Namur, development of vassalage in, 25–6
Narbonne, 86; Council of, 215
Neifen, Gottfried von, 101
Nerra, Fulk, Duke of Burgundy, 78
Nevers, John, Duke of, 254
Nevsky, Alexander, 266
Nibelungenlied, 50, 52, 60, 63, 74

Nicholas III, Pope, 190
Nicholas IV, Pope, 252
Nicopolis, crusade of, 254–5, 330
Nobility, becomes separate from knighthood, 32
Nogaret, Guillaume de, 245, 252, 253
Nogent, Guibert de, 205
Northallerton, battle of, 194, 198
Northmen, 53, 74–5, 77
Noya, siege of, 201
Noyelles, John Traiment de, 35–6
Nur-ed-Din, 232
Nuremberg, 'robber' knights war with, 37

Odo de Déols, 216
Okeghem, Jean d', 297
Oliver, 55–6, 57, 58, 75, 146
On the art of loving honestly (Anreas Capellanus), 133–7
Orable-Guibourc, Princess, 59, 60, 66, 75
Orange, 59, 86
Orange, Guillaume d', 53, 58–60, 61, 62, 63, 66, 75
Orange, Raimbaut d', 85
Orbigo bridge, *Passo Honroso* at, 179
Ordericus Vitalis, 78
Orgeluse, 116
Oriana, 318, 319
Orlando Furioso (Ariosto), 315–16
Orlando innamorato (Boiardo), 315
Orléans, Erneis d', 59
Orléans, siege of, 200
Otto I, Emperor, 38; crowning of, 39

Otto of Bavaria, Count, 40
Otto of Freising, 30, 161
Outremer, Frankish settlements of, 222, 223, 224, 235, 237, 238–9, 251
Ovid, 72, 107, 136, 137, 138, 139, 140
Oxford, Provisions of, 34

Padilla, Doña Maria de, 287
Padua, jousts at, 300
Palaeologos Pasha, 256
Palestine, military Orders in, 222, 226–40, 247, 248, 262, 267–8, 286, 288; castles of, 238–9; decline of, 239–40; dissensions among, 235–6; independence of action of, 235, 236; lack of discipline, 196–7, 236; rashness of, 236–7; relations with Muslims, 238, 268, 282
Palmerin of England, 320
Papacy, 141, 143, 199; as a temporal power, 217; blesses military expeditions, 217; raises armies, 214
Paris, Etienne Tempier, Bishop of, 133
Paris, Matthew, 162
Parthians, mounted archers of, 18
Parzival, 114–18, 119, 144, 146
Pas d'Armes, 95, 106, 148, 151, 178–80, 188, 189, 297, 298; at Orbigo, 179; at St Inglevert, 178, 189; at St Omer, 180; at Sandricourt, 178; at Tarascon, 179–80; at Valladolid, 179; *see also* Tournaments
Passau, Bishop of, 40